Élie Halévy

# INTELLECTUAL HISTORY
# OF THE MODERN AGE

# ÉLIE HALÉVY

Republican Liberalism
Confronts the Era of Tyranny

K. STEVEN VINCENT

**PENN**

UNIVERSITY OF PENNSYLVANIA PRESS

PHILADELPHIA

Published by
University of Pennsylvania Press
Philadelphia, Pennsylvania 19104-4112
www.upenn.edu/pennpress

Printed in the United States of America on acid-free paper

1 3 5 7 9 10 8 6 4 2


Library of Congress Cataloging-in-Publication Data

Names: Vincent, K. Steven, author.
Title: Élie Halévy : Republican liberalism confronts the era of tyranny /
K. Steven Vincent.
Other titles: Intellectual history of the modern age.
Description: First edition. | Philadelphia : University of Pennsylvania Press,
[2020] | Series: Intellectual history of the modern age | Includes
bibliographical references and index.
Identifiers: LCCN 2019046217 | ISBN 978-0-8122-5203-3 (hardcover)
Subjects: LCSH: Halévy, Élie, 1870–1937. |
Historians—France—Biography. | Intellectuals—France—Biography. |
France—Intellectual life—19th century. | France—Intellectual life—20th
century.
Classification: LCC DA3.H28 V56 2020 | DDC 941.0072/02 [B]—dc23
LC record available at https://lccn.loc.gov/2019046217

*For Ana*

# CONTENTS

# Introduction

Élie Halévy (1870–1937) was a highly respected intellectual of his era, and he has remained among the most famous and well-regarded liberal French historians. In the Anglo-American world, he is best known for his three-volume history of British Utilitarianism and for his multi-volume history of nineteenth-century England.[1] In his native France, his reputation rests on his association with the *Revue de métaphysique et de morale*, a philosophical journal that he founded in 1893 with his friends Xavier Léon, Léon Brunschvicg, and Alain (Émile Chartier); on his participation in the defense of Alfred Dreyfus; and on his lectures on the history of European socialism given every other year between 1902 and 1937 at the École libre des sciences politiques (henceforth, Sciences Po).[2] He is famous in both contexts for his post–World War I analyses of the growth of radical movements on the Left and the Right, during what he labeled "the era of tyrannies."[3]

This intellectual biography examines the entire range of Halévy's works, as well as the contexts within which these works were written: his neo-Kantian philosophical orientation; his incisive analysis of British Utilitarianism (an analysis still debated by historians of political thought); his involvement in the Dreyfus Affair; his stance of "socialist liberalism" in the years before World War I; his thesis about the importance of religion and mores in modern England (the so-called "Halévy thesis"); his principled stance during World War I; his new views of socialism and nationalism after the war; his arguments concerning the era of tyrannies.

As this list indicates, Halévy was intimately involved with a wide range of philosophical, political, economic, and historical issues of his era. He provides an entry, for example, into the neo-Kantianism that animated the *Revue de métaphysique et de morale* and, more broadly, that informed much of the philosophy produced in France during the 1890s. His neo-Kantianism, however, was inflected with a dialectical form of Platonism, which he analyzed in his thesis published in 1896, *La théorie Platonicienne des sciences*.[4] In Part I of the book, after introducing the Halévy family, I examine how his modified neo-Kantian perspective remained an important framework: for his early articles about epistemology and education; for his stance toward the new disciplines of psychology and sociology; for his thinking about British Utilitarianism. Halévy began his professional career as a philosopher, and the first section of my book argues that this is an essential framework for understanding the distinctiveness of his thought, and the disagreements he expressed with contemporaries like Henri Bergson, Émile Durkheim, Théodule-Armand Ribot, Vilfredo Pareto, and others.

Unlike many of his contemporaries who remained closely attached to investigations in philosophy and science, however, Halévy turned as a young man in his twenties to history, economic theory, and the wider problems of socio-political justice. He continued to participate in debates with the major philosophers and sociologists of his era at sessions of the Société française de philosophie, but his primary attention turned to the history of England and to the history of European socialism. He lectured on both at Sciences Po, and wrote dense histories of English thought and institutions. The themes that he explored in his histories of England drew from a rich French tradition (that includes Voltaire, Germaine de Staël, Hippolyte Taine, Émile Boutmy, among others) but also reflected the influence of his close associates in England, where he spent several months every year (thinkers like Beatrice and Sidney Webb and Graham Wallas). His focus on England influenced his views of France and, beyond this, his views of modern politics and the rise of modern tyranny.

Halévy's move from philosophy to history is analyzed in Part II. This part opens with an account of an important event—the Dreyfus Affair—that deeply affected Halévy and overlapped with the shift in his intellectual orientation. The Affair reinforced his commitment to study not just philosophy but also socio-political ideas and movements, and to analyze the complex nature of historical change. It also drew Halévy into politics. His activities during the Dreyfus Affair demonstrated his strong commitment to the constitutional and juridical institutions of the Third Republic, even as they also revealed his impatience with many of the politicians who led it. He became more concerned with the fragility of modern liberal democracies.

The years between the Dreyfus Affair and the outbreak of World War I were immensely productive for Halévy. He published on English history and European socialism, and presented famous lectures on both. He became a historian-philosopher, widely respected in both England and France, and developed an orientation—one that informed all of his subsequent work—that viewed thought and politics as historically conditioned. Different societies, he argued, because of the curiosities of their historical development and the distinctiveness of their cultural traditions, confronted the problems of liberty, equity, and justice differently. There was no uniform program of action that was universally applicable; politics and culture were each a "sedimentation of practices," to borrow a phrase from Françoise Mélonio, and they needed to be approached comparatively.[5] In his subsequent writings Halévy demonstrated that he believed that only historically informed analysis would offer insight into the complexity of economic developments, social changes, intellectual movements, and cultural traditions, and hence only such historical sensitivity could provide the understanding needed for prudent and progressive action. As Raymond Aron has pointed out, Halévy continued the tradition of Montesquieu and Tocqueville, but updated to encompass the profound changes of the late nineteenth century and World War I.[6]

The Great War was a transformative experience for Halévy, as it was for most Europeans of his generation. He stopped teaching and put aside his scholarship during the war, and worked in hospitals that attended to the wounded and dying. When he returned to his scholarship after the war, he remained interested in British developments and in the broader issue of the tension between liberalism and socialism, but the chronological focus shifted to events that had led to war, and to the changes that were a consequence of the war and its attendant revolutions. This is the focus of Part III of the book. He remained a supporter of liberal democracy, but was deeply concerned about the increased vulnerability of European countries as they confronted the diplomatic and economic challenges of the postwar era, faced the impatient expectations of popular movements, and were challenged by the emergence of authoritarian figures. This is the period when he wrote his famous essay on the era of tyrannies. He feared that liberal democracies, in this new era created by war and revolution, and inhabiting a world order populated by charismatic leaders able to "organize enthusiasm," would be forced, if they were to survive at all, to change in unfortunate ways.[7]

Élie Halévy has been difficult to classify on the spectrum of modern French ideologies. He always referred to himself as a "liberal,"[8] which he certainly was, though it is necessary to add the qualification, as did François Furet in 1996, that Halévy was a liberal "in the widest sense of this term . . . which is to say that [he] belonged in thought to the philosophy of the

Enlightenment and in politics to the Left."[9] Like all liberals, he stoutly defended the civil and political principles identified with the French Revolution—civil equality and popular sovereignty—but he was extremely sensitive to the problems and inequities created by industrialization and its attendant social effects. A strong defender of individualism, he did not believe, as did Frédéric Bastiat or British Manchester Liberals, that the market was naturally self-regulating or produced an equitable distribution of riches. Political institutions and social organizations were necessary to ensure the protection of liberties and to rectify economic injustices. He seriously confronted, in short, the conflicts at the heart of modern industrial democracies: how to safeguard precious individual liberties while at the same time addressing socio-economic needs; how to foster individualism while at the same time recognizing the broadening administrative responsibilities of the state; how to balance individual emancipation, one the one hand, with political and socio-economic organization, on the other. It is the argument of this book that Halévy belongs to a distinctively French tradition of liberalism that first emerged during the French Revolution but that evolved as it confronted the dislocations of modernity.

What is unusual about Halévy—and one of the main reasons that it has been difficult for French scholars to categorize him—is that he approached these issues as a historian, not as a political theorist or political activist. Moreover, he was a historian not of France but of Britain. Though his lectures on the history of socialism encompassed French thinkers and movements, and though his correspondence demonstrates a deep concern for French and more broadly European affairs, his primary scholarly focus was Britain. Halévy began a serious study of things British in 1896, which led to the publication of his three-volume *La formation du radicalisme philosophique* in the early years of the new century.[10] Subsequently, he devoted much of his scholarly attention to his multi volume history of England in the nineteenth century,[11] though *en route* he wrote articles about British Methodism and books about Thomas Hodgskin and the British Empire.[12] Even after the war, when he turned to analyze the troubled state of world politics, England and British developments remained one of his central concerns, and were used comparatively to assess developments in other countries, including France. It is perhaps not surprising, given this scholarly focus, that his reputation is greater in the English-speaking world than in France.[13] The marginal, quasi-oppositional stance Halévy adopted toward his own country is elegantly captured by François Furet: "He constantly remained on the margins of the French scene, and even indefinable in his relationship with it: professor who deliberately held back from grand institutions, like the Sorbonne; intellectual who was passionate about public affairs without loving French politics; democratic republican who became the adopted son of a semi-aristocratic monarchy [England]; grand bourgeois who was touched by the socialist idea while refusing Marx and Jaurès; French patriot who hated French nationalism."[14]

Though Halévy is primarily known as a historian and intellectual, his actions during the Dreyfus Affair and after World War I demonstrated his commitment to moral responsibility and political engagement. How his liberalism evolved to address the social and economic problems thrown up by industrialization, and to address the international and domestic issues thrown up by war, revolution, and interwar instability, are central themes considered in part III of this book. The subtitle of the book—"Republican Liberalism Confronts the Era of Tyranny"—highlights this interwar era. Equally significant, however, were Halévy's contributions to philosophy and history, topics addressed in parts I and II. Another subtitle, considered but ultimately rejected, yet nonetheless equally accurate, would be "Socialist Liberal Historian During the French Third Republic."

## A Note on Sources

When I began working on this project in 2011, it was necessary to use a variety of dated editions of Halévy's writings and to work with the Halévy papers located in the archive at the École normale supérieure in Paris.[15] I expected and hoped that these extensive papers—there are ninety-five cartons of them—would offer new insights into Halévy's published works and help provide a framework for understanding the chronological development of Halévy's thought. To be sure, there was important earlier scholarship: biographies by Michèle Bo Bramsen[16] and Myrna Chase;[17] critical analyses by Raymond Aron,[18] Charles Gillispie,[19] Melvin Richter,[20] and François Bédarida.[21] Also available was newer scholarship on Halévy that reflected, in part, the increased interest in French liberalism consequent of the decline of revolutionary illusions and of *marxisant* frameworks of analysis following 1968, reinforced by the more general decline of the Left following the end of the

Cold War in 1989 and the implosion of the Soviet Union in 1991. In 1995, a critical edition of *La formation du radicalisme philosophique* was published.[22] This was followed, in 1996, by a valuable volume of Halévy's correspondence, with a superb introduction by François Furet.[23] In the same year a volume devoted to the Halévy family appeared, one that grew out of an exposition organized by the Musée d'Orsay.[24] More recently, works by Ludovic Frobert,[25] Stéphan Soulié,[26] Vincent Duclert,[27] and Marie Scot[28] (to name some of the most important) were published. Even more recently, there were conferences devoted to his thought that led to new analyses of various aspects of Halévy's *oeuvre*.[29]

The most significant new development for scholars, however, was the publication in 2016 of the first three volumes of a new critical edition of Halévy's *Oeuvres complètes*. Under the direction of Vincent Duclert and Marie Scot, and published by Les Belles Lettres, the volumes of the *Oeuvres complètes* promise to assist significantly future scholarship on Halévy.[30] This is especially evident in the volumes that focus on his posthumously published works. Volume 2 of the *Oeuvres complètes* is devoted to the *L'ère de tyrannies*, originally published in 1938. The earlier volume had been brought together by Halévy's widow, Florence, and his close friend Célestin Bouglé, and it contained not only the famous 1936 discussion of "L'ère de tyrannies," but also important articles written by Halévy about socialism, war, and problems facing post–World War I Europe. The new critical edition supplements these original articles with extensive critical notes and with other writings, conference presentations, and correspondence that touch on these issues. It also includes scholarly reflections about Halévy and his contributions written after his death, many of them relevant to themes he raised.

Volume 3 of the *Oeuvres complètes* is devoted to the *Histoire du socialisme européen*, originally published in 1948. The new critical edition analyzes how the editors (the group included, most importantly, Florence Halévy, Célestin Bouglé, and Raymond Aron) constructed the original volume from handwritten lectures and student notes. Again, the new critical edition includes extensive notes and other writings by Halévy related to the issues raised. Perhaps most important of all, it dates the various chapters of the 1948 publication, helping one to interpret the evolution of his thought.[31] Other scholars will wish to join me in expressing gratitude to the editors Vincent Duclert and Marie Scot. Having personally spent many months with the Halévy papers, I found it a luxury (and a relief) to have so many of the manuscript lectures and notes chronologically identified and published.

## A Note on Methodology

The ensuing chapters offer a densely contextualized intellectual biography of Élie Halévy. While wider socioeconomic and cultural factors are considered, especially as they exerted an influence on Halévy, the focus is on the development of his thought and his life. This distinctive focus inevitably involves trade-offs. Most obviously, it frames broader historical issues in relationship to the life of one individual and his immediate milieu. I make no apology for this but wish to note that I have attempted to provide sufficiently "thick" contextual analyses to avoid the subordination of issues to Halévy's distinctive perspective.

In defense of contextual intellectual biography, perhaps a few comments are not inappropriate. While structural and institutional forces obviously merit the close attention of historians, and have been weighed in what follows, I believe the best historical accounts include considerations of personal agency, motivation, ideology, actions, and the wider impact of these on society. The natural way to provide such an account is to look at men and women, their backgrounds, their temperaments, and their thoughts, and to give attention to how these unfolded in broader historical contexts—intellectual, cultural, political, social, and economic.

I've come to view historical scholarship—better, my own historical work—as a deep sort of "reflective travel" (the best metaphor I can think of). It is the type of study that offers, I believe, a salutary form of learning. In an obvious sense, of course, we are always in and of our own culture. But reflective travel pushes against this embeddedness—minimally providing a pleasurable respite from our own culture (the result, perhaps, of any deeply absorbing work) but, more significantly, encouraging a receptivity to another culture, another historical era, and their broader significance. On the rebound, moreover, it is able to foster a fresh view of one's own historical situatedness, with all its assumptions and peculiarities. It offers, in its best moments, a useful comparative perspective. I believe that this is especially useful when considering the familiar but fraught issues that occupied Halévy's attention—liberalism, socialism, war, revolution, liberty, and justice—issues that are central to the intellectual biography that follows. It goes without saying that they remain relevant today. In the conclusion of the book, I offer some reflections on the history of French socialism and liberalism.

# PART I

Neo-Kantianism and
British Radicalism

## CHAPTER I

# The Early Years

There is a virtue that I place above all others: sincerity. It is the
condition of social life.
—Élie Halévy, "Journal," 18 May 1888

I am neither Protestant, Catholic, nor Jew. True religion is true Bud-
dhism, which denies the immortality of the soul, the divinity and
existence of one or several gods, and limits itself to affirming as
unique dogma *that the truth is true*, and that reason is worthy of
dominating passion and suppressing grief. These things, however, are
true only because they are truths, not because Buddha said them.
—Élie Halévy to Xavier Léon, 17 September 1897

Élie Halévy was born into a prominent wealthy Parisian family that touched
many centers of the artistic and intellectual life of nineteenth- and early
twentieth-century France. The family was so extraordinary that in 1996 the
Musée d'Orsay in Paris organized an exposition that focused exclusively on
it.[1] A brief summary of a few of the high points of the family history will
provide a glimpse of the milieu in which Élie Halévy was raised.[2]

The Halévy family had Jewish, Catholic, and Protestant roots. Élie's
paternal great-grandfather, Élie Halphen Lévy, was born in 1760 in Fürth,
close to Nuremberg, but moved with his family to Metz in 1789 and then to
Paris in the mid-1790s, moves that probably were connected with the liberal
revolutionary reforms that granted French citizenship rights to Jews (by the
legislation of 1790 and 1791). Élie Lévy became a cantor at the synagogue on

the rue de la Victoire in Paris and, because of his language skills, an intermediary between the Jewish and Christian communities. He changed his name in 1808 to Halévy. In 1818, he became connected with the journal *Israélite français*, founded in the same year. Two years later, he published *Instruction morale et religieuse à l'usage de la jeunesse israélite*. He died in 1826.

Élie Halévy (Élie Halphen Lévy) had two sons. The eldest, Fromental (1799–1862), entered the Conservatoire de musique de Paris when he was ten years old and subsequently had a successful career in music, becoming one of the principal composers in France during the first half of the nineteenth century. His opera *La Juive* (1835) was a great success, as was his comic opera *Les Mousquetaires de la reine* (1846). Fromental entered the Institut and the Académie des beaux-arts in the mid-1830s. His wife was a member of the Rodrigues family, famous bankers and entrepreneurs of the Second Empire. Fromental's daughter Geneviève married Georges Bizet, the great nineteenth-century composer, forming a family connection that would be important for her cousin Ludovic Halévy, about whom I have more to say below. Moreover, after Bizet's death, she remarried and became a significant figure in the social scene in Paris. One of her friends was Marcel Proust, and some have claimed that she was a model for the duchesse de Guermantes in *À la recherche du temps perdu*.

Élie's second son, Léon (1802–1883)—the grandfather of our Élie Halévy—had an equally successful career in literature. He was sent to the Lycée Charlemagne, where he befriended fellow students like Sainte-Beuve, and at a young age, between 1823 and 1825, served as the last secretary (following Auguste Comte) of Henri de Saint-Simon. In 1825, he published *Resumé de l'histoire des Juifs anciens*; this was followed in 1828 by a companion volume, *Resumé de l'histoire des Juifs modernes*. In these works, Léon Halévy called for a "complete fusion" between Jews and their compatriots, taking a strong assimilationist stance that counseled relegating religion to the private sphere. He was a co-founder of *Le Producteur*, a co-editor of *L'Opinion: Journal des moeurs, de la littérature, des arts, des théâtres et de l'industrie*, and subsequently taught French literature at the École polytechnique (1831–1834), worked at the Institut and for the Ministry of Public Instruction, and from 1868 to 1876 was a frequent contributor to the Parisian *Journal des débats*. His call for assimilation reflected his own life story: he married Alexandrine Le Bas, who was Catholic and the daughter of the famous Parisian architect Hippolyte Le Bas. All of the children of the union of Léon Halévy and Alexandrine Le Bas were baptized.

Before he married Alexandrine Le Bas, Léon Halévy had fathered a child with Lucinde Paradol, an actress at the Théâtre français. This child remained close to the Halévy family but was legally recognized by François Prévost and therefore named Anatole Prévost-Paradol. Anatole Prévost-Paradol (1829–1870) was a very successful and influential writer during the Second Empire, connected with the *Journal des débats* (1857–1870), author of *Études sur les moralistes français* (1865) and *La France nouvelle* (1868), and a member of the Académie française (elected in 1865). An Orleanist liberal, he was a critic of the Empire and was very close to his half brother, Ludovic Halévy, the father of the Élie Halévy, who is the subject of this study.[3]

Ludovic Halévy (1834–1908), the son of Alexandrine Le Bas and Léon Halévy, grew up in two worlds: the corridors of the Institut; and the milieu of the Opéra (where his uncle, Fromental Halévy, remained influential). Ludovic attended the Collège Louis-le-Grand, where he made connections that led to a close association with the duc de Morny and positions in the government administration, including that of *secrétaire-rédacteur des débats du Corps législatif.* The second musical world was more important, however, especially when he teamed up as a libretist with Jacques Offenbach, Henri Meilhac, and Bizet (his cousin by marriage, as we have seen). He had an immensely successful career. In 1855, at the young age of twenty-two, he wrote his first light opera with Offenbach, *Ba-Ta-Clan*; and during the following years he worked with Offenbach on, among others, *L'Impresario* (1856) and *Le Docteur miracle* (1857). By the late 1850s, he was writing comic operas on his own (like *Rose et Rosette*, 1858), and collaborating with others, like Hector Crémieux (on *Orphée aux Enfers*, 1858). His association with Meilhac began in 1860, when they worked together on *Ce qui plaît aux hommes*. The partnership quickly grew into a regular collaboration, and together they wrote around fifty works. During the 1860s, Offenbach, Meilhac, and Halévy teamed up to produce a string of incredibly popular opéra bouffes, including *La Belle Hélène* (1864), *Barbe-Bleue* (1866), *La Vie parisienne* (1866), and *La Grande-Duchesse de Gérolstein* (1867). These works of "Offenbach-mania" brought all three notoriety and fabulous wealth. Halévy's connection with Bizet took off during the 1870s. The most famous collaboration was when Halévy and Meilhac wrote the libretto for Bizet's opera *Carmen*, adapted from the novel by Prosper Mérimée.

In 1868, Ludovic Halévy married Louise Breguet, a member of the prominent and wealthy Protestant family that produced Swiss watches, but also a family that became famous, after returning to France during the revolutionary era, for building precision instruments and being pioneers in telegraphy and aviation. Louise's parents lived in an *hôtel particulier* on the quai de l'Horloge on the Île de la Cité. Her cousin was the famous French chemist Marcelin Berthelot.[4]

In 1870, during the siege of Paris in the midst of the Franco-Prussian War, Ludovic and Louise fled Paris, taking refuge on the Normandy coast at Étretat. This is where Élie Halévy, the subject of this book, was born, on 6 September 1870, five days after the military loss of Sedan, and two days after the proclamation in Paris of the Republic. After ten months, the family returned to Paris, and Ludovic continued his musical successes for the next few years. He gave up the theater after 1881, the date of his last composition, and devoted himself to writing, something with which he had already had some success when, in 1872, he published his accounts of the Franco-Prussian War, *L'Invasion: Souvenirs et récits*.[5] In December of the same year, another son was born, Élie's brother, Daniel, who was to become a celebrated literary figure.[6]

The family lived during Élie's and Daniel's youth on the rue de Roche-foucauld, then rue de Douai, in the Pigalle quartier. One of the neighbors and frequent visitors to the rue de Douai was Edgar Degas, the famous painter, who remained a close family friend until a break during the Dreyfus Affair, a break that was precipitated by Degas's strident anti-Semitism. Upon the death of Louise's father in 1883, Ludovic bought the five-floor Breguet residence at 39 quai de l'Horloge. Ten years later, he bought a house and estate in the countryside southeast of Paris at Sucy-en-Brie. In the years between, in 1886, he was elected to the Académie française.

"Quelle famille!" to borrow the phrase of François Furet.[7] Born into this wealthy extended family (Figure 1), the young Élie had as privileged a life as was possible during the early decades of the Third Republic. In the words of his close friend Célestin Bouglé, Élie inhabited a society with "the richest and most varied traditions, which opened for him views of the world of the Insti-tut as well as that of the Opéra, the worlds of foreign politics as well as the minor events of the boulevards."[8]

Élie was, by all indications, a studious, serious, extremely gifted child (Figure 2) and adolescent. One gets glimpses of this from entries in a private "journal" that he kept while growing up, a journal discovered only after his death. When seventeen years old, for example, he criticized the pretensions of those looking for recognition, and held up the value of "sincerity."

# The Halévy Family

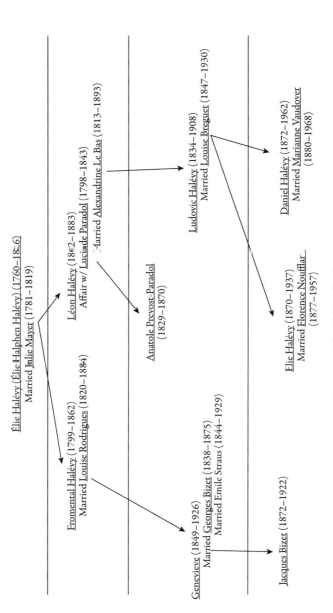

Élie Halévy (Élie Halphen Halévy) (1760–1826)
Married Julie Mayer (1781–1819)

Léon Halévy (1802–1883)
Affair w/ Lucinde Paradol (1798–1843)
Married Alexandrine Le Bas (1813–1893)

Anatole Prevost-Paradol
(1829–1870)

Ludovic Halévy (1834–1908)
Married Louise Breguet (1847–1930)

Daniel Halévy (1872–1962)
Married Marianne Vaudoyer
(1880–1968)

Fromental Halévy (1799–1862)
Married Louise Rodrigues (1820–1884)

Élie Halévy (1870–1937)
Married Florence Noufflar
(1877–1957)

Geneviève (1849–1926)
Married Georges Bizet (1838–1875)
Married Emile Straus (1844–1929)

Jacques Bizet (1872–1922)

FIGURE 1. The Halévy family tree.

FIGURE 2. Élie Halévy at nine years old (about 1879–1880). Reproduced with the permission of the Société historique et archéologique de Sucy-en-Brie, and of the chairman of this society, Michel Balard.

Honor, the bragging of *honnêteté*, disgusts me. . . .

There is a virtue that I place above all others: sincerity. It is the condition of social life. There is nothing as fatiguing as the lie, as the pretension, this life of taste and of spirit [*esprit*]. . . . All my efforts are directed here: to be sincere. There is no reason to become involved [*s'engrener*] in any coterie, literary or other; [rather, it is necessary] to guard my complete independence of thought, of language; [it is necessary] not to be obliged to anyone, even to myself, for my opinions; not to allow any invasion [of this independence] because of friendship or doctrine; to have clear ideas with the perfect liberty to act as I wish.[9]

Élie goes on to refer to a passage of Seneca that counsels against regretting the passage of time. "You see," he writes, "that the Stoic inspiration is the source of my conduct."[10]

Other passages in this journal reflected Halévy's desire to devote himself to a moral and intellectual life that made no compromises with the constraints of practical life—an idealistic, even absolutist stance not so uncharacteristic of youth. This philosophical framework also informed the "intellectual crisis" that he experienced when he was twenty. "I feel clearly the nature of the revolution that operates within me. There is in me an old Jewish [*sémite*] and Protestant foundation that becomes each day more exhausted and desiccated. Protestant by heredity, Kantian for two or three years, Plato swept it all away. But it is necessary that Plato be organized in my mind inside of the Protestant and Kantian forms. This is the problem in its psychological form."[11]

## Secularism

The religious orientation of Élie Halévy—or, more precisely, its absence—was an outgrowth of his heritage and upbringing, but it also was deeply influenced by his education and milieu. His mother was responsible for what limited religious training her two sons received, and therefore, to the extent that Élie subscribed to any religion, it was to Protestantism (in predominantly Catholic France). Even this, however, exaggerates his religiosity. The Dreyfus Affair, as we shall see, forced him to confront his "objective" identity as a Jew because of the family name, but he did not so identify himself. This was expressed clearly in a letter to his friend Célestin Bouglé in November 1897, written at the moment Élie realized that Dreyfus was innocent. "I am almost certain that Dreyfus . . . has been the victim of a frightful plot, that reasons of state and of electoral interest have commanded dissimulation. But I carry a Jewish name and am Protestant: am I the victim of an illusion of caste?"[12] He wondered if his Jewish or Protestant heritage had in some way influenced his judgment, asking his friend to reassure him that it had not. This provides clear evidence that he recognized this background, but it does not indicate any close identity with either. Moreover, we know from other sources that he pushed back against any such identification.

Such a stance was not uncommon for individuals in assimilated Jewish and Protestant families during the Third Republic. Jews and Protestants, of course, were granted full civil rights and citizenship during the French

Revolution, and many embraced the civic, cultural, and economic opportunities these rights afforded. Some scholars have argued that Judaism and Protestantism, stripped down to their ethical cores, were fully compatible with contemporary French culture, and that, therefore, embracing Frenchness did not entail giving up Jewishness or Protestantness. This blending was encouraged by the pedagogical policy of the Third Republic, which stressed secular regenerative education.[13] Other scholars see the embrace of secular French republicanism as inevitably diminishing essential elements of Jewishness or Protestantness. This is a debate that has accompanied many movements of "secularization" and "assimilation." Diana R. Halmann has suggested that for French Jews of the generation of Élie's grandfather, this created "a palpable tension in the balancing of their lives as *citoyens* and *israélites*, a tension that led to a certain ambivalence toward their heritage and the religion of their birth."[14] Whatever tension and equivocation this produced, however, did not inhibit Fromental and Léon's moves toward assimilation. Léon, Élie's grandfather, recommended intermarriage with gentiles in his writings, suggested that religion should be relegated to the "private" sphere, and married a Catholic.[15] This did not entail entirely giving up his Jewish identity, nor a lack of engagement with Judaic culture, but it does suggest a commitment to an intellectual and cultural fusion with non-Jews. This was even more common a half century later, when our Élie Halévy was coming of age. There is no evidence that Élie experienced any psychological tension or ambivalence about heritage or "identity." So far as is known, he never questioned or denied his family's mixed heritage, but his identity seemed firmly centered on being French.

That being said, anyone who had knowledge of the historical experience of Jews and Protestants in France, as Halévy certainly had, could not ignore the prejudices that had existed in the past, nor be oblivious to the continuing strength of conservative Catholic ideologues who insisted that French identity was reserved for Catholics. Nor could one easily ignore the political implications of this narrow view of French identity. This helps explain why Jews and Protestants, as well as individuals whose ancestors were Jewish or Protestant, tended to be staunch supporters of the civil and political rights introduced during the Revolution and guaranteed by subsequent regimes. Jews and Protestants were also prominent among those who desired the reduction of the influence of the Catholic Church, and who supported the secularization of French education. Élie Halévy, for one, was always vocal in his support of the "constitution" of the Third Republic, especially of its judicial protections, and he was in favor of the expansion of *les écoles laïques*.

Such issues became especially important when rights were threatened by conservative and reactionary forces, as was the case during the Dreyfus Affair, discussed in chapter 4. Sensitivity to these issues helps explain the resistance on the part of Halévy and his associates when faced with the nativist cultural nationalism celebrated in novels like those of Maurice Barrès, to say nothing of the disgust they felt when they confronted the crude anti-Semitism in writings of people like Édouard Drumont. This sensitivity also helps explain why individuals of Jewish and Protestant heritage tended to move in certain cultural circles and be attracted to certain institutions. Some schools, like the Lycée Condorcet, were viewed as especially open and tolerant, and it comes as no surprise that it was favored by assimilated Jews, Protestants, and their descendants.

Halévy embraced modern French culture and institutions, which does not mean that he rejected his Jewish or Protestant heritage. But neither heritage seemed especially important. Halévy mentioned his Jewish identity only in passing, and generally only when anti-Semitism showed its ugly face. Halévy's identity with Protestantism was similarly weak. Though exposed to Protestantism by his mother, and sometimes identifying himself as a Protestant, Halévy wrote to his brother, Daniel, in 1893 (he was twenty-two years old at the time), "I distrust new cults, and pardon only very old religions. It is better to be Stoic than Christian."[16] Two years later, in July 1895, he wrote to Bouglé, "I see no reason to believe in the immortality of the soul, nor to assign the universe another end than the universe itself."[17] A few months after this, he stated succinctly, again to Bouglé, that one of the "embarrassing problems" for any religion was the question of "faith." "What is faith?" he asked rhetorically; what is it, he answered, other than "the resistance of custom to reason." In fact, it is, he pointed out, only "prejudice."[18] "Religious emotion," he suggested in July 1900, "is an aesthetic emotion attributing a moral value to its object."[19]

As these statements indicate, Halévy was a secular rationalist who distrusted passion and intuition. This would be reflected, as we see below, in the philosophical orientation of the *Revue de métaphysique et de morale*, the journal that Halévy founded with his friends Xavier Léon, Léon Brunschvicg, and Émile Chartier (Alain). Upon the appearance of the first numbers of this journal, Halévy proudly proclaimed to Xavier Léon: "We have demonstrated . . . that one is able to be idealist without being Christian, and a free thinker without being a follower of [Herbert] Spencer, in other words that in France in 1900 one is able to revitalize the Greek philosophy of 400 years before Jesus Christ."[20]

Halévy's colleague and friend Brunschvicg wrote after his death that "the *oeuvre* of Élie Halévy is to be explained by his fidelity to the inspiration of Plato. . . . To Élie Halévy's eyes, the connection of theory and practice is the reason for the existence of philosophical effort."[21] While I believe Brunschvicg's statement exaggerates the importance of Plato and understates the importance of neo-Kantianism, it is an accurate characterization of the high value Halévy placed on reason, and on the connection of reason to practice. These particulars of his philosophical orientation were formed during his education at the Lycée Condorcet, reinforced during his years at the École normale supérieure, and remained the animating philosophy of the *Revue de métaphysique et de morale*.

## Education at the Lycée Condorcet and the École Normale Supérieure

Élie went to the Lycée Condorcet in 1880 and remained there until 1888.[22] At the lycée he met many of the males who remained his close friends for life. Two of his classmates were Léon Brunschvicg and Xavier Léon, who joined with Élie in 1893 to create the philosophy journal *Revue de métaphysique et de morale*. This is discussed below.[23] It was also at the Lycée Condorcet that all three became deeply influenced by the Kantian perspective of their philosophy teacher, Alphonse Darlu.[24] Stéphane Mallarmé, the symbolist poet, also taught at the Lycée Condorcet at this time, but Élie seemed little influenced by him, though he took his classes. His younger brother, Daniel, who followed Élie into the lycée two years later, was more influenced by Mallarmé and subsequently pursued a more literary path.

Élie was by all accounts a serious, intellectually intense young man. Robert Dreyfus, a classmate of Daniel's, recalled how he and his friends were a bit intimidated in his presence. "I saw Élie Halévy again at the Lycée Condorcet, austere *philosophe*, laureate of the *concours générale*. . . . This was the time when Marcel Proust sent to me one day a sort of psychological confession, advising me with anxiety to hold it secret, and not even to show it to our friend Daniel [Halévy] nor above all to his brother Élie, of whom he was particularly fearful of his sarcastic disapprobation. Élie Halévy, our elder, greatly intimidated Marcel Proust, and I believe that at this period he also intimidated me a little. Since then, I have often felt all that was indulgent in his manner, even what was tender."[25]

FIGURE 3. (*Standing*): Élie Halévy, Daniel Halévy (Élie's brother); (*seated*): Valentine Halévy (Élie's aunt), and Alexandrine Halévy (Élie's paternal grandmother) (about 1890, around the time Élie would have been attending the École normale supérieure). Reproduced with the permission of the Société historique et archéologique de Sucy-en-Brie, and of the chairman of this society, Michel Balard.

Accounts indicate that Halévy retained this serious bearing throughout his life. Posthumous recollections by friends and acquaintances noted his intellectual honesty and moral bearing, but also the absence of pretense or interest in honors. Julien Benda, for example, obviously deeply moved by Halévy's unexpected death in 1937, wrote the following:

> I see again Halévy in his study at Sucy [Halévy's residence on the
> outskirts of Paris after 1911]. I see again this tall, slim, elegant man,
> the perfect model of the aristocratic republican. I see him as he was,
> so simple, so little pontifical, so scornful, without any boastfulness,
> of the honors that were assigned to him, so free from any bitterness
> before the clever and brilliant historians and the din of their glory.
> When I discover once again, in reading his books, how this simplic-
> ity covered knowledge, disinterested labor, lofty views, original
> ideas, I think that I have been given, at least once in my life, the
> privilege of approaching a great practitioner of the human heart and
> mind. Such individuals are a consolation to the human race.[26]

At the end of his years at the Lycée Condorcet, Halévy sat for the *concours général de philosophie*, and, as Robert Dreyfus's statement above indicates, he was ranked first. As a result of this high placement, he was admitted to the École normale supérieure, the premier humanities school in France (Figure 3). He resided at the École normale from 1889 to 1892 and there encountered other lifelong friends: Célestin Bouglé, who became a highly regarded sociologist and, in 1935, the director of the École normale; and Émile Chartier, the philosopher, journalist, and pacifist who became famous under the pseudonym Alain.[27] At the École normale, the Kantianism that Halévy had absorbed from Darlu at the Lycée Condorcet was reinforced.[28] He took classes from Émile Boutroux, who had studied in Heidelberg in 1869–1870 and had been influenced by Eduard Zeller and Hermann von Helmholtz, German neo-Kantians. Though Élie came to differ from Boutroux on several fronts, he was deeply respectful and appreciative of Boutroux's philosophical stance.[29] Halévy finished second in his graduating class, behind Alain, and in the same year, 1892, received his *agrégation de philosophie*. In 1893, he was named professor of philosophy at l'École Jean-Baptiste Say.

## CHAPTER 2

# Revue de Métaphysique et de Morale

It is necessary [for us] to act against the miserable positivism from
which we are extricating ourselves, and from the irritating religiosity
in which we risk getting stuck—to found a philosophy of action and
of reflection—to be rationalists with rage.

—Élie Halévy to Xavier Léon, 31 August 1891

The importance of neo-Kantianism in late nineteenth-century European
thought has been commonly noted.[1] We cannot review here the various
forms that this took in France and elsewhere, but it is important to understand how it provided the essential philosophical framework for the secular
rationalism of Halévy, Xavier Léon, and Léon Brunschvicg, and of the
journal these three young men founded in 1893, the *Revue de métaphysique
et de morale*.[2] All three had absorbed a neo-Kantian perspective as students
in the philosophy class at the Lycée Condorcet taught by Alphonse Darlu,
a man who continued to exert an influence on the general philosophical
orientation of the journal.[3] There are many complexities to their stance,
but the essential aspect is how it positioned their philosophy between the
narrow empirical "positivism" of Auguste Comte and the expansive subjective "spiritualism" of Alfred Fouillée and Henri Bergson. It also informed,
as we shall see below, how Halévy and his cofounders defined their relationship to the empirical psychological theory of Théodule-Armand Ribot
(founder of the *Revue philosophique* and holder of the chair in "experimental and comparative psychology" at the Collège de France) and the sociological theory of Émile Durkheim.[4]

## Neo-Kantianism and the *Revue de Métaphysique et de Morale*

The Kantianism of the directors of the *Revue de métaphysique et de morale* made them secular rationalists who rejected ontology for epistemology.[5] In a revealing statement after Halévy died in 1937, his close friend Célestin Bouglé characterized the orientation of Halévy, Xavier Léon, Léon Brunschvicg, and the *Revue* in the following manner: "It appeared to them urgent to react at the same time against the current of positivism, which stopped at the facts, and against mysticism, which led to superstitions. For this project, [it was necessary] to redress the mind, to render it confident in its original forms, to deliver it from the 'fascination of the object,' to make [one] aware that the mind is the central cord of morality as well as of science."[6] As this indicates, the "metaphysics" in the title of the journal did not carry a religious meaning for the founders of the journal. Its inclusion in the title was meant to announce their dedication to the search for the contributions of the human mind to our understanding of the world, and to philosophical and rational principles. An essential task of philosophy, in the founders' eyes, was to resist being confined to ordering empirical data, as recommended by positivists, and to strive to find the principles and theories that human reason provided for an understanding of the world and its inhabitants.

This was a principal reason that Xavier Léon insisted on keeping the term "metaphysics" in the title. He wished to distinguish their endeavor from that of the positivists, who argued that there were no absolute principles and insisted that philosophy should be restricted to empirical knowledge. The inclusion of the term "metaphysics" did not entail, however, any sympathy for a religious or a mystical perspective. Halévy had at first worried that the term would carry such associations, but he became convinced, as he told Léon in a letter, that it was appropriate if carefully defined. "Having reflected on it all, I withdraw my objections to the word: metaphysics, if you mean by this not a separate science, discussing in isolation a determined number of special problems, but a method, opposed to the *positivist* method of observation."[7]

The other term in the title, of course, was "moral," and this also signaled the orientation of the founders. They insisted that the rationalist orientation that they adopted should avoid a self-referential philosophy unconnected with real human actions. Philosophy was not to be an abstract and unworldly idealism; rather, it was to inform human activity in society and in history. As Brunschvicg put it in his tribute to Halévy after his death, the title of the journal included *morale* because the founders "wished to underline their ambition to act. . . . For Élie Halévy, the connection of theory and practice is the *raison d'être* of the philosophic effort—the connecting theme of the articles that he wrote."[8]

It was important, as Xavier Léon wrote in his first signed text in the *Revue*, to attack the "intellectual and moral anarchy" of the era, and to do this he planned "to write a book to propose a discipline of *moeurs* for the young."[9] This combination of philosophy and morality was defended explicitly by Léon when contemporaries raised questions about the focus of the journal.[10] He wrote, for example, to the philosopher Octave Hamelin: "If we were permitted to summarize in two formulas the spirit of our direction, we would say willingly that the *Revue de métaphysique et de morale* pursues a double goal: that of bringing together the philosophy of the sciences on terrain other than that of facts, that is, on the terrain of ideas; and that of bringing together the philosophy of morals on a certain other than that of faith in sentiment, that is, on the terrain of Reason."[11]

As this neo-Kantian agenda suggests, the founders of the journal wished to distance themselves from a scientism that pretended to furnish a dogmatic explanation of the universe that dissolved all mystery—of what at the time was referred to as "scientific mechanism." But they were equally opposed to skeptical theories that rejected scientific explanations as providing true knowledge. It was necessary, in the words of the "manifesto" of the journal, to reinforce the "lumière de la raison" against the reigning culture that finds itself "in the midst of these incertitudes, between the current positivism that stops itself at the facts and the mysticism that leads to superstition."[12]

This stance was shared with neo-Kantians in Germany, and both groups believed that they had found in Kant's philosophy the foundations of a unified scientific and moral view, in opposition to the fragmentation of thought represented by the emergence of different scholarly disciplines and marked by the growing recognition of the diversity of social forms and traditions.[13] Kant's philosophy was attractive because it provided a unity—an epistemological theory that pushed back against the bold metaphysical theories of the post-Kantians, and a philosophy that addressed not just epistemological issues but also those of moral action and aesthetic judgment. On the epistemological front, neo-Kantians were convinced that Kant's transcendental method demonstrated that the *a priori* intuitions of time and space and the *a priori* categories of the mind successfully accounted for the basis of scientific knowledge. This was true even as there were disagreements among late nineteenth-century neo-Kantians concerning whether these categories were biological or logical. Moreover, on the moral front, most neo-Kantians were convinced that Kant's philosophy had successfully integrated the fields of epistemology, morals, and aesthetic judgment—that is, that the three *Critiques* provided a philosophy of non-problematic unity and coherence.

One of the issues that concerned neo-Kantians was how to accommodate the evolving nature of scientific knowledge. It was widely accepted that Kant had based his critical philosophy on the assumed truth of Newtonian physics. As scientific knowledge evolved, especially with the introduction of evolutionary theory and, later, of relativity theory, some wondered if the system would be flexible enough to accommodate these changes. Various neo-Kantians argued that the system of *a priori* categories would need to evolve in ways that accommodated our advancing knowledge. Others, of course, concluded that Kant's epistemological theory was inadequate and, breaking with the epistemological orientation of Kant, came to look for other philosophies to ground their thought. Halévy and his cofounders pushed back against this rejection of Kant.

Another difficult issue for neo-Kantians was the relationship of the noumenal and phenomenal realms, an old philosophical chestnut that reemerged in the debates of the late nineteenth century. Kant had famously argued that our scientific knowledge was restricted to the phenomenal realm. This left open the issue of how to conceive of the noumenal realm of "things-in-themselves." For some, the noumenal realm had no independent meaning and no independent existence; the sensible, intelligible manifold of experience was ordered by our mind, and this simply *was* reality. For these thinkers, the beauty of Kant's transcendental system was that it protected scientific knowledge from metaphysical assumptions and claims, implying that arenas of "knowledge" beyond the phenomenal were postulates of limited value. For others (including Kant himself), the importance of postulates (like the existence of God) were central, especially for the construction of moral principles, the making of aesthetic judgments, and the conceptualization of how to act. This left open the difficult issue of determining the relationship of these arenas to the wider issue of "being." In short, were there irreconcilable tensions among the truth claims of the three *Critiques*?

Halévy and his associates at the *Revue* believed that Kantianism provided a comprehensive framework for scientific, moral, and aesthetic knowledge, and that it was necessary to keep these three realms distinct. Halévy, for example, in a letter to Bouglé in April 1903 stressed the importance of keeping different types of knowledge distinct: "I have no new enlightenment to bring to you on the problem of final cause: reread the *Critique of Judgment* [of Kant]. You know that I consider neither science capable of resolving, or abolishing, metaphysical problems, nor metaphysics capable of making discoveries in the manner of science."[14] Halévy and the other editors of the *Revue* argued that both scientific and moral truths were available, and that both were essential.

Concerning scientific knowledge, they believed that advances in our understanding of the world were underpinned by an evolution of principles and theoretical frameworks, and that these in turn were situated on firm experimental and philosophical bases. They argued that Kantian theory, properly understood, supported these theoretical frameworks and furthered scientific progress.

This stance becomes clearer when one considers their embrace of Henri Poincaré's "conventionalism." They were attracted to Poincaré's famous argument that theories were "commodities" that offered different frameworks for understanding the universe, and they were convinced that this did not undermine the idea of scientific truth. Poincaré argued that theoretical frameworks were the principles, definitions, and "conventions" that humans have selected as organizational guides for revealing the relationships among the various phenomena of the world. Objective reality, he argued, is nothing other than these relationships. Truth, therefore, is never a fixed set of ideas true for all time, as might be suggested by religious thought, Platonic forms, or even Kantian things-in-themselves. Truth is limited to the complexities of conventions, definitions, and principles that meet our human need for a stable, objective understanding of the world. This did not mean that Poincaré viewed truth emerging from arbitrary thoughts or intuitions. Scientific knowledge, and more broadly our general knowledge of the world, is to be based on experiments that lead to scientific agreement, and more broadly to moral and legal accords that structure human relations.[15]

This was very appealing to the directors of the *Revue*, who agreed with Poincaré that scientific truth was a progressive rational understanding of the world and its laws. Brunschvicg, for example, wrote: "Some have made him [Poincaré] say that science was indifferent to the search for truth, and that one was authorized by this pretended indifference to find elsewhere the center of human preoccupations, in order to raise above science a *je ne sais quoi* which one calls truth, and of which the proper character will never be able to be verified. Poincaré did not accept this."[16] There was a fundamental difference, in the eyes of Brunschvicg, between the embrace of an "arbitrary" stance toward truth and the "conventional" view of truth that he shared with Poincaré.

Halévy and his cofounders wished to embrace science and to share its criticism of any radical relativism or mysticism that suggested that the truths of science could be dissolved by claims of all-embracing subjectivity. At the same time, they wished to insist that philosophy had a legitimate role *along-side* the scientific disciplines: namely, to bring reasoned criticism to forms of knowledge, including scientific knowledge; to analyze the consistency of the claims of the various sciences; in short, to provide *"l'esprit de réflexion cri-tique."* Halévy was quite strident about this in a letter to Léon. "It is necessary [for us] to act against the miserable positivism from which we are extricating ourselves, and from the irritating religiosity in which we risk getting stuck—to found a philosophy of action and of reflection—to be rationalists with rage."[17]

## Between "Spiritualism" and "Positivism" (Between Alfred Fouillée and Auguste Comte)

Halévy's first article in the *Revue de métaphysique et de morale*, published in 1893 and co-written with Léon Brunschvicg, provides evidence of the desire to stake out a path between "spiritualism" and "positivism." The article was devoted to defending "science" against religion and positivism, and to recommending the creation of chairs in logic and morality to join the other chairs at the Collège de France.[18] Halévy and Brunschvicg focused on the Collège because it was one of the most important cultural institutions of France; in their own words, "destined to direct the intellectual life of a people." Because of this important role, they insisted that it had to remain flexible enough to "change with the times."[19] They noted that the Collège had traversed two periods in the nineteenth century—a first period represented by Michelet, Quinet, and Mickiewicz and a second period identified with Renan—and they then pointed out that the school was currently led by defenders of science who had created two new chairs: one devoted to the history of the sciences, and a second devoted to experimental and comparative psychology. Unfortunately, in their opinion, the general orientation of those holding these chairs, *and* of those occupying the positions in Greek and Latin philosophy and in modern philosophy, focused on the history of their disciplines rather than on the underlying principles of these disciplines. "The philosoph-ical teaching at the Collège de France," Halévy and Brunschvicg wrote, "lacks nothing except philosophy. Dogmatic and skeptical: the ones because they impose on philosophical problems a solution determined in advance, in front of which free reflection has no rights; the others because, in an absolutist fashion, they do not wish to pose philosophical problems, believing that it is, on these matters, either dangerous or unuseful to open discussion publicly."[20] Halévy and Brunschvicg clearly wished to recommend a different orientation, one that correctly conceptualized the importance of both science and philo-sophy.

The major thrust of the article, entitled "La Philosophie au Collège de France,"was to defend what Halévy and Brunschvicg termed the "rational method" against the unfortunate "corcordat" that has been established between mysticism, on the one hand, and positivism, on the other. Both approaches were flawed because they failed to address appropriately the criti-cal questions facing reason. They were either too empirical or too idealistic, too positivistic or too religious. Halévy and Brunschvicg rejected Comtean positivism, arguing that positivists assumed that knowledge of the universe was limited to piecemeal studies. "While science [as viewed by the positivists] no longer pretends to be, in any degree, an absolute and definitive systemati-zation of things, it is conceived as constituted by a set of procedures that experience teaches us. The positivist faith is free to affirm [incorrectly, in their opinion] that these procedures always succeed, that we are habituated by long experience never to be deceived; but religious faith is equally free to regard science as an artificial construction, and to regard its results as conve-nient formulas imposed on the mystery of things by human caprice."[21] As this quotation indicates, Halévy and Brunschvicg also rejected a religious framework, arguing that it was too divorced from any connection with empirical reality and therefore had the tendency to make assumptions and reach conclusions that were unverifiable. "The ones [the positivists] are attached to the pure givens of experience, and prevent themselves from draw-ing from them any practical system, resigned in advance to the slow and fatal evolution of things; the others [the mystics/the religious] dream of forcefully introducing into the facts rudimentary principles born of their imagination and their needs."[22]

The solution, according to Halévy and Brunschvicg, was for science to retake possession of itself, to consider its work "neither blind, nor arbitrary." And for this to be so, "it is necessary that the universal order appear as being neither a coincidence, nor a fiction; because reason does not admit chance and does not admit miracle."[23] It was necessary to investigate with critical reason the interrelationship of science, empirical reality, and human action. "It is impossible for reason not to pose philosophical problems; impossible for speculative reason not to search to coordinate the laws of nature and practical reason, to fix the rules of human conduct; and it is impossible that this problem, posed by reason, is able to be treated and resolved by anything except a rational method. . . . It is not a question of giving a particular school an official approbation, nor of creating a dogmatism: it is a question of encouraging and stimulating the critical spirit, of instituting an order of discussion."[24] The goal of reason is to continually search for a coherent view of the universe that avoids the partiality of positivism and the caprice of religion. "To place intelligence in front of nature, and to show how it organizes the phenomena by the simple development of its constitutive laws; briefly, to teach reason to rediscover itself in the science that it has made."[25]

To situate themselves in the philosophical debates of the era, Halévy and his cofounders were careful to distinguish their stance not only from the positivists but also from "spiritualists" like Alfred Fouillée.[26] Fouillée shared their neo-Kantian anti-positivism but differed on how consciousness functioned. He argued that ideas are not "epiphenomenal" and passive; rather, ideas must be considered as forces that inform our actions and underpin the manner in which we experience the world. Halévy and Brunschvicg summarized it this way: "The root of sensation is activity, appetite. . . . From this point of view alone, one is able to conceive how so-called abstract ideas act and live, and are *forces*. The ideas of time and space, ideas of the absolute, of infinity and of perfection, the idea of liberty are *idées-forces*; their psychological action constitutes and defines their metaphysical value."[27] But while they applauded the anti-positivism of Fouillée, they did not like his embrace of spontaneous consciousness, arguing that it skirted too close to spiritualism and mysticism. "Briefly, if M. Fouillée invokes, against the materialist formula of evolutionism, the irreducibility of consciousness [*conscience*] to material facts, we invoke in our turn, against the psychic evolutionism of M. Fouillée, the irreducibility of reflection to the simple givens of spontaneous consciousness."[28] Fouillée's embrace of "spontaneous consciousness" suggested to Halévy that the mind operated as an experimental aesthetic enterprise, that consciousness was creative but subjective. Halévy maintained that the mind was more structured, that consciousness was creative but objective, and that it provided the basis for intelligent judgment.

## Halévy's Early Philosophical Writings

The other articles that Halévy published in the 1890s focused on philosophy, specifically on epistemological theories of "sentiments" and "associations" and on the role of reason (or lack thereof) in psychological theories. All of these articles reflected the neo-Kantian perspective that he shared with the other founders of the *Revue de métaphysique et de morale.* In an article published in the *Revue* in 1896, Halévy examined the issue of the relationship of reason and will, on the one hand, with psychological theories that relied on the idea of "association," on the other.[29] He argued that these theories often ignored the importance of human volition and human reason. He contrasted two psychological theories. The first theory assumed that there were certain laws of a regular succession of psychological images and states, laws analogous to mechanistic laws of the motions of the heavens. The second theory rejected the idea that there is a mechanistic relationship of mental ideas and psychological states, and argued that "certain notions which . . . appear to us essential to the organization of our thought" escape such purported "laws of association."[30] Halévy clearly favored the second theory, which left room for the role of will and reason.[31]

Halévy published an article in 1897 that focused on the role of emotions and the relationship of emotions to physiology and intelligence.[32] He devoted most of the article to a refutation of the philosophical claim, attributed to William James among others, that emotions were explained solely by reference to physiological modifications. Halévy argued that this could not be scientifically proven and, further, insisted that the mind played an important role. Without denying that physiological reactions were often associated with emotional states, he maintained that the activity of cogitation also was central. What he termed "the work of intelligence" frequently—perhaps always—intervenes between sentiment and muscular-physiological movements.[33] "In order to organize our subjective impressions, it is necessary for us to assign to them some conditions susceptible of being represented to our intelligence; in order to know our soul, it is necessary to know our body."[34] Halévy did not equate emotions with the "immediate givens of sensible consciousness"—that is, with the inherent ordering performed by the pure *a priori* "intuitions" of time and space, and the *a priori* "categories" à la Kant. But the mind nonetheless intervened. "If, moreover, agreeable sensations and disagreeable sensations are opposed as two natural groups, it is because of certain intellectual habits, of certain judgments about the useful or harmful character of these impressions in relationship to the conservation of life."[35]

Halévy concluded that many sentiments should be categorized as "immediate consciousness," as those individual reactions that are to a large extent subjective, and whose accuracy cannot be legitimately questioned. He contrasted these with "reflective consciousness," which are more refined and connected with reasoned conclusions. Both, however (as the phrases imply), are products of the work of our intellect.[36]

The following year, Halévy revisited related issues in an article devoted to "psychological intensity."[37] Again, his main point was to emphasize how much the mind intervenes in our psychological processes. He argued that the mind decomposes the sensations that we receive, even ones of great intensity, and comes to new syntheses through analysis. He also claimed that it was a mistake to assume, as some empiricists did, that the intensity of a sensation or of a reflection was synonymous with its truth. Halévy mentioned, in this regard, the contrasting convictions of Galileo and the inquisitors who persecuted him: all, he pointed out, had an equal intensity of belief. There were numerous cases, in short, in which the intensity of belief was not an assurance of its truth, which required analysis and reasoned reflection.

In 1900, Halévy repeated his philosophical stance against what he termed "sensualism," the assumption that consciousness was made up exclusively of immediate sensations.[38] He insisted, in contrast to the "sensualists," that the mind was involved in all experience. As he put it in an earlier letter to Bouglé, "It will be necessary to write a *Critique of Sensations*, in order to demonstrate, in examining all the supposedly simple givens of empiricism . . . that these givens are not simple, but are already products of reflection."[39]

Halévy's argument paralleled Kant's attack on the epistemology of Hume. "In reality," Halévy wrote, "the exterior world is interior to thought; and even its exteriority is constituted by its conformity to the laws of thought, if laws of thought exist. . . . Our thesis is that association determines the very nature of associated sensations, that all sensation is, by definition, an association of elements. . . . *To sense is to associate.*"[40] "In short, the principle of association is a principle not regulating, but constitutive of sensation."[41] The role of the mind, of reason, was central for Halévy because he believed that it was important to move beyond a radical Humean skepticism that reduced knowledge to a nominalism of disparate sensations. Rather, we must recognize that order is provided by reason. As Halévy's friend Alain (Émile Chartier) put it after reading Halévy's article on psychological intensity, "I see very clearly where you are going . . . you believe that sensation implies reason and consists of this implication."[42]

Logic had a role to play in the scientific advance of reason, but Halévy and Brunschvicg insisted that it must be connected to experience and nature. "Logic does not remake science, it assumes science already given." Halévy was here making a distinction similar to Kant's famous insistence that logic should only be employed as a "canon" of knowledge, and not as an "organon" of knowledge.[43] As a "canon," logic was *applied to* reality; as an "organan," it was inappropriately assumed that it could *create* reality. Halévy made a similar distinction, one closely connected to his rejection of religious mysticism. He argued that the universe should not be assumed *a priori* to follow a specific form of logic; such regularity was a result of reason being applied to nature. Unfortunately, the ascendancy of positivists, on the one hand, and mystical religious thinkers, on the other, had left a hiatus between facts and principles. There was, Halévy wrote, "no elaboration of a dialectic that would permit one to justify the principles by the facts, to judge the facts by the principles."[44]

Halévy favored a specific sort of dialectic, the nature of which he explored in his dissertation on Plato, *La Théorie platonicienne des sciences* (published in 1896).[45] Again it is necessary to be brief, but the thrust of Halévy's book was to insist that Plato's use of the dialogue form indicated a "dialogic" and "dialectical" philosophy. Moreover, Halévy argued that Plato's dialogues take two different forms. "The first are purely critical in their development, purely negative in their conclusion: they demonstrate the impossibility of defining without contradiction such and such a notion, proposed at the beginning of the philosophical examination. The dialectic renders us intelligent not in the positive sense that it furnishes us with new knowledge, but in the entirely negative sense of delivering us from the illusion of knowing: to know, in this philosophical sense, is to know that one does not know."[46] This "regressive dialectic" was critical. Its purpose was the "decomposition" of extant truths. Its goal was to "deliver us from the illusion of knowing."

Halévy contrasted the "regressive dialectic" with a "progressive dialectic" that Plato employs in other dialogues. The purpose of this "progressive dialectic" is "recomposition." "In the other dialogues, on the contrary, Plato pursues and attains a positive end: definition of justice, definition of science, deduction of a social system, exposition of a system of nature. The dialectic is no longer here simply a critical method, but rather a method of demonstration and organization."[47] In sum, there is a "double face" to the Platonic philosophical method: it is "at the same time critical and constructive, negative and positive."[48]

Halévy contrasted the dialectical reasoning recommended by Plato with modern judicial dialogue that wished only to refute the arguments of adversaries and to convince others of the truth of a particular point of view. Plato had a more comprehensive view. "The Platonic dialogue wants purely and simply *to be*; it pursues no goal, its only rule is to develop in conformity with its internal principle, which is not to imply contradiction, and to suppress itself when it implies contradiction. [In] this free progress of dialectical thought, . . . Plato employed, at different times, the most energetic expressions in order to characterize it: 'it is necessary to follow reason,' 'it is necessary to go where the paths of our reason lead us,' 'there where the wind of reason carries us, it is necessary to go.' "[49] Halévy was attracted to the dialogic/dialectical nature of Plato's method—of the tension between the "regressive" and the "progressive"—and employed it in his subsequent historical investigations. He also found it attractive because he believed that scientific and moral progress would result only from a pragmatic "dialectical" stance that relied on a similar philosophical commitment to dialogue, negotiation, and ongoing rational reflection.[50]

His early philosophical writings, to summarize, demonstrate that Halévy embraced a Kantian idealism that insisted on the constitutive role of human consciousness for all knowledge, but a Kantianism inflected with a Platonism that insisted on the dialogic nature of reason. This, he hoped, would provide a solid foundation for thought and action. In an article written with Léon Brunschvicg for the *Revue de métaphysique et de morale* in 1894, Halévy made clear that he hoped the journal would foster a "philosophic public." "The object of the *Revue*," they wrote, was "to work to show, against current prejudice, and taking existing philosophy as the text for our study, that this philosophy has a determined orientation, that it takes account of the truth toward which it tends, and finally that this truth is capable of rallying spirits and of constituting, by the spontaneous accord of individual tendencies, a philosophical public worthy of the name."[51] As Brunschvicg pointed out in his *homage* to Halévy in 1937, Halévy's thesis on Plato already looked to not just analysis but also to justify some ideas, condemn others, and to act for the "salvation of the city."[52]

All of his philosophical writings of these years indicate that Halévy worried about the power of spiritualism and its close associate mysticism. He pushed back at philosophical arguments that skirted too close to either. He was not confident that the rationalism favored by the *Revue* would prevail, as evidenced in a 1900 letter to Bouglé. "The times are against us, and I point out to you . . . that in the matters of *shivers*, of *enthusiasm*, and of lyricism, rationalism is not worth as much as mystic spiritualism, and that the cymbals of Bacchus always make more noise than the lyre of Apollo. . . . The great mystic orgy has begun. *La Revue de métaphysique*, will it live long enough to permit the reaction of reason to operate in its columns?"[53] For all his hand-wringing, however, Halévy could exult to his coeditor Xavier Léon that their new journal was helping to revive philosophy and reason. "My dear friend," he wrote in March 1898,

> It is eleven o'clock; I just returned home; I glanced again at the last
> number of the *Revue*, and I write to you, in the fullness of my joy,
> in considering the *oeuvre* that we have, that you have realized. We
> have succeeded, after five years have passed, to have gotten accepted
> by the public a volume of one hundred and fifty pages, in which all
> questions are treated from a philosophical point of view, in five
> articles, all of which are good. Does there exist in France, does there
> exist in the entire world, a review that publishes, of five articles, five
> good articles? [Does there exist a review] that adopts a method for
> resolving all problems, or at least for working toward the solution of
> all problems? [Does there exist a review] that, in conclusion, is able
> to take the right of treating a question that no other review dares to
> treat with the same spirit of liberty? To all these questions, it is
> necessary to respond *no*.

In the same letter, celebrating the fifth anniversary of the appearance of the *Revue*, Halévy characterized its distinctive philosophical orientation.

> We have demonstrated that the alternative: seventeenth century *or*
> eighteenth century, theology *or* philosophy of the Enlightenment,
> does not apply, that one is able to be idealist without being Chris-
> tian, a free thinker without being a Spencerian; to put it in other
> terms, that in France in 1900 one is able to give rise again to the
> Greek philosophy of 400 years before Jesus Christ. . . . It is a miracle
> that we still exist, as it was a miracle of constant attention that the
> fire of the vestals was maintained, as it is a miracle that civilization
> persists in a humanity naturally barbarous, that life persists in a
> material universe.[54]

## Henri Bergson and the *Revue*

Henri Bergson (1859–1941) was the most famous French philosopher of his generation.[55] A decade older than Halévy, Léon, and Brunschvicg, Bergson established his reputation with the publication of *Essai sur les données immédiates de la conscience* in 1889.[56] This was followed by teaching at prestigious lycées in Paris, an appointment as a *maître de conférence* at the École normale in 1889, and then a chair at the Collège de France in 1900, where he gave popular public lectures. During this period, he published a series of influential philosophical works, most notably *Matière et mémoire* in 1896, *Le Rire* in 1900; and *L'Évolution créatrice* in 1907. He was elected to the Académie française in 1914, by which time he had become an internationally recognized intellectual. In 1927, he was awarded the Nobel Prize for Literature.

Bergson had a complex relationship with the directors of the *Revue*. He had been asked, but declined, to write an article for the first number of *Revue* in 1893, but he continued to be active in the Société français de philosophie that was founded by Léon in 1900. He also remained tangentially connected to the journal and published his article "Introduction à la metaphysique" in the *Revue* in 1903. Nonetheless, there were some serious philosophical differences between Bergson and the founding members of the journal.[57]

Bergson descended from a French spiritualist tradition that dated back at least to Descartes, a philosophical tradition that recognized intuition, not sense perception, as the sole immediate given of all true knowledge. Intuition was viewed by Bergson as the special act of consciousness that was the privileged way to knowledge, and his writings endeavored to disengage this knowledge from all the superstructures, associated ideas, acquired habits, conventions, and prejudices that conventionally surrounded it. Like the neo-Kantians, Bergson criticized scientific mechanism and narrow positivism, but he did not share their epistemology or their commitment to reflective reason. He did not believe that an *a priori* framework of mind was sufficient or that analytical science offered exhaustive knowledge of the natural world. He argued that these were at best limited, for they did not explain or allow us to grasp the reality of creativity and time. These truths could be approached only through the special act of consciousness that he referred to as intuition.[58]

The most famous of the intuitive truths Bergson championed was the experience of temporal "duration" (*durée*), which he insisted needed to be distinguished from measurable, quantitative "time." This was a major theme of his *Essai sur les données immédiates de la conscience*, where he argued that traditional understandings of time had been dominated by spatial categories and were inextricably linked with the tendency of our sciences to reduce qualities to quantities, unique experiences to repeatable abstractions, and new phenomena to old patterns. According to Bergson, there was in fact no time in the material world; it was an internal experience. "The interval of the *durée* exists only in us, and because of the mutual penetration of our conscious states; outside us one would find nothing but space, and thus simultaneities, of which one may not even say that they objectively succeed each other, as any succession is conceived of by comparing the present to the past."[59]

Halévy and his cofounders resisted Bergson's notion of duration because they interpreted time as a constant of the manifold of perception for all humans, not as an immediate given of *individual* experience that is grasped by intuition. Moreover, they distrusted Bergson's celebration of intuition or "spontaneous consciousness," something that, as we have seen, also distanced them from the philosophy of Fouillée. In an 1894 article summarizing philosophical publications of 1893, Halévy and Brunschvicg characterized Bergson's philosophy as a version of psychological monism that embraced "a subjectivism without reserve."[60] Louis Couturat, a philosopher belonging to the inner circle of the *Revue*, complained to Halévy in 1897 that Bergson's philosophy was a "false metaphysics" that suffered from a troubling anti-intellectualism.[61] These philosophical differences created a strain in relations with Bergson, as Halévy pointed out in a letter in 1908: "In spite of all our courtesies and all our persistence, there is among us some hostility toward his [Bergson's] philosophy, and in the *Revue* there is a foundation of dogmatic rationalism that he distrusts."[62] It was a distrust that would grow for different reasons during World War I, as we shall see in Chapter 7.

## Between Psychology and Sociology
### (Between Théodule-Armand Ribot and Émile Durkheim)

The Kantianism of the founders of the *Revue* explains their criticism not only of Bergson but also of many of the psychological and sociological theories of the era. In opposition to some of the psychologists who wished to insist on the determining role of sentiments, Halévy and his cofounders, as we have seen, insisted on the contribution of reason and intelligence. Halévy mentioned, in a letter to Bouglé in March 1901, that one of his potential intellectual projects, unfortunately never realized, was to write "a treatise on rational psychology."[63] As this suggests, there was some tension with competing psychological theories, but not a clear rupture. There was a shared recognition of the important role that the realm of the nonphysical played in determining action, and therefore there was a shared opposition to materialist biological theories or reductionist sociological theories that eliminated the role of sentiment and individual reason. Halévy, Léon, and Brunschvicg were suspicious of claims that sentiments determined human actions if this claim did not take into account the dimensions of reason and conscience. In short, there was resistance by the founders of the *Revue* when it appeared as though psychologists were suggesting that the explanation for actions could be reduced to a psychological dimension that excluded the input of critical reason. They also resisted sociological theories that reduced human action to reflections of wider social forces; that is, that excluded psychology and human reason. As Stéphan Soulié concisely put it: "The intellectualist rationalism denounces the excess of the biologicization and the mechanization of psychic lives and [also] resists theories that underline too clearly the role of the unconscious and of 'obscure' forces. . . . [They advance] not a negation of the unconscious but the affirmation of a conception of the unconscious that does not limit the prerogatives of consciousness. . . . The progress of mind passes through a progressive rationalization in reflective understanding."[64]

This explains why Halévy and Brunschvicg were critical of the theories of psychologists like Ribot and sociologists like Durkheim. Ribot embraced a physiologically based psychology that claimed that all human action was a result of physiological-chemical interactions, and that character did not involve intelligence, because it could be reduced to questions of sentiment and emotion. In 1893, for example, Ribot wrote: "That which is considered fundamental in character are tendencies, impulsions, desires, sentiments, all of these things, and nothing but these things."[65] And in 1896, in *La psychologie des sentiments*, he wrote: "Everything may be explained on physiological-chemical grounds."[66] Concerning the interrelationship of emotion and intelligence, he wrote: "The foundation of the affective life is appetite or its contrary, that is to say, movement or stops of movements; that in its origins, it is a tendency, an act in the nascent or complete state, independent of intelligence."[67] In Halévy's estimation, these views did not sufficiently take into account the role of reason and reflective understanding.

The criticism of Ribot was implied in the article on the Collège de France that Halévy and Brunschvicg published in 1893, because in fact the article was occasioned by the creation at the Collège of a chair in experimental and comparative psychology for Ribot. "It remains the case," they wrote, "that philosophical instruction at the Collège de France is, if one wishes, complete; it lacks nothing except philosophy. . . . Science appears as a discipline that is imposed on thought in the same way that religion is imposed on thought, [with the assumption] that it ought to accept this state of affairs without examination and without control . . . , the spirit that creates science is banished from science."[68] Halévy was more blunt in his correspondence. After reading Ribot's 1896 book *La psychologie des sentiments*, Halévy wrote to Bouglé: "Ribot is certainly an honest man, and his analyses and descriptions are conscientious, but what philosophical anemia! What security in sophisms! What lack of intelligence in the true sense of the word!"[69]

The sociological theories of Durkheim and his school had similar deficiencies, though the relationship with him was closer. In the 1894 article in which Halévy and Brunschvicg characterized Bergson's philosophy as a "subjectivism without reserve," they criticized Durkheim's sociology as a version of scientism that squeezed out the essential role of individual critical reason. The relationship with Durkheim was complex. Not only did Durkheim contribute articles to the *Revue* and participate in social gatherings at Xavier Léon's house, an indication of cordial social relations; in addition, there was respect for Durkheim's stances on education and politics.[70] The directors of the *Revue* shared with Durkheim a desire to return to philosophy, and they all believed that their intellectual activities were valuable beyond the walls of the academy. That is, they believed that social and political benefits would result from their theoretical analyses.[71]

Nonetheless, there were some notable theoretical strains. Halévy and Brunschvicz criticized Durkheim for his exggerated ambition for sociology, and for advancing a theory of knowledge that reduced epistemological questions to sociological ones. Not only did this offend their Kantian notions of the organizing power of the mind; it also ignored the importance of psychology.[72] They argued that Durkheim mistakenly advanced a "sociological method" that consisted "of excluding all psychological elements."[73] "This elimination is not only arbitrary, it is of the nature to sterilize and to paralyze the science; in effect, what remains for the sociologist once he empties society of its content?"[74] His method of exclusion, in Halévy and Brunschvicg's opinion, would permit Durkheim to categorize societies in the manner that zoologists categorize animals, but little more. Such an approach would "obtain only an abstract and formal schemata." It lamentably would be unable to explain social organization and social change, because individuals were instrumental in the creation of these.[75] "It [the thrust of Durkheim's sociology] is to violate the law of causality . . . and puts the individual outside history."[76] As Halévy put it in a letter to Bouglé in 1906, Durkheim had not converted him "to the theory according to which everything that exceeds the purely biological and material level of existence ought to be considered as social, and only social."[77]

By this time (1906), of course, Durkheim had moderated his claims concerning the exclusion of the psychological from the sociological, in essence embracing a position that gave considerable room to socio-psychological concepts. For example, while in *De la division du travail: Étude des sociétés supérieures* (1893), he had focused on "the volume of society," "the degree of concentration of the mass," and "dynamic density" to explain the power and nature of religious ideas, by the time he published *Le Suicide: Étude de sociologie* (1897) he was shifting his focus to the foundational nature of "collective representations" like religion and to the transformations of collective sentiments and beliefs. In an 1897 review of Antonio Labriola's *Essais sur la conception matérialiste de l'histoire*, Durkheim even suggested that economic factors in part depended on religion, essentially reversing the position he had taken in *De la division du travail*.[78] Nonetheless, his emphasis remained on social phenomena at the expense of other factors, and this irritated Halévy and the other core members of the *Revue*.[79]

Halévy and Brunschvicz also criticized Durkheim in 1893 for believing that "a scientific notion of moral obligation" was possible. They were unhappy with the manner in which he moved from a mechanistic account of social relations to moral judgments, as when he "transform[ed] the unconscious laws of society into the reflected method of evolution."[80] In essence, they were not convinced that he could legitimately move from a classification of societies to claims about the desired moral goals of society—from "is" to "ought." Durkheim, they suggested, in claiming that the determining foundation of everything was social, legitimated unexamined social instincts, social traditions, and social tendencies. Collective representations were valorized at the expense of individual conscience; social norms at the expense of rational and/or universal ethics.[81] Halévy and Brunschvicg pushed back. "It is here clearly demonstrated," they wrote, "that the scientific study of societies cannot in any way suppress the moral problem."[82]

Durkheim subsequently addressed the issue of moral rules and the closely related issue of "sacredness," believing that his sociologically oriented "scientific study" of morality would lead to a position from which to criticize and, he hoped, modify that which exists. He believed, in sum, that his sociological

explanations, while they would not provide a basis for judging *between* societies, nor provide a formula for *universal* moral ideals, would point to a single
set of moral judgments for each society.[83] Halévy and Brunschvicg never
accepted this characteristically Durkheimian move.[84]

This criticism was closely connected with the perception of the directors of the *Revue* that Durkheim was so intent on establishing the credentials of the new discipline of sociology that he would not allow certain
fundamental philosophical questions to be broached. "M. Durkheim wants
philosophy to be a science of principles and of fundamental notions: but
when one poses the problem of knowing what is fundamental, what is a
notion, what is a principle, this is what M. Durkheim will never permit."[85]
Halévy and the other directors of the *Revue* wished to make philosophy the
capacious discipline that framed questions and assessed other disciplines,
including sociology. Philosophy was to be "indissolubly a system of ideas
and a critical movement of thought."[86] Durkheim, on the other hand,
wished to make philosophy, including moral philosophy, a province of
sociology.[87]

The editors of the *Revue* adopted a stance between Ribot and Bergson,
on the one hand, and Durkheim, on the other. They appropriated elements
of Ribot's psychological theory and Durkheim's sociological theory but
insisted that the actions of individuals could not be reduced to physiology or
intuition, nor could they be reduced to reflections of social forces. They
concluded by reaffirming their neo-Kantian philosophical perspective. "Philosophy is essentially organizing: it transfigures nature from which it discovers
not a fixed substance and a mass of facts, but a system of ideas and a strictness
of thought."[88] They wished to insist that individuals have free thoughts that
organize the universe. But they also wished to insist that the activity of free
thought is always in nature, "en face de la nature."[89] Science, they claimed,
is a structure that is invented by the mind but controlled by nature. "Scientific laws are neither necessary forms, nor necessary moments of thought;
without contradiction they would be able to be other; they are not any more
pure fictions, while they succeed; they are inventions thanks to which intellectual activity assimilates things; scientific laws are, in the last analysis, the
habits that form liberty, because uniformity and regularity are able . . . to be
only a form of chance and of indetermination."[90] Philosophy was the discipline that questioned the assumptions upon which the other disciplines,
including psychology and sociology, were built. It provided the essential
rational and critical framework.

Where morality and human motivation fit in to this neo-Kantian frame-work was not clearly conceptualized by Halévy at this time. Kantian "will" was welcomed, but the abstract nature of Kantian philosophy seemed to leave little room for an analysis of how moral ideals intersect with the variety of human actions. In his writings of the late 1890s, Halévy made assertions that there were fundamental motivations upon which morality was situated. He never provided a fully developed framework, however. In his article on "the association of ideas," for example, he wrote:

> If it is necessary to opt, in the associationist doctrine, for the associa-tionist idea against the sensualist idea, and if the principle of associa-tion appears, in the last analysis, as constitutive of sensation, if it takes into account, in particular, the intellectual origin of impres-sions of pleasure and pain, then the order appears as our own nature; the conservation of order, as the principle of morality; the love of order, as the most fundamental of our motives, to which one is able to demonstrate all our motives come down to, despite their apparent diversity. Thus the principle of the association of ideas, defined in its purity, restores to morality the ideas of constant relation and of rational determination, from which, by a strange paradox, the [sen-sualist, skeptical] philosophy of liberty had become detached.[91]

There is a sense here, implicit but nodding toward changes to come, that Kantian intellectualism is not adequate to deal with the complexity of mod-ern experience. I consider below how Halévy pushed back against the abstract intellectualism of Kantian reason, especially Kantian "practical reason," and how this coincided with a growing intellectual engagement with economic and political theory and their intersection with history. Halévy never repudi-ated Kantianism, but he became dissatisfied with its abstractions, which were unable to provide insight into the multi-dimensional structure of modern life and the complexity of historical reality.

## Gabriel Tarde

Gabriel Tarde (1843–1904) was a well-known French magistrate, crimino-logist, and sociologist during the late nineteenth century, obtaining the chair of modern philosophy at the Collège de France in 1900. He based his sociological theory on the psychological interactions among individuals—most famously "invention" and "imitation"—and was a persistent critic of Durkheimian sociology.[92] He began teaching at Sciences Po in 1896 (his first course, "La Politique," was a presentation of his views of sociology), so when Halévy joined the faculty in 1898 they became colleagues. There is no evidence of close association or friendship; nor is it possible to discern any direct influence of one on the other. But there were some significant overlapping concerns that merit attention.

Tarde sustained a Rousseauist view of man, arguing that human beings are born good, and that corruption is a result of society. Also like Rousseau, he argued that humans are driven by what Rousseau termed "sentiments prior to reason," relabeled by Tarde as "sentiments du coeur." Human action is not explained by physical and material factors; rather it is conditioned by how sentiments are directed by human conscience and will. Through personal moral struggle, a society would be able to create "harmony between the diverse filters of the heart—pity, indignation, admiration, anger, enthusiasm." This social accord might be advanced, Tarde suggested, by the intervention of "some apostle, some founder of religion, some great popular or mystical reformer."[93] But it was mostly a factor of humans imitating the positive actions of their fellow humans.

As this suggests, man is a free and conscious being who reacts to "sentiments." And these, in the best of circumstances, would be pursued in a positive or benign direction, with resulting actions sustained through willful effort. Lacking this, Tarde argued that there would be an increase in immoral actions, corruption, and crime. He rejected the notion that there is moral determinism. Following Émile Boutroux, Tarde believed that determinism is only a "surface phenomenon" that frames our understanding of the movements of the physical world. Below this surface "contingency" rules. "To be," according to Tarde, is "to act" in this world of contingency; and "to act" is to recognize the psychological character of will and the importance of morals. Tarde argued that humans are endowed with a "rational instinct," a form of direct intuition of rational realities analogous to our aesthetic sense of taste. He was optimistic concerning the ability of human beings to struggle for progress, and he was confident that a universal humanism would lead humanity to superior federalism, and to transcendent and international patriotism. While he was critical of any organic metaphor, he believed in progress, in a certain evolution of humanity.

Tarde's sociology was built on the claim that he had divined the psychological roots of human action: exemplary causality, imitation, beliefs, and desires. Individuals act in a semi-conscious manner, he claimed, and social life is commanded by psychological forces. Societies have their own structures and laws, and they survive and prosper when the members of a given society have beliefs ("myths") and desires in common. Tarde was generally optimistic about the success of social conglomerations, believing that there is a general movement toward harmony due to the prestige of leaders, the seduction of prestige, and the psychological power of the impulse to "imitate" success.

Tarde's conception of human nature and social action made him critical of the biological determinism of Italian criminologists like Napoleone Colajanni and Cesare Lombroso, and his optimism made him critical of Durkheim's claim that criminality is an integral part of all societies. Like Auguste Cournot, who exerted a profound influence, Tarde did not believe that there was a "science" of society. Even the impersonal social constants of language, religion, economics, and associative institutions are the result of individual ideas and accumulated individual initiatives. This made them powerful forces, but ultimately they were "contingent," and therefore susceptible of change through human action.

Tarde was critical of the sociology of his immediate predecessors and of many of his contemporaries. He was critical of the "social organicism" of Alfred Espinas, arguing that this was a false metaphor for human interrelationships. He was equally critical of the "social evolutionism" of Herbert Spencer, arguing that the "struggle for life" failed to capture the creative spontaneity, solidarity, and harmony that human interrelations revealed. And he was critical of the sociology of Durkheim, arguing that it was based on a false sociological ontology that was shot through with myths like "conscience collective" and the "âme des groupes." Tarde argued that there were only inter-personal psychological relations like "imitation" and "invention," and that these more accurately accounted for the growing similarity within and between modern societies. Tarde was, in short, a methodological individualist in the sense that everything in society could be explained in terms of individuals, while Durkheim insisted on the ontological primacy of social facts. To Durkheim's claim that "remove individuals and society remains," Tarde responded: "Remove the individual and nothing remains of the social."[94] Against Durkheim's argument that criminality is a natural part of all societies, Tarde insisted on the centrality of the moral conscience of each individual and on the variability of levels of criminality in different societies. He argued that to explain modernity Durkheim's sociology relied too heavily on abstract notions like the increasing "volume" and "density" of societies, and therefore underestimated the importance of accident, individual genius, and the disruptive force of the irrational.[95]

Bouglé, Halévy's close friend but also a disciple of Durkheim, criticized Tarde's claims of presenting a scientific sociology.[96] He took issue with Tarde's assertion that everything in society could be reduced to the individual.[97] Espinas was even more severe, arguing that Tarde was mistaken when he wished "to transform his inter-psychology into an apparent sociology."[98]

There was some convergence in the views of Tarde and Halévy. Both believed that philosophy was not content simply to register the facts. Rather, its agenda was to search beyond and underneath the facts, to "complete" science. But there were notable differences. Tarde viewed science through the lens of a Leibnizian philosophy, a "monadological" philosophy that focused on the ontological richness of each individual, and claimed that each individual was "a center of force" that had innate tendencies of movement, generation, and imitation. Halévy, as we have seen, was a neo-Kantian who believed in the transcendental method, and he was less dismissive of social forces. Tarde was also more politically and socially conservative than Halévy and was especially critical of socialism. They both viewed society as centered around individuals, however, and both rejected Durkheim's view that morality was a result of socially existent standards, a view that they argued left out ideals.

Halévy was also critical of Tarde's historical optimism. Like Tocqueville, Tarde believed that the movement toward democracy was irreversible and that the centralization of the administration and government of France was a result of changes that dated back to the Old Regime. Halévy focused less on these administrative and political elements of French history, though he was supportive of the civil and republican dimensions of the Third Republic. Where all three men came together was in their belief that *moeurs* were more powerful than laws in the historical becoming of societies. All three, as well, provided a nuanced consideration of individualism and its problems. Halévy shared with Tarde a belief that the state was an essential institution for the production of social harmony; here, he moved away from Tocqueville, who was more of a federalist and regionalist than either of the late nineteenth-century thinkers. Halévy was closer to Tocqueville methodologically, however, because he insisted on a historically informed comparative analysis of societies, which made him sensitive, like Tocqueville, to the diversity of cultures. Tarde was not historically inclined, using history as a repertoire of transhistorical facts from which to fashion universal laws.[99] This was a historically deaf sociological framework toward which Halévy became more and more critical.

## Human Nature: Inquietude and Critical Thought

How did the neo-Kantianism of Halévy and his position vis-à-vis the psychological and sociological theories of his era influence his view of human nature and society? As we have seen, Halévy was a "conceptualist," who did not believe that human nature was determined exclusively by early ego development or by the psycho-physical forces emphasized in the emerging psychological literature of his era. Like other neo-Kantians, he believed in the "transcendental method" that sought the prior conditions of knowing and willing. And, like other neo-Kantians, he was an idealist who believed that knowledge was not simply grasped; it was constructed. He wished to combat psychological theories that appealed exclusively to physiological mechanism, as well as those that suggested a relativism of values growing out of intuition and personal experience. He also wished to combat the profoundly sociologized notions of human behavior that the new discipline of sociology was beginning to stress. While his neo-Kantianism opened the way for an alternative to the relativity of values implicit in some of the mystical and psychological theories of his era, it also informed his opposition to the deterministic implications of some sociological theories. He never accepted a theory that psychological or structural forces were *determining* of human action, though he never failed to recognize the importance of psychological and social forces. These were constituent elements of human action, along with the rational dimension that reflected his neo-Kantian philosophical background.

The convergence of these psychological, sociological, and philosophical notions informed Halévy's conception of human nature.[100] Halévy worked periodically on an account of human nature that attempted to capture this complexity. One of the essential elements of the makeup of human beings, he claimed, was "inquietude," a disposition that he believed was a central constituent element of moral action. "I have written a plan, and some fragments, for an essay on liberty," he wrote to Bouglé in 1902, "where I demonstrate that *inquietude* is the moral essence of man; that all conscientious moralities imply it, even when they pretend to be moralities of solidarity, of submission to the laws of nature and to the laws of society."[101] "Inquietude" referred to an emotional state characterized by agitation and feverishness; the term comes from the Latin *inquietus*, which literally means "unquiet" or "stormy." Halévy's use of the term indicates that he was part of a long French tradition that viewed individuals as continually apprehensive, uncertain, and restlessly seeking satisfaction.[102] This anxious state led humans to act in various ways, according to Halévy, some preferable to others. He worried that inquietude could lead to an embrace of unreasonable enthusiasm, lyricism, or mystical spiritualism.[103] He worried about "accumulated superstitions" associated with Christianity and, more generally, about the power of state religions (especially Catholicism) that believed in "the unanimity of religious consciousness."[104] And he was especially concerned about the dangers of the "new and excessive sentiments" connected with modern patriotism.[105] Finally, he expressed "a lively antipathy for aristocratic, religious, and provincial sentimentalism," claiming that this antipathy was, as he put it, "the most tenacious prejudice of my nature."[106] In short, inquietude could lead in directions that Halévy found disturbing. Inquietude clearly did not lead "naturally" to benign or positive social interactions; it did not lead "naturally" to reasonable action.

In fact, Halévy rejected the notion that the first social sentiments of individuals were ones of peaceful coexistence.[107] And he was skeptical of the tendency of some thinkers to assume that human cooperation could be easily universalized.[108] How, then, could positive attitudes and moral actions be encouraged? He argued that they must be based on a firm moral foundation and on carefully constructed traditions of sociability. Writing to Bouglé in 1900 about individual pleasure and the nature of social stability, he emphasized the centrality of individual morality. "There is social equilibrium, about which the politician ought to know the laws, and which in part is the condition of the equilibrium of individual functions. But society, being itself composed of individuals, cannot remain well ordered if the individuals of that society do not first make order prevail within themselves. What one can say precisely on the subject of morality, is that it is the science of equilibrium."[109]

This emphasis on individual morality—what we might term "self-mastery"—was important because individuals were not, according to Halévy, naturally sociable. "The individual," he wrote in an unpublished manuscript, "is an *anti-social* phenomenon; however, he has need of society to exist and to develop."[110] In another fragment, he referred to the tension between the needs of individuals and society.

> One is able to declare with Rousseau, without doubt, that the existence of all social institutions is absolutely contrary to the development of the faculties of the individual, and that the individual ought to free himself of all species of social intrusions that prevent the ability to live a happy, safe, free, and good life. But Rousseau has

also written the *Social Contract*, and in the *Social Contract*, he singularly extended the rights of society over the individual. It seems, in the last analysis, very difficult to sustain, without contradiction, that the individual has no need of society for the safe development of his highest faculties. The question is to know if society, which is the necessary condition for the development of individual faculties, ought to be, once these faculties are developed, the unique object of their activity.[111]

Halévy did not believe that society should be the unique object of individual activity. But he did believe that it was necessary to arouse in individuals, and in society more generally, adequate motivation for unselfish action. There was a preoccupation with overcoming strictly individual satisfactions, and with fostering what he referred to as "the idea of obligation" or "the morality of obligation."[112] "Morality," he wrote in an unpublished manuscript, "commands that the individual regulate his relations with other individuals in a manner such that, in the city, the common interest of all individuals results."[113]

These issues of morality were inextricably intertwined with considerations of character, in particular with the valorization of self-restraint, perseverance, strenuous effort, and courage in the face of adversity. These were obviously efforts of will, of the voluntary actions that were required to overcome giving in to the immediate gratification of impulse or to avoid submitting to weak habits.[114] In a letter to Bouglé in 1897, Halévy challenged the two of them to recognize that "the approach in matters of individual morality was in need of being entirely renewed. The ancients were on a good path, but Christian civilization lost everything: one now proposes as the content of individual morality only obligations toward others and toward God, that is to say, to act because of the fear of others and of God."[115] Halévy clearly wished to situate morality on more robust and positive foundations. "It is better to be Stoic than Christian," he wrote to his brother, Daniel.[116]

In an intriguing interchange with Vilfredo Pareto in 1904, Halévy carefully considered the relationship between individuals and society. He focused on Pareto's arguments in favor of "individualism" but suggested that there were in fact three overlapping levels of meaning that should not be confused.[117] The first level of "individualism," Halévy suggested, referred to a method of interpreting societies that assumed that all social phenomena were additions of individuals. He cautioned against this, arguing that "there is something that is irreducible to the phenomena of individual psychology, and inexplicable by the phenomena of individual psychology, [and] that society constitutes a whole [*un phénomène d'ensemble*] that dominates and extends beyond the individual."[118] Methodologically, both individual actions and social forces needed to be considered, though he warned against sociological theories that ignored the individual.

The second meaning of "individualism" defined the end toward which human activities should be directed: the goals of individual freedom, of individual development, of what John Stuart Mill had termed "individuality." Halévy was sympathetic to this notion of what we might term "expressive individualism," but he insisted that this goal should not be confused with the *means* used to attain it. Even Marx, he pointed out, agreed that "individualism" was the appropriate goal of historical change. Where Marx and Halévy differed from radical "individualism" was on the third level, which focused on the appropriate means to attain this goal; that is, it focused on politics and on social policy. "Individualism" on this third level called for the limitation of the role of the state. Halévy was unconvinced, objecting that there needed to be institutions that transcended the individual.[119]

What institutions were necessary? Perhaps most important in the modern era were nation-states. Opposed to both classical liberals and revolutionary syndicalists, Halévy insisted that states performed a critical role in protecting individual liberties. They were "essentially the instrument for the defense of all individuals against all groups. One cannot thus, without absurdity, under the pretext of protecting the liberty of individuals, reduce the functions of the state to nothing, as called for by the anarchists, or reduce the functions of the state to a defined minimum, as called for by classical liberals."[120] Halévy expressed similar defenses of state action in the final volume of *La formation du radicalisme philosophique*. "It should not be said that men were born free and founded the State to increase their security at the expense of their liberty. It should be said that men wanted to be free, and that, insofar as they wanted to be free, they constituted the State to increase simultaneously their security and their liberty."[121] The goal of individualism, in short, required institutions like the state.

Were other institutions also important? Halévy, to the best of my knowledge, never answered this question categorically; he never produced an abstract socio-political theory. He approached such questions as a historian, insisting that different societies had developed different institutions, and that these institutions had cultivated different cultures, some more supportive of liberty than others. His analysis of England, however, suggests that religious groups that fostered a stern morality were especially important, and that religion often cultivated more or less attractive social *moeurs*. In the notes he took when reading the works of Tocqueville, Halévy recorded the latter's point that there was nothing in Christianity that was absolutely contrary to modern societies, and many things favorable, especially "the ideas and passions" that Christianity instilled.[122] Nonetheless, Halévy articulated the familiar liberal opposition to the intolerant stance taken historically by the Catholic Church, and obviously approved of religious toleration. England, he argued, benefited from the diversity of churches.

> Briefly, if one wants to understand the difference that exists between the history of modern England and the contemporary history of the other nations of Europe—we think particularly, being French, of France—it is always necessary, if our analysis is correct, to be alert to the silent action exercised on the nation by the autonomous churches of the petite bourgeoisie. . . . Because of the existence of these free churches [in England], the two watchwords, revolution and reaction, lose all their significance. The idea of church is not identified with a single church to which the state is viewed as uniquely giving support; nor do the people, when they protest against governmental abuse, revolt at the same time against all spiritual discipline.[123]

Beyond this salutary separation of state and church, Halévy also argued that England benefited from having numerous churches that performed the function of comforting the disadvantaged in times of economic crisis, while at the same time instilling a morality of tolerance and compromise. "They [the Protestant sects of England] offered a distraction from the despair of the proletariat in times of hunger and misery, providing an obstacle to the propagation of revolutionary ideas, and replacing a despotism of laws with a despotism of *moeurs*."[124]

Halévy was less forthcoming about other associations, though he wrote warmly of cooperatives, unions, workers' *syndicats*, and educational institutions. In November 1901, he visited Albi and admired the workers' cooperatives that had been established by glassworkers.[125] In 1903, he visited dairy cooperatives in Ireland.[126] He found appealing the view that labor was creative and social, and he was attracted to the stance of those who recommended associations of producers and, more generally, peaceful and cooperative economic relations. He also found appealing the "spontaneous collectivism" developed by societies of "individuals who consider themselves co-proprietors of social capital."[127] He also expressed admiration for associations, viewing them as important "centers of resistance to the 'great tides' of society," as stable social forces against the "unreflective and organic movements of popular opinion."[128]

The overall result was a view of the relationship of individuals, societies, and institutions that recognized the importance of individuals and of larger forces, and that insisted on the responsible recognition of the interdependence of individuals and societies. Halévy provided his own definition of what was desirable:

> It implies that we are conscious and reflective, capable of reasoning about our acts and about other things: the culture of our reason, understood in the development of our individuality, is thus a necessary part of our notion of what is desirable. Society ceases to appear to us as a sentimental fusion, in which the personalities of the members who compose it is lost, in order to become a reflective collaboration of individual intelligences: where there is recognition of the necessity of relations of collaboration and even of subordination. It is thus that a rational individualism accepts some limits to the excessive loosening of the social bond, which seems the desired result of the radical application of the individualist principle.[129]

This quotation points to two additional elements that informed Halévy's view of individuals and their relationship to society: first, the importance of sentiments other than egoistic self-interest; second, the importance of reason. An important element of Halévy's discontent with Utilitarian theories was the limited nature of their understanding of human nature, reducing it to considering the individual "as a purely egoistical being." Fortunately, according to Halévy, sociologists had come to recognize the importance of empathy and altruism. "The new sociological method," he wrote, "distinguishes itself from the old Utilitarian method in that it accepts sympathy, or altruism, as an irreducible given of experience, and considers as primitive not the individual, but the social fact as such. . . . Is it not much better to avow that sympathy cannot be deduced from egoism, and that our social existence implies the presence in us not only of personal sentiments, but also of disinterested sentiments . . . ?"[130]

Equally important for Halévy were reason and critical thought. He never identified culture with sentiment; no society should be ruled by unreasoned emotions. As he put it in a letter to Bouglé in 1899, "Where ideas are lacking, the passions become masters."[131] Society should always be led by those who exercise rational deliberation. "It is necessary to consider that humanity has at its disposal an almost inexhaustible fund of enthusiasm; and that reflection, if it recognizes the true limits of its power, can accomplish the modest and useful task of regulating and controlling enthusiasm."[132] This did not mean that there existed some abstract standard of reason that, insensitive to context, should guide action. The standard Halévy recommended was social action that did not *contradict* reason. "I remain devoted to the truth, with Socrates and Descartes, who demanded of social life not to contradict the progress of reason, of wisdom, of speculative thought: there is a 'provisional' morality, which is eternal."[133] This stance illustrates how closely Halévy remained attached to the neo-Kantian agenda of the *Revue de métaphysique et de morale*.

## Practical Philosophy

In the second installment of their 1894 article, Halévy and Brunschvicg made it clear that, in addition to pure philosophy, they were examining theories of practical philosophy. A reasonable approach, they suggested, was to imagine how action and speculation could be fruitfully combined for social and individual reform. They insisted that the solution was to find a sociological and psychological stance that avoided acceptance of the status quo, on the one extreme, and, on the other, utopian dreams. It was necessary "to discover for societies a realizable goal, and by that to free ourselves at the same time from the absolute traditionalism of the conservatives and the blind illusions of the rationalists."[134]

The correct procedure would be to recognize that the psychology of individuals is inextricably intertwined with the social forms that exist and that are central to any movement toward another, better social order. In the language of Montesquieu, Rousseau, Tocqueville, and others, it was essential to consider the importance of social mores, of what Halévy would prefer to call *esprit*, and what we would probably call social psychology. "A true science of societies is not that which studies the genesis of societies by placing itself outside all psychological facts: it is that which would see the social law surge from individual consciences by the spontaneous movement of *esprits*, and interpret it as the expression of common ideas and common sentiments."[135] This meant that individuals must be considered, not in isolation, but as inhabiting interactive societies. "It is arbitrary to reduce psychology to the study of individual facts; because among the facts of consciousness figure ideas and wills, in which several individuals are able to participate. Beside individual psychology, there is social psychology."[136] Individual autonomy could not be analyzed without taking into consideration wider social elements. But it was equally important to avoid reducing individual responsibilities to social actions. "The primary obligation of the individual toward the group of which he is a part," Halévy wrote in 1905, "is to exist for oneself."[137]

Halévy and Brunschvicg, in their article of 1894, were particularly complimentary toward Tarde's analysis of imitation and invention, and his argument that social reality had its source in individuals and in the psychological interrelationships that unite individuals. "By making in the history of societies a place for individual factors and by recognizing that the individual is something other than the simple result of a competition of social forces, M. Tarde poses in its true terms the problem of the relationship of the individual and the state, the relationship that materialist socialism misunderstands when it transforms the individual into a function of the state. All social facts suppose two elements: invention, which is individual, and the other, imitation, which is strictly social."[138] Neither invention nor imitation—neither the individual nor the social—is primary; both are creative, and each in different contexts influences the other. Analysis must remain flexible enough to encompass both individual and social frameworks.[139]

One result of this framework was a criticism of absolute idealism (as opposed to a Kantian "transcendental idealism") and of crude materialism. It was the latter that informed Halévy's critique of the thought of the classical economists and of Marx. Both, Halévy argued, embraced an unduly narrow conception of human motivation.[140] He believed it was essential to consider sentiments that were not *au fond* tied to the economic substructure. As he put it in a letter of December 1901 to Bouglé:

I think that a critique of historical materialism ought to be founded ... on a refutation of the doctrine according to which knowledge is an accident of the struggle for life, a contingent product of desire and of the will to live: because all desire presupposes a thought, an

idea, and is not able to be conceived except as the life, the persistence
in time, of an idea. Besides, in order to understand historical materialism strictly (the evolution of human thought tied to modifications
of the forms of production), the vicious circle is evident: it is human
science that created these forms of production. . . . If the forms of
the economic world exercise an uncontestable action on the ways of
human thinking, in scientific, philosophical, and religious matters,
it is necessary to see there only a reaction, on the human mind, of a
milieu that the human mind itself has created.[141]

Ideas and material reality, in short, must both be seen as causative.

This rejection of crude materialism led Halévy, in ways discussed below,
to analyze societies generally, and socialist movements specifically, in relationship to their national contexts, with all the nuances of institutions, culture,
and *moeurs* that this implies. While Halévy always recognized that material
reality had a profound impact on human action and human social development, he insisted in addition on the importance (and often the precedence)
of ideas and beliefs.

For materialism, I stop myself at this formula. The idea, essentially,
precedes the act, but it is not able to foresee that which it will
become, once entered into the act, once entered into the domain of
facts. The idea of mechanization preceded, by more than a century,
modern mechanization; but mechanization offers us the spectacle of
a division of social classes, not foreseen by Bacon or Descartes. . . .
Sociology, understood, according to its definition, as a study of
social forms, ought to be accompanied by a study of the reciprocal
relations of beliefs (philosophical, religious, scientific, moral) and of
social forms.[142]

This is of a piece with Halévy's criticisms of liberal economists who
failed to take into consideration forces beyond the rational self-interest of
individuals. Political economy was too often presented with insufficiently
examined assumptions. It was assumed, for example, that there existed a free
market in which "all individuals act only in conformance to the clear and
distinct knowledge of their interests, and in which all interests are naturally
and necessarily in harmony." The problem was that this view was based on
an assumed reality. "The economist did not ask himself if this state was

realizable: he supposed this realized state, because it was the condition of the possibility of his science; he did not pose the critical problem of knowing if the abstractions of political economy were legitimate in the same way as those of physics, astronomy, and geometry." One of the additional problems with this orientation, in Halévy's opinion, was that economists refused to consider qualitative questions concerning wealth, especially the distribution of wealth. Nor did they consider "the spiritual significance and the moral value of life."[143]

Halévy was unwilling to embrace a radical individualism. He noted that positivism had come, in the thought of the followers of Comte (in the thought of, for example, Renan and Taine) to focus less and less on society and more and more on the individual. And he took critical aim at those who argued that individualism was both the objective law of existing society and the preferred goal of society—a contradiction between what purportedly "is" and what purportedly "ought to be" that was, according to Halévy, simply sloppy thinking.

The trick, of course, was to work toward a goal that was recognized as such (and not taken as an empirical fact), and that was possible—that is, not "utopian." In Halévy and Brunschvicg's words, the individual should be faced with a goal "that is something more than a momentary fancy of the imagination, [a goal] that corresponds to a reality."[144] Halévy and Brunschvicg referred to such a goal as something that would fulfill the "double expression of invention and discovery:" "The truth is invented, because it consists of an intellectual synthesis, because it responds to a need of unification which is in the mind; it is discovered, because it does not disappear in order to be reborn with each act of our imagination, because, being necessary, it is eternal, and in this sense objective. And this is true of social laws just as it is true of natural laws."[145] This conflation of social and natural laws indicates that Halévy and Brunschvicg embraced a goal that insisted on the centrality of imagining the rational basis of human justice.

The final pages of Halévy and Brunschvicg's 1894 article addressed the issue of morality, revealing the difficulty they had in conceptualizing a rational morality that took sufficiently into consideration the psychological and sociological dimensions. They insisted that the modern individual was imbedded in a specific society and that moral value was inextricably intertwined with wider concerns growing out of this context. But they also claimed that morality was not something based on devotion to a specific society or nation, nor something based on a specific religion. Rather, it

should be based on a reasoned consideration of the "general forms of knowledge," of "what is general and profound within each individual."[146] This
would lead to "the free union of minds" that recognizes the solidarity of
humanity, and "contains the idea of unity which is the principle of the ideal
society."[147] There is an implicit cosmopolitanism in this stance, which
denotes a retreat into a neo-Kantian universalist ethic. Halévy and Brunschvicg did not reject national specificity but they did insist that one must look
beyond societal or national norms to universal principles.

## Beyond Kant

The tension between this implicit cosmopolitanism and the focus on social
specificity was closely related to the move Halévy began to make at this time
from Kantian universalism to a more historically grounded and politically
engaged perspective. He became concerned less and less with philosophical
"truth," and more and more with the resonance and influence of ideas in
specific locations. This shift took place in three stages.

The first stage was marked by Halévy assuming a central role in the
launching of the "questions pratiques" section of the *Revue* in 1895.[148] This
section, as the name implies, was to focus on contemporary issues that
extended beyond metaphysics and abstract discussion of moral principles.
Halévy encouraged his friends to contribute articles on neutrality in international politics, on "sociology and democracy," and other timely issues. The
first series of articles in the "questions pratiques" section focused on a public
debate over the competing roles of science and religion. In part, this debate
was a continuation of the long-standing conflict in France between religious
and secular thought and institutions, a conflict that often focused specifically
on who was to control educational policy. Catholic intellectuals frequently
had complained about the overreach of science and of the secularization that
they claimed science represented, and clearly they wished to see the Catholic
Church oversee moral instruction in the schools. In January 1895, this dispute
took a noisy and public turn, precipitating a debate over the so-called "bankruptcy of science."[149] A specific flash point was created by Ferdinand Brunetière, who published an article in the *Revue des deux mondes* (he was the editor
of this journal) entitled "Après une visite au Vatican," in which he claimed
that there was a stark choice concerning the source of ethical knowledge:
science or the church.[150] He argued that science was unable "even to pose the

only really important questions, those questions that touch on the origin of man, on the laws of his conduct, and on his destiny," implying that these questions could be and should be answered by the Catholic Church. Though Brunetière was not himself a believer, his wider political point was that in the French context the Catholic Church should be respected as the fountain of morality and, therefore, should oversee education.

The response of secular scientists and their philosophical supporters was immediate. They published rejoinders in various journals. And they organized a "banquet for science" in April 1895, at which a series of toasts were made not just to science but more specifically to one of its luminaries, the famous chemist Marcelin Berthelot, who had challenged Brunetière in an article published in the *Revue de Paris*.[151] The *Revue de métaphysique et de morale* took a firm stand in favor of science and secular education, making its position clear in an anonymous "introduction" to the "practical questions" section that was almost certainly written by Halévy.[152] Moral guidance should come from reason, not from religious dogma; the institutions within which ethical thought should be developed were the collèges and universities, not the Catholic Church. This was followed in subsequent numbers of the *Revue* by articles devoted to the religious-secular issue: one by Alphonse Darlu, the neo-Kantian mentor of Halévy, Brunschvicg, and Léon from the Lycée Condorcet, that was strongly critical of Brunetière[153] and a second, by Frédéric Rauh, a frequent contributor to the *Revue*, who took a more conciliatory position on religious instruction, but firmly pushed back against Brunetière's argument for a Catholic privilege.[154]

The second stage of his turn away from abstract neo-Kantianism was the growing interest Halévy took in political economy.[155] This entailed a new interest in economic theories, in specific types of economic and industrial change, and in the manner in which these changes unfolded in different societies. The anti-formalism of this new perspective was expressed baldly in a review in the *Revue* focusing on John Hobson's 1901 book *The Social Problem*. "It is a profound understanding of political economy that allows Mr. Hobson to speak about social concerns in rigorous language, and to escape from both the formalism of Kantian doctrine on law and the sometimes abstract, sometimes metaphorical, formalism of contemporary sociology, and finally, instead of refuting or defending the abstract theory on the rights of man, to revise, complete, or in some sense, *fill it in*."[156]

The third stage, finally, was a growing concern with socio-political *movements*, including socialist movements, rather than with socio-political ideas.

In a letter to Xavier Léon in November 1902, Halévy made the point that in his preparations for his course on the history of European socialism at Sciences Po (discussed below) he was absorbed in "the history of economic doctrines." A little more than two years later, he wrote, again to Léon, that his courses were "less and less courses in the history of doctrines" and more and more about "history *and* doctrines."[157]

In sum, between 1895 and 1905, Halévy came to realize that he needed to be concerned not just with formal philosophy but also with practical issues like educational policy and the church, with theories about political economy and society, including socialism, and with the interaction of these practical issues and theories with broader historical forces. To appreciate the importance of these dimensions for Halévy, we need only mention the analysis of eighteenth- and nineteenth-century England that he was beginning to develop during these same years. He came to view England as exceptionally fortunate to have entered the modern period animated by "les moeurs publiques" that fostered "voluntary obedience" and "spontaneous organization."[158] This, Halévy would famously argue, was inextricably intertwined with the unusual British combination of high culture informed by bizarre varieties of Utilitarianism and a popular culture informed by religious movements like Methodism. It was this culture that was primarily responsible for the stability of modern England, according to Halévy, though he also gave extensive attention to its political institutions (so central to the analyses of predecessors like Montesquieu or Constant), and to its economic power (central to the analyses of those enamored of English industrialization). This area of Halévy's thought is examined in Chapter 6.

Halévy would use a similar framework in his analyses of nineteenth-century European socialism. Again, he was concerned with the psychological, sociological, and philosophical assumptions that underpinned various socialist doctrines and movements. And, again, he insisted that these needed to be interpreted as embedded in, deeply influenced by, and in turn deeply influencing, specific national histories. How Halévy viewed the emergence and development of socialism in different European societies is the topic of Chapter 5.

Before we turn to either of these areas of Halévy's scholarship, however, we must discuss Halévy's work on British Utilitarianism and the impact of the Dreyfus Affair. The Dreyfus Affair, considered in chapter 4, led Halévy into the messy world of political engagement. The research he conducted in England on Bentham and "philosophical radicalism" led him into the complex world of historical analysis. This is the focus of the following chapter.

CHAPTER 3

# British Utilitarianism

## (1896–1904)

Political economy has only the appearance of an exact science, and the numbers on which it operates can never be other than arbitrarily chosen numbers, out of all relation to the real. . . . It is necessary to recognize that Ricardo's political economy has in many respects now been refuted for a century.
— Elie Halévy, *La formation du radicalisme philosophique*

The illusion of the Utilitarian economists was to found the abstention of governments not on an acknowledgment of our powerlessness to correct the imperatives of nature, but on an act of faith in the beneficence of natural laws: they travestied a natural scepticism, which remains quite legitimate, into a rationalistic optimism which was certainly sophistical.
— Elie Halévy, *La formation du radicalisme philosophique*

Halévy became famous as a historian of England and its people. While his colleagues at the *Revue de métaphysique et du morale* continued to focus on philosophy and science, Halévy turned toward history and economics. Before 1902, the result of this turn was scholarship that focused more on ideas than on broader historical issues. His first extensive project was a history of the evolution of the philosophical, political, and economic thought of the British Utilitarians, beginning with Jeremy Bentham. This was published in three volumes in the early years of the new century under the title *La formation du radicalisme philosophique*.[1] This chapter focuses on this work and what it reveals about Halévy's intellectual evolution. First, however, a few words about the French tradition of English analysis and a brief look at Halévy's early encounters with Britain and the British.

## The French Tradition

Halévy continued a long French tradition of thought that insisted that human nature was unstable and variable, and that social peace and political order were difficult to achieve.[2] Like many of his French predecessors, Halévy offered reflections about human nature and social interrelationships that proceeded comparatively, and like them he turned to England for a comparison with France. During the eighteenth century, the French writers who made such comparisons often were motivated by patriotism and nationalism. Aggressive and denigrating depictions of England and the English were especially common in periods of war between the two nation-states—during the Seven Years' War, for example, and during the upheavals surrounding the American and French Revolutions.[3] At other times, positive views of England and its mores were intimately connected with critical views of French national character, and of the institutions that surrounded and nurtured this distinctive character. Eighteenth-century Anglophiles like Voltaire gave high marks to the English for their respect for private property, habeas corpus, public jury trials, and the political institutions that separated and balanced power.[4] Nineteenth-century Anglophiles like Germaine de Staël, Benjamin Constant, and François Guizot carefully studied English institutions for hints of how to avoid the political instability that plagued France after 1789.[5] Alexis de Tocqueville studied the patterns of aristocratic landholding, local institutions, associational activity, juridical traditions, and commercial growth to divine the positive manner in which England had dealt with the growth of equality.[6] Anglophobes, on the other hand, noted the turbulent but melancholic character of the English, the disorderly political behavior of English "factions," the national tendency for aggressive imperialism, and the seeming indifference to the plight of the underclass.[7] It should come as no surprise that the alleged vices of the English, and the perceived shortcomings of their political institutions, were commonly recorded by Old Regime defenders of the absolute monarchy in France. Perhaps less commonly noted is the frequency with which English foibles were noted by writers like Rousseau who wished to emphasize the shortcomings of all extant political institutions,[8] and by Physiocrats who preferred agrarian France to commercial England.[9] On the other hand, the alleged virtues of England and the English were recorded by those wishing to highlight the deficiencies of France and the French. These latter comparisons often carried the implication that the author, unlike his or her trapped compatriots, had transcended the national stereotype and enjoyed a broader cosmopolitan perspective.

Both positive and negative comparisons frequently dealt in hasty generalizations about both countries, and commonly they contained glosses that ignored regional or class differences. They often included stereotypes about the causative weight of climate, of the environment, of the legal framework, of political institutions and traditions, and (especially in French depictions of England during the nineteenth century) repeated clichés about the stability provided by tradition, religious toleration, and "mixed" government. The reductive nature of many of these can be viewed as the occupational hazard of simplistic comparative analyses.

Halévy's writings reflected this broader cultural movement. Halévy was influenced, as his reading notes indicate, by the masters of French thought: Pascal, Voltaire, Montesquieu, Rousseau, Constant, Tocqueville, and so on.[10] He was equally influenced by prominent intellectuals of his era: by authors like Hippolyte Taine and Émile Boutmy, who wrote positively about English mores, religion, and culture;[11] by sociologists like Alfred Fouillée, Gabriel Tarde, and Émile Durkheim. And he was influenced by the contemporaneous theories that focused on what Ernest Renan termed the "national spirit" of different populations, and on what Théodule-Armand Ribot termed the "ethnological psychology" of a people.[12] Halévy's writings about England are distinctive, however, because imbedded in his dense histories of nineteenth-century England and its thought. They are expressive of his tenacious fascination with detail and of his resistance to simplistic generalizations. And, I wish to suggest, they were informed by a comparative agenda that looked to England as a society not troubled by the distinctive peculiarities of French culture and politics, a society that had not had to endure what Halévy termed "the long years of political anarchy" in his own country.[13] He looked for ways that this history could provide his own countrymen with salutary comparative lessons.

French intellectuals during the eighteenth century who wished to distinguish France from England—Voltaire is perhaps the most famous—emphasized the civil freedoms enjoyed in England but lacking in France. Thinkers during the nineteenth century, like Constant and Guizot, looked to representative politics as the distinguishing characteristic of England, again highlighting elements lacking in France. By the late nineteenth century, of course, France enjoyed these advances: the Third Republic had given France civil guarantees and representative politics. Perhaps it should come as no surprise that Halévy, in attempting to explain why England remained distinctive, focused on those elements that remained markedly different from those in France. Perhaps it is not surprising, that is, that he focused on England's intellectual tradition of Utilitarianism, its moeurs, and its religious culture.

## First Visits to Britain

Halévy made his first trip to England when he was twenty-two years old, in October 1892. He returned to France in December but then returned to visit England, Scotland, and Ireland from January 30 to March 27, 1893. He was captivated by England and its people from these first visits, and he subsequently resided in England for several months every year (except for a brief hiatus during World War I). His initial reaction was critical fascination. In one of his first letters to his mother, he wrote that the English are very different from the French, because the former "have opinions about everything, but theories about nothing." It is the opposite for the French: "One declares that the French are not reasonable, when, in fact, their crime is to be too reasonable and to prefer reason to good sense."[14] A month later, in a letter to his family, Halévy referred to the English as "brutes." "I say brutes in the most noble meaning of the word. Brutes by their incapacity to reflect, by their scorn of theories, by their frankness, their courage, their love of the open air, their pride."[15] To René Berthelot, Halévy reflected that the English oscillate between Scottish sangfroid and Irish imagination but remain poorly equipped for metaphysics.[16]

Halévy was soon giving more qualified assessments, however, and everything points to a quickly evolving seduction by all aspects of "Englishness." Visiting Oxford in November 1892, he wrote to his mother: "There is not a university in Europe, nor in the world, where it would be better to live than Oxford, where one has the best impression of peace, of sanity, and of quietude."[17] He was increasingly enamored of English society and English mores, even though the English remained somewhat enigmatic to him—in 1898, he wrote that the English were "the most indecipherable of all people";[18] in 1900, he referred to them as "inscrutable and difficult to understand";[19] in 1902, he noted that they were "silent, fatalistic, optimistic";[20] and in 1905, that they were characterized by a "singular mélange of religious exaltation and imperturbable coldness."[21] In 1912, he remarked on the "phlegmatic temperament of the nation."[22] In his letters to Bertrand Russell in the early years of the new century, he criticized the English tendency to embrace an ahistorical form of laissez-faire.[23] And in his book about the British Empire, published in 1905, he acerbically noted that British imperialism increasingly was driven by chauvinistic, racist, and self-serving motives: "The English tend thus, with the growth of their Empire and by the mere fact of their imperialism, to become a nation composed no longer of industrialists, traders, and workers, but of capitalists and administrators, no longer men who work, but men who, in order to live, automatically deduct a part of the labor of others."[24]

Halévy's turn toward English thought, especially Utilitarianism, and to British history more broadly, occurred in 1895–1896. He wrote to his friend Célestin Bouglé in September 1895 that history would be his new scholarly focus. Why? "Because this is unfortunately my only way to make science." Moreover, his focus would be England because of its importance in modern history. He worried about being too partisan but demurred. "The true peril that one encounters in studying too exclusively England, it is to become Anglophile. But what is one to do? . . . It is certain that, for the past two centuries, it is England that has given to Europe political lessons."[25] For months, he struggled to decide what orientation to take. As he informed Bouglé in a letter in November 1895, he was working "to organize [his] intellectual life" but finding a specific direction difficult. The letter referred to the breadth of his interests: "I should write a *Theory of Juridical Relations* (what is a right? what does one mean to say when one says that there is a right? what is the value of the search for origins? for utopias? etc.). Then it would be necessary (imperative always conditional) to write some volumes on the relation of man to woman (the prerogative/right of and the difference of the sexes), on the relation of man to child (the prerogative/right of and the difference of age), on the diverse forms of association, on the relation of the rich to the poor, or the patron to the worker."[26] His correspondence indicates, however, that Halévy was beginning to find his way. On 26 June 1896, he wrote to Bouglé that he was "studying the biography of Bentham. . . . Once Bentham is buried, I will pass to his works, and I glimpse the abyss of legislative projects, of financial plans and of castles in Spain. Then, after that, what will it lead to? A theory of society? Or a theory of modern democracy? Or a history of England? The future will reveal me to myself, and tell me in which of these three concentric circles I should enclose myself."[27] Less than a month later, he was more explicit: "I will not write a history of England. I will write a philosophy of history, or a critical examination of fundamental social notions, or something entirely different in this order of ideas. . . . Right now, I belong to Bentham."[28]

Halévy's focus on Bentham and British Utilitarianism was reinforced in December 1896 when he was asked by Émile Boutmy, the director of the École libre des sciences politiques, to organize some conferences devoted to Bentham. These took place in March 1897. The following year, 1898, Halévy was named a professor at the school and was charged with teaching a course entitled "The Evolution of Political Ideas in England." This class, taught every other year, would come to focus on different aspects of British history, but initially it focused on what Halévy decided to call British "philosophical radicalism." In 1902, he began teaching a second course at Sciences Po, on the history of European socialism, a course that again would have a different focus each time it was offered. Except for the brief hiatus of the war (1914–1918), these courses, alternating, were taught every year of his life. He was, by all accounts, an exceptionally talented lecturer. Jean-Marcel Jeanneney, for example, provided this memory in 1938: "He held himself either standing, with two hands on the back of his chair, or sitting very straight, strong and tall, head held high, beard thick and short, training his gaze on the attentive audience. The amphitheater listened with passionate intensity to his voice, even and full, sometimes ironic, sometimes gruff. The sentences, which were neither precious nor rhetorical, attained an elegance by the purity of a simple style, where the words were expressed forcefully with their full meaning and where the phrases, one after another, struck one and engraved themselves on the mind."[29]

Though distracted by the Dreyfus Affair in the last years of the century, discussed in Chapter 4, Halévy worked energetically on his new British project. He gained access to Bentham's manuscripts in 1898 and discovered, as he told his father, "a mountain of illegible and poorly classified documents."[30] Seemingly the first scholar to utilize this archive, he established a chronology of Bentham's works and even discovered some works that had not been published.[31] The second volume of his project on British Utilitarianism was accepted as his French-language *thèse de doctorat*, defended in March 1901.[32] Halévy probably did not imagine, when he began, that it would take eight years before the third volume of his trilogy on Bentham and the Utilitarians was published in 1904. The result was an impressive history of British Utilitarian thought up to the Reform Bill of 1832. The volumes were well received at the time and continue to be of interest to scholars of Utilitarianism.[33]

## The Formation of Philosophical Radicalism

Halévy attributed the rise of British philosophical radicalism—what is often referred to as British Utilitarianism—to the convergence of an intellectual impulse with wider historical forces. The former, deriving from the Enlightenment, was the hope of finding moral and social laws that were as rational and regular as the laws Newton had posited to describe the regularity of the natural order. The wider context was the "crisis in society" that attended the unsettling effects of the industrial revolution and the sociopolitical turmoil unleashed by the French Revolution in the late eighteenth and early nineteenth centuries—"a crisis," Halévy wrote on the first page of the first volume, "which called for transformations of the judicial, economic, and political regimes and gave rise to schemes for reform and to reformers without number, a crisis, finally, which demanded a unique principle capable of uniting into a single theoretic whole so many scattered notions."[34]

As this quotation indicates, Halévy intended to examine the emergence of Utilitarian doctrine on various fronts: philosophical, judicial, political, and economic. The Utilitarians believed that these various fields could all be situated on an objective science of behavior, one that drew from the associationist psychological theory of Hume, Hartley, and Priestley, and that calculated appropriate action by appealing to the utilitarian principle of the greatest good for the greatest number. They believed, in short, that all these fields could be placed on a scientific basis if there was a careful quantification of pleasures and pains, and a judicious calculation of what actions and which institutions would bring humanity the most benefit. They were enthusiastic that such a "science" would put an end to subjectivism in morals, and an end to the appeal to abstract ideals in legal and political affairs.

This did not mean that the philosophical, juridical, political, and economic doctrines of the Utilitarians developed simultaneously. One of the things that make his history of the movement so engaging is the care with which Halévy examined the development of mainline Utilitarian thought on divergent fronts. This also allowed him to apply a distinctive analytical framework to his historical account. As Halévy examined different fronts on which the Utilitarians moved, he perceived a fundamental tension, one that he returned to throughout his extensive work. There was, he argued, a tension between those fronts on which the Utilitarians assumed there was a "natural identity of interests," on the one hand, and those fronts, on the other, on which they argued there was an "artificial identification of interests." What intrigued Halévy was that the main thinkers of the tradition had noticeably divergent assessments of how humans acted in different arenas. In the arenas of law and politics, the Utilitarians believed that there was no spontaneous fusion of interests; that is, egoistic actions by individuals were not immediately or ultimately harmonious with the general interest. The implication of this was that there needed to be a legal system and an administrative-political framework to bring personal behavior into some rough conformance with the general interests of society. Because there was no "natural identity of interests," it was necessary to create the framework for an "artificial identification of interests."

Quite other was the economic realm. In this arena, there was a strong presumption that there was a "natural harmony of interests," or what Halévy also referred to as a "spontaneous harmony of egoisms."[35] While there was a need for some limited administrative intrusion by the state to provide for public works (like roads) and public institutions (like schools)—because the expense of these would likely dissuade any individual from viewing the creation of these as being in his or her personal self-interest—there was an assumption, more broadly, that the general interest would be best served by allowing individuals to act selfishly. This was true because the Utilitarians believed that, in the economic realm, there was a "natural harmony of interests."

While Bentham and James Mill were strong supporters, therefore, of Adam Smith's optimism about the spontaneous identity of interests within the framework of a market economy (more on this below), they were not so disposed in the political realm. Here, they believed that the legislator must actively intervene to bring about the identification of interests between individuals and/or between individuals and the larger polity. Moreover, on this front, Benthan, especially in his early writings, tended to be an authoritarian. Bentham, Halévy noted, wished to effect political reform based upon his utilitarian calculus, but he was largely "indifferent to the means which governments might employ."[36] Bentham argued that morals and legislation should be founded on an objective science of behavior, a science that was emerging from the understanding of human psychology deriving from the "associationism" of eighteenth-century British philosophy. Halévy perceptively noted, however, that the "associationism" Bentham favored hearkened back more to the "rationalism" of Helvétius than to the "naturalism" of David Hume.

Bentham argued that this new science would support a rejection of common law. And it would justify a transformation of the abstract legal terminology that appealed to unrealizable ideals such as "liberty" and "equality." Both could be replaced with a systematic codification of civil and penal law that would be directed toward the adjustment of human behavior for the realization of the common good. The result was a theory of law that, in Halévy's words, "was neither liberalism nor sentimentalism."

> Bentham would not include liberty as one of the ends of civil law: he considered it only as a secondary form of security. He did not wish that liberty would be the means employed to bring about the general interest. His philosophy is essentially a philosophy written for legislators and men of government, that is to say for men whose profession it is to restrict liberty. . . . The disciple of Helvétius, he [Bentham] regarded man as an animal, capable of pleasure and pain, and the legislator as a wise man who knows the laws obeyed by human sensibility; he did not hope to eliminate suffering, but rather he highjacked, in favor of the legislator, with his knowledge of what is useful, the power of inflicting punishment in order to bring about an artificial identification of interests. It is left to the reason of the legislator to see to it that, by despotically and methodically imposing suffering on individuals, heedless of their instinctive and sentimental protests, that finally, for the collectivity, the sum of pleasures outweighs the sum of pains.[37]

After he met James Mill in 1808, Bentham came to accept universal male suffrage, the secret ballot, and annual elections—that is, he came to accept the program that came to be associated with mature "philosophic radicalism."

He remained attached, however, to the principle of utility and to the belief that there was a scientific foundation for judicial and political reform. What changed for Bentham after meeting Mill was a new view of the preferred means for the recognition and realization of these "scientific" reforms. His embrace of universal male suffrage did not make him a liberal, however. "He merely passed from a monarchic authoritarianism to a democratic authoritarianism, without pausing at the intermediary position, which is the position of Anglo-Saxon liberalism."[38]

On the economic front, Halévy interpreted Bentham and Mill's doctrine as closely following the theories of Adam Smith, though Halévy judged Smith to be the more subtle and interesting theorist. Smith's approach, according to Halévy, was a mingling of inductive reasoning, in the form of historical analysis and empirical observation, with deductive reasoning, to come up with preliminary principles. This led Smith to view political economy as intermingled with politics and legislation; it was not strictly a deductive science. Moreover, these observations steered him to believe that the state needed to take responsibility for things like public works and education. Smith also had a more subtle understanding of human nature, appreciating the role of emotions like sympathy. The Utilitarians, on the other hand, were rationalists who transformed Smithian theory into a rigid deductive science.

> A major difference exists between Ricardo and Adam Smith. They do not both understand the expression "political economy" in the same sense. For Adam Smith, political economy means the sum of the practical applications of a certain number of observations bearing on the phenomena of the industrial and commercial world. . . . Adam Smith, the friend and disciple of Hume, wanted to proceed as an observer and as a historian. . . . According to Ricardo, the object of political economy is *laws*; and this expression is significant; is not encountered in the work of Adam Smith. Thus political economy, which for Adam Smith was a branch of politics and legislation, became for Ricardo the theory of the laws of the natural distribution of wealth.[39]

Nonetheless, Halévy was critical of Bentham's, James Mill's, David Ricardo's, *and* Smith's economic theories, especially in the third chapter of the first volume of *La formation du radicalisme philosophique* and in the conclusion to the third volume. "Clearly the future deductions of Ricardo and

of James Mill are present in germ in the *Wealth of Nations*."[40] The framework
of Halévy's analysis was the degree to which Smith and the others viewed
individual market actions leading to a "natural harmony of interests." Halévy
came to the conclusion that in the Utilitarian view of market rationality flew
in the face of empirical evidence to the contrary. One central issue was the
assumption that individuals acted rationally. Halévy, in reaction, raised questions about the complex psychological dimensions of market interactions.
When discussing the value of exchange, for example, Smith and Bentham
argued that it was a function of the interaction of the quantities of supply and
demand. Halévy asked about the psychological orientation of participants in
the market exchange. "But is it not permissible to inquire why such a given
quantity and not another was brought from each side? A psychological element is implied in the very idea of demand: a demand is a desire or a need."[41]
Moreover, desires and needs were not always the expression of a rational
calculation. Halévy queried why Smith and Bentham wished to minimize the
importance of nonrational psychological factors, and why they insisted on
attributing "a universal value to the principle of the identity of interests."[42]

Halévy also suggested that the issue of the scarcity of products raised
similar psychological issues. Scarcity, of course, could make things very valuable in the market, especially when these things were strongly desired. On
the other hand, if the commodity could be produced in unlimited quantity
through human labor, then the price would fluctuate depending upon the
exertion of labor and the production of the commodity; its value would be
"a function not of scarcity but of the difficulty of obtaining the object by
labor." The commodity's value, therefore, was viewed as a result of "the
nature of things."[43] Again, Halévy raised the issue of the psychological dimension of desire, of demand, suggesting that this needed to be factored in to
any market calculations.

Halévy, in addition, was interested in how Smith used many juristic
expressions to describe value but reduced "just" value to "the natural state of
things in which objects are exchanged proportionally to the labor which produced them, without legislative intervention": "Adam Smith complains, for
instance, that 'the sacred rights of private property are sacrificed to the presumed interests of pubic revenue.' Or again, . . . he forbids the 'sacrifice of
the ordinary laws of justice to an idea of public utility, to a sort of reason of
state, to an act of legislative authority which ought only to be exercised,
which can only be excused, in cases of the most urgent necessity.' . . . The
liberty of each individual to seek his own interest in his own way is always

defined as a right." As Halévy cogently pointed out, Smith "postulates as much as proves the principle of the identity of interest."[44]

Halévy suggested that such postulated claims ignored the contingencies of historical situations and the complexities of specific contexts. "One is therefore entitled to ask if Adam Smith's theory of the division of labor and of exchange value, instead of having given a demonstration of the principle of the natural identity of interests, did not in fact *postulate* the truth of the principle in order to make it possible to neglect the exceptions to which, in fact, his theory of exchange suffers."[45] In sum, Halévy argued that the Smithian "postulate" of the principle of identity of interests was not based on empirical evidence.[46] It "*presupposes* that individuals who are perfectly selfish are also, as a general rule, perfectly reasonable."[47] Halévy was unconvinced.

Even more troubling, according to Halévy, was the failure of Smith to consider the modifications of his abstract theory when one considered the effects of profit and rent, and when one considered the privileged position of some members of society over others, in terms both of intelligence and of power.

> [Smith] acknowledges that the violation of natural liberty is legitimate in certain definite cases where it would endanger 'the security of the whole society.' But, in the particular case of contracts between masters and workmen, the interests of the two parties are in no way the same; and, moreover, the masters, being richer and less numerous, are in a permanent and unjust coalition against the laborers. Adam Smith states this; but he does not ask for any state intervention; he does not even ask that the men should be allowed the freedom to combine; he merely denounces, in general terms, the spirit of combination and of corporation, and criticizes the complicated system of governmental socialism that England had inherited either from the Middle Ages or from the sixteenth century.[48]

Halévy obviously was troubled by the fact that Smith was wedded to the thesis of governmental nonintervention in the economy and to the presumed positive interrelatedness of individual interests. Smith's complaint against all laws by which a government might try to intervene in the economic life of the nation, Halévy claimed, was related to the belief that laws on this front were inefficacious. Halévy did not agree.[49] He pointed out that Smith recognized the disparities of wealth distribution but nonetheless insisted on government nonintervention.

Even in the work of Adam Smith, is it possible to find, as we have tried to show, reasons to affirm that the identity of interests of the wage-earner, the landlord and the capitalist is not spontaneously realized, and that, consequently, an intervention by the state in economic relations is useful, even necessary, in order to support the principle of utility? The Fundamental idea in political economy is the idea of exchange; and the postulate implied in the principle of the identity of interests is the idea that exchange gives labor its recompense, that the mechanism of exchange is just. But, in reality, the laws of exchange conform with justice only in cases when the individuals affected by the exchange are both workers, deriving an equal produce from an equal labor. If this condition is not realized, does not the principle of utility prescribe that, when the two notions of *exchange* and *recompense* no longer coincide, the notion of *recompense* should be put before the notion of *exchange*, and recognize that legislative artifices should be conceived to assure that all work receives its proper recompense, and every need its satisfaction?[50]

According to Halévy, Bentham simplified Smith's economic doctrine even further by focusing almost exclusively on the role of capital at the expense of considering the principle of exchange and the division of labor—central elements of Smith's theory. The result of Bentham's turn to economic problems in the 1780s was the popularization of a rationalistic "scientific" model of economic relations that deeply influenced Anglo-American thought. It centered on the conviction that there was a spontaneous identity of interests in the economic realm, and that government intervention should be limited to providing knowledge and encouraging the study of the useful sciences. Halévy's assessment was sharply critical. "The liberal thesis seems to imply the principle of the identity of interests as its necessary principle, while the examination of the distribution of wealth in society composed of workers, capitalists and landowners reveals natural divergences of interest."[51]

Halévy was clearly not convinced by Smith and Bentham's rationalistic model of the market. It too frequently ignored psychological issues; it pushed aside the consideration of historical context; it embraced abstract principles, presumed to be scientific, at the expense of the interests of labor and the disadvantaged segments of society. Halévy was even critical of the famous analysis in the first chapter of Smith's famous book *The Wealth of Nations* of the division of labor. Smith viewed the division of labor as an effect of exchange, not, as previous thinkers like Francis Hutcheson had argued, the cause of exchange.

Halévy was even more impatient with Ricardo's penchant for abstractions —abstractions that again refused to take into consideration the weight of conflicting empirical evidence. In a letter to Malthus, Ricardo had expressed frustration that people continued to produce objects that were not selling in the market, writing: "I can scarcely account for the length of time this delusion continues." Halévy's criticism was pointed: "The instinct of the logician and rationalist, who, in order to work out the fundamental principles of science, needs to isolate the principles, and to make abstractions of disturbing causes, and, finally, in order to understand better the abstraction, persuades himself that the abstraction is identical with the real."[52] Ricardo's theory of the "natural identity of interests," in short, was flawed because it failed to take into account the real behavior of individuals.

Ricardo was not just the theorist of the "natural identity of interests." He also proposed the policy of free trade. Halévy argued that Ricardo was so wedded to the cause of free trade that he sacrificed his other theories to it. "Now the theory of exchange, defined as it is by Ricardo, justifies the policy of free-trade in many respects; but on certain points it tells against it. Does Ricardo therefore sacrifice the cause of free-trade in order to preserve intact his theory of value? It is the opposite which happens. In order to strengthen the free-trade cause, and demonstrate that the policy of free-trade is truly favorable to the interests of the English people, Ricardo modifies the law of value and the psychological theory on which it is based."[53] In an interesting analysis of the *popularity* of Ricardo's position, Halévy did not argue that this support was entirely a consequence of the analytical power of Ricardo's abstractions. Rather, he suggested that it was caused by the wider historical forces. As he concisely put it, "The imperative need felt by the industrial classes in England about the year 1817 for universal free-trade, is the historical fact which doubtless explains the success of the new doctrine."[54]

Halévy concluded his extensive history of Utilitarians with a criticism of their abstract rationalism and a rejection of their simplistic theory of human nature. Their abstract/rationalistic theories were flawed because they failed to take into consideration the complexities of historical difference. Their egoistic theory of human nature was flawed because it failed to take into consideration the complexity of human sentiments. The egoistic theory of human nature also was morally flawed, because it rejected the notion that self-denying actions were sometimes required to act morally. "The Utilitarians were really trying to bring about a revolution in the conception of virtue," he wrote. "One will not understand their attempt to reconcile the individual interest and collective interest if one does not see in their philosophy, first and foremost, an attempt to discredit self-abnegation and to rehabilitate egoism."[55] But it was absurd, Halévy reasoned, to reduce the notion of "virtue" to acting "on condition that your goodness always serves indirectly your own interest."[56] In his eyes, this was to reduce morality to the narrow view that it was synonymous with self-regarding economic actions; it was an attempt to reduce the moral "ought" to the economically selfish "is."

This stance offended not only the neo-Kantian moral sense of "duty" Halévy espoused. It also offended his assessment of what concretely would be beneficial for modern populations. It was unconvincing, he claimed, to believe that everyone acting in his self-interest would lead to everyone's interests being attended to. In a powerful segment in the conclusion to the final volume, Halévy argued that such a theory was, at best, a prettified Hobbism. Hobbes famously argued that individuals, because of their recognition of the dangers they faced, and because of the fear they experienced, agreed to hand over absolute power to a sovereign ruler. As a consequence, the sovereign was made responsible for bringing about the "harmony" among "interests"— interests that were not naturally in harmony. The Utilitarians argued that there *was* a natural "identification of interests" in the economic realm and that, therefore, no government intervention was needed to address individual dangers and fears. This market theory then influenced their orientation toward government intervention more broadly.

> The morality of the Utilitarians is their economic psychology put into the imperative. Two centuries earlier Hobbes had based a complete system of social despotism on the doctrine of utility; and in fact, the principle of the artificial identity of interests, on which Bentham's juridical theory rests, justified such an interpretation of Utilitarianism: it is the threat of punishment inflicted by the sovereign that establishes for the individual the connection between interest and duty. But, insensibly, the progress and the triumph of the new political economy had determined the preponderance within the doctrine of another principle, the principle according to which egoisms harmonize by themselves in a society that is in conformity with nature. From this new point of view, the fundamental moral

notion, for the theorists of Utilitarianism, is no longer that of obligation, but that of exchange; the motive of moral action is no longer
fear, but rather trust.[57]

Halévy believed that this was "insensible." He accused the Utilitarians of
"optimistic quietism."[58]

Utilitarian theory, Halévy asserted, made unjustified assumptions about
human nature and about societies. As he put it more bluntly in a letter to
Bouglé, his history of Utilitarianism was "the history of a dogma."[59] Rather
than accept Ricardo's claim that "egoistic individuals . . . pursue exclusively
the satisfaction of their material needs and the acquisition of the greatest
possible quantity of wealth," Halévy argued that it was obvious that an individual also acted for "social motives" like the "love of his native soil" and
"family feelings."[60] Rather than accept the idea that government intervention
in the economy was ineffective or worse, he argued that it could have a
positive impact. Government intervention could help to limit poverty
through actions like fixing a minimum wage, by providing a forum within
which divergences of interests could be discussed, negotiated, and, one
hoped, reconciled. This did not entail an embrace by Halévy of extensive
governmental action. He did not view government intervention as a panacea
for all problems. In fact, he claimed that government actions sometimes lead
to problems; in his own words, they "run the risk of making the evil we want
to cure worse." To do nothing was cruel, however, and was based on a naive
faith that there were economic "natural laws" that were beneficent. Empirical
evidence suggested the contrary. "From the moment that the laws of nature
cease to be the laws of harmony, why should not human science intervene to
correct their disastrous effects?"[61] "We know that the laws of nature are
unjust. . . . The illusion of the Utilitarian economists was to base the abstention of government not on an acknowledgment of our powerlessness to correct the imperfections of nature, but on an act of faith in the beneficence of
natural laws: they travestied a naturalistic skepticism, which remains quite
legitimate, into a rationalistic optimism which was certainly sophistical."[62]
Rather than believe naively in beneficent "natural laws," Halévy argued that
governments should intervene to help correct injustice and help the disadvantaged. "In so far as a rational science of political economy is possible, the
intervention of governments in the production and exchange of wealth
appears to be a necessity, and in so far as economic science continues to make

regular progress, it seems natural to believe that governmental interventions will make corresponding advances."[63]

## Halévy's Scholarly Agenda

There is a pragmatism in Halévy's stance that is in fundamental opposition to the rigid rationalism of the Utilitarians. Halévy wished to understand how modern societies could be best organized to arbitrate the values of equality and freedom, and to balance the goal of individual emancipation with a requisite level of sociopolitical organization. This was connected with his concern to understand what ideas would be most helpful for this arbitration to take place peacefully and for this balance to be sustained. His analysis of British Utilitarianism was oriented to address these larger issues. Halévy was concerned not only to identify the central principles of Bentham's doctrine, and to explain the logical contradictions within it, but also to show how the central principles spawned conflicting goals in public policy—conflicting goals that were advanced by different figures within the larger "movement."

This is closely related to another aspect of Halévy's scholarship on British Utilitarianism that needs to be emphasized: its methodology. Halévy had once commented to Bouglé that "the most disgusting thing would be to have a sterile philosophy like that of Lachelier."[64] It now becomes clear what he meant by this. Jules Lachelier was an important neo-Kantian philosopher in France, but Halévy indicated that he had come to view his focus on epistemological theory and metaphysics as not sufficient. To avoid being "sterile," theory needed to be considered in interaction with its application. This did not entail moving away from the careful analysis of theory; indeed, Halévy continued to excel in the analysis of complex structures of thought, and in the demonstration of their internal contradictions. He continued to display his competence in philosophy. But in addition to this focus on internal coherence, he was interested in how theories were applied in practice, and especially in how theories were mobilized in discrepant ways. To put it another way, while he was still interested in the theoretical sophistication of theory, he was just as interested, indeed more interested, in the juridical, political, and economic applications of the theory. He was no longer a philosopher or simply a historian of ideas; he had become an intellectual historian. Moreover, he was an intellectual historian who was interested in thinkers and doctrines not because of their originality or philosophical sophistication but rather because of the importance of the historical movements that emerged from these doctrines.[65]

In the letter to Bouglé in May 1896, mentioned above, Halévy had pondered where his intellectual energies might be directed after he finished his work on Bentham and his thought. "A theory of society? or a theory of modern democracy? or a history of England?"[66] He decided to pursue the latter, but in fact his future volumes on the history of England implicitly addressed theories of society and modern democracy as well.

In several passages in *La formation du radicalisme philosophique*, Halévy stepped back from an analysis of the thought of the Utilitarians to ask the historical question of why it had emerged in England when it did. That is, he was led to ask the obvious historical question of why it had become such a strong current of thought in England, knowing as he did that it was less important in France. He was struck by this historical peculiarity and wished to explain it.[67] One way to get at this was to compare British and French political and intellectual trajectories, and to analyze diverging historical forces that might explain this. Such broader historical issues were alluded to in *La formation du radicalisme philosophique*, but only in a very general, even vague manner. He suggested, for example, that Bentham's theory was a response to the peculiarities of the English legal system and English common law.[68] He mentioned how in Britain in the early nineteenth century there was "the imperative need" felt by the industrial classes for "universal free-trade."[69] He implied the need for a class analysis when he noted the rise of new tensions in England between manufacturers, landowners, and labor at the end of the Napoleonic Wars.[70] And he mentioned, in sweeping fashion, "England's insular position, the American Revolution, the French Revolution, twenty years of universal war, the discovery of important coal-fields; finally, the actions of a small number of individuals who were intelligent and energetic, passionately philanthropical, endowed with the systematic spirit and with the taste for intellectual domination."[71] These, however, were more hints about what forces might explain the rise of free trade and Utilitarian theory than a sustained historical analysis. They indicate, too, the direction Halévy was moving intellectually. They point toward later writings that would include not just an analysis of intellectual theories, their internal contradictions, and how they were received and applied, but also more detailed analyses of how these theories and their application were situated within broader political, economic, and cultural movements.[72] They point to Halévy's *History of the English People in the Nineteenth Century.*

The objections Halévy had to the Utilitarians' narrow view of government action also point in a direction that would gain more and more of his attention. He was asked in the winter of 1900–1901 to teach an additional course at the École libre de sciences politiques on the history of European socialism.[73] This course began in 1902 and would be offered every other year (alternating with his class on the history of England) until his death in 1937. Socialism in its various forms would remain a central intellectual concern for Halévy, and a central aspect of this concern would be the governmental and organizational dimensions at its center.

In reverse order, these topics—the history of England and the history of European socialism—are taken up in the central chapters of part II ahead, where we turn to Halévy's scholarship in the years before the outbreak of World War I.

In addition, we need to confront Halévy's anxiety concerning the fragility of France's liberal democracy. This was caused by the explosion of the Dreyfus Affair. We turn to this first, to consider how the affair, and Halévy's activities during it, shaped Halévy's political orientation and commitments.

# PART II

French Politics,
European Socialism,
and British History

## CHAPTER 4

# The Dreyfus Affair

## (1897–1901)

I was not socialist [in 1902]. I was "liberal" in the sense that I was
anticlerical, democrat, republican—to use a word which was at this
time heavy with meaning, I was a "Dreyfusard."
            —Élie Halévy, "L'ère des tyrannies," 28 November 1936

Élie Halévy was drawn into politics by the Dreyfus Affair. Generally committed to his scholarship, he was stunned into action in November 1897 when
he read in *Le Temps* the famous letter of Senator Scheurer-Kestner that questioned Dreyfus's guilt. Halévy immediately contacted friends and began
mobilizing support for Dreyfus, a response that indicates his deep commitment to the Republic and to the civil and political principles on which it was
based.

   The case against Dreyfus began innocuously enough, in 1894, and initially it received slight attention. A cleaning lady, who worked in the German
Embassy but also was paid by French intelligence, found in an embassy
wastebasket an incriminating unsigned letter and a list of French military
secrets (the *bordereau*), which she quickly passed along to her French contacts. After a hasty investigation by the French intelligence service (the Statistical Section), suspicion fell on Captain Alfred Dreyfus. Dreyfus was from a
wealthy Jewish family that had left Alsace in 1871 after the Franco-Prussian
war to avoid giving up French citizenship. He had advanced quickly in the
military, becoming the highest-ranking Jewish officer in the French Army. In

1892, thirty-three years old, he was appointed to the General Staff. Two years later, on 15 October 1894, he was arrested for high treason. Vigorously protesting his innocence, he nonetheless was convicted by a military tribunal on 22 December 1894. He was stripped of his military rank in a humiliating ceremony at the École militaire on 5 January 1895 and was sent on 21 February 1895 to Devil's Island off the coast of French Guyana to serve a life sentence.

The case against Dreyfus was weak. Handwriting experts differed on whether the handwriting in the incriminating letter matched that of Dreyfus. From a wealthy family, he had no obvious need of the meager sums that espionage might bring him. A devoted family man from a patriotic family, he seemed the exact opposite of a potential traitor. The prosecution proceeded in part because of the public uproar created by Édouard Drumont's anti-Semitic paper *La libre parole*, which claimed that the "Jewish lobby" was attempting to undermine the army and the Republic, and was using its nefarious influence to gain the release of a traitor. In early November 1894, the paper printed illustrations of a hook-nosed "Judas Dreyfus" wearing the spiked helmet of the German Army.[1] The prosecution probably succeeded because of this overheated atmosphere, but also because the prosecution submitted dubious and forged documents, the "secret dossier" that was never shown to Dreyfus or his attorneys.

Initially, there was little reaction except by members of the Dreyfus family, who insisted on Alfred Dreyfus's innocence. Halévy seems to have given the case little thought at the time and is reported by his brother, Daniel, "to have believed blindly in the culpability of Dreyfus" in 1894–1895.[2] By the end of 1896, however, others began to have doubts about the conviction. New evidence of espionage was uncovered in the trash from the German Embassy, indicating at the very least that there was another traitor. More important, Lieutenant Colonel Georges Picquart, named chief of the Statistical Section in July 1895, concluded in August 1896 that the author of the bordereau was not Dreyfus but rather Commandant Ferdinand Walsin-Esterhazy. This is now generally accepted by scholars.

Questions about the conduct of the case and opposition to the conviction grew in the months that followed. In September 1896, the existence of the secret dossier was made public in the newspaper *L'Éclair*. In November, 1896, Bernard Lazare published a pamphlet attacking the weakness of the case against Dreyfus.[3] The same month, the General Staff curiously transferred Picquart to eastern France, then to North Africa. Halévy, busy with other activities, remained largely unmoved by the case at this time. These were the years when he went to Berlin and Leipzig to study philosophy (March–July 1895); when he finished his thèse on Plato (published in 1896);[4] when he was involved in organizing the conference on Bentham at Sciences Po (March 1897); when he visited Tunisia and Algeria (April–May 1897); when he and his friends were occupied with the early issues of their new journal, the *Revue de métaphysique et de morale*.

Nevertheless, in November 1897, Halévy and his brother, Daniel, were drawn into the affair earlier than most other Parisian intellectuals.[5] This was due to the convergence of several factors. The first was the letter of Senator Scheurer-Kestner published in *Le Temps* on 15 November 1897, making public his rejection of the outcome of the trial of 1894. Daniel read Scheurer-Kestner's letter while on the train en route to his parents' new estate on the outskirts of Paris at Sucy-en-Brie. When he arrived, he shared the article with his brother, who reacted immediately. Élie contacted his friends at the *Revue* and at the École normale supérieure in the days that followed, asking their opinions and sharing his suspicions.[6] A second factor was the influence of their father, Ludovic, who, at a dinner in Paris on 18 November, spoke with Anatole France and others knowledgeable about questions raised by critics of the conduct of the trial. Ludovic was in contact, too, with Lucien Herr, the librarian at the École normale who also had come to the conclusion that a grave injustice had been committed.[7] Ludovic shared his concerns with his two sons. A third factor was the growing power of nationalist and anti-Semitic currents, which likely led Élie and Daniel to question the motives of the prosecutors. One might argue whether Élie and Daniel were, up to this point, culturally Jewish, half-Jewish, or French; but there is little doubt that the unfolding of the affair made them more conscious of their Jewish heritage.

By 21 November, Daniel, Élie, and Ludovic had become convinced of Dreyfus's innocence, and they immediately moved to action. They were, therefore, early Dreyfusards. Élie and Daniel became very active enlisting the support of their friends and colleagues, and circulating petitions among intellectuals protesting the violation of judicial procedures in the trial of Dreyfus and demanding revision. They applauded the late-1897 articles of Émile Zola in *Le Figaro* and his famous subsequent attack, "J'accuse: Letter to the President of the Republic," published in Clemenceau's newspaper *L'Aurore* on 13 January 1898. They were instrumental in gathering support for the petitions that appeared in *L'Aurore* and *Le Siècle* between 14/15 January and 4 February 1898.[8] They also worked within the framework of organizations like the Ligue des droits de l'homme et du citoyen, created at this time to demand a reconsideration of the verdict. Daniel was most active in the salons and editorial offices in Paris; Élie spent his time soliciting the support of friends and contacts at the École normale supérieure and the *Revue de métaphysique et de morale*.[9]

As mentioned, the affair made the Halévys sensitive as never before to the strength of bellicose French nationalism and anti-Semitism.[10] In December 1897, Élie wrote to Bouglé that he perceived a shift in popular prejudice in France: while formerly it had focused on Jesuits, now it was obsessed with Jews.[11] A few months later, he suggested that anti-Semitism was a "powerful coalition" because it appealed, on the one hand, to the old aristocracy and to the traditionalist Catholic bourgeoisie because of its attack on "financial feudalism and the *nouveaux enrichis*," while, at the same time, it appealed to socialists because Jews symbolized capitalism.[12] When anti-Semitic riots broke out in France and Algeria in January and February 1898, the Halévys, quite predictably, were appalled by the ease with which "a band of screaming actors [*une bande de cabotine hurleurs*]" could stir up urban crowds.[13] In a later letter to Bouglé, Élie glossed a short history of the rise of anti-Semitism in France after 1885, noting its emergence in the writings of people like Paul Déroulède during the Boulanger Crisis and the Panama Scandal.[14] Clearly, he was shocked by its strength in France. It even led to painful breaks with close family friends, for example with the painter Degas, who revealed himself during the affair to be a strident anti-Semite.

Élie worried about how the country would exit from the crisis. He was deeply troubled by the 1899 assassination attempt on Fernand Labori, the lawyer defending Zola and Dreyfus. He worried that frustrated anti-Dreyfusards might stage a coup against the Republic if the verdict was overturned.[15] All of these developments increased his skeptical attitude toward the popular classes, who during the entirety of the affair demonstrated a worrying propensity to follow the lead of right-wing demagogues.

The affair also reinforced Élie and Daniel's reservations about the class of active politicians, especially the members of the Orleanist elite who, in their estimation, failed to take action to protect individual rights. They were disappointed when relatives like René Berthelot refused to support the Dreyfusards.[16] They were upset that some of the prestigious intellectuals of the previous generation—Ferdinand Brunetière, Jules Lemaître, Pierre Duhem, Marcel Dubois—came out in opposition to Dreyfus and his supporters. Many politicians, it became clear to them, were attracted to a dangerous nationalism, and many were attached more to their selfish ambitions than to

FIGURE 4. Ludovic Halévy (Élie's father), Élie, and Daniel (Élie's brother) at
the burial of Émile Zola (5 October 1902). Reproduced with the permission of
the Société historique et archéologique de Sucy-en-Brie, and of the chairman
of this society, Michel Balard.

the needs of the polity. This skepticism of politicians did not change in
the years following the affair, when the Radicals took over control of the
government. They shared the perspective of Élie's close friend Alain, who
argued that the Dreyfus Affair remained the exemplary event that demonstrated the arrogance of those in power, but also the efficacy of responsible
citizens who insisted on exerting some control over public affairs.[17] The
Halévys attended the funeral of Zola when he died, four years after his celebrated attack (Figure 4).

The manner in which the affair distanced Élie and Daniel from the
political elite, however, differed. As Vincent Duclert has pointed out, Daniel
remained the "romantic" that he was, throwing himself into organizations
that he hoped would save the soul of France, and would continue to influence
the politics of the Republic after the end of the affair.[18] This was his agenda
for helping to organize, in October 1899, the first Université populaire in the
faubourg Saint-Antoine, for example. The Universités populaires were created

by Dreyfusard intellectuals to dissuade workers from embracing crude nationalism and anti-Semitism. For Daniel, this was an important step toward his solidarity with elements within the working class and his embrace of non-authoritarian socialism. He adopted a militant stance that led to the embrace of a curious blend of revolutionary syndicalism and attachment to *la France profonde*. Daniel also collaborated with journals like *Pages libres* and Péguy's *Cahiers de la quinzaine*. Daniel's socialism during these years grew out of the Proudhonian tradition and merged with Sorelian syndicalism. He condemned the Marxists within the Socialist Party and disagreed with socialist leaders like Jean Jaurès, who he felt compromised "French" traditions with his embrace of a rigid Marxism. Within a few years, however, as prominent revolutionary syndicalists took a militant stance against bourgeois intellectuals like himself, Daniel would become disenchanted with syndicalist militancy and move to the Right. Through it all, he retained a sympathetic attitude—at once tender, naive, even utopian—toward the traditions of *ancienne* France. This presaged his later move toward the traditionalist, antidemocratic Right.[19]

Élie shared much of the stance of his brother but never gave up his attachment to the institutions of the Republic. He also entered the affair with high hopes of promoting social justice through the mobilization of intellectuals, through the activities of what came to be called at this time "the intelligentsia."[20] And he also hoped to promote social justice through popular education. But he never had illusions about the reasonableness of la France profonde. He was more concerned about the moral and intellectual consequences of the affair, distancing himself from the movement after the trial in Rennes in 1899 (which led to the reconviction of Dreyfus, but with "extenuating circumstances") and the pardon of Dreyfus by the president of the Republic. When Dreyfus accepted the pardon (on 19 September 1899), Élie returned to his scholarship.

The affair made Élie even more suspicious of politicians than he had been previously. Like his brother, he was critical of prominent figures on the Right and the Left, distressed to see the moral enthusiasm of the affair all too quickly replaced by a return to empty phrase making and public posturing—a thin facade behind which, he believed, lurked selfish ambition. His critiques of the Orleanist elite during and after the affair, and his criticisms of Radical politicians of the *bloc des gauches*, are reminiscent of Tocqueville's critiques of the political elites of the July Monarchy.

Like his brother, Élie was sympathetic toward those movements on the Left that rejected the Socialist Party and looked for *ouvrieriste* solutions—

cooperatives, syndicates, and so forth. Unlike his brother, however, he did not express any nostalgia for ancienne France, which he viewed as fundamentally flawed politically and socially. He had no sympathy for the church or for the old aristocracy, the forces favored by the nationalist Right. The real division with his brother, however, was the attachment Élie had to the Republic and its institutions. He was much more suspicious than his brother of the antirepublican, revolutionary rhetoric of the syndicalist and Marxist Left. Part of this was his suspicion of enthusiasm and passion, especially as these influenced political and social movements. He was never attracted to the movements animated with religious enthusiasm or by Sorelian "myths." He called for a rationalization of religion and expressed a hope that reason and dialogue could lead to mutual understanding.

Halévy's experience of these years strengthened his attachment to science and reason, and it made him more critical of the Catholic Church.[21] Years later, in an epistolary interchange with the English translator of his *Histoire du peuple anglais*, he made clear how the affair had reinforced his critical view of the church. The translator, E. I. Watkin, in 1927 expressed discomfort with how Halévy, in the first volume of the "epilogue" to the *Histoire* (published in 1926), depicted British Catholicism. Halévy claimed that there had been a pre–World War I decline of individualist Protestantism in Britain and a growth of Catholicism, but that this so-called renaissance of Catholicism (this was the irritating part to Watkin) was in fact a "decline of Christian faith," an expression of "moral lassitude and intellectual timidity" that marked nothing short of the "euthanasia" of Christian faith.[22] Watkins, a convert to Catholicism, took offense, writing to Halévy that the depiction of the Catholic revival as "the euthanasia of the Christian religion" and of the broader Catholic movement as "a phenomenon of the senile decay motivated by intellectual timidity and moral weakness" was fundamentally misdirected. Moreover, he went on, "What is really painful in your letter is your plain avowal that you do not believe in toleration and religious liberty. In England we have on the whole a 'free Church in a free state' since no man is penalized for not being an Anglican. You evidently admire our political system and spirit. I am I must admit *shocked* to find you reject one of the keystones of the building."[23]

The most intriguing part of Halévy's response to Watkin zeroed in on the intolerance of the Vatican and the Gallican Church, while at the same time emphasizing that it was critical to consider the different national contexts within which the Catholic Church operated. A free Catholic Church in a free state like England, he wrote, would mean that Catholics could freely worship. A free Catholic Church in a free state like France, on the other hand, would mean that the Catholic majority, unless its actions were restricted by the state, would dictate policy to non-Catholics. This was because neither the Gallican Church nor the Vatican believed in doctrinal tolerance. As Halévy put it in his letter to Watkin: "The formula: 'A Free Church within a Free State' does not make for liberty, if it means merely a Church free from all kind of State control, and at the same time free to control spiritually everything and everybody, and free moreover to define where the spiritual ends. Catholicism does not make for liberty, and that is why I remain an impenitent enemy of Catholicism."[24] In a subsequent letter, Halévy reminded Watkin that the post–Dreyfus Affair legal restrictions against religious teaching orders in France (restrictions that Halévy, in fact, had not supported) were a direct result of the affair, "all through which you will admit . . . the Church had not been fighting a battle for liberty. It brought persecution upon his [sic] head."[25] Halévy went on to point out that the law restricting religious teaching orders had, in fact, never been rigorously applied, and religious teaching, especially for young women, remained widespread in France. The interchange indicates how far the shadow of the Dreyfus Affair extended. It clearly reinforced Halévy's secularism and the suspicions Halévy had of the Catholic Church.

It is curious that the affair did not have a greater effect on the *Revue de métaphysique et de morale*. The founders of the *Revue* were, like Halévy, secular republicans with Jewish family backgrounds. The affair forced recognition of their "objective" Jewishness, and all became Dreyfusards. Nonetheless, the *Revue* largely avoided direct reference to the affair. It is difficult to know precisely why this was the case, but likely there were overlapping reasons: confidence in republican values; fear that their active participation would stimulate anti-Semitism; prudence of a new review that did not wish to alienate potential collaborators.[26]

The unfolding of the affair corresponded chronologically with the period that saw Halévy moving from philosophy to history. He became less interested in the truth of doctrines and more interested in how doctrines had significant historical impact. In the words of Vincent Duclert, "The Dreyfus Affair conducted Élie Halévy to practical philosophy and to political criticism."[27] He focused his subsequent scholarship on theories that had enjoyed significant support within, and exerted significant influence upon, democratic societies of Western Europe. He continued his research into Utilitarian "radicalism" in Britain, examined above. In subsequent years, he would turn his attention to socialist theories and socialist movements, and also to a broader history of England in the nineteenth century that examined economic, political, and cultural dimensions. In this work, his critical examination of doctrines made him sensitive to historical differences: how similar ideas could have widely discrepant practical effects; and how similar theories spawned divergent movements in different historical contexts. He became more cognizant of the complex interaction of ideas and context, recognizing, in short, that neither operated as the independent variable to which the other was entirely dependent.

Élie Halévy's political values are not easily situated in the normal organizational categories of French politics. A man suspicious of most political figures, Halévy was nonetheless a firm supporter of the institutions of the Third Republic. The Dreyfus Affair made him nervous that, given the opportune crisis, the Republic could be taken over by an intolerant right wing: either a rigid regime controlled by a conservative, oligarchic, self-serving elite or an unstable regime buffeted about by populist outbursts and nativist-reactionary demagogues. Halévy feared that right-wing forces of either type would restrict the Republic's inclusiveness and capaciousness. This made him a man of the Left. But, which Left? The answer: the liberal, republican, moderate socialist, nonrevolutionary Left. Though during the years of the Dreyfus Affair Halévy was primarily critical of the Right, he became just as critical of revolutionary socialists and revolutionary syndicalists of the Left. He believed that they too threatened the stability of the Republic, even as he voiced support for the redistribution of wealth and expressed sympathy for moderate socialism. The politics he embraced—respect for civil liberties, for constitutional order, for secularism, for educational expansion, for economic reform—continued to inform his outlook, as we see in detail below. This did not make him a political activist, however. He remained primarily a scholar, but a scholar who spoke up when the Republic appeared to be in danger: during the affair; during and immediately following the war; during the era of tyrannies.

The affair was a central event in Halévy's coming to political consciousness. Halévy recognized this himself. In November 1836, while presenting his famous analysis of modern "tyrannies," he referred to his intellectual formation at the turn of the century in the following manner: "I was 'liberal' in the sense that I was anticlerical, democrat, republican—to use a word that was at this time heavy with meaning, I was a 'Dreyfusard.'"[28]

## Marriage to Florence Noufflard

The years surrounding 1900 not only affirmed Halévy's intellectual and political orientation, they also settled Halévy's personal life. In July 1901, Élie met
Florence Noufflard while she was visiting his family in Sucy-en-Brie (Figure
5). His brother, Daniel, and his wife, Marianne, had met Florence earlier in
the year in Florence, Italy, while visiting Marianne's relatives. They were
impressed with the young woman, twenty-four years old at the time, and
they promptly arranged with Daniel's father, Ludovic, for her to visit the
family home outside Paris. Not only were they intrigued by Florence, they
also believed that she might be a possible partner for Élie, who family and
friends worried was so committed to his intellectual pursuits that he might
never marry.[29] He certainly seemed reluctant, for reasons that he attempted
to explain to Célestin Bouglé in March 1901. "You counsel me, moreover, to
add the matter of marriage, when I don't see a fortnight in my life when I
could accommodate the engagement. It is necessary to become married when
destiny would have it, not otherwise. . . . It is not necessary to become
married because our parents desire that we put another chain around our
necks. . . . It is necessary that marriage, in order to be consecrated by Destiny,
appear as an encounter fortuitous and necessary."[30]

For all his reticence, Élie obviously took to Florence immediately. Some
suggest that it was *le coup de foudre* ("love at first sight"); others suggest that
Élie was "struck by the intelligence, the naturalness, the kindness, and the
beauty" of Florence.[31] The two spent time together in Sucy, and then with
Daniel and Marianne they made a hastily organized trip to visit Chartres,
Versailles, Maintenon, and Le Mans. Élie clearly had fallen in love, and after
the passing of several weeks he followed Florence to Jouy-en-Jonas, a suburb
southwest of Paris, where she was staying with Daniel and Marianne. On 5
September, following a walk in the forest, they announced that they were
engaged. A little over a month later, on 17 October 1891, they married in the
city that carried Florence's name and spent their honeymoon in Portofino,
where they remained until the end of the year.

Who was Florence Noufflard (1877–1957)? Her father, Georges Noufflard, was descended from a French family that manufactured cloth in Lou-
viers, east of Le Havre. He traveled extensively as a young man, and while in
Tuscany met a young Italian woman, Emilia Landrini, whom he subsequently married. Georges and Emilia had three children: Jeanne, Florence,
and André. Georges died in 1897 at the young age of fifty-one, and his young

FIGURE 5. Florence Noufflard at Sucy-en-Brie (1901). Reproduced with the permission of the Société historique et archéologique de Sucy-en-Brie, and of the chairman of this society, Michel Balard.

widow took the family back to Florence to be close to her family. This meant, of course, that Florence had a part-French and part-Italian upbringing. André Noufflard, Florence's younger brother, became a well-known artist and married another equally well-known artist, Berthe Langweil. The two would often spend time with Élie and Florence.

All accounts testify that Florence and Élie were a perfectly matched couple. Florence became very close to Élie's longtime friends in France, and to those in England as well. They both loved to travel, making trips (to give a few examples) to Italy and Ireland in 1903; to Italy and Egypt in 1904; to Egypt and Sudan in 1905; to bicycle in the Auvergne and the Dordogne in 1910. And this, of course, was in addition to the three months they, on average, spent in England every year. They also shared an enthusiasm for hiking and often traveled to the Alps in the late summer. Moreover, Florence enjoyed working in the London archives with Élie, no doubt a significant element of support and comfort for her bookish husband. As he related to his mother immediately after their marriage, "We already have made order reign in our apartment, separating our time into hours of working and hours of going for a walk; evidently, we resemble each other; evidently, we have the same active and peaceful conception of existence."[32] A week later, he reassured Célestin Bouglé that his intellectual work was not suffering because of his marriage (he was reading Marx's *Capital* at the time, in preparation for his first course on the history of European socialism at Sciences Po). "I am very happy," he wrote, "and domestic happiness does not seem to compromise the lucidity of my mind. My wife, besides, has a mind as lucid as mine. I have told her already to consider you a friend."[33] Florence and Élie had no children, but they often spent time with the children of their relations.

Florence survived Élie by twenty years, remaining in their house in Sucy-en-Brie—"la Maison Blanche"—that they had built on the estate of Élie's parents in 1910–1911.[34] There is little evidence of Florence's activities outside the family, beyond, that is, her extensive work to preserve Élie's papers and to arrange the posthumous publication of Élie's unpublished works. She gave money in support of feminist causes, but there is no evidence that she was personally active.[35] After her death in 1957, the house, along with Élie's library and voluminous papers, were overseen by Florence's niece Henriette Guy-Loë, the daughter of Florence's brother. André Noufflard, and his wife, Berthe. Henriette became instrumental in arranging the publication of her famous uncle's correspondence.[36]

## CHAPTER 5

# L'École Libre des Sciences Politiques
# and Socialism

## (1902–1914)

Socialism: grand, powerful, and formidable doctrine that we are not
able to appreciate in France.

—Élie Halévy, "Journal," 18 May 1888

I recognize that socialism contains the secret of the future. But I am
unable to decipher this secret, and I am unable to say if socialism
will lead us to the universalised version of the Swiss republic or to
European Caesarism.

—Élie Halévy to Célestin Bouglé, 1 October 1913

Economic doctrine above all, modern socialism affirms that it is possible to replace the free initiative of individuals with the organized
action of the collective in the production and distribution of wealth.

—Élie Halévy, *Histoire du socialisme européen*, 1948

Halévy is best known in the Anglo-American world for his volumes on British Utilitarianism and his multivolume history of England during the nineteenth century. In his native France, however, his reputation is associated
with his directing role of the *Revue de métaphysique et de morale*, examined in
Chapter 2, and for his lectures on the history of European socialism given

every other year at the École libre des sciences politiques between 1902 and 1937.

It is this last arena of Halévy's work—writings about and lectures on socialism—that provide the focus for this chapter. The publication of Halévy's lectures on socialism was planned, following his untimely death in 1937, by a group of friends and disciples, led by Célestin Bouglé, Robert Marjolin, Étienne Mantoux, and Raymond Aron. Publication was postponed, however, by the outbreak of World War II, and the volume finally appeared in 1948.[1] The book is a compilation of handwritten lectures that Halévy had delivered at Sciences Po, supplemented with lecture notes of students. It is a curious mix. There are fascinating lectures on English political economy, on German state socialism, on Marx's thought, and much more, but there is no sustained argument and even some tension among the various chapters. This is perhaps not surprising, as the volume analyzes widely discrepant European socialist movements. Some sections are descriptive, others are critical, especially those on socialisms in authoritarian states. This critical regard fairly reflects Halévy's stance after World War I, when he argued that there was an unfortunate convergence of socialism with nationalism. In his postwar essays, which I examine in detail in a later chapter, he expressed a deep concern about the changes introduced and/or reinforced by the war: the expansion of state power; the burgeoning faith in bureaucracies and technocrats; the more frequent intrusions into the public sphere of mass movements informed by sectional or private interests. This translated into a skeptical stance toward many socialist movements. Moreover, it was a stance that corresponded with that of Aron, the editor who brought the book to completion after the liberation of France (other editors, like Bouglé, had died before publication). The lectures, as presented, support the view that Halévy was a liberal opposed to socialism.

We now have more information about Halévy's evolving views of socialism, however, suggesting that a reconsideration of Halévy's stance on socialism is in order. A portion of Halévy's correspondence has been published,[2] and in this correspondence Halévy frequently discussed his preparations for his courses at Sciences Po, with mention of socialist works read and his likes and dislikes. Even more important, one can now consult the early manuscript versions of his lectures on the history of socialism, held at the École normale supérieure in Paris.[3] This has led to some important scholarly work, most notably by Ludovic Frobert, who has published an article that focuses on these early lectures and also a book on Halévy's economic thought before

World War I.[4] In addition, there is new scholarship on the wider context: on the varieties of French socialism; on the philosophical and sociological thought of the era; on the nature of the French state; on the widespread interest in France in social reform.[5]

All of this is related to the focus of this chapter: how to understand Halévy's interpretation of European socialism before World War I. Halévy had a complex relationship to socialism, one that was influenced by his philosophical background, by his assessment of the socialist movements of his era, and also by his analysis of the national contexts within which these movements developed. He was convinced of the importance of socialism but was both attracted and repelled. At times, he sounded like an enthusiastic supporter, as when he wrote in 1906: "Universalized liberty is democracy; and universalized democracy, when it is extended from the political field to the economic field, is only socialism."[6] At other times he was critical. He was, in short, ambivalent. As he confessed to Bouglé in 1913, "I recognize that socialism contains the secret of the future. But I cannot decipher this secret, and I am not able to say if socialism will lead us to a universalised version of the Swiss republic or to European Caesarism."[7]

His ambivalent stance was closely related to the view Halévy took that there was a fundamental tension at the core of socialism. On the one hand, there were laudable socialist analyses of socioeconomic inequities, and there frequently were combined with commendable demands for working-class emancipation and a more just distribution of wealth.[8] On the other hand, there were organizational elements within the socialist tradition that Halévy found less attractive. These disturbing strains, moreover, were often connected with impatient calls for revolution, which he judged to be dangerous. Moreover, the prospects of the implementation of the administrative, political, and economic reforms that he favored and feared were, in his mind, closely related to the national contexts within which such reforms were to take place.

Halévy noted as early as 1895 that there was a fundamental tension at the heart of European socialism between emancipation and organization.[9] His most famous articulation of this dichotomy, however, is in the opening paragraph of his article "The Era of Tyrannies" (originally published in 1938): "Socialism, since its birth in the early years of the nineteenth century, has suffered from an internal contradiction. On the one hand, it is often presented by its partisans as the outcome and fulfillment of the Revolution of 1789, which was a revolution of liberty, as a liberation from the last remaining subjection after all the others have been destroyed: the subjection of labor by capital. But it is also, on the other hand, a reaction against individualism and liberalism; it proposes a new compulsory organization in place of the outworn institutions that the Revolution had destroyed."[10]

This chapter examines the analysis Halévy made before 1914 of the historical strains of European socialism. It is framed by his philosophical stance (the curious combination of neo-Kantianism and dialectical Platonism, discussed above) and by his consideration of the emerging fields of psychology and sociology (also discussed above). The body of the chapter, however, is a close look at Halévy's lectures and early writings about European socialism. It will conclude with a look at the assessment Halévy made of the French socialist movements of his own era. The argument advanced here is that before the Great War, his liberalism was strongly inflected with aspects of socialism, and that this was a not uncommon characteristic of French liberalism of this era.

## Early Reflections on Socialism

His early notes and correspondence indicate that Halévy was initially attracted to socialism but repelled by some of its popular versions. He noted in his lycée journal, when he was eighteen years old, that he planned to study strikes, and he mentioned in passing that socialism was the "grand, powerful, and formidable doctrine, which we are not able to appreciate in France."[11] In November 1894, however, now in his early twenties, he wrote to his close friend Célestin Bouglé that "the rhetoric of [Jean] Jaurès and the insults of [Henri] Rochefort are slightly unappetizing. Besides, historical considerations make me always hesitate on the threshold of socialism."[12] There is no indication of what these specific "historical considerations" might have been, but they were likely related to the revolutionary stance of French socialists like Jaurès and to the demagogic tendencies of figures like Rochefort. The resistance to an embrace of socialism also could have been provoked by the authoritarian tendencies of socialism observed in Germany, where Halévy studied from March to July 1895. As he wrote to his brother, Daniel, at this time, "[Germany] marches strait to industrial socialism—Moreover, I'm wondering if socialism is not the form taken by industrialism in a country that worships military and administrative discipline, [and] respects legal fictions and religious ceremonies."[13] These reservations, however, were joined by expressions of sympathy for reforms that addressed economic inequities and for the German state policies that provided workers with insurance.[14]

The interest Halévy showed in socialism intensified after 1898, the year Émile Boutmy approached him about teaching a course on the history of European socialism at Sciences Po. Halévy accepted, and though the course did not begin until January 1902, he began reading more widely and preparing lectures. This was the occasion for his first sustained encounter with many of the important socialist thinkers of the nineteenth century.

His correspondence shows a cautious sympathy for the cooperatist, associationist, and nonauthoritarian strains of the French tradition, though Halévy disliked the utopianism of some French socialists and the aggressive patriarchalism of others. In February 1902, for example, he wrote to Bouglé that he was reading Constantin Pecqueur, who he suggested was the source of Marx's later theory of capitalist concentration.[15] A year later, he mentioned that he was reading (again) Charles Fourier and Pierre-Joseph Proudhon, giving them a mixed assessment. Fourier, he wrote, "is mad . . . but I am managing to understand the state of the Fourierist mind." Proudhon was similarly unattractive: "He repelled me two weeks ago, and not for the first time."[16] Halévy repeated this critical view of Proudhon in his short review, published in 1905, of Gaston Isambert's *Les idées socialistes en France de 1815 a 1848*, where he referred to Proudhon as "a systematic denier."[17] He was similarly critical during an exchange on the nature of Proudhon's thought that took place at La Société française de philosophie in February 1912.[18] Opposing the more sympathetic sociological interpretation of Proudhon advanced by Bouglé, Halévy argued that Proudhon was an intransigent proponent of individualism, patriarchy, and the economic contract, and lamentably was opposed to any more developed notion of social or political organization.[19]

In spite of his reservations concerning Proudhon's radical contractarianism and his patriarchicalism, however, Halévy was generally sympathetic toward the wider tradition of early nineteenth-century French thought and mid-nineteenth-century French socialism. He spoke positively of the ideal of "solidarity" advanced by Pierre-Simon Ballanche.[20] And he suggested during his debate with Bouglé that he found "the language of [Philippe Joseph Benjamin] Buchez or of Pierre Leroux" more appealing than that of Proudhon.[21] A central positive element of the French tradition of sociopolitical thought, according to Halévy, a tradition that included the socialists, was its emphasis on morality. He wrote to Dominique Parodi in February 1901 about this moral dimension. "It is from the moral point of view that I believe one would be able to determine the common attitude of [Étienne] Vacherot, [Charles] Renouvier, and I would add, perhaps Proudhon; because Proudhon is, I believe, the founder of independent morality. The essential core of the ideas on which his disciples still live was, I believe, very different from the 'socio-economic' materialism of Karl Marx."[22] In 1904, he wrote to Bouglé: "While working on my class [at Sciences Po], the French Proudhonians came to my attention, and I came to understand that there was, in the last part of the last century, a republican and specifically French manner of thinking, that we know very well, exactly because it is so close to us."[23] Halévy was sympathetic especially to the moral criticisms that early socialists brought to bear on the inequities created by the spread of industrialization. Rather than being content with some presumption of the "harmonious character of economic phenomena," the early French socialists followed early critics of industrialization like Sismonde de Sismondi, who pointed out the pervasiveness of working-class misery and the frequency of economic crises of overproduction.

Halévy was attracted to numerous socialist recommendations for reform. He was, for example, sympathetically inclined toward recommendations for the creation of producers' and consumers' cooperatives. In November 1901, he visited Albi and admired the workers' cooperative that had been established there by glassworkers.[24] He found appealing the view that labor was creative and social, and was attracted to the stance of those who recommended associations of producers, and, more generally, peaceful and cooperative economic relations. He also found appealing the development of "associations of producers"—societies of "individuals who consider themselves coproprietors of social capital."[25] He did not believe, however, that producers' associations—what he termed in his lectures "spontaneous collectivism"—would resolve all social conflicts; he remained, as he wrote to Bouglé after his visit to Albi, "skeptical concerning the universalization of cooperatism."[26] Halévy did not believe that social reform would spontaneously emerge from working-class organizations; intervention of the state would be necessary to address the "disharmony" of economic exchange, which when left unregulated "constitutes a system for the artificial distribution of wealth."[27]

Halévy also supported working-class associations, including those of public workers, which was a controversial issue in the late nineteenth century. There is an entertaining letter from Halévy to Bouglé pointing out that while the formation of a "syndicat" by public workers was legally prohibited in

France, they could easily skirt the law by forming an "amicale"—that is, a friendly society—that could then ask to belong to the organizations of Bourses de Travail.[28] During the railway strikes of 1910, when the government mobilized troops to keep the trains running, Halévy complained that the state was willing to support only the railway companies and unfortunately failed to work for the amelioration of "the conditions of life" of rail workers or for improvement of railway equipment.[29] The early socialists and their syndicalist descendants raised issues about socio-economic inequity and labor organization that Halévy responded to sympathetically.

## Halévy's Early Lectures on Socialism at Sciences Po

His reflections about the moral orientation of the early socialists highlighted a divergence that Halévy would continue to emphasize: the contrast between this moral attitude and the purported scientism of the classical economists and the socialists who followed in their path. In his extensive analysis of British Utilitarianism, he had criticized Jeremy Bentham, David Ricardo, and James Mill for embracing simplistic social and economic models that *posited* laws rather than constructed generalization based on empirical study. In 1911, he put it this way: "No attempt was made to determine, by observation, the existence of empirical laws. Nor was there any recourse to a statistical method. Political economy, according to Ricardo and James Mill, proceeds by a series of hypothetical constructions."[30] This same issue received extensive treatment in Halévy's first lectures at Sciences Po on the history of European socialism.[31]

Halévy's lectures at Sciences Po, which began in January 1902, were a great success. We have testimony attesting to the popularity of his lectures. Jean-Marcel Jeanneney, for example, recalled the scrupulous and rigorous nature of Halévy's analyses.[32] Daniel Guérin wrote to Bouglé after Halévy's death that Halévy's "wonderful course . . . was, for me, the first step towards socialism."[33]

The first lecture Halévy gave in 1902 focused on the social and economic thought that emerged from the doctrines of the British political economists. As he wrote in his notes: "The point of departure of the evolution that we study, the initial doctrine of which we study the transformations [is] the political economy of Smith and Ricardo."[34] He claimed that there were three fundamental characteristics of this doctrine: (1) an individualist ideal; (2) a rationalist method; and (3) a noninterventionist theory of politics.[35]

The individualist ideal was the belief that society is "an abstraction, a simple collection of individuals," and that these individuals "constitute the only *realities.*" Even the definition of the "nation," Halévy suggested, was often viewed as "a grammatical invention . . . , a *non-entity,* something that had existence only in the brains of political men." The broader implication of this individualist ideal was that individual interests should not be subordinated to the interests of this "non-entity;" in sum, the "national interest" was only "a sum of individuals' interests." Moreover, it was assumed that the equilibrium of all individual interests would emerge naturally, thanks to the division of labor within each society, which naturally and spontaneously would inform the culture and structure the industry demanded by the environmental conditions of climate and landed resources. The assumption of this ideal, according to Halévy, was that individualism implied cosmopolitanism.

The second characteristic of English political economy was the "rationalist method." Given the assumption of individualism, it was claimed that individuals always acted in an egoistic and reasonable manner. "Since [the individual] is the absolute reality, sufficient unto himself, not only does he propose his personal interest as the sole end, but he is capable of attaining it; he is *perfectly intelligent.* Given a *plurality* of individuals thus constituted, *exchange* appears as the means for them to realize simultaneously their personal interests: from exchange results the division of labor and all the mechanisms of the commercial and industrial world." Halévy went on to point out that this supposed "rationalism" extended to the construction of laws about accumulation, profits, and salaries.

The third characteristic of English political economy, finally, was its embrace of "non-interventionist politics": "Not only do they not want national governments isolating the interests of individuals of one nation from those of the individuals of other nations (anti-protectionism); but they do not want the government of each nation to take for its domestic mission to protect the interests of a class presumed oppressed, against those of another class presumed oppressive. . . . It is governments, not natural laws, which, according to this doctrine, are essentially oppressive." Halévy suggested that in England this doctrine was defended by people like Ricardo to refute protectionism, while in France the same doctrine was defended by people like Frédéric Bastiat to refute socialism.

Halévy noted the curious nature of this so-called social science. While most sciences attempted to determine natural laws so that humans could modify the natural environment for the protection and benefit of humanity, the political economists argued that the economic laws that they had divined were natural laws that we ought not to modify. "Ricardo and Bastiat are content to demonstrate the harmonious character of economic phenomena, provided that science does not intervene to modify it. It is a return to an ancient conception, Pythagorean (the science that reveals to us the harmony of the spheres), biblical (the science that is content with the glory of God)." There is, he pointed out, a religious character to this theory: "Nature is the work of God; it is impious for mankind to want to ameliorate it. If the economists use analogies in order to define their science, they take over those of astronomical science, necessarily passive and contemplative."

Halévy turned next to the German reaction to this theory. While most German economic theorists remained descendants of Adam Smith (the exception is Adam Müller), there was a broader cultural reaction against the individualism, rationalism, and noninterventionism at the heart of English political economy. Against individualism, it was argued that "national society, in all its complexity, is the sole reality." The individual was able to be separated from it "only by abstraction, a simple logical fiction analogous to the atom in physics." For the same reason, the cosmopolitan dimension of this individualism was also contested; each national society had its distinctive manner of conceptualizing and contextualizing the individual. The reaction against cosmopolitan individualism was especially strong throughout the Germanies because of the influence of "the idealist philosophy of Hegel and of Schelling, diametrically opposed to the nominalism of Hume and James Mill."

The Germans also rejected the deductive rationalism of British political economy. They favored empiricism. In their consideration of the nation, for example, the German theorists rejected the idea that it was a conglomeration of abstract and simple individuals. Rather, the nation "is infinitely complex, immersed in the obscure past and, on the other side, in the even more obscure future; each nation, besides, has its own past, its own destination, irreducible to tradition and to the destination of every other nation." It was not abstract reason that revealed this complexity but experience and history.

Finally, the Germans rejected the noninterventionist stance of the English political economists. Rather than assume that the laws of the economy were peculiarly sacrosanct, and therefore immune from the intervention of human beings, the critics of Ricardo argued that some intervention could produce benefits for society. Halévy also pointed out that there was no convincing defense of profits in Ricardo's theory, and that conservatives and especially socialists quickly came to advance theories claiming that intervention was necessary "to correct an imperfect nature, if one wishes to realize the interest of the greatest number."

Halévy turned next, in this first lecture, to the socialist response that emerged in reaction to the noninterventionist stance of the political economists. He argued that there were two important movements that emerged in the second half of the nineteenth century: socialism and colonialism. Both, he suggested, were responses to the growth of capitalism. Because capitalism needed new outlets for its products and new land for industrial exploitation, there was the search for colonies. And because capitalism caused domestic irritations—especially among those who labored and were poorly paid, and who therefore had a precarious existence in the midst of increasing wealth—there was the rise of socialism. Halévy noted the diversity of early socialism and argued that Marxism "came to crystallize" the various elements of the movement. I turn to Halévy's interpretation of Marx's writings later in this chapter.[36]

Halévy made it clear, however, that in his consideration of socialist doctrine he would not assume, as did Marxism, that humanity was approaching its final state of economic organization and social stability. He noted that this "illusion" was similar to the promises of religious leaders who had predicted the end of worldly misery, and also similar to the hopes of secular theorists of "progress" like those of Condorcet, who predicted the nearness of the era of liberty and equality, or of writers like Comte, who announced the arrival of the era of positivism. Halévy also chided these theorists for their presumption of having divined changes that would affect the entire globe; they foolishly believed they had the solutions to problems that encompassed all of humanity.

If these apocalyptic and utopian elements could be put aside, however, Halévy suggested, there were important elements of socialist theory that should be seriously considered. First, socialism helped define the manner in which the political economy of European societies had developed historically. And it suggested ways to move ahead practically. On this latter front, socialists had suggested two forms of "collectivism." The first was spontaneous and led to forms of cooperatism. The second was administrative and implied the intervention of the state.

Halévy noted in the final words of this first lecture that he would consider both forms of "collectivism" in future lectures. He also claimed that the idea of a society without government was very exceptional and he indicated that he would trace its origins to British writers of the eighteenth century. From there, it had informed anarchist ideas in the nineteenth century and continued to influence Hegelian speculations about the "final condition of humanity," where it was imagined that the conflict between state and society would be abolished and that the tensions between functionaries and citizens would disappear. Halévy also promised to consider German economic theorists who addressed this problem and to return to examining how socialists had addressed a central question that remained pertinent: how much of the public economy should be absorbed into the state economy.

Subsequent lectures did exactly that. Halévy's second lecture focused on Friedrich List and the nationalist political economy in the Germanies during the middle of the nineteenth century.[37] In 1841, List criticized the free-exchange doctrines of Adam Smith and his followers in his book *Système nationale d'économie politique*. He argued that Smith and company had failed to consider, in their focus on individual material production, the future value of investments in such things as education and productive forces. And, by focusing on the individual and the world, they also had failed to adequately consider national interests. To adequately address these dimensions, it was necessary, according to List, to give attention to the historical peculiarities of each nation, including the intellectual, moral, and aesthetic elements that were ignored by the English political economists. He considered his productivist and historically sensitive perspective as descending, not from the scientism of the physiocrats, but from the historicism of Montesquieu.

The state was assumed by List to have a central role: to help develop productive forces and to advance industrial education to stimulate progress. And, in direct opposition to the free-exchange theory of the political economists, he argued that infant manufacturing enterprises would often need to be protected from the adult enterprises of neighboring countries to prevent the former from being "smothered in their cribs" by the latter. List went on to argue that the free-trade theories of Smith were adopted in the late eighteenth century by the British because of self-interested motives; that is, because they gave an obvious economic advantage to British manufacturers. Halévy did not dispute the importance of List's historical analysis, and he implied that there were many cases in which the protection of infant industries would be justified. He questioned, however, List's claim that the advancement of free-trade programs was driven by conscious duplicity, suggesting instead that the theory "is better explained by the unconscious suggestion of interested motives."[38]

Another important element of List's economic theory, according to Halévy, was consideration of the needs of future generations and their relationship to present political and economic decisions. National debt was one obvious issue here (debts could serve the economic interests of the present population at the expense of future populations). Also important for List were questions of infrastructure and institutions, and of the geographic extent of the nation. His concern for the integrity and independence of European national economies led List to make statements justifying territorial aggrandizement for nationalist reasons, and also for the subordination of colonial populations to the needs and interests of the European colonial powers. These issues were, of course, controversial. But, in spite of these, Halévy suggested that List had raised the important issue of the economic intervention of the state. "Statistics and history teach," wrote List, "that the action of the legislative power and of the administration becomes everywhere more necessary to the degree that the economy of the nation develops."[39]

Halévy devoted his third lecture to German historicism, which emerged in reaction to the rationalism of classical political economy.[40] German economists viewed the general rules (like Ricardo's theory of rent) as insufficiently empirical; the rules failed to take into account many exceptions and therefore ceased to merit being designated general rules. Moreover, classical political economists frequently claimed that these general abstract rules were "natural" and, therefore, "moral." German philosophers reacted to this claim, arguing that this was a confusion of "is" and "ought," and that there was nothing to recommend accepting what existed as "naturally just" when human intervention could create a more just world.

Halévy suggested that the German reaction was rooted in the critique of Anglo-French philosophy of the eighteenth century. The latter assumed that abstract theory, especially in its mathematical and Cartesian form, could exhaust the understanding of reality. German thinkers argued that classical political economy, drawing from this tradition and utilizing its categories, was not a sufficient framework for interpreting the complexity of empirical reality. German philosophers, in general, argued that the conflict between thought and reality could be transcended only by religious intuition (Schelling) or by dialectical reasoning (Hegel). More specifically, German economic theorists like Wilhelm Roscher, Bruno Hildebrand, and Gustav Schmoller argued that political economy had to reject the static "science of abstractions" of Ricardo and his ilk, in favor of a "science of the real" that combined quantitative analysis, qualitative historical observation, and a methodology devoted to comparison, analogy, and historical development.

## Halévy on Hodgskin and Marx

Halévy had great admiration for Marx, whose writings he began to study seriously at this time. He argued that Marxism "crystallized" various elements of the socialist movement and he believed that the theory continued to exercise considerable influence on European socialist movements because Marx "knew to concentrate in a single system so many diverse experiences."[41] Halévy devoted central lectures of his course at Sciences Po to the analysis of Marx's theoretical contributions.[42] In a letter to Bouglé on 9 November 1901, he baldly stated, "I belong entirely to Karl Marx (assuredly you have read the chapters on the division of labor). Marxism will be the pivot of my course this winter; if it becomes a regular offering, this course will be able to be entitled 'Critique or critical appreciation of modern socialism.'"[43] This in fact was the case, as central lectures of Halévy's course focused on Marx's theories. In subsequent letters to Bouglé, Halévy noted that he was reading volumes 2 and 3 of *Capital*.[44] In 1913, he still referred to Marx as "a man of genius in the clearest sense of the word."[45]

Halévy believed that Marx's historical materialism was an advance over previous economic theories, even though, as we see below, he objected to what he viewed as the apocalyptic and reductionist elements of Marxist doctrine. Halévy was impressed especially with Marx's analysis of modern economic relations and noted how his theory had evolved between the publication of *Critique de l'économie politique* in 1859 and the publication of the first volume of *Capital* in 1867. According to Halévy, Marx had correctly noted how modern industry had led to the concentration of capital, though, as mentioned above, Halévy noted that Pecqueur had preceded Marx in this analysis.[46] And, according to Halévy, Marx had advanced an important criticism of Ricardian economic thought and its labor theory of value. Marx emphasized the importance of the difference between "use value" and "exchange value." This allowed him to explain the emergence of profit ("surplus value"), which was the result of the dialectical interaction of the two types of value; that is, of the contradiction between "use value," synonymous with the salary paid the workers who made the products, and "exchange value," which added to "use value" the profits ("surplus value") retained by the capitalists.

Marx's theory was also an advance on Ricardo's theory, according to Halévy, because the latter did not adequately account for the role of capital and profits. Capital intervened in ways that made the identification of value with labor unconvincing, or at best contradictory. There was "fixed capital," which was the investment in machines, and from which investors expected profits in the form of interest. And there was "variable capital," which was the amount of money required to pay the salaries of workers. More significantly, Marx argued that Ricardo did not appreciate that profits were a result of the "surplus value" produced by the labor that was brought into the productive process by variable capital. That is, he did not recognize that the labor power purchased by capitalists was the place where profits were realized. Halévy argued that Marx's thinking on this front offered a bold historical analysis that focused on the new economic relationships that were replacing earlier forms of family production.

One of the writers who stimulated Halévy's analysis of Marx's thinking about these issues was Thomas Hodgskin. Halévy wrote to Bouglé in May 1902 that the study of Hodgskin "is interesting not only for the knowledge of sources, but also for the critique, of the Marxist theory of value."[47] A year later, he published a small volume devoted to Hodgskin and his thought.[48] Hodgskin accepted the Ricardian labor theory of value but rejected Ricardo's political economy, according to Halévy, and Marx made a similar move. Hodgskin claimed that there were "natural and just laws" for the valuation of goods, which should be based on labor, but he argued that equitable distribution had been distorted under capitalism. This was because "exchange value" in capitalist societies was not based on labor; rather it resulted from the juridical framework created by bourgeois society, a framework that violated "natural" labor value in favor of the powerful possessing class. Hodgskin reasoned that if the legal structure that protected capitalist wealth was eliminated, the natural order would return, and the workers would cease being exploited. Halévy emphasized Hodgskin's anarchist framework: the degree to which he believed that there was a "natural" providential order that was just and the manner in which he used this normative "natural" order as the basis of his criticism of the existing order. Hodgskin argued that capitalism was, in the words of Halévy, "a historical accident, the result of conquest, which is not able to undermine, neither in a very profound manner, nor in a very durable manner, the natural equilibrium of economic phenomena."[49] Contrary to Hodgskin, Halévy was far from rejecting the beneficial role of political institutions and laws. Labeling Hodgskin's stance a version of "the anarchist prejudice and the juridical prejudice," he rhetorically asked: "Would the libertarian socialism of Hodgskin be found to differ much from the free-trade philosophy of the Ricardians?"[50]

According to Halévy, Marx found Hodgskin's theory attractive in two ways. Marx agreed that the injustices of the current economic order were much as Hodgskin analyzed them; that is, he agreed with Hodgskin that many of the inequities of capitalist society were a result of a juridical order that provided the bourgeoisie with the legal means to add "surplus value" to the value of commodities created by the labor of workers. This was the thrust of the theory of "exchange value." And, according to Halévy, Marx also favored the future emergence of a just society that was anarchist in its framework: an association, in which the free development of each is the condition for the free development of all," as Marx and Engels put it in *The Communist Manifesto*.[51] This was similar to the future just society that Hodgskin imagined, though Marx never described the features of this future society in any detail. The principal difference between Hodgskin and Marx (an extremely important one in Halévy's opinion) was that Marx placed this analysis in the framework of Hegelian historical thought. The great advance Marx made over Hodgskin was that he integrated the analysis of value and exploitation with a developmental view of the world, one that insisted that nothing was permanent and that historical change was central.[52]

Marx therefore rejected the economic theory that insisted that demand would always equal supply (the illusion of orthodox Ricardians like Jean-Baptiste Say, James Mill, and John McCulloch). And he rejected the idea that the dire consequences of the role of capital and the market could be neutralized if workers were paid for all of the value that they created (the illusion of Pierre-Joseph Proudhon and a number of English socialists, like Hodgskin). Neither of these groups accounted for the historical changes that had been introduced by capitalist industries and would be transcended by future changes. Halévy was impressed with Marx's theories on this front. He explained his admiration in part by pointing to the influence of the new dynamic views of history that had arisen in German thought, and that contrasted so sharply with the static views of eighteenth-century thinkers. Hegel, of course, was central, as he had made evolutionary conceptions of constant change the center of his philosophy, but with the important added element

that he insisted on the dialectic. Halévy insisted that Marx remained a Hegelian because he embraced the evolutionary and dialectical elements of Hegel's
philosophy. But Marx, following the lead of Bruno Bauer and Ludwig Feuerbach in his writings of the 1840s, insisted that the idealism of Hegel must be
transformed into a materialism that viewed as primary, not *Geist* or God, but
humanity, productive and in action. Marx extended this critique of Bauer
and Feuerbach into an attack on the state and insisted on the primacy of
economic forces and concrete human activity. But he remained deeply influenced by German philosophy. "If Marx had been a Frenchman of the time
of Proudhon, he would speak, in order to announce the new era, a juridical
language, predicting the reign of justice; if he had been English, he would
speak the language of utilitarianism, and would announce the future harmony of interests. But he is German, still speaks the language of the philosophers of liberty, announces 'the integral development of the individual,' 'the
free development of each with the free development of all.'"[53]

Halévy concluded this lesson with some general observations and questions. He observed that Marx perceptively analyzed certain contradictions
within capitalist society: the contradiction in the interior of each enterprise
between workers and owners; the contradictions in the wider market economy between different enterprises because of the competitive forces of the
market. And, of course, Marx predicted the concentration of capital and (in
Halévy's words) "the upheaval of capitalist society and the revolutionary
arrival of integral collectivism."

Halévy was critical, however, of a number of elements of Marx's theory.
Like Hodgskin, Marx remained wedded, in his analysis of extant economic
relations, to the labor theory of value, though qualified by Marx as "labor
power." This meant that he failed to take into consideration marginal values,
analyzed by Austrian economic thinkers during the nineteenth century.
These thinkers also insisted, as Marx did not, that scarcity had an impact on
market value. Halévy, in addition, suggested that Marx had failed to take
into consideration the importance of interest, another variable that added to
the price of commodities when exchanged. And, Halévy suggested, Marx was
mistaken when he argued that the concentration of capital explained the
division between agrarian and industrial production. Even when attention
was confined to the industrial sector, Halévy was not convinced that the
concentration of capital would progress uniformly, suggesting that in some
contexts "associations of small capitalists" would likely emerge. Perhaps most
seriously, however, Halévy did not foresee industrial concentration leading

to an inevitable "falling rate of profit," working-class immiseration, and cataclysmic revolution. Marx's "solution" had been to insist that the economic dynamics of the nexus of capital investment and market economics would produce crises of overproduction and, ultimately, a class revolution. Halévy was skeptical, closer to the revisionist position of Eduard Bernstein than to the orthodox Marxist stance of, say, Karl Kautsky. Halévy, in sum, was impressed with the depth of analysis Marx gave of the interaction of the forces and relations of production, and equally with his insistence that these be placed in a historical framework—that is, be understood dialectically. But he had some serious reservations.

Halévy also raised some fundamental methodological issues. He questioned, for example, the degree to which Marx's theory was driven by a materialist logic. He ended one of his lectures with a query about the adequacy of the Marxist theory of historical materialism. Does this theory adequately address "the relationships of thought and action?" One of the unfortunate consequences of the focus Marx puts on the interplay of economic forces and economic relations, according to Halévy, was his rejection of the efficacy of fiscal reform or, for that matter, of any reforms introduced by the state. Halévy saw the state differently: as an essential institution for socioeconomic change. It was not simply a reflection of underlying socioeconomic relations. The state could redistribute wealth, and it could (and did) protect individuals against powerful groups and individuals. As Halévy put it in a letter to Bouglé: "I believe that the state, in its essence, is not tyrannical; it is, essentially, the organ for the defense of the whole society against particular societies, of all individuals against all the groups. It ceases to respond to its essence when it becomes the organ of defense of groups and of particular societies. But when it fills its function, when it works to fight against the preponderance of particular societies and groups frightened of its action . . . [it becomes] the sole means that is in our power to defend liberty."[54]

## "The Principles of the Distribution of Wealth" (1906)

Halévy's defense of the state was related to his conviction that markets were not "natural" but rather were organized by the legal framework in which they operated, and that this legal framework was, in turn, determined by political contestation. This consideration of the wider context within which markets functioned was at the heart of an important essay Halévy published in 1906 on the distribution of wealth.[55] He had hinted to his friends in 1905 that his course on socialism might lead to a small publication, "but not more than an article for now."[56] In fact, he published several important essays in the early years of the new century, of which the essay on the distribution of wealth is arguably the most impressive.

"Les principes de la distribution des riches," fifty pages in length, is the clearest articulation of the economic views Halévy held at this stage of his life. He emphasized that economic facts were not part of a "science" that allowed the formation of universal abstract laws but rather had to be understood in relationship to their historical and institutional contexts. This was especially true of distribution, which, even more than production, was dependent on human will and moral choice. Halévy was critical of the theories of the classical economists, who insisted, mistakenly, that markets and exchange relations were "laws" related to production and to the presumed rationality of actors. "The distribution of riches," he wrote, "results from a series of conventions concluded between diverse associated classes for the production and co-ownership of the social base [*fond social*]."[57]

Halévy believed that the market was essential for the distribution of goods but that the manner in which this market worked was determined by the "tacit and express conventions" of society.[58] The market, he wrote, "is a political institution . . . it is necessary that there are rules, a police, in brief an intervention of the state."[59] This obviously entailed a rejection of the laissez-faire liberalism of the Manchester school in England and propounded by Frédéric Bastiat and Vilfredo Pareto on the Continent.

> It is false to believe that exchange is a notion that cannot be analyzed, and that the laws of exchange are, in some manner anterior to all juridical institutions, analogous, for men living in society, to the laws of molecular attraction for inanimate nature. Exchange supposes a system of juridical institutions, elaborated by human society in view of determined ends. Far from it being the case that the distribution of wealth ought to be considered as explained when its properties are reduced to laws of exchange, it is rather exchange that is susceptible to an explanation and an inverse reduction: it constitutes a mode of the artificial distribution of wealth.[60]

The market of classical economic theory presupposed the existence of a society composed of independent property owners, which Halévy argued was itself a society based on the consent of its members. "Exchange has as its first condition the consent, express or implied, of the society to the possession, by the individuals between which the exchange is made, of a certain foundation: soil that they occupy, capital that they inherit, objects that their labor has produced. It is this social consent that 'consecrates' possession, to speak the mystical language of the jurists, which transforms possession into property."[61] Moreover, exchange presupposed the existence of a legal and political order: "This market, where the sellers and buyers encounter each other, is a political institution: in order for it to exist and for it to be an effective place of encounter for all who wish to exchange their products, there must be rules, a police, in short an intervention of the State. Free trade supposes, not . . . the absolute dispersion of individuals, but rather their concentration by an act of social authority."[62]

The goals that needed to provide the framework for the market were those determined by what constituted a just distribution of wealth. "Exchange defines itself by its end, which is to accord to each member of the social body a part of the riches proportional to his economic productivity. It therefore supposes a series of rules." Such rules "have for their object not to correct the inherent defaults of exchange, considered as a natural phenomenon, but on the contrary to realize the perfection of exchange, considered as a juridical phenomenon. Because exchange is an artificial mode of the distribution of wealth, desired or consented to by the majority of the members of the society where it functions, the conflict of economic forces will be perfectly ruled, according to the laws of exchange, when each finds himself remunerated for his work."[63]

Halévy was optimistic that the "laws of exchange" would change in ways that diminished the disparity of wealth. He based this optimistic prediction on his observation that there was an ongoing "democratization" of society. This had political and economic dimensions. It was more evident in the political realm, where European constitutions were giving more and more power to the lower classes. It was slower in the economic realm, where the "the enormity of gross fortunes, acquired by the bank, commerce and industry, assaults the eyes. It is the perpetual object of popular denunciations."[64] But this also was changing. Halévy believed that there was a shift in "the mental constitution of the human race" occurring at the time he was writing. Looking back to 1848, he suggested that socialist demands for equality had failed to be successfully implemented because the mental attitude of society had remained "aristocratic," meaning that the lower classes widely accepted the disparity of income and riches. They still assumed, socialist rhetoric notwithstanding, that some members of society were more deserving of wealth than others. But, as time passed, and as attitudes and expectations changed—as they were "democratized"—this disparity would recede. In short, equalization would be brought about by a cultural change. "Liberty universalized is democracy; and democracy universalized, extended from the political domain to the economic domain, there is only one word to designate it: socialism."[65]

The institutions that Halévy believed would likely mark the "democratization" of the economy were workers' organizations, cooperatives, and industrial enterprises administered by municipalities and the state.[66] "If the theoretician is idealistic, curious to divine that which in the present prepares the future, he will search, among the economic institutions of the present, those that are of the nature to prepare a more equal distribution of tasks and wealth. The syndicates, the cooperatives, the industrial enterprises administered by the state or by municipalities are, in the most advanced industrial nations, some of these institutions."[67] Looking to the future, Halévy was hopeful that these organizations would contribute to a peaceful transition to a more equitable society. They could provide some of the loci where workers could articulate their demands and exert their influence. Halévy hoped such institutions could effectively sideline the confrontational demands of revolutionary syndicalists and the revolutionary demands of the socialist leaders of the Section Française de l'Internationale Ouvrière (SFIO—French Section of the Workers' International). He clearly was searching for ways to forestall a violent resolution of the class differences that, he believed, were constitutive components of the modern industrial economy. He was encouraged that the power of workers could grow within and through these institutions, and he hoped that this would facilitate the peaceful negotiation of class conflict.

For Halévy, therefore, it was necessary to revise the rules that structured economic ownership and exchange according to the changing demands of concrete situations. The process by which these decisions should be made, he suggested, was dialogue, conciliation, and compromise—they should be made within the broader arena of political contestation. This would lead to the progressive equalization of wealth. The utopian socialists of the mid-nineteenth century, Halévy wrote, "were correct when they defined justice by the principle of the equality of salaries or by the principle following which each receives according to his needs. . . . The progress of democratic notions and institutions consists in the progressive equalization of needs."[68] Their mistake, according to Halévy, was to assume that this could be achieved immediately. In fact, the transition from "aristocratic society" to "democratic society" would require a long education of *mentalités*. Halévy was optimistic, however, that discussion and education, combined with the creation of institutions like syndicates and cooperatives, could lead to the rules of society being modified to bring about this greater equality. The article also defended state intervention to redistribute wealth and insisted that there was no necessary "antithesis between liberty and socialism."[69]

The assessment by Halévy of how quickly change would occur was, in fact, partly dependent on where he was looking. His assessment of the strength and orientation of associations in Europe, for example, was quite positive. In 1903, Halévy referred favorably to associations in England, especially those that had resisted the bellicose and imperialistic enthusiasms of popular crowds. "The great utility of associations," he wrote to Bouglé, "is to furnish some centers of resistance to the great tides of society."[70] And a few months later: "The useful role that they [associations] are able to play [is] to resist unreflective and organic movements of popular opinion."[71] Halévy was less optimistic, as we see below, when he turned his attention to France.

## "Saint Simonian Economic Doctrine" (1907–1908)

The essay on the distribution of wealth was followed by two long essays that analyzed the thought of Saint-Simon and the Saint-Simonians.[72] While his early lectures on the history of European socialism focused mostly on English and German socialism, with only infrequent references to French theorists, Halévy clearly was not neglecting French traditions. He alerted Bouglé in 1904 and 1905 that he had begun a study of Saint-Simon and his followers.[73] The result was the two lengthy articles in the *Revue de mois*, published in 1907 and 1908.

Halévy claimed in these articles that "the real inventors of Marxian socialism were all those theorists, dead before the middle of the century, whose varying doctrines Marx was able to bring together into a single system."[74] Moreover, one of the most important of these was "the great precursor," Henri de Saint-Simon (1760–1825).[75] Halévy's objective in these two essays was to describe and analyze the significant contribution that Saint-Simon and his followers, the Saint-Simonians, had made to modern socialism. Halévy pointed out that Saint-Simon had begun his examination of society with a framework derived from classical economics and from constitutional and parliamentary ideas associated with the French Revolution. But what especially interested Halévy was the progression from this "liberal" stance—which informed his thought in 1814–1817, and which he shared with Charles Comte, Charles Dunoyer, and his young secretary, Augustin Thierry (all connected with the journal *Le Censeur*)—to the more critical, authoritarian, and "socialist" stance at the time of his death in 1825.

Saint-Simon, Charles Comte, Dunoyer, and Thierry shared the general orientation of the economists that privileged the economic dimension over that of political institutions and procedures. But Saint-Simon and his cohort emphasized the importance of industry and production, unlike the classical economists who tended to focus less on production than on distribution. Moreover, the Frenchmen of *Le Censeur* did not assume that the market would naturally regulate itself, and they believed as a consequence that an economic elite would necessarily arise. Charles Comte and Dunoyer looked for the spontaneous emergence of such an elite; Saint-Simon came to believe that it should be formed by leading industrialists, scientists, and intellectuals, whose duty it would be to direct society. This was a sign of an authoritarian element that became progressively more pronounced in Saint-Simon's thought as the years passed—an element that drove Thierry away and brought in a new secretary, Auguste Comte, who, arguably, became not just another secretary but a collaborator.[76]

This authoritarian dimension in Saint-Simon's thought was joined by an "organizational" one after 1819, a dimension that was probably influenced by the works of the "theocrats," Joseph de Maistre and Louis de Bonald. Together, these resulted in a new prominence given to ideas of authority and discipline, which Saint-Simon and Auguste Comte defined as the rejection of the "negative" juridical and constitutional frameworks associated with the French Revolution, and as the embrace of the "positive" managerial frameworks associated with industry and science. Saint-Simon called this, famously, the replacement of "government" by "administration." It was a nondemocratic, nonparticipatory element that would deeply influence the organizational ideas of his followers, the Saint-Simonians—an element of which Halévy was deeply critical.

The Saint-Simonians, following Saint-Simon, tended to focus on production rather than on consumption, and, also following Saint-Simon, they wished to have social wealth distributed among those who had produced it, at the expense of the "idle." How productivity was assessed, however, and how as a consequence the rewards for productivity were to be distributed, were issues of some tension and ambiguity for Saint-Simon and for his followers. Saint-Simon called for "industrial equality," which meant that "each person draws in benefits from society in exact proportion to his social investment [*sa mise sociale*], that is to say, to his positive capacity, and to the use which he makes of his means [*ses moyens*], among which, needless to say, his capital must be included."[77] This formulation leaves many questions unanswered about how to measure the "social investment" and "means" of an individual, and also about how to evaluate the productivity of capital or the legitimacy of rewards derived from inherited wealth. But there was a clear commitment to a new framework for the distribution of wealth, which was to favor those who participated in the productive process.

Similarly, Saint-Simon's followers called for distribution "to each according to his capacity," which suggested that an individual was to be rewarded according to the part of the produce of collective labor that was proportionate to the effectiveness of his labor. This not only assumed an unequal distribution but again did not clearly specify the methods of measurement. Moreover, Halévy suggested, the Saint-Simonians had difficulty clearly thinking through the problems of interest and inheritance.[78] But, they all—and this was the essential point according to Halévy—called for an early form of socialism. They proposed "a centralized organization of industrial labor and a planned distribution of social wealth."[79] The development of industry specifically, and the economy more generally, was not to be left to happenstance or to the anarchic play of market forces; it was to be organized for the benefit of society.

Halévy devoted many pages to consideration of how the Saint-Simonians wished decisions to be made. Like Saint-Simon, they favored "administration" rather than "government" and argued that an effective administration should be dominated by bankers and industrial leaders. Their orientation, again like Saint-Simon's, was decidedly not democratic, and therefore not socialist in the sense that decisions about production and consumption were to be debated and discussed. Halévy suggested that this separated Saint-Simon from "modern socialism," which was "an essentially democratic doctrine."[80] The Saint-Simonians, similarly, in Halévy's words, had not entirely foreseen "the democratization of industrial production."[81] After World War I, as we shall see, Halévy viewed such authoritarian orientations as quite common among socialists, though they were connected with old-fashioned nationalistic forms of government that promised workers security, and not with the progressive industrial organizations imagined by the Saint-Simonians.

Halévy had serious reservations about the theory that recommended decisions be made by an economic and technocratic elite, as he would have reservations about the "state socialisms" that emerged after the Great War. He was, however, more sympathetic to other aspects of Saint-Simonian theory. Concerning human motivation, for example, Saint-Simon and the Saint-Simonians argued that the desire to enrich oneself was often tempered, fortunately, by social enthusiasm. This contrasted sharply with the view of the economists, who reduced motivation to the desire for material gain, tempered only by the fear of being condemned.

> Saint-Simon did not think it enough to appeal to the egoism of individuals to bring about the harmony of interests. On this point, his "positivism" was opposed to the utilitarianism of Bentham and the English school. . . . He relied, then, not on considered egoism but on the "force of moral sentiment" to end the crisis thwarting mankind. "The truth in this regard [wrote Saint-Simon]—a truth established by the march of civilization—is that the passion for public welfare is much more effective in bringing about political amelioration than the egoistic passion of the classes to whom such changes ought to be most profitable." . . . Here we are as far as possible [Halévy continued] from Helvétius and Bentham. The condition for the harmony of interests is that each member of society not only knows his own interests, but is capable of elevating himself to a consideration of the general interest.[82]

Halévy was also sympathetic to the insistence of Saint-Simon and the Saint-Simonians, again in stark contrast to the economists of their era, that competition was not an independent force that should remain unregulated but instead a force that could be organized for the benefit of all members of society. "The Saint-Simonians agreed, and we do too, following them, to conceive society as an association, not for the abolition of competition, but for its organization."[83]

Finally, Halévy was sympathetic to the Saint-Simonian insistence that economic relations could not be isolated from the wider social and historical context in which they existed. Political economy was part of the cumulative history of the human race, they had argued, and it had to be oriented toward providing an assessment of extant relations within society, and of the wider forces weighing on society. The purpose of this analysis was to facilitate the movement toward a better organization.[84] Halévy raised critical questions about the optimistic assumptions that undergirded the Saint-Simonian view of "evolution" and "progress"—he termed this view their inclination "toward a finalist, metaphysical, and religious interpretation of progress."[85] But he was complimentary about their comprehensive approach. Rather than considering the "division of labor" as permanent, for example, why not consider it, as they did, "a special and crude form of a more general phenomenon—the 'combination of efforts' toward a known goal." This liberated political economy from the straitjacket of the classical economists, who reduced it "to the proportions of a special science, whose concern is isolated from the totality of social relations."[86] In sum, the Saint-Simonian method of analysis was broadly social and historical. This was a significant step forward. It cleared the path for a democratic socialism, which would share this broad view but would conceptualize differently the process by which social and economic decisions were to be made.

The positive model that Halévy no doubt had in the back of his mind when he wrote these essays about Saint-Simon and the Saint-Simonians was the deliberative model that he had presented in his 1906 article on the distribution of wealth. It shared the concern with rewarding those who were productive. It insisted on considering humans as driven by more than their economic interests. It considered economics not as the determining "science" but as one dimension of societies also marked by cultural and historical forces. But, unlike the Saint-Simonians, who called for "administration" by an elite, Halévy called for deliberation, negotiation, and compromise.

## Halévy's Socialist Liberalism

Halévy demonstrated a profound engagement with socialist thought. His lectures, his writings, his interventions in meetings of the French philosophical society demonstrate an intense engagement with the debates of the period around the issue of socialism. This is indicative of the shift away from the philosophical orientation of his earliest writings—an orientation that was informed by Kantian universalism—toward a perspective grounded socially and historically. As noted above, Halévy was no longer devoting as much attention to issues of philosophical "truth" and was turning instead to political economy, the history of socialism, and nineteenth-century British history.[87] The next chapter will analyze how this contributed to the formulation of the "Halévy thesis" concerning British stability.[88] The present chapter has demonstrated that this turn also led Halévy to analyze not just the doctrinal dimension of socialism but also the political, social, cultural, and national environments within which these socialist doctrines developed.

The national comparison that most frequently informed Halévy's perspective was that between England and France. This would be most in evidence in his published works after World War I, when he analyzed the changes taking place in British socialism.[89] Already before the war, however, he was acutely sensitive to the differences in national traditions. Already he viewed German socialism as "an enormous and inert mass, penetrated with admiration for itself and for the totality of German civilization."[90] Already he contrasted this with English reasonableness, which translated into a socialism that was reformist and nonrevolutionary.[91]

Conversely, he was critical of the culture of France, which seemed unable to support reasonable socialism. Halévy suggested, for example, that French socialist demands for equality during the Revolution of 1848 failed for cultural, not economic, reasons: because, he wrote, "the mentality [of society] was entirely aristocratic."[92] More generally, he worried that the French, unlike the sober English, were "gay, light-hearted, expansive, and frivolous," and because of this cultural complex they would have difficulty developing a moderate socialism. In fact, his analysis of French culture was more nuanced, because Halévy was also impressed by, and worried by, the rigid form of rationalism that animated French intellectual life. He worried about the ideological stridency and "disastrous eloquence" that prevented compromise, here echoing an evaluation of French culture made by Tocqueville, among others.[93] This cultural combination had helped to nurture forms of socialism in France that Halévy found unappealing.

The early years of the Third Republic were, of course, volatile, especially for French socialism. The Left was still reeling from the repression following the French Commune of 1871, which had forced many prominent figures into exile, at least until the amnesties of 1879 and 1880. When they returned to France, many were unwilling to compromise with what they considered to be the corrupt and repressive Republic. The 1890s saw the first significant number of socialists elected to the Chamber of Deputies, but they also brought a wave of anarchist violence and new repressive legislation. The ideological influence of Proudhon, who had attacked politics, and Blanqui, who had advocated revolution, was still strong; the influence of Marx was just beginning. Halévy, in fact, was one of the first to read Marx carefully, along with Georges Sorel, Jean Jaurès, and Charles Andler. These were also the years when the *bourse* movement developed, followed by the emergence of revolutionary syndicalism. Halévy's first lectures on the history of European socialism in 1902 corresponded with the opening of syndicalism's "heroic period," with leaders of the Confédération Générale du Travail (CGT—General Confederation of Labor) calling for workers to take control of enterprises through direct action. These were also the years when socialist factions realized a tenuous unity in the SFIO, notable for its rejection of "ministerialism" and its rhetorical commitment to revolution.

His correspondence indicates that Halévy responded forcefully to these various stances and peculiarities of the French Left. He celebrated the move by French working-class groups to find common ground. In September 1912, for example, he wrote the following to Bouglé about the meeting in Le Havre of the Congrès national corporative of the CGT: "I have read the summary of the debates at Le Havre. . . . The time of the split among syndicalists and among socialists is past. Among syndicalists on the one hand, and socialists on the other, the split is something much more serious and respectable than the quarrels between Broussists, Guesdists, Allemanists, twenty years ago. Cooperative unity is being formed. These are some very happy symptoms."[94]

More common, however, were critical remarks about socialist leaders. Halévy found men like Jules Guesde, an influential socialist militant who embraced a crude Marxism, dogmatically misguided. He was equally critical of syndicalist intellectuals like Georges Sorel, who embraced the myth of the general strike and rejected political action. He even was critical of many of the reform socialists, because they flirted with revolution. He wrote to Bouglé in 1894, as mentioned above, that he found the "the [revolutionary] rhetoric of Jaurès . . . slightly unappetizing."[95] He was relieved in the late 1890s when some Parisian socialists began to defend the Republic and support the retrial of Alfred Dreyfus. In February 1898, he wrote to his father: "I [had] believed Parisian socialism was [Henri] Rochefort. It appears that I was wrong."[96] Nonetheless, Halévy remained critical of the leaders of the French socialist movement and expressed his concern in his correspondence. "What good is the attractive enthusiasm of Jaurès," he complained to Bouglé in September 1905, "if it is necessarily overwhelmed by the fanaticism of [Gustave] Hervé."[97] Three months later he lamented: "Why doesn't Jaurès defend the

Republic, or why does he assume, in order to defend it, an outlook so revolutionary and complicated?"[98] A few months later, he contrasted the moderate socialists of the Labour Party in England, whom he referred to as "mutualists," with the more radical socialists in France, like Jaurès and Victor Griffuelhes (the secretary-general of the CGT), who employed "revolutionary phraseology" and demanded "social revolution."[99] To his wife, Florence, in a letter from 1906, he spelled out his frustrations:

> When I hear—as yesterday at the Société de philosophie—a French revolutionary socialist ramble on for three solid hours, with the respectful attention of about thirty teachers, I wish to have a religion, a king, to respect established institutions, in order to give life a good foundation, and to feel that something around me and in me [opposes] the tumult, the violence, the incoherence, and the disastrous eloquence. I spoke, poorly, because I spoke not in order to express ideas or to bring to bear some facts, but only because of my irritation. . . . It is necessary, in order to deal with the state of French affairs, to create a school for training in wise behavior . . . in order to cohabitate with fools who have lost their heads. Difficult exercise . . .[100]

Halévy's impatience did not diminish as the years passed. He complained that the French too often appealed to revolutionary illusions rather than reasonable programs. In 1908, after reading Jaurès's history of the French Revolution, he wrote to Bouglé: "Yes, heroic convulsions would be better than this dull mess. The misfortune is that so many heroic convulsions result in this dull mess. If the Revolution had had neither the massacres of September nor the drownings of Nantes, nor the guillotining in Paris, and if it had finished, by some fortuitous path, with a Washington, or even finished with Bonaparte, I would have liked it better."[101] Halévy did not want the *disappearance* of the anarchists and socialists in France, because they fulfilled the important service of raising critical issues. The anarchists, he mused, "have their utility in a poorly constituted society. They will therefore be useful for a long time."[102] He also valued the existence of the Socialist Party, which was "an integral part of the modern large state." But, he was not comfortable when republicans came to regard Jaurès as the "guardian of their conscience."[103] Socialism might contain "the secret of the future," as he put it to

Bouglé,[104] but unfortunately the secret was hidden under layers of enthusiastic rhetoric. Even Jaurès—especially Jaurès—tended to intoxicate himself, and intoxicate the young men who were swayed by his speeches, with humanitarian ideals to which reality did not correspond.

Closely related to the critical stance Halévy took toward individual French socialists of the era was his assessment, more broadly, of French moeurs. Unlike the English, who were animated by a "moderate individualism [*individualisme tempéré*]" that fostered "voluntary obedience" and "spontaneous organization,"[105] the French were "gay, light-hearted, expansive, and frivolous,"[106] as mentioned above, but also had a "military soul."[107] These sentiments, which supported revolutionary emotionalism, were curiously connected with a deep cultural commitment to a rigid form of rationalism that appealed to abstract reason.[108] In Halévy's mind, this abstract rationalism and volatile emotionalism led to an unfortunate alternation between an exaggerated respect for authority, on the one hand, and, on the other, an equally exaggerated embrace of revolutionary change.

In his correspondence, Halévy expressed freely his frustrations concerning French moeurs, and explicitly articulated his anxiety that this was intimately related to the instability of French politics. In October 1892, he wrote to his mother: "The problem [of the French] is to be too reasonable and to prefer reason to simple good sense. And this is why there is always a conservative party in England because *all* the English are conservative, while there has never been a conservative party in France because *not one* Frenchman is conservative. I know well that there are some anarchists in England; but these are *eccentrics*, classed and tolerated as such, who have some clubs and whose eccentricity enters into beautiful harmony with the English people taken as a whole."[109] In France, the anarchists and revolutionaries were more numerous. Many people, he suggested, could not conceive opposing governmental policy without calling for an insurrection, without a stormy rejection of dialogue and compromise. "It becomes fatiguing," he complained in 1906, "to belong to a people perpetually inflamed [*perpetuellement passionné*]." "A weighty moderation, spread in all of the levels of the population, would have spared us *the entirety* of the Dreyfus Affair, from the condemnation to the rehabilitation; wouldn't that have been delicious?"[110]

Halévy often worried, in addition, about the tractability of the popular classes in France. During the Dreyfus Affair, as we have seen, he was appalled by what he termed "a band of screaming actors [*une bande de cabotins hurleurs*]" that stirred up the crowds into hysterical anti-Semitism.[111] He was thankful that there were institutions and laws in France that protected the minority, and impressed by the "logical" arguments of Fernand Labori (the lawyer who defended Zola and Dreyfus during the Affair). [112] But he also criticized the inclination of the majority of French "men of letters" towards a rigid conservatism that undermined the laws protecting basic civil liberties.[113] In short, he was concerned that French moeurs did not support political stability. In 1894, in a letter to Bouglé, he lamented: "Is it not more and more evident that this country [France] is incapable of governing itself? . . . The absence of government and decadence, are they synonymous?"[114] A decade later, again to Bouglé, he worried: "The French are only good at two things: to be governed and to quarrel about doctrines. This was true at the time of Abélard and of Guillaume de Champeaux; it was true at the time of Pascal, of Bossuet, of Fénelon; it was true at the time of Proudhon, of the Saint-Simonians, of the Fouriérists; it will again be true tomorrow."[115]

Halévy had an ambivalent relationship to socialism before World War I. He respected the critical stance of the early socialists in opposition to the rigid rationalism of the English Utilitarians and the Manchester liberals. He admired how the writings of socialists analyzed the concentration of wealth and recurrent crises of overproduction. He was deeply sympathetic to their calls for greater equality and their exposure of the injustices of industrialization. He respected the moral fervor of their demands for reform; and he responded warmly to the critical and emancipatory elements within most strains of socialist thought—many of which had their origins in early French socialism. He was favorably disposed to state intervention to redistribute wealth, to what he referred to (in his first lecture on the history of socialism in 1902) as "administrative collectivism." But he refused to call himself a socialist and insisted that he was a liberal.[116] In part, this was because many socialists focused too exclusively on material interests and on a limited range of human sentiments. Others, Halévy charged, embraced an unduly reductive sociological perspective. He judged these too narrow to capture the complexity of human action; they offended his neo-Kantian view of human rationality, human nature, and human motivation.

Equally important, however, was that the refusal of Halévy to call himself a socialist was due to the close connection of pre–World War I French socialism with revolutionary Marxism and revolutionary syndicalism; that is, he disliked the forms of socialism that had emerged in France, with their demands for radical change through revolution and violence. The loudest voices in the ranks of French socialism scorned the sort of state-directed reform he favored; and, they threatened to tear apart the society that, for all its faults, enjoyed the most progressive political institutions in Europe, with the protection of civil liberties and universal male suffrage. Finally, he refused to call himself a socialist because he worried that French moeurs would likely undermine implementation of even the moderate socialist reforms that he favored. "What is socialism?" he rhetorically asked Bouglé. "In England, that which one calls the *Labour Party* is a party of mutualists, and the principal theoreticians of socialism are the Webbs. . . . All that scarcely resembles the social revolution of which Griffuelhes—and Jaurès—dream. For the historian, the French point of view is without doubt more amusing; but for the sociologist, the English point of view is without doubt more serious."[117]

In another context (say, England) or in another time (say, when socialism in France was associated with the republican reforms of the Second Republic), Halévy likely would have embraced socialism. This, of course, remains speculation—injudicious speculation, perhaps, given his insistence that any reasonable assessment must carefully take into account the complexities of the historical context (with overlapping political, social, economic, and cultural variables). Halévy recognized the weight of his own historical milieu on his own socio-political identity. He stated in 1936 that if he had entered the École normale a few years later than he did, he likely would have been a socialist.[118] But he insisted on his identification as a Dreyfusard and a liberal.

Halévy's liberalism had elements that in most contexts would be considered socialist. Socialism, of course, can have many meanings. It can refer to the integration of labor into economic decision making; or to the implementation of redistributive social legislation; or to the state assuming a robust role in the economy; or to the rejection of the price mechanism of the market; or to the collective ownership of the means of production. Halévy agreed with the first three of these elements but not the last two. From an Anglo-American perspective, this would have made him a moderate socialist. In France, it made him a socialist liberal.

CHAPTER 6

# British Affairs

## Empire, Methodism, and English Socialists
## (1905–1914)

The English have transformed England into a vast *debating society*
[this phrase in English] where, all questions are discussed, but none
are worth dying for. They have domesticated riot, domesticated civil
war.

—Élie Halévy to Florence Halévy, 2 July 1903

British individualism is a moderate individualism, where there is
mixed together, almost to the point of being indiscernible, the influence of Evangelicalism and the influence of Utilitarianism.

—Élie Halévy, *Histoire du peuple anglais au XIXe siècle*

His lectures on the history of European socialism did not mean that Halévy
had turned away from England. He continued to spend several months in
England every year, and every other year his course at the École libre des
sciences politiques was devoted to some aspect of the history of England. His
scholarly reputation, as we have seen, was largely based on his three-volume
analysis of British Utilitarianism, *La formation du radicalisme philosophique*,
published from 1901 to 1904.[1] Moreover, his continuing work on Britain led
to new publications. First came a short book on empire, *L'Angleterre et
son empire*, published in 1905.[2] This was quickly followed by two long
articles (appearing in 1906) that analyzed modern English religious culture,

"La naissance du Méthodisme."[3] Then, in 1912, he published with Hachette what was to become his most famous book on the history of England, the initial volume of his expansive, multivolume *Histoire du peuple anglais au XIXe siècle*. This large volume (620 pages) was subtitled *L'Angleterre en 1815*.[4]

In the last two of these publications, Halévy argued—in what became known as the Halévy thesis—that English Protestantism, especially the evangelical forms of English Protestantism associated with Methodism, was a key element of Britain's sociopolitical stability.[5] This deep-seated religiosity, he argued, was supportive of British liberalism and British philanthropy; it was responsible for an England that, in his own words, "governs itself, in place of being governed from above."[6]

The other distinctive component of English culture, examined extensively in *La formation du radicalisme philosophique*, was Utilitarianism. Halévy was fascinated by the popularity of this doctrine in English high culture. This chapter focuses on how Halévy brought together his analysis of the Utilitarianism of British high culture and his analysis of the religiosity of British popular culture to advance a theory of why the English had not been as radical and revolutionary as the French. The new attention Halévy gave to evangelical Christianity shows the evolution that had taken place in his thinking since the publication of the final volume of *La formation du radicalisme philosophique*. In this earlier work, he had focused on the logic and inherent contradictions in the theory of Bentham and his followers, and had argued that these were central to understanding the different tendencies within the movement of Utilitarianism. In his new publications, he combined this history of doctrine with a broader history of the political and economic development of England, and with a thesis that highlighted its distinctive religious culture.

First, however, a brief look at his book on the fascination in Britain with its growing empire.

## *England and Its Empire* (1905)

Halévy's correspondence indicates that he was disturbed by the new belligerency of British attitudes toward foreigners, and the new aggressive policy of the British as demonstrated in South Africa and elsewhere.[7] Halévy and his wife, Florence, traveled to Egypt and Sudan in November 1904, a trip that included, along with visits to famous sites, discussions with British officials.

Halévy returned committed to write a short book. The result was *L'Angleterre et son empire*, which focused, as its title indicates, on British imperialism during the second half of the nineteenth century.[8] Halévy began by noting that English foreign policy following the Napoleonic Wars had been devoted to free trade and support of the emancipation of Spanish colonies in South America. The purpose of the British Empire at this time, he wrote, was to provide an outlet for excess industrial products and to provide a place of settlement for a growing population. In general, he suggested, there was less focus on domination than on commerce. The second half of the century saw a change, with Britain giving less attention to Continental affairs and more attention to intervention—often armed intervention—in its colonial empire. This was true of governments of both parties, but the man who epitomized this new more aggressive policy was the Conservative prime minister Benjamin Disraeli, who was in power between 1874 and 1880. His predecessor, William Gladstone, at least during his first ministry (1868–1874), had favored the Manchesterite policy of nonintervention recommended by Richard Cobden and John Bright. Disraeli, on the other hand, "invented imperialism," favoring what Halévy referred to as "Asiatic imperialism . . . which is monarchic, military, administrative and fiscal."[9] Subsequent governments of Gladstone and Lord Salisbury embraced an even more aggressive imperialism.

The conclusion of the book raised broader issues that would continue to concern Halévy in future works about England. He pointed out that there was vigorous popular support for empire in England in the late nineteenth century and suggested that this enthusiasm was bringing about a shift in British mores that would not serve England well in the long term. This was in part because the strong support for empire might lead to holding on to colonies beyond the date when it was economically advantageous to do so. That is, the upwelling of popular support might lead to an empire policy in which the high cost of maintaining and defending the colonies would outstrip the economic benefits. Other issues, equally if not more important, were less economic than political and ideological. While Halévy claimed that liberal British imperialists were more democratic than their counterparts elsewhere, he suggested that they still were not willing to treat indigenous peoples as equals. It was assumed that in empire the function of colonial subjects is "not to cooperate with the government of the empire, but to serve it. These are not citizens, these are subjects who are expected, in order for the empire to prosper, to work under the orders and for the benefit of their Anglo-Saxon masters."[10] In short, the empire represented an unequal distribution of "rights," which Halévy believed was a violation of justice.

The third troubling result of the establishment and maintenance of empire, according to Halévy, was cultural. He suggested that administering an empire was eroding positive British moeurs. "The English tend thus, with the expansion of their empire and by the fact of their imperialism, to become a nation composed no longer of industrialists, of merchants and workers, but of capitalists and administrators, no longer of men who work, but of men who take, in order to live, a part of the work of others. But is it not by this idleness, to which the exercise of the functions of command condemns them, that the superior races degenerate, and finish by one day permitting the inferior races to be rescued from a prolonged subjugation?"[11] Halévy was, in essence, echoing an analysis dear to the heart of Alexis de Tocqueville about the domestic cultural impact of empire. The impact of empire, however, was diametrically opposed in the analyses of the two. Tocqueville had been impressed by the link between French colonial action in Algeria with more robust "virtue" and patriotism among French citizens. He celebrated this effect of French empire on French moeurs. Halévy, on the other hand, argued that the popularity of empire in England similarly involved a heightened patriotism, but he was critical of its wider cultural impact. British empire, he argued, stimulated a patriotism that unfortunately spilled over into aggressive nationalism, and it also coincided with a new and disturbing loss of commitment to a robust work ethic.

Halévy ended his analysis questioning whether the British Empire would survive in the long term. He noted that the English were "the least pedantic and the least tyrannical of the colonizing people," but he nonetheless concluded that "the British Empire will decline." This was not likely to happen quickly, however. Halévy argued that industrial and commercial concentration would continue, and that these would favor the military and political concentration of the great powers—North America, Russia, Japan. The twentieth century, he reasoned, would be "the century of empires."[12]

Given Halévy's interest in British imperialism, one might expect a similar consideration of the French Empire, which also was expanding during this period, and which also was having an impact on the mores of French society. The documents related to Halévy's reaction to this are, unfortunately, very thin. There is, to the best of my knowledge, nothing in Halévy's published writings about the French Empire. Since he did not publish anything directly analyzing French society or French politics, perhaps this is not surprising. Nonetheless, the silence is deafening. The one source that permits limited insight into his views is his correspondence during a brief trip that Halévy made to Tunisia and Algeria in the spring of 1897. This correspondence indicates that he was shocked both by the poor conditions of the indigenous population and by the brutality of the French. There is nothing complimentary in this correspondence, however, about the non-French. He wrote that "it is a very mediocre civilization that we are demolishing by entering here."[13] But passages discussing the French colonial population are even more critical. "Above all, I have been overtaken by a disgust, impossible to overcome, of the proceedings of the colons vis-à-vis the colonized," he wrote on 24 April 1897.[14] Two days later, after commenting unfavorably about the indigenous culture, he went on to say: "It is a very lamentable civilization that we have put in its place. . . . I fear that this is above all the fault of the French 'colons.' "[15] There seems to be the commonplace assumption of the superiority of French civilization, but a lament that the French colonial population and the French administration are failing to bring this to North Africa. "We reproach the Arabs for having too much originality, and for not assimilating to our civilization. All this would be possible, if we had a little political genius. But we do not."[16] Halévy clearly did not wish to justify French colonial behavior; quite the contrary. There is no evidence, however, that he was concerned to provide a broader criticism of French colonial policy.

## "The Birth of Methodism in England" (1906)

In 1906, Halévy published in *La revue de Paris* a two-part article on the birth of Methodism in England.[17] They were the first articulation of a thesis that would come to be closely associated with Halévy's scholarly reputation, especially in the Anglo-Saxon world: namely, that Methodism was extremely important for understanding the mores of modern England and, further, that it was one of the elements that helped England avoid revolution during the early nineteenth century.

The two parts of the article combine a discussion of how John and Charles Wesley came to embrace the doctrines and techniques associated with Methodism with a broader analysis of why this peculiar form of Puritanism spread so quickly in early eighteenth-century Britain. Halévy also was intrigued that evangelical Protestantism continued to have such resonance in

British society. The Wesleys, he pointed out, came from a High Church Anglican background but were influenced in 1738 by two foreign movements. The first was the Moravian Brothers, represented by the individual Peter Böhler, who insisted that true Christian faith consisted of believing in two essential things: that sins would be forgiven when one recognized the merits of Christ; and that this faith was to be secured suddenly through a kind of "instantaneous" miracle. That is, a true Christian must be convinced of the necessity of faith in a redeeming God and in the instantaneity of conversion. Halévy suggested that the Wesley brothers were susceptible to Böhler's attention and solicitation when they returned to Britain physically exhausted and deeply disappointed after a failed missionizing trip to America. "Thanks to him [Böhler], the two brothers awaited the moment when Christ would desire their conversion and grant to them the conviction of salvation, a postponement too full of impatient expectation not to be satisfied in the end. One cannot hover dizzily at the brink of an abyss for three months without eventually stumbling in."[18]

The other influence on the Wesleys was the revivalist method of teaching that their compatriot George Whitefield learned from Welsh Nonconformists like Griffith Jones, Daniel Rowland, and Howell Harris. In Wales, John Wesley first experienced the remarkable effects that this display of rhetorical eloquence and enthusiasm could have on large crowds, especially when he preached, not in a church, but outdoors. Halévy argued that it was the convergence of the Moravian doctrine of instantaneous conversion and the Welsh methods of preaching that led to Methodism. "If the Moravians had not taught Wesley what he must preach in order to capture hearts, would Methodism have come into being? And is it any more likely that Methodism would have come into being if the Welsh preachers had not demonstrated to Whitefield [and Wesley] how he must preach in order to give the inception of a sect the aspect and importance of a popular revolution? Methodism consisted in the propagation of Moravian and Welsh enthusiasm in England."[19]

But why did Methodism gain such a strong following in England? And why did it continue to have such a robust influence on English culture? To answer these questions, Halévy expanded his account to include broader economic, political, and cultural factors. He argued that Methodism built upon a strong base of Protestant passions that had persisted in England but was no longer serviced by High Church Latitudinarians, Nonconformist rationalists, or philosophical Radicals. Even Dissenting ministers, who had stirred up religious passions during the stormy seventeenth century, "preached a doctrine more and more like Deism" in the early eighteenth century.[20] Halévy argued that there was a great deal of "latent religious sentiment" among the popular classes in early eighteenth-century England, and that there was a "reverence for the incomprehensible" waiting to be tapped by Wesley and Methodism.[21] "To produce such a revival of faith, what was needed was a combination of the ecclesiastical zeal of certain of the clergy, and the Protestant piety of the mass of the faithful. Was Methodism anything but this?"[22]

The enormous success of Methodism required more than this, however. It also required an economic downturn that stirred up popular agitation and discontent. This created a crisis for the government of Robert Walpole and its policy of peace. That is, Halévy argued that, contemporaneous with Wesley and Whitefield's conversion to revivalist preaching methods, there was an economic crisis of overproduction that led to growing unemployment, which led to working class activism in the form of marches and demonstrations, and to a renewal of English bellicosity, personified by William Pitt. The new enthusiastic religiosity identified with Methodism built upon this discontent. In Halévy's own words, "The despair of the working class was the raw material to which Methodist doctrine and discipline gave a shape."[23]

This raw material, however, did not lead, as it might have, to violent militancy. Lacking a leadership from the middle class that embraced a militant ideology, working-class enthusiasm instead was channeled in a direction that was not revolutionary, not irreligious, and not republican. Discontent, instead, was channeled into Methodism, which of all the Protestant sects "was at once the most conservative in the political opinions of its members, and the most hierarchical in its internal organization."[24] The result was the growth of a passionate and emotional movement that was not threatening to the social order.

> England experienced a crisis of industrial overproduction of extreme gravity, which reduced the lower orders of the manufactories to poverty and made them accessible to all forms of collective emotion at a time when scientific rationalism had not yet been disseminated among the lowest strata of the bourgeoisie. This is why English Protestantism, suddenly resuscitated and consolidated by this crisis, did not evolve in the direction of philosophic rationalism as among the German Lutherans. This is why in modern England there are

no genuine lay parties of social and political revolution. This, in other words, is why after a half century in which it seemed that free thought must triumph, England reawakened a Puritan nation, and has remained so until our day.[25]

It was important, according to Halévy, that Methodism combined emotional preaching with a hierarchical organization that emphasized the distinction between ministers and laymen, and also emphasized the importance of discipline. It was this combination that made it popular but also relatively conservative.

Methodism is the High Church of Nonconformity. It is a Nonconformist sect established by Anglican clergymen who wished to remain faithful to the Church of England. From this stemmed the success of Methodism at a time when England was weary of the Christian republicanism of the seventeenth century and when a new kind of republicanism had not yet arisen elsewhere in Europe to wage war on the very concept of religion.

In Wesleyan organization, the hierarchical and the egalitarian principles were combined in equal portions. A moderately conservative Protestantism was substituted for the revolutionary Protestantism of the seventeenth century. In 1649, the English Puritans had beheaded a king. It is generally agreed that the influence of Methodism contributed a great deal, during the last several years of the eighteenth century, to preventing the French Revolution from having an English counterpart.[26]

There has been a considerable historiographical debate since Halévy's time concerning the impact of Methodism on the English popular classes. Some scholars have argued that it is more complex than Halévy claimed, and that it is important to recognize that some workers turned to Methodism *and* to radical activities at the same time. That is, Methodism did not always act in a conservative manner; it was not always an "opium" of the people.[27] More widely accepted is the other part of Halévy's thesis, namely, that Methodism influenced other groups in English society—Dissenters, the Anglican Establishment, even secular opinion. While scholarly disputes remain, there is more general agreement that religiosity has been foundational for English culture.[28] Halévy claimed that this was related specifically to the "birth" of Methodism.

> Even today, whenever a Methodist preacher brings a popular audi-
> ence together at a street corner to read the Bible, sing hymns, and
> pray in common, whenever he induces a "revival" of mysticism and
> religious exaltation, in a region or throughout the nation, the great
> movement of 1739 is being repeated in the pattern fixed by tradition,
> with climactic changes of mood that everybody—passionate partici-
> pants and disinterested spectators—can foresee in advance. A force
> capable of expending itself in displays of violence or popular upheav-
> als assumes, under the influence of a century and a half of Method-
> ism, the form least capable of unsettling a social order founded upon
> inequality of rank and wealth.[29]

## History of the English People in the Nineteenth Century, Volume 1: England in 1815 (1912)

Halévy's history of the birth of Methodism was an element—an important but not dominant element—of his larger project to produce a history of England during the nineteenth century. He wished to weave his analysis of Methodism into a broader analysis of British culture and science, and more generally integrate these strands with an account of the political and economic phenomena.[30] He explained in a letter to Lucien Herr that his purpose in the first volume of this history—published in 1912 as *Histoire du peuple anglais au XIXe siècle*, volume 1: *L'Angleterre en 1815*—was to provide an introduction to the longer history that he intended to write. "This first volume—a general tableau, an introduction—is an attempt to define in its general traits, in order to explain by their origins, the system of English institutions and beliefs. Political liberalism; economic individualism; *Protestantism* and industrialism combined."[31] In the preface, he put it this way: "I do not propose to recount the episodes of military, diplomatic, or parliamentary history, but to study simultaneously, under their opposed aspects, British civilization and society as a whole, and to understand how diverse orders of phenomena—political, economic, and religious—combined with one another and reacted against each other."[32] The book, remarkable in its erudition and expository

FIGURE 6. Élie Halévy on the Thames (about 1907–1908). Reproduced with
the permission of the Association des amis d'Élie et Florence Halévy, and of the
president of this association, Vincent Duclert.

power, provides a detailed analysis of how these forces overlapped. Characteristically, Halévy resisted the notion that a single variable was sufficient to
explain historical change.

Part I of the first volume focused on politics. Halévy devoted many
pages to analyzing the working of the parliamentary system, with the complex
interrelationships of monarch, prime minister, parties, bureaucracy, judiciary,
local constituencies, and public opinion. He noted the power of oratory
among solicitors and barristers, and argued against Montesquieu that there
was no real separation of power. "The British government," he wrote, "is not
a government where all the powers are clearly distinguished. It is a government where all the elements are mixed up, where all the powers encroach
upon others." This "confusion," he suggested, operated in such a way that it
was a "detriment of the monarchical principle."[33]

This confusion also, more generally, limited the power of the central
government. Though the state delivered the mail, collected taxes, and commanded the army and the navy, it had a very limited reach. There were
no government-provided schools, roads, or poor relief. The electorate was

composed of only a small fraction of the nation, so effective control of politics in the country was left in the hands of the aristocracy of wealthy landed proprietors, who controlled both central and local government. The head of state, as a consequence, was "without power, or almost without power."[34]

Halévy also discussed the complicated nature of British representative politics: local power and regional differences within England; strong government support among parliamentary representatives from Scotland; and control in Ireland by a Protestant minority that "exploit[ed] the country like a colony, without any other preoccupation than to extract as many advantages and as much money as possible."[35] Nonetheless, he concluded that politics in Britain was less arbitrary than on the Continent, and he noted in passing that it would begin to be reformed in 1832.

Part II analyzed the economy. Halévy discussed the importance of industrial growth; the effect on the economy of the restoration of peace in 1814–1815 at the end of the revolutionary wars; the impact of the opening of postrevolutionary trade on the presumed "equilibrium" between agriculture and industry; the troubling exploitation of the popular classes; the actions of Luddites and working-class radicals; and, the recurring crises of overproduction.

The attention Halévy gave to politics and economics was intertwined with his attempt to understand why the English peasants, artisans, and industrial workers had not been as radical or as revolutionary as the French. He was fascinated with what J. Bartlet Brebner termed "the operative morality of British liberalism."[36] And this led him, as suggested above, to his analyses of Methodism and Utilitarianism. Halévy concluded that English stability did not have much to do with English politics or with English economics. Neither English political institutions (emphasized by previous French thinkers like Montesquieu and Constant) nor its economic growth (the focus of those enamored of the prosperity created by English industrialization) were sufficient, in his mind, to explain the peculiarly nonrevolutionary nature of British society in the nineteenth century. The English constitution, in Halévy's opinion, did not give to the government sufficient authority to overcome radical opposition; and he judged the electoral system "incoherent, disorganized."[37] Moreover, English industrial growth was characterized by cycles of overproduction and unemployment (he followed, here, the analyses of Sismondi). These recurring economic crises were not created by the imprudent actions of the government, according to Halévy (as mistakenly argued

by the "free-exchange party"); rather, they were created "by the general organization of commerce and industry."[38] The result was a troubling social *instability*. In short, Halévy judged English politics to be chaotic, and he believed
English economic growth to be unstable.

To explain the peculiar stability of nineteenth-century England, it was
necessary to look elsewhere. To understand the relatively peaceful history of
England, it was necessary to focus on culture—on "les moeurs publiques"—
that encouraged social peace.

> In no other country in Europe have social changes been accom-
> plished with such a marked and gradual continuity. Where must
> one search to find the sources of this continuity and comparative
> stability? It is not, as we have come to see, in the economic organiza-
> tion of the country. It is not, moreover, in the political organizations
> of the country: we have seen how, taken by themselves, the political
> institutions of England were unstable and anarchic. It is necessary
> for us, therefore, to search some causes, to take a new approach, to
> analyze a final category of social phenomena: beliefs, emotions, and
> opinions, as well as the institutions and groups in which these
> beliefs, emotions, and opinions take a form suitable for scientific
> inquiry.[39]

This was the focus of part III of the book. Here, Halévy suggested that
what was distinctive about British culture was how the peculiar form of British Protestantism—especially the influence of Methodism—combined with
the new ethos connected with the industrial revolution—Utilitarianism—
and how both of these reinforced the "old Whig political traditions." These
together were what made up the distinctive character of British liberalism.
Repeating the argument he had made in his publications of 1906, Halévy
claimed that the influence of Methodism was especially weighty for the
peaceful continuity of English institutions and society, of "the miracle of
modern England, anarchist but orderly, practical and businesslike, but religious, and even pietist."[40] But in *L'Angleterre en 1815*, Halévy was concerned
to illustrate how this religious culture interacted with the new scientific and
empirical philosophy. He argued that it was the unusual British combination
of a high culture informed by bizarre varieties of Utilitarianism and a popular
culture informed by religious movements like Methodism that explained the

stability of modern Britain. Methodism and Utilitarianism were the antidotes to instability.

What traits of Methodism were so important, according to Halévy? First, it embraced the Protestant doctrine of the mysterious personal relationship of the individual with God, as well as the traditional Protestant belief in justification by faith alone. Unlike some other Protestant denominations, however, it remained hierarchical in its internal organization and defended itself against a rigorous embrace of predestination that would have threatened to sterilize human effort.[41] Second, Methodists, and English evangelicals more broadly, took conscience seriously, meaning that it emphasized deep reflection about moral behavior and supported, more generally, sober social mores. When he explored the issue in 1906—in the two-articles entitled "La naissance du Méthodisme en Angleterre"—Halévy claimed that Protestant-ism had produced "grave, reserved, silent, and melancholy" Englishmen, who experienced a sense of awe at the "incomprehensible mystery" of the uni-verse.[42] He also suggested that the reservoir of Protestant emotionalism tapped by Methodism came, more broadly, to inform the Anglican Church and British society. It led to the formation of numerous voluntary societies "to combat vice and to edify the faithful."[43] Halévy suggested, in sum, that Protestant religiosity stimulated English associational life and helped incul-cate a culture of self-imposed restraint. It provided the "mystic foundation of English liberalism" among the popular classes, and therefore helped save the country from the revolutionary turmoil that visited countries like France at the end of the eighteenth century.[44] Halévy made a parallel argument in *L'Angleterre en 1815*. As he put it on the final page of the book: "Method-ism is the true antidote to Jacobinism, and the free organization of the churches is, in the country that it governs, the true principle of order. Saying 'England is a free country' means, if one goes to the foundation of things, that England is the country of voluntary obedience, of spontaneous organiza-tion."[45] "Voluntary obedience," "spontaneous organization"—these were the critical contributions that Methodism and evangelicalism made to British culture. The result was a relatively peaceful society in which liberty was divorced from rebellion. " 'Liberty' now signified 'spontaneous voluntary dis-cipline' in opposition to a discipline forcibly imposed by a government."[46]

What of Utilitarianism? What contribution did Utilitarianism make to English culture? In a curious way, the English Utilitarians, in Halévy's accounting, also embraced an ascetic way of life, closer to the stoics than the epicureans, and therefore also supportive of "organization" and "obedience."

Though Bentham and his associates were animated by a "thoroughgoing rationalism which was in striking contrast with the emotionalism of the evangelicals,"[47] their morality was based on sagacity, prudence, and the postponement of immediate pleasures. Their view of proper ethical comportment did not conflict with the moral constrains recommended by the evangelicals.

Halévy's extensive analysis of what he labeled "philosophical radicalism" was penetrating, as we have seen,[48] in its exposure of the contradictions at the heart of the theory and in its critique of the authoritarian tendencies of its legal and political philosophy. But Halévy was nonetheless respectful of the impact it had on English society. In the closing pages of the second volume of his history of British "philosophical radicalism," he noted that by 1815 the principle of utility was "the very foundation of English understanding. All English thinkers, conservatives or democrats, communists or partisans of individual and hereditary property, partisans of free-exchange or protectionists, refer instinctively to this principle."[49]

Utilitarian theory was based, as noted, on a relatively simple notion of human motivation and on a straightforward associationist psychological theory. Bentham, Halévy argued, had recognized the importance of "sympathy" (an important sentiment in the moral theories of predecessors like Francis Hutcheson and Adam Smith), but he had emphasized egoistic sentiments. "Bentham was inclined to admit, like Hume but with fewer reservations, that egoism was, if not an exclusive, at least a predominant influence on human actions: more narrowly yet, he declared that 'of all the passions, that which is the most accessible to calculation' . . . is the passion 'that corresponds to the motive of pecuniary interest.' "[50] In short, the economic drive for personal gain—what Bentham would call the "dogmatic of egoism"—was stronger than any other sentiment. In addition, Bentham was a rationalist, believing that humans acted by rationally weighing benefits in terms of the quantity of pleasure or pain that actions would produce. And, on the basis of this simple idea of human motivation, Bentham believed he could "establish morality as an exact science,"[51] erecting on this foundation a program of juridical, political, and economic reform. These would be based on the famous ethical maxim—"the utilitarian principle"—that one should always act in ways that would produce the greatest good for the greatest number.

At the heart of Halévy's analysis of Bentham and his followers, as analyzed in chapter 3 above, was his claim that there was a tension at the heart of utilitarian philosophy. On the one hand, Utilitarians assumed that unrestrained selfishness was beneficial, or at least sufficiently benign, for there to be no need for intervention, governmental or otherwise, to prevent injurious activity. This "natural harmony of interests" was true for the economy, where the Utilitarians followed the economic theories of Adam Smith. On the other hand, it was not assumed that unrestrained human action in the juridical or political realms was moral or benign. Here, Utilitarians argued that government intervention was needed to create an "artificial harmony of interests" that would maximize good. This undergirded an authoritarian strain, according to Halévy, that was especially strong in the thought of Jeremy Bentham. "Morals, for him [Bentham] has a commanding, governmental nature; or again, if you like, he accepts the principle of utility in the specific form of the artificial identification of interests. The science of human nature permits the conquering of human nature for the good of mankind, just as, in the interest of mankind, the science of physical nature permits the conquering of physical nature. Further, he writes, in language directly inspired by Helvétius, 'that it is the business of government to work to increase social happiness, by punishing and rewarding.'"[52] Halévy concluded that Bentham's philosophy of law "is essentially a philosophy written for legislators and men engaged in government, that is to say for men whose profession it is to restrict liberty."[53]

Halévy, as we have seen, had a more complex understanding of human nature than Bentham.[54] He disagreed with the assumption of Bentham that individuals always acted selfishly and rationally. He distrusted the tendency of the Utilitarians to pronounce general theories under which empirical variations were subsumed and eliminated. In *La formation du radicalisme philosophique*, he had criticized the tendency of the Utilitarians to push aside empirical evidence that conflicted with their theories—"to postulate the truth of a principle, in order to be able to neglect the exceptions."[55] The analysis in *L'Angleterre en 1815* was similarly critical: "The Utilitarians neglected as useless the learned research, the knowledge concerning the evolution of law. Their method, as they fully realized, was radically opposed to the 'historical' method that German professors were in the process of bringing into fashion."[56] Halévy preferred a methodology respectful of empirical complexity: there were overlapping variables; there were empirically demonstrated variations within societies; and there were historically demonstrated divergences between different societies and nations. Utilitarian doctrine was too often insensitive to these important dynamics.

This is important to emphasize. His analysis of the conflict at the heart of Utilitarian doctrine—the tension between the presumed "natural harmony of interest" and the "artificial harmony of interest"—led Halévy to consider carefully the divergent views of social dynamics that this suggested, and the divergent views of human nature that were ignored by this utilitarian view of these social dynamics. How could thinkers embrace such contradictory analyses of social dynamics? What did this say about their social theories? In pondering these issues, Halévy was led to consider the complexity of historical developments.[57]

Nonetheless, Halévy was impressed, despite his appreciation of the divergent theories in the ranks of English Utilitarians, by the popularity of the rigorous, even ascetic, strain of thinking that the Utilitarians inserted in the culture of the middle and upper classes in England. He suggested that its pervasiveness had instilled in the English people a stern and very sober view of moral action. "The morality of utility is not a generous morality that distributes pleasure without measure, because pleasure is good; it is an economic morality, to use Bentham's expression, which measures the immediate pleasure of individuals from the perspective of guaranteeing for them the future possession of pleasure."[58] In short, Halévy was convinced that the early Utilitarians like Bentham and William Godwin shared a stern moral outlook. Later Utilitarians like James Mill and Ricardo, for all their talk of happiness, were no different; they too embraced what Halévy termed a "reflective egoism." Happiness was based on "sagacity, prudence, and all the egoistic virtues." Utilitarianism was responsible for spreading "a plebian or rather bourgeois morality, made for working artisans and sensible tradesmen, [a morality] which teaches subjects to take up the defense of their interests; it is a reasoning, calculating and prosaic morality."[59]

> The Utilitarians are much less preoccupied with freeing instinct, and of establishing the right of everyone to all the pleasures, than to defining the conditions, which are often painful, which nature puts in the way of the satisfaction of needs, and, to use a Malthusian expression, the "moral restraints" which are the logical consequence of these conditions. . . . It is necessary to work and to save in order to live happily. Also one must know how to accept inevitable suffering. . . . Without going back to the sages of Greece, one is able even to establish certain analogies between the moral temperament of the Utilitarians and that of all the Puritanical sects which modern England has produced. . . . In short, ethics, according to Bentham and his disciples, is a laborious act.[60]

*L'Angleterre en 1815* was, therefore, a general history of England in 1815, but it was also intended to address a broad question: "Why has modern England, of all the countries of Europe, had the least revolutionary history, been the most free of violent crises and sudden changes?" Not, Halévy argued, because of its political institutions. In fact, the British constitution was "anarchic." England's "political institutions were such that society might easily have lapsed into anarchy had there existed in England a bourgeoisie animated by the spirit of revolution." Nor was the relative peacefulness of English society a result of economic growth. Again, there were class divisions, as analyzed by Ricardo and Marx, and there were severe industrial crises, as analyzed by Sismondi. These could easily have "plunged the kingdom into violent revolution." What explained, then, the relative peacefulness of England? Halévy nodded to the geographical insight of Montesquieu, who had pointed to the isolated island nature of England as providing a safeguard from a Continental invader. And he nodded to the later argument of Tocqueville, who pointed to the absence of a centralized bureaucracy. But, for Halévy, these theses were insufficient. Also central, he famously argued, was the conservative and antirevolutionary spirit that derived from the Methodist revival of the eighteenth century and the reinforcing "moral restraints" provided by Utilitarianism.

> Why has modern England, of all the countries of Europe, had the least revolutionary history, been the most free of violent crises and sudden changes? We have sought in vain the explanation of this by an analysis of her political institutions or of her economic organization. Her political institutions are such that social order might easily have degenerated into anarchy had there existed in England a bourgeoisie animated by the spirit of revolution. And a system of economic production which is effectively anarchistic could easily have plunged the kingdom into a state of insurrection if the working classes had found in the middle class some men to provide an ideal, a doctrine, a program of definite action. But the elite of the working class, the hard-working bourgeoisie, is, because the effects of the evangelical movement, animated with a spirit which presents no danger to the established order.[61]

What was this spirit? "The sects, in their free diversity, are in agreement among themselves, and in agreement with the national authorities, to impose on the nation a rigorous moral conformism, and at least an outward respect for the Christian social order. The passion for organization combines with the passion for liberty, . . . and the authority of moeurs replaces and renders almost useless the authority of law. This is modern England."[62] Methodism and the evangelical movement, Halévy claimed, came to influence the High Church, the movement of Protestant Dissent, and even secular British opinion.

Like the earlier articles on the birth of Methodism, therefore, Halévy's new book focused on the movement created by Whitefield and the Wesleys, but the emphasis now was on the continuing influence that this movement had on the mores of English society. And, importantly, this influence supported the government and helped resist "French" revolutionary ideas. "Jacobin principles did not prejudice the Methodist propaganda. The new type of Nonconformity, evangelical and pietist, was gaining ground every year [against the Anglican Church, but also against the more radical and rational doctrines expressed by older Dissenters like Richard Price and Joseph Priestley]."[63] Its influence, according to Halévy, extended to the gentry, which earlier had been attracted to the radical views of Voltaire and Rousseau. By 1815, they had become more restrained, more pious. "They were still disposed, during the first fifteen years of the nineteenth century, to entertain the same belief [that England was the country of freedom fighting despotism], but the word 'liberty' no longer had for them the same sense it had had in the mouths of their fathers. 'Liberty' now signified 'spontaneous voluntary discipline,' in opposition to a discipline imposed by governmental constraint. . . . The change in the opinion that the English had of themselves is incontestably the work of Methodist propaganda, continued by the Evangelical party."[64]

The influence of the Utilitarians on British culture was also important, and, in Halévy's accounting, it reinforced the asceticism of the evangelicals. Like the pages in *La formation du radicalisme philosophique* that analyzed the constraining aspects of Utilitarian morals, the pages in *L'Angleterre en 1815* similarly emphasized their laborious nature.

It would be incorrect to irreconcilably oppose the morality of the Utilitarians to Christian morality, on the grounds that logically there is no possible reconciliation between a morality founded on pleasure and a morality founded on sacrifice. This is because Utilitarian morality should not be defined, absolutely, as a morality of pleasure.

It rests simultaneously on two principles. The first of these, it is true, identifies what is good with what is pleasurable; but the second, equally important, is that man, because of the natural conditions of his existence, should always sacrifice a present pleasure in hopes of a future pleasure, to purchase pleasure with labor or suffering.[65]

Halévy concluded his volume with a warm recommendation of "the spirit of private initiative" that was the outgrowth of Methodism and Utilitarianism. "English individualism is a moderate individualism [*individualisme tempéré*], where there is mixed together, almost to the point of being indiscernible, the influence of Evangelicalism and the influence of Utilitarianism."[66]

Halévy's later assessments of English culture would consistently emphasize the importance of Utilitarianism and Methodism. Even when Halévy noted significant cultural changes, as he did, for example, in his historical examinations of England written after World War I, he stressed continuity.[67] In these volumes, for example, while he elaborated on a theme he had mentioned in *L'Angleterre et son empire*—the disturbing growth of "decadence" in England on both the religious and the economic fronts—he nonetheless stressed cultural continuity. He worried about the decline of the individualist form of Protestant Christianity.[68] And he was concerned that the form of socialism gaining power in England was one that undermined the "spirit of productivity" in British industry.[69] But, while noting these cultural changes, he recognized the persistence of what he referred to as a "permanent foundation." "In England, today as yesterday, all is instinctively trial and error, mutual tolerance, and reciprocal adjustment, under the action of this moral and religious constitution of its people, the nature of which we have analyzed previously. This constitution remains, in its major traits, unchanged: it remains the foundation of these admirable political moeurs, loathed but at the same time envied by all those who, on the continent, be they in parties of the right or the left, profess the philosophy of violence."[70]

As indicated above, Élie Halévy continued a long French tradition of thought that proceeded comparatively and that turned to England to highlight what was different in France.[71] He looked to England as a society not troubled by some of the peculiarities of French culture and politics, which had helped it avoid what he referred to as France's "long years of political anarchy."[72] He was looking for ways that British history could provide his own countrymen with salutary lessons. Where he differed from his predecessors was his focus on Utilitarianism and Methodism. French intellectuals during the eighteenth century who wished to distinguish France from England—Voltaire, for example—emphasized the civil freedoms enjoyed in England but lacking in France. Thinkers during the nineteenth century—Constant and Guizot, for example—looked to representative liberal politics as the distinguishing characteristic of England, again highlighting something lacking in France. By the late nineteenth century, these did not mark a divide between England and France. The Third Republic had instituted civil guarantees and representative politics. To explain why England remained distinctive, Halévy emphasized aspects of British development that were markedly different from those in France. He focused on England's intellectual tradition of Utilitarianism, the prudent and tolerant aspect of English moeurs, and the continuing influence of eighteenth-century Methodism that channeled religious fervor in socially and politically conservative directions.

## The Webbs and Graham Wallas

In the years before the outbreak of World War I, Halévy, in addition to working on his histories of England and socialism, became acquainted with leading Fabian socialists like Sidney Webb, Beatrice Webb, and Graham Wallas. In his letters to family and friends, he mentions meetings with Sidney and Beatrice Webb and their circle, indicating cordial relations even after intellectual differences became pronounced.[73] The most notable of these differences were over empire and the political-administrative context for socialist reform. The Webbs supported empire, which Halévy opposed, and they favored a bureaucratic top-down socialism, which he viewed as dangerous. Years later, during the discussion of his famous 1936 essay "The Era of Tyrannies," he gave a succinct account of the importance of the Webbs for his own intellectual development, while also noting the aspects of their socialism he found troubling. He explained that, when he came of age in the 1890s, he was a "liberal," meaning that he was anticlerical, democratic, republican—in short, a Dreyfusard. He then went on to clarify why he did not wish to call himself a socialist.

> I was not a socialist, but I already knew quite a lot about socialism, as much from what I could already observe in France as from what I learned through my experience of things English. I had already, at this time, made prolonged and frequent trips to England over a

period of three or four years; and already I had established a friendship with two distinguished personalities of the *Fabian Society*, Mr.
and Mrs. Sidney Webb. I have remained their friend; and today I
feel that we are contemporaries; but, at that time, the ten years that
separated us meant a great deal. I was a young man of twenty-five
or thirty talking with two older people of thirty-five or forty, people
who had already written books that have remained classics. I listened
to them with respect; and they explained to me the principles of
their socialism, which was essentially anti-liberal. They were not
fighting Conservatism or Toryism, about which they were quite
indulgent, but Gladstonian Liberalism. It was the time of the Boer
War; and the advanced Liberals and the Labourites, who were beginning to organize themselves into a party, defended the Boers against
British imperialism out of generosity and a love of liberty and
humanity. But the two Webbs, along with their friend Bernard
Shaw, formed a group apart. They were ostentatious imperialists.
The independence of small nations could well mean something to
believers in liberal individualism, but not to them, precisely because
they were collectivists. I can still hear Sidney Webb explaining to me
that the future was with the great administrative nations, governed
by bureaucrats, and where order was maintained by policemen.[74]

Halévy had closer political and intellectual ties with Graham Wallas, an
important English social democrat whose intellectual trajectory also moved
him away from the Webbs.[75] Wallas (1858–1932) came from an evangelical
family, was educated at Oxford, and became an early member of the Fabian
Society, joining in 1886. He was also one of the founders of the London
School of Economics in 1895.[76] Close to the Webbs in the late 1880s and early
1890s, he was Sidney's best man when he married Beatrice Potter in July
1892. Like other Fabians, Wallas was influenced by the moral socialism of
William Morris, by Positivism, and by Darwinism and science. A moral
socialist and a Progressive Radical, he pushed back against the materialist
prognosis and revolutionary predictions of Karl Marx. Wallas also rejected
the various individualist arguments—political, economic, scientific, and
moral—that claimed that the moral regeneration of individuals and their
acceptance of responsibilities and duties were sufficient to address the social
and economic problems that England confronted. He insisted that there were
economic and structural causes of poverty that the state could and should

address. He shared the Webbs' expansive theory of rent, which claimed that "rent" was the unearned income enjoyed by those who owned productive land, who controlled industries, or who benefited from accumulated wealth. "Rent," the Fabians argued, was the price paid for differential advantages in production to those who owned or controlled economic assets—the fortuitous advantage of owners of land who rented this land to peasants, the advantage of industrialists who hired cheap labor, and the advantage of speculators and the moneyed class who received interest on the capital they lent. These gains, according to this analysis, had little to do with the *ability* of the landowner, employer, or *rentier*; rather, they grew primarily from inherited land and wealth (rent and interest were viewed as comparable), and from the advantages provided by the legal system constructed to favor individuals and families with these riches.

By the time Halévy met him in the late 1890s or early 1900s,[77] Wallas's relations with the Fabian Society and with the Webbs had weakened. They diverged over educational policy, something that Wallas, who served on the London School Board and the London County Council for years (1895–1907), was intensively committed to reforming. He opposed any reform that would retain government support for religious teaching in the schools; the Webbs, on the other hand, were willing to accept reforms that included continued public support for religious "voluntary schools," provided the reforms raised the level of efficiency and widened the scope of education. The relationship between Wallas and the Webbs became even more difficult with the outbreak of the Boer War. The Webbs, along with George Bernard Shaw (as Halévy's statement above indicates) supported the "bureaucratic imperialism" of the British government against the Boers, while Wallas opposed the war, arguing that it was driven by the interests of speculators searching for new markets and by the encouragement of dangerous—that is, jingoist—nationalism. The tensions between Wallas and the Fabians came to a head in 1904, when the Webbs and Shaw indicated that they also could embrace a protectionist policy if it would provide leverage for realizing the state-directed economic reforms they favored. Wallas opposed protectionism and used this occasion to leave the Fabian Society, though he remained on cordial terms with the Webbs and Shaw.

Wallas shared with the so-called New Liberals like J. A. Hobson, L. Hobhouse, and the Hammonds a concern that Fabianism was drifting too close to an elitist administrative absolutism.[78] Like Wallas, they preferred the encouragement of public morals and intelligence to make them effective forces for progressive democratic political and social change. From this point until the outbreak of the war, Wallas shared with other New Liberals a socialist liberal agenda that emphasized its distance from both Marxism and Fabianism. They favored a redistribution of wealth but not revolution or the destruction of property. They advocated economic reforms implemented by the democratic state but not the imposition of economic efficiency through the actions of a confiscatory state bureaucracy. Like other New Liberals, Wallas remained committed to liberal democracy, to the realization of socioeconomic reform through peaceful means, and to a belief that education was one of the most important vehicles for the encouragement of social responsibility and altruistic sentiments. He did not believe that reforms should exceed the wishes of the population.

Halévy shared these views, and it is not a great surprise that he and Wallas became closer. Halévy's correspondence indicates that Élie and Florence enjoyed dinners and other social occasions with Wallas and his family.[79] The Wallases—Graham, his wife Audrey, and their daughter, May—became good friends. The relationship thickened during and after World War I, and when the Halévys returned to London in the postwar years, they often socialized with the Wallases.

Wallas, like Halévy, believed that bringing about significant reform would not be easy, nor would it ever be fully realized. In his 1889 article "Property under Socialism" in *Fabian Essays*, Wallas took pains to explain that he had "dwelt . . . upon the necessary difficulties and limitations of Socialism" rather than on grand designs or the contours of future society. He was critical of the propensity of early socialists to provide "a complete description of Society as it ought to be," arguing that this was utopian.[80] Committed to reform, he believed it was necessary to "take men as they now are,"[81] and that it was naive to think that the division of labor could be miraculously transcended or that the drudgery of industrial society could be entirely eliminated.[82] He also condemned revolutionary syndicalism, arguing that Sorelian notions of direct action animated by "myths" of violence and regeneration were anti-intellectual and counterproductive. Wallas was in favor of what he termed a "tentative and limited Social-Democracy."[83]

One of the distinguishing characteristics of Wallas's orientation was attentiveness to psychology.[84] After leaving the Fabian Society, Wallas turned his attention to social psychology and its importance for understanding political behavior. His investigations led to two important publications before the outbreak of World War I: *Human Nature in Politics* (1908) and *The Great*

*Society: A Psychological Analysis* (1914).[85] Wallas was particularly concerned that citizens in democracies seemed little interested in public affairs, and that their political decisions rested not on reason but on "unconscious or half-conscious inference fixed by habit."[86] Political action therefore took place largely "off stage," remote from these average citizens. He worried that a small cadre of individuals could effectively dominate political decisions, and that democratic politics was so deeply affected by advertising that it was becoming "the conjuring trade."[87] Political leaders, in sum, could manipulate the popular will.

Wallas also worried about the erosion of traditional mores. His sensitivity to the potential pathologies of individual psychology and to the propensity of groups to follow dubious leaders reinforced his rationalism; he called for the subordination of "Instinct" to "Thought." He worried that modern society was leading to more social and economic insecurity and that this could be channeled too easily into demands for "increased national armaments," "increased internal coercive authority," and a general yearning for extreme politics.[88] Such ideas would find echoes in Halévy's analyses of nationalism during and after the war.[89]

After the war, Wallas (again, like Halévy) rejected Bolshevism and pushed back against the Guild socialism of G. D. H. Cole, who argued that labor organizations would be able to provide a better foundation for social action than the state. Wallas did not reject the importance of unions and of other labor organizations, but he believed Guild socialists exaggerated the unselfishness of vocational organizations generally and of individual workers specifically. As we see below, these views were shared by Halévy.[90] Both remained committed to practical reform and progressive administration but had no illusions that workers or their organizations were the privileged means for achieving reform. They also resisted the embrace of organic metaphors that were common in the thought of other New Liberals: the paradigm of the "hive" common in the thought of Hobson; the overtones of purpose and destiny present in the thought of Hobhouse. Wallas seems to have been less influenced by the Hegelianism of T. H. Green than other English socialist liberals of his generation. Halévy's neo-Kantianism made him similarly resistant to idealist metaphysics and, like Wallas, attracted to a pragmatic orientation that stressed the difficulties of progressive reform.[91]

# PART III

World War I and
the State of Europe
in the Era of Tyrannies

## CHAPTER 7

# World War I

## (1914–1918)

The day Jaurès was assassinated and the conflagration of Europe was ignited, a new era opened in the history of the world. It is foolish to believe that in six months this could be extinguished, and that the same parties, the same groups, the same individuals, would be able to resume the course of their combinations as if nothing had passed in the interval. Don't make me say, in the style of today, that Europe goes to be regenerated, purified, by this baptism of fire. I say that Europe will be changed by it; and I say that it is not at all ready to emerge from it.

—Élie Halévy to Xavier Léon, 24 March 1916

If Germany emerges victorious from the conflict . . . what triumph for the Prussian and monarchical idea of the state! What punishment for the people who have believed in the benefits of liberty!

—Élie Halévy to Xavier Léon, 25 February 1917

It is impossible to overestimate the degree to which World War I transformed Europe and the life of its inhabitants. Major modern wars tend to shrink civil society, or at least attenuate their complexity. Perhaps this is not surprising, since nation and family demand more attention during wars than during peacetime, leaving less time for the pursuit of other activities or the contemplation of other issues. Such it was for Élie Halévy, who quickly concluded that the war was changing irrevocably the world that he had known. When the conflagration began, Halévy was forty-three years old. Much of his attention in the late summer and fall of 1914, not surprisingly, was devoted to the safety of his immediate family; what energy remained was largely consumed by his anguish over the fate of his country. Halévy followed carefully the day-to-day news from the fronts, relying more on Italian, Swiss, and English papers than French ones. In September 1914, he was relieved, predictably, when the German thrust toward Paris was stopped with the Battle of the Marne, but he continued to be very attentive throughout the war to the movements of troops, to changes in military tactics, and to the prospects of victory or defeat. He was also, as discussed below, concerned with the international implications of the conflict, and with its wider political and cultural consequences. World War I forced Halévy to reassess the nature of European societies, measure the consequences of modern warfare on political and social values and institutions, and reconsider the appropriate role of intellectuals in this new environment. It is this experience and these issues that provide the focus of this chapter.

## The Halévys During the War

When the war broke out, Élie and Florence were visiting a spa at Mont-Dore in the Auvergne, where Élie was attending to a bout of bronchitis. He was not mobilized, due to his age, but soon assumed duties in a military hospital close to their home in Sucy-en-Brie on the outskirts of Paris. He and Florence moved briefly to Touraine when the hospital was moved during the Battle of the Marne. Then, in February 1915, they settled in Albertville, Savoy, where Élie took up a position as a military nurse, soon expanded to include other administrative duties, in the military hospital directed by his cousin Alfred Fuchs (Figure 7). The Halévys remained in Albertville until March 1918.

Halévy had other options for employment during the war but found all of these alternatives unattractive. Teaching at Sciences Po struck him as "the most ridiculous of sinecures," given that most of his students were at the front, so he suspended his classes.[1] Moving to Paris to work at a ministry or to write propaganda, proposed at various times by Halévy's friends and supporters, he judged to be too compromising of his independence and intellectual integrity. "All the small political and parliamentary noises," he wrote to his friend Xavier Léon, "produce in me real pain."[2] This was closely related

FIGURE 7. Élie Halévy in the uniform of hospital worker in Albertville during World War I (1915–1918). Reproduced with the permission of the Association des amis d'Élie et Florence Halévy, and of the president of this association, Vincent Duclert.

to Halévy's caustic assessment of the pervasiveness of unprincipled nationalism, about which more below. He could not imagine himself becoming involved in such a position.

> I do not blame people for having the taste for political intrigue, any more than I blame them for having the taste for *la vie mondaine*, or the taste for the literary life. But I have neither the first, nor the second, nor the third of these tastes. And I sense . . . that I am not cut out to play the role of a political or politico-diplomatic agent. If I were such an agent, I would die of ennui, or perhaps of disgust at the idea of all the half-lies that, orally or in writing, I would of necessity be affirming with more éclat than if it was a question of verifiable scientific propositions. . . . Let us protect our intelligence for the day when we are able to give it full liberty.[3]

In addition, Halévy judged most diplomatic and propaganda activities largely irrelevant to the essential issue of the outcome of the war, which he believed could only be decided by the military. "I am . . . exactly of the opinion of René [Berthelot] on one point," he wrote to Léon in a characteristic passage in July 1915, "this war, as all war, is able to be finished only by a military decision. Any peace that intervenes before that will be only a phantom of peace."[4] But if the irrelevance of diplomacy given the nature of the war was important, Halévy's refusal to consider diplomatic or propagandistic activity was driven even more by his refusal to compromise his intellectual independence. As Vincent Duclert has put it, "Liberty of thought is for Élie Halévy too precious to be placed in the service of combat."[5]

This did not mean that Halévy did not occasionally feel isolated, nor that he did not desire a more exciting life. Already in the Fall of 1914, he was adjusting to the rigors of the alternation of activity and repose, and he was conscious that this required an emotional adjustment. "The war teaches you the philosophy that it is able to teach: the art of living day to day, of accepting the necessities of each moment."[6] In March 1915, he complained to Léon that "Nothing is more monotonous than a war of ten months. . . . I live in a hole, where it is very difficult for me to adopt the attitude of an informed man."[7] Unable to pursue his historical scholarship, he looked for other activities outside the military hospital. He read widely: Michelet, Balzac, Rousseau, Eugène Sue, Anatole France, Arnold Bennett, Byron, and Gibbon. The histories of Michelet and Gibbon gave him special pleasure; he found some solace in their depictions of other eras that demonstrated, like the current war, "the stupid grandeur of historical events and the powerlessness of individuals."[8] When his official duties were light, he also devoted some time to investigating the popular culture in Savoy, in essence becoming an amateur ethnographer. He conducted interviews and studied local customs, activities that allowed him to periodically "forget the war, the sons and husbands at the front," and to listen to peasants recounting their "extraordinary histories."[9] In the words of Marie Scot, "This inquiry allow[ed] the exile to root himself in the land of refuge and to insert himself in local sociabilities. It also permit[ted] the *philosophe* historian to appropriate the ethnographic method of participant observation."[10] He would use his new ethnographic skills when he visited the mines in Wales in 1919.

In addition to his hospital work, amateur ethnographic investigations, and extensive reading, Halévy pursued other intellectual activities. He continued to be extensively involved with the *Revue de métaphysique et de morale*, seeing this as an essential instrument for combating the troubling intellectual paralysis caused by the war. We return to this below. He also embarked on a translation of Hobbes's *De Cive*, which provides insight into his anxieties about modern citizenship. This, in turn, was closely related to his ongoing reflections about the fate of liberty in modern society, and about how the changed conditions introduced by the war affected the framework in which the "democratic spirit" might flourish. Again, these are issues to which we return below.

As the war dragged on, Halévy felt that his talents were not being sufficiently utilized, and he told his correspondents that he would welcome the opportunity to put to good use "his knowledge of the English language and society."[11] In 1916, he even contacted friends in England about the possibility of some position there.[12] He worried that the war would "paralyze all thought" and spoke of how he had "tried, twenty times without success, to put something on paper on the subject of the war. But I never found anything to say which had any value. We are too directly engaged."[13] He occasionally contemplated devoting himself to an occupation that would contribute in some way to the "direct and material preparation for war." No such positions materialized, however, and he steadfastly resisted the allure of Paris. He was not attracted to what he characterized as the "half-intellectual half-warrior occupations" in the capital, where he "would be condemned to say or suffer a heap of foolishness. In the interest of the nation, I would like to do something useful. But because of my intellectual *amour-propre,* I would rather change bandages than talk nonsense."[14] In short, he preferred to remain at work in the hospital, where he could assure himself, as he put it, of "the direct utility of my actions."[15]

## Halévy's Understanding and Assessment of the War

Halévy was uncommonly perceptive concerning the conduct and immediate consequences of the war. His correspondence is filled with remarkable analysis and reflections. He quickly came to the view, for example, that an offensive military strategy would not lead to victory. In November 1914, he baldly stated that an offensive war had become "impossible," a view that he frequently repeated.[16] Victory would be determined, he argued, by the determination of the men in the trenches, by the condition of societies, by the will of the states, and by the spirit of national institutions.

Given the carnage at the front, Halévy was impressed by the determination and quiet bravery of the soldiers that he met in the hospital at Albertville. He was not surprised that these soldiers did not "profess this foolish love of combat of which the [Paris newspapers] *Echo de Paris* and the *Matin* speak." But he was astonished that these wounded soldiers did not speak of peace. "All [these soldiers] are getting ready for a second winter campaign. All prepare for it with a sigh, but add 'What is necessary is necessary. While so many Germans are in France and Belgium, one is not able to make peace.' "[17] Halévy was moved that, though there was no evidence of "warrior enthusiasm," there was a quiet determination, even "resignation," that the fighting and the war must continue.[18]

Halévy was convinced that it was deep divisions between the belligerent nations that had led to the conflict, and he therefore concluded that the war would not be easily brought to a conclusion. "We have before us ten or fifteen, or thirty years of war," he wrote in November 1914.[19] He also recognized that the war was creating enormous economic difficulties for all the participating countries.[20] He did not believe, however, that this would facilitate a quick end to the conflict. The war, he wrote to his brother in July 1915, was an affair "as vast as the Thirty Years' War, the wars of the reign of Louis XIV, the wars of the Revolution and Empire."[21] This was a constant refrain in his correspondence. In a characteristic passage to Léon from June 1915, he wrote: "This war, or this succession of wars, will last a long time. If it is not able to go on a long time with the armies constituted as they are at present, then one will change the type of armies. If the armies fall to half of their current levels, one will fight with half armies."[22]

Halévy was convinced that the war would end, not with an armistice, but only when there was a full military defeat of Germany, which had to include the liberation of all the territory German armies had occupied. Anything less would not provide the basis for a permanent peace; it would be only a "fugitive truce."[23] "This war, this total war," he wrote in 1915, "will finish only with a military decision. All peace which intervenes before that will be only a phantom peace. . . . I don't wait for a triumph in the immediate future. I know all that it will cost in order to defeat the pride of a great people."[24]

The prospect of a settlement that was less than a full military defeat of Germany was deeply unsettling to Halévy, for reasons that in retrospect look remarkably cogent. In December 1916, he wrote the following: "From here, twenty years. I do not see how the enormous questions which have been unleashed by this war, and that this war has rendered more acute than ever, are able to be resolved in less time, and otherwise than by war. I foresee, as I have always claimed, a weary peace [*une paix de lassitude*] intervening in the very short term, after the check of the next allied effort, for example. And after? Germany, with its growing demands, founded on the increased sense of its power, will impose very quickly, for good or ill, a new war on its neighbors."[25] "This war, or this cycle of wars, will end the day Prussian militarism is destroyed."[26]

Halévy analyzed the resources, strategy, and morale of the various belligerent countries, and these made him cautiously optimistic that the Entente would ultimately be victorious. He was periodically anxious, however, about the political organization of France, picking up a theme that was prominent in his correspondence before the war. France, he believed, was burdened with a political culture that fostered intellectual posturing rather than sensible compromise. The weight of this anxiety became heavier as the war dragged on. In 1915, Halévy worried about the "weakness of the internal politics" of the country.[27] In 1916, he was concerned by the rise of pacifism.[28] In August 1916, he wrote that the peril facing France was not clericalism, but "apathy, indolence, carelessness."[29] By the end of the year, he was so disenchanted by the political leaders that he suggested any French victory would be due to exertions of the military and bureaucratic functionaries, *not* the leaders of the government or the members of the Chamber of Deputies. Fortunately, he wrote, France had a "complicated constitution" dating from 1875, and such constitutions were favorable to liberalism.[30]

In early 1917, Halévy's anxiety concerning the dysfunction of the French government became acute. This was a critical period, of course: some troops were in mutiny; pacifist movements were growing; the February Revolution threatened to take Russia out of the war; domestic strikes were multiplying; and the "union sacrée" was splintering. During the ministerial crisis of March 1917, Halévy wrote long critical letters that lambasted the political leaders. The Chamber of Deputies, he wrote, "is incapable of governing itself," and therefore incapable of governing the country. The "old evil" of factionalist bickering and ministerial instability had resurfaced. This might be tolerable in peacetime, he wrote, but in wartime "a new remedy" was required. Perhaps what the country needed was a reinforcement of the executive power and the creation of a single assembly to replace the Chamber and the Senate. Praising the government functionaries who kept things running, he castigated the politicians, fearing that if the system were not changed, "France will have another Bonaparte."[31]

It is sad that the war has not been for us the occasion to change our methods, to make in this urgent situation the series of reforms that, for ten years, have been needed. To purchase goods from foreigners without counting, to distribute subventions to hands that are already full, to allow everyone to spend wildly everywhere, to wait for the day of famine in order to throw all responsibility onto "the ministers," and emerge from all these difficulties by a ministerial crisis that has the unique advantage of creating room, for six months, for a new squad of Deputies. That is the entire politics of the Parliament, without a word of satire or exaggeration.[32]

By this time, the general state of civilian mores was not much better, according to Halévy. "It is . . . militarily that we have the most incontestable value. It is when it is a question of exploiting our land, or administering our riches, or establishing taxes, that we are truly mediocre."[33] Fortunately, in spite of the political disorder at the political center and the lamentable state of French moeurs, circumstances intervened to pull the country back to its senses. "The German government will always arrange the necessary number of atrocities to revive French patriotism."[34] And he believed that the "war-making abilities" of the nation would allow it to survive the war "with relative impunity."[35] It was the spirit of the soldiers that gave Halévy hope, in contrast to the spirit of civilians in or out of government. France, he concluded, was always an enigma for the political observer: "Is one ever able to say if it is liberal in the direction of anarchy, or foolishly reactionary?"

Halévy spoke more and more, as the war dragged on, of the long-term consequences for France and for Europe. In late 1917, he wrote: "France was saved on the Marne; and, since that day, by a constant flood of Anglo-Saxons, [and] by the increasing value of our army, our strategic position has been affirmed. I know that there is a large region of Belgium, Lorraine, Alsace that is doomed to destruction. I know that the entire world, and France in particular, will leave exhausted from this struggle. But the world has seen such things many other times; and the century has not yet arrived when the human species will find the means of developing without wars and without revolutions."[36] Halévy seemed resigned to the perennial aggressiveness of the human species, and to the fact that wars and revolutions were endemic to human history. He was confident that France would survive the war but recognized that it would inhabit a dangerous world. Moreover, it would be only a second-rank power.

We are intelligent enough to know that all of us, French, English, Germans, are the inheritors, the transmitters of the same civilization; intelligent enough also to understand that European civilization has a national, not international form, and that it is within the framework of the French nation that our action will need to be exercised in order to be useful. This will be a difficult role to fulfill, due to a combination of circumstances that will not at all resemble those of the milieu in which we grew up, to circumstances in which France will no longer be a declining great nation, but rather an extremely formidable second-level nation.[37]

## Nationalism

The outbreak of the war led to an outpouring of nationalist rhetoric on both sides of the Rhine. In France, intellectuals and scientists were prominent among those who articulated a bellicose hostility not only to the German military and German leaders but also to German culture and, at times, all things German. Halévy resisted these extremes. He condemned German aggression, was a firm critic of what he termed "Prussian militarism," and never wavered in his desire to defeat the German Army and liberate Belgian and French territory. But he insisted that French patriotism not lead to a condemnation of German culture.[38]

Halévy had long appreciated that patriotism and nationalism were strong forces that needed to be balanced with cosmopolitanism. "Patriotism is a sentiment analogous to sentiment of family," he wrote in 1901, "more abstract in its object and thus more amenable to reasoned use. I don't dream of praising or blaming it; the problem is simply to control its usage."[39] He believed that "patriotism" could be directed toward positive ends. In 1904, for example, he wrote to his close friend Célestin Bouglé: "I am convinced that *right now*, the patriotic sentiment is a powerful sentiment, which is able to be and ought to be employed in the sense of civilization."[40] He noted that such "enthusiasms" should be, and could be, controlled by reasoned reflection; and he seemed confident that Europe was moving toward peace and unity.[41] Immediately before the war, however, Halévy had become concerned at the growth of more aggressive nationalist sentiments. In 1910, he wrote to his mother that his own patriotism was "offended" by the doctrines of the Action française, which was pushing its reactionary agenda of "integral nationalism."[42] A similar reaction led him to write to Bouglé in 1912 that it was important not to "allow patriotism to be monopolized by the admirers of the Middle Ages."[43] But he still favored patriotism, worrying that its erosion because of the pacifist campaign of men like Gustave Hervé and Jean Jaurès was weakening France vis-à-vis neighboring countries like Germany. In 1904, he had recommended a "neutral attitude" between pacifists and militarists.[44] But as the influence of pacifism grew he became more critical of its power to undermine patriotic unity. In 1905, he argued that it was necessary, in his words, "to democratize, not to suppress, the military spirit."[45] He insisted that it was important to keep patriotism and nationalism out of the hands of the radical right wing, but generally it was a positive force. "In the current state of humanity," he wrote to Bouglé in 1912, "one is able to civilize mankind only by making appeal to their national sentiments."[46]

Unfortunately, this moderate patriotism came under assault with the outbreak of the war. Nationalist enthusiasm, unmediated by reflection and untempered by reason, became the default stance of most segments of the French population. This included many members of the French intelligentsia, who condemned everything German, demanded the cancellation of subscriptions to German publications, and campaigned to sever ties with German academics and cultural figures. This was especially true after the publication in France in October 1914 of the famous/infamous "A Call to Civilized Nations" that German intellectuals issued to defend German military aims.[47] This manifesto shocked intellectuals in France because it came on the heels of news of war crimes by the German army in Belgium—accusations that it had murdered Belgian civilians—and of news that the library at the University of Louvain had been burned and the cathedral in Reims had been shelled by German artillery. And all of this, of course, came after the violation of Belgium neutrality and the invasion of France in August 1914. The German manifesto—quickly called the "Manifesto of the Ninety-Three" in reference to the ninety-three signatures—was especially inflammatory. Signed by a who's who of German scientists and scholars, it claimed that it was not true that Germany had caused the war, violated Belgian neutrality, ignored international law, or committed atrocities against innocent civilians. Rather, Germans were a peace-loving and cultured people led by an emperor committed to maintaining "universal peace."[48]

French reaction was intense.[49] The faculties of the universities issued rejoinders; various Paris academies published condemnations; the Institut de France voted to remove signatories of the German manifesto from honorary membership; writers, artists, scientists, and men of letters wrote critical essays and joined forces to issue their own "French Manifesto of the One Hundred" in March 1915. All were critical of the actions of the German military. But, as already mentioned, many moved to condemn German culture *tout court*, to see the root of Prussian militarism and pan-Germanism in the thought of cultural figures like Johan Gottlieb Fichte, G. W. F. Hegel, and even Immanuel Kant.[50]

Halévy, on the other hand, counseled against hasty rushes to judgment. After news spread that there had been German atrocities against Belgian civilians (atrocities that historians have subsequently verified), Halévy worried about the escalation of reprisals. French troops, he wrote to Léon, "are firmly convinced of the reality of German atrocities; but since they believe, because of this, that they are justified in their retaliation, one can never know, at the end of the day, who started it. There are some questions, all things considered, into which an intelligent person should not venture."[51] He also insisted that it was necessary to distinguish German military aggression from German culture. This entailed avoiding the rabid nationalism that was spreading in both nations, and it required avoiding the condemnation of German science and German philosophy. Halévy was not greatly *surprised* by the widespread support of German militarism by German intellectuals, because he observed a similar reaction in France and assumed that intellectuals generally gave in, like others, to bellicose nationalism. "The state of spirit of these men [in Germany]," he wrote to Xavier Léon, "astonishes me less than you; how many men of letters, intellectuals were able under Napoléon to brave the warrior sentiment?"[52] He understood but nonetheless condemned. He considered writing an article to draw attention to German intellectuals who had *not* signed the manifesto, mentioning Georg Simmel, Richard Strauss, Hugo von Hofmannsthal, David Hilbert, Georg Lasson, and Hermann Cohen; but he decided, upon reflection, not to do so, fearing that such an article would only cause trouble for these individuals.[53]

Much to Halévy's displeasure, the growth of aggressive nationalism among French intellectuals was not confined to extreme right-wing figures like Maurice Barrès. This was not unexpected, given Barrès's association with Action française, which had long been hostile to Germany. But there were also attacks on German culture by colleagues with whom Halévy and his *Revue de métaphysique et de morale* partners Léon and Brunschvicg had had close relations. Émile Boutroux, for example, a neo-Kantian of the previous generation who had been a mentor to the founders of the *Revue*, dropped his

Kantianism after 1914 and depicted the war as a civilizational clash between classical Catholic France, which he claimed stood for universal values, and a barbarous anti-Enlightenment Germany, which stood for narrow nationalism.[54] In a 1914 letter to the editors of the *Revue des deux mondes*, Boutroux argued that German intellectual life had become captivated by the desire to impose German culture on the world.[55] Henri Bergson, similarly, in a speech he gave at the Académie française on 4 August 1914, characterized the war as a struggle of French "civilization" versus German "barbarism."[56] And when Bergson assumed the presidency of the Académie des sciences morales et politiques in December 1914, he continued his attack, railing at German intellectuals and arguing that an "artificial" culture and a "mechanistic" worldview had come to dominate German culture.[57] In sum, the patriotism of Boutroux and Bergson spilled over into a nationalism that condemned not just German military aggression but also German culture.

Halévy wished to separate the two. As early as October 1914, he was writing to his friends that it was important to defeat the German military but to respect German science, German philosophy, and German music. "This state of overexcitement that reigns in the Parisian journals against all German 'culture,' is it profound or rather passing and superficial? Is it a 'war' hysteria that will pass away with the peace? I hope that we have not abandoned ourselves to it too quickly, and that I shall still be able to listen to Wagner, read Hegel, and admit that Nernst is a great chemist and Klein a great mathematician." It was important, in short, "not to become slaves of an exclusive nationalism."[58] When Bergson stirred up nationalism in December 1914, Halévy was appalled. "In times of war, if pacifist eloquence sounds false, warrior eloquence sounds even more false."[59]

## Revue de Métaphysique et de Morale

Halévy recognized that nationalism, enflamed by the war, would be difficult to overcome. He hoped that the *Revue de métaphysique et de morale* would be one of the vehicles to stanch the flow of nationalist hatred. The publication of the *Revue* was interrupted by the outbreak of war but resumed in mid-1915.[60] The letters Halévy wrote to Xavier Léon are filled with his thoughts about the general role to be played by the *Revue*, as well as his ideas about the contents of specific numbers. As early as September 1914, he was writing that it was necessary to put the *Revue* back in circulation because "we owe to

France not to suppress, indefinitely, all French culture."[61] In December, he dictated to Léon a draft notice for subscribers of the *Revue* that would explain the suspension of publication and give promise of its reappearance.

> [Our readers] will have understood that at this time, when most of the collaborators of the *Revue de Métaphysique et de Morale* are performing their duty as soldiers, at a time when, for those who remain, the liberty of thought that pure speculation demands is difficult to find, they will have understood that it has been singularly difficult for us to follow through with our accustomed tasks. Not that we are not impatient to resume them. The *Revue de Métaphysique et de Morale* and the *Bulletin de la Société française de philosophie* are expressions of an essential aspect of French thought; and, if, in order to maintain this double path of spiritual life, we had need of an encouragement, we have found it in the touching witnesses of sympathy that, during these past months, we have received from our collaborators. . . . The *Revue de Métaphysique* and the *Bulletin de la Société française de philosophie* will reappear when circumstances permit, which we hope will be in the very near future.[62]

Halévy saw the *Revue* as instrumental in addressing the need, as he put it in September 1915, to "revitalize national intelligence."[63] He also hoped that it would help revitalize European culture. "It is necessary to save intelligence, European intelligence, from the peril it courts of being annihilated under the bloody ruins."[64] "The uninterrupted publication of a *Revue*, mercilessly serene and impartial," he wrote in September 1916, "is yet a way, for the country, to throw a challenge to the world."[65]

But what orientation, what focus, would provide this "challenge"? First, the *Revue* should "not take on the aspect of a patriotic pamphlet."[66] Rather, it should emphasize, in Halévy's opinion, rationalism, cosmopolitanism, and international scientific discussion. One way to transcend the narrow view that threatened to reduce intellectual interchange to *national* dialogues was to encourage a pan-European discussion of important issues, and to devote space to *universal* topics. Halévy was firm on this point. "There is not any true science without a *radical* internationalism."[67] He suggested that the "practical questions" section of the *Revue* should be revitalized to discuss issues raised by the war: international law; justifications for the use of force;

feminism; education reform; the functions of a society of nations; the relationship of democracy and war; the relationship of socialism and war.[68] And he suggested that the *Revue* should organize international conferences to examine important issues: the relationship of nationalism and imperialism; the role of small nations in history.[69] In April 1915, he proposed publishing a translation of Kant's "Project for Perpetual Peace."[70] In November 1915, he wanted to include an hommage to the German neo-Kantian philosopher Wilhelm Windelband, who had recently died. "All other manner of making war seems to be detestable," he told Léon.[71] In short, Halévy wished to press a broad cosmopolitan agenda, but one that would not bring into question the patriotism of the journal or its editors.

This orientation involved a commitment to universal moral values, a stance that was underpinned by their philosophical neo-Kantianism. Several articles in the *Revue* addressed this issue by discussing the relationship between "force" and "right," and criticizing the tendency of German Hegelians to confuse the two.[72] Dominique Parodi, for example, criticized thinkers for insisting that force and right were "interdependent and inseparable" and for "desiring to see in one the sign of the other," a position that, he claimed, entailed the "loss of a universal base for morality."[73] Charles Andler attacked the influence of Fichte and Hegel, and their effect on German culture: "For Hegel war is eternal and moral. . . . The military theoreticians of Prussia today will not forget this moral teaching that they draw from diffuse Hegelianism [and] that has not ceased to pervade nineteenth-century Germany."[74] While the philosophical stance of the *Revue* was to support cosmopolitan universal values, these positive values were implicitly and explicitly tied to French traditions, in a binary opposition that frequently contrasted French with German thought. Nonetheless, the editors were at pains to avoid castigating *all* German thought and culture, as their continued Kantianism indicated.

In no issue of the journal was this cosmopolitan stance more apparent than in the number devoted to the Reformation. Halévy was anxious to devote significant space to a discussion of the meaning of the Reformation, hoping that it would appear in 1917, the fourth centennial of Luther's bold nailing of his theses on the door of the church in Wittenberg. It was published, however, in 1918.[75] Halévy insisted that there should be an array of articles on the Reformation in its various geographical locations, providing a panoramic view of its influence and thereby demonstrating that "the Reformation was something other than an explosion of German nationalism." The point, he suggested in the same letter to Léon, was to show that "it was a great moment in the history of European civilization."[76] He obviously wished to avoid offending French Catholics unnecessarily but also wished to counter French narrowness and German nationalism, and to assign Protestantism "its place in the general movement of history."[77]

Halévy wrote the introduction to this number of the journal, which he lifted, almost verbatim, from a letter previously written to Léon.[78] He wrote that the Reformation had contributed to the constitution of "the conscience of modern Europe," but that it had to compete with the doctrine of eighteenth-century *philosophes* who "dreamed of founding a religion of reason, a religion of humanity." He summarized the main ideological thrust of the collection of articles in the following manner:

> To show that Prussianism does not exhaust the essence of Lutheranism, nor Lutheranism the essence of Protestantism; to show that, if the somber mysticism of the aristocratic warrior is derived from peculiar forms of the Reformation, it is also one of the sources from which political democracy has taken its political dogma, its faith in the liberty of individuals and of peoples, and its belief in universal justice. In short, it is to show that Protestantism, whatever its destiny may be, has not been the creation [*avènement*] of one race, but a general fact of the history of Western civilization, a grand movement of the human soul, the fertile influence of which has crossed the seas. We must struggle, in our manner, against the poison of German nationalism.[79]

Halévy, it should be pointed out, and as we have seen above, was much more sympathetic, as were most French citizens of Jewish heritage, to Protestantism than to intolerant French Catholicism. He had seen the danger of the latter during the Dreyfus Affair, when right-wing "integral" nationalists articulated a closed nationalist identity that excluded Jews and Protestants.

## Translation of Thomas Hobbes's *De Cive*

While stationed in Albertville, Halévy translated Hobbes's *De Cive* (*On the Citizen*) into French.[80] This translation has been lost, unfortunately, but his dedication to this task indicates the degree to which he was thinking about the issues of politics and citizenship. We have little hard evidence to help us understand why he chose to translate this particular work, but there are some aspects of Hobbes's book that would have made it attractive. Hobbes begins this famous work by pointing out that there is a natural right to self-preservation, and he also argues that individuals have the right to defend themselves against violence. The defense of France against German aggression in 1914 was often couched in just such language, and we know that Halévy shared this idea of national defense. It is difficult, therefore, not to assume that he would have been sympathetic to this aspect of Hobbes's thought.

Hobbes also famously argued, as he later did in *Leviathan*, that humanity has aggressive and selfish inclinations, and that without the collective judgments that created political communities, there would be, as he put it, a "war of all men against all men."[81] He wrote that people were naturally self-serving, stating that (in a description in *De Cive* that anticipated one provided in *Leviathan*) they were "few, savage, short lived, poor and mean, and lacked all the comforts and amenities of life which *peace* and society afford."[82] But Hobbes also argued that people had the capacity to alter these passions through will and "right reason."[83] Halévy had a similar view of human nature, both of its negative attributes and of the possibility of these being altered and controlled by reason and will. Such unkind sentiments and aggressive passions, needless to say, were on bold display when he worked on his translation. And he would also have been sympathetic to Hobbes's claim that individuals and societies have a legitimate interest in defending themselves against violence; and that protection against these dangers was to be provided by a sovereign state created by the reasoned democratic collective judgments of the people confronted with these dangers.

There are other elements of Hobbes's book that might have made it attractive to Halévy. There is a democratic thrust to Hobbes's argument in this book, curious given Hobbes's well-deserved reputation of being an apologist for absolute monarchy. This is present in the manner in which in *De Cive* Hobbes describes the emergence of a political community, of the commonwealth. He argues that the creation of the sovereign (a sovereign given immense power in Hobbes's system) is a democratic act that results from the rational action of a people. This act requires that each member of the prospective society, in Hobbes's words, "oblige himself, by an Agreement with each of the rest, not to resist the *will* of the *man* or *Assembly* to which he has submitted himself; that is, not to withhold the use of his wealth and strength against any other men than himself (for he is understood to retain the right of defending himself against violence)."[84] As Richard Tuck has pointed out, this argument veered dangerously close to the contractual argument advanced by some opponents of the absolute monarchy in the mid-seventeenth century, and was likely one reason that other monarchists of this era opposed Hobbes's theory.[85] For, if this democratic act *created* the sovereign, could the members of society not also dismiss the particular sovereign while retaining the sovereign power of the commonwealth? Hobbes did not come to this conclusion,[86] and he eliminated hints of such democratic-sounding elements when he wrote *Leviathan*. But, to return to Halévy, I think the democratic implications of parts of *De Cive* cohered nicely with his understanding of the creation of sovereignty and to the continuing power of the populace. Equally attractive to him, I believe, was Hobbes's insistence that once in power, the sovereign (man or assembly) was expected to exercise power and enjoy the respect of the people. Halévy, as we have seen, worried about the divisiveness of French politics during the war, and he was willing to see an expansion of executive power, though this power should again be restricted after the end of hostilities. As he put it in a letter to Bertrand Russell in 1919: "Strongly as I believe in the necessity of dictatorship, with all its worse [*sic*] implications, in time of war, I hope that war is now over, and that the blessed day of thought and anarchy is dawning again upon us."[87]

What I'd like to suggest, therefore, is that Halévy would have encountered several themes in Hobbes's work that positively resonated with his own thinking about the instability of societies in a dangerous and violent world; that is, in the kind of world France found itself inhabiting during World War I. The greatest difference between their political views was Halévy's insistence that sovereignty, during peacetime, should be open to change via deliberation of the members of the polity. During war, however, Halévy was perfectly willing to see executive power expanded. Hobbes, as I've suggested, though slightly ambiguous about the power of the sovereign, ultimately gives the executive extraordinary powers. He argues in the latter part of *De Cive*, for example, that the sovereign—in his era, the monarch—must not only be invested with great powers once the commonwealth is created but rightfully can expect the "crowd" of inhabitants of the commonwealth to be obedient.[88] I suspect that in 1917 Halévy, when was translating Hobbes's book, was not unsympathetic to such an argument. Once the war had ended, however, he was concerned about exactly such executive power, as I discuss in the next chapter. Was it the extreme authoritarian conclusion of Hobbes's book that led Halévy to decide after the war against publication of his translation? Or was it, rather, that other engagements quickly took precedence? We shall, perhaps, never know, though I suspect that it was a combination of both of these factors.

## Dominique Parodi and Wartime Propaganda

Halévy's reluctance to work closely with the French government, or to write propaganda for the war effort, was not universally shared by his colleagues.[89] Some, like Xavier Léon, shared Halévy's reservations and, consequently, took a position as a hospital administrator, not unlike the position taken by Halévy. Célestin Bouglé also worked in army hospitals as an orderly, and he later helped to found and administer an *école des mutilés* in Clermont-Ferrand, to assist amputees; however, he also wrote pamphlets to boost morale during the war.[90] Léon Brunschvicg was more active, working for the Maison de presse attached to the Bureau d'information diplomatique du Ministère des affaires étrangères.[91] These men shared Halévy's dislike of Bergson and Boutroux's shrill nationalism, but they believed their support of republican France at war required a more active role than that taken by Halévy.

This was true also of Dominique Parodi, who was closely connected to the *Revue*. His case, and its contrast with Halévy's, illustrates the different directions taken by the group at the center of the *Revue*. Parodi (1870–1955) was born in Genoa into a Franco-Italian family but was raised in France. Like Halévy, Léon, and Brunschvicg, Parodi fell under the influence of Alphonse Darlu at the Lycée Condorcet, and like Halévy and Brunschvicg, but a year later, he entered the École normale supérieure. Awarded an *agregé* in philosophy in 1902, he taught in the years before the war in lycées in Rodez, Limoges, Bordeaux, Rouen, and finally Paris. He wrote books and articles on education, morals, philosophy, and politics, and in addition to his connection with the *Revue* belonged to the group around Durkheim's *l'Année sociologique*, though he later became critical of sociological theory in ways similar to Halévy.[92]

In June 1915, Parodi became attached to the vice-consulate in Vintimille as an interpreter (his Italian was flawless), and at the end of the year he moved to the Institut français de Florence to help build French-Italian cultural relations.[93] Both of these activities were supported by the French government, designed to reinforce the rapprochement between the two countries during the period when Italy was entering the war on the side of the Entente. Parodi supported the view that "Latin nations" shared a distinctive culture, defined by a juridical orientation that defended harmony and liberty, and that it was opposed to the Germanic "spirit" that was founded on principles of oppression and authority, and that defended strict organization and servitude.

Parodi came to present more nuanced views, however. Returning to Paris in September 1916, he took up his duties teaching philosophy at the Lycée Condorcet, while also continuing his activities for the French propaganda service, even traveling to Provence in 1917 and to the Ain in 1918 to give patriotic speeches to boost home-front morale. He continued to draw a distinction between the Entente, on the one side, fighting for liberty, democracy, and the right of sovereign people to choose their own governments, and, on the other side, Germanic governments and armies whose agenda was to organize the world under pressure of a heavy-handed authoritarianism. But he now pushed back against blanket characterizations of German culture, insisting that one must distinguish the more liberal culture in the south of Germany from the militarism and the glorification of force that characterized Prussian Pan-Germanism. His lament was that mystic Pan-Germanism had prevailed over the idealism more prevalent in the south.[94]

Parodi also pushed back against the "spiritual" versus "material" dichotomy that informed the rhetoric of many French nationalists. Now he argued that both French and German cultural traditions had elements of materialism and spiritualism. The important issue was which of these elements was ascendant. The significant struggle, in his mind, was to defend rationalism and idealism against crude materialism, and also against both the mythic nationalism present in Pan-German thought *and* the vitalist spiritualism that remained such a potent element in French culture. As this indicates, in important ways Parodi continued to frame issues in terms of the "spiritualist" versus "rationalist" dichotomy that had been a central element of French philosophical debates of the 1890s. What was new was his belief that the mystical strain was being encouraged in both Germany and France by a divinization of force during the war—by a belief in a "warrior mysticism" that encouraged immoral actions under cover of a militaristic Pan-Germanism or, in France, under cover of defending the *patrie* against the Pan-German onslaught. Parodi called this tendency to subordinate truth to action "pragmatism," a move that he believed undermined the autonomy of reason.[95] He expressed this as the dichotomy between "force" and "law and right" in an article published in *Revue* in 1916, mentioned above. He argued that Germany had unfortunately fallen under the spell of a power "that revealed itself and realized itself by force." France and its allies, on the other hand, fought to realize the ideals of "Order, Reason, Equity, and Beauty. It is not Force first, of which law is only the shadow; it is Law/Right [*le Droit*] first, of which force is only the instrument."[96] Parodi, in sum, continued to defend a rational ideal of morality and justice.

Parodi and Halévy shared a great deal. Both believed that France had a right to defend itself against German aggression. Both desired to be "useful" during the war. And both were "secular rationalists" who refused to reduce moral issues to sociological forces. Both insisted that there was a tension between patriotism and nationalism, and that the former was a positive sentiment, while the latter was dangerous. They both worried that the enthusiasm for force and the fascination with sublime violence—emotions that had become energized by the wartime struggle—were dangerous for the stability of France. Parodi believed this "warrior mysticism" was a not uncommon cultural development attendant on violent struggles. It was, in his eyes, one of the most dangerous outgrowths of the war. Parodi and Halévy both opposed pacifism but worried that "warrior enthusiasm" and unbridled nationalism were undermining reasonable patriotism.[97]

Parodi, like Halévy, saw this warrior enthusiasm as suspiciously close to Bergson's notion of vitalist spiritualism. They both believed it was important to control such cultural manifestations and insisted that it was necessary to reassert the importance of French rationalist idealism. This, as we have seen, reflected a long-standing disapproval of Bergson's spiritualist philosophy.[98] During the war, they saw Bergsonian spiritualism undergirding Bergson's unguarded emotional nationalism. They were at pains to separate this from their own view of what was commendable in French culture, the "secular rationalism" that they had spent years defending in the pages of the *Revue*.

What separated Halévy and Parodi was Parodi's willingness to make aggressive public statements about Germany and German culture. Halévy was not opposed to patriotic propaganda, but he disliked the nature of much of the propaganda that he encountered, fearing that public pronouncements too frequently encouraged the warrior enthusiasm he opposed. He was also temperamentally unsuited to the role of a propagandist, believing that it would compromise his intellectual independence. Halévy wrote to Léon in 1915 (this was the period when Parodi was active in Italy), "I am not like Parodi, and I am perfectly happy to escape from the civil life, in order to disappear into the services in the rear [*services d'arrière*]. . . . All the small political and parliamentary noises produce in me real pain."[99] During the war, he was unwilling to make cultural generalizations about nations and cultures (he would be less constrained after the war),[100] fearing that this would undermine cosmopolitanism and internationalism. He was unwilling also to submit to state censorship or the inevitable self-censorship that were necessary concomitants of being a propagandist for the war. In a revealing letter to Léon in 1916, he wrote: "If I don't blacken [pages with words], it is that the war exhausts me as it does all the world; exhausts me directly, because it is not to live intellectually to be always suspended in wait of the news of tomorrow; exhausts me indirectly, because I always have the vague feeling that to think freely is to betray the cause of freedom. To be toward oneself, while one writes, one's own censor, no."[101]

In his analysis of Parodi's wartime writings, Stéphan Soulié astutely observed that "the frontier is uncertain between intellectual sincerity and the discourse suitable to the service of propaganda. Evidently, there was for Parodi, as for many intellectuals, a split personality of discourse [*une forme de dédoublement du discours*], an intimate conflict between one's performative designs, immediately political, and the obligations of rational critique."[102] Parodi walked this precarious line because he was convinced that propaganda for France during the war was critical for the defense of his democratic and republican politics, and also for the defense of his rationalist convictions against mysticism and spiritualism. Halévy shared these goals, but he had no taste for the duplicity of censorship and self-censorship that he believed writing propaganda inevitably entailed.

## Halévy and Alain

The depth of the changes in Halévy's thinking occasioned by the war is the topic of the next chapter. There can be no doubt, however, that the war years had a significant impact. As Vincent Duclert has put it, "The first world conflict marked Élie Halévy for ever."[103] Evidence of the impact of the war is provided by the dialogue that took place between Halévy and Émile Chartier (Alain).[104] Halévy and Alain had met in October 1889, when they both entered the École normale supérieure. They quickly became close friends, and after passing their agrégation de philosophie in 1892 and going their separate ways, they corresponded regularly. Alain first took a position as a professor at a lycée in Pontivy, in Brittany, but subsequently moved to Lorient, to Rouen, and then to Paris, where he taught at the Lycée Condorcet and the Lycée Michelet, and then after 1909 at the Lycée Henri IV.[105] He became a much-loved professor, wrote numerous articles for the early numbers of the *Revue de métaphysique et de morale*, and, especially after the war, published extensively.[106]

The dialogue during the war is interesting because Alain was a pacifist who firmly pressed Halévy on his stance toward the war. In spite of the strains this caused, however, they remained close friends. Though a pacifist, Alain served in the army during the war, honoring a promise he had made to himself in 1888 when he had been excused from military service for being a student. Once the war had broken out, he believed it was unconscionable to remain a civilian when "the best" were being sent to the front to be massacred. He saw horrific evidence of the fighting during his years in the army, though he worked a telephone for an artillery company and, therefore, was not in the trenches. In May 1916 he was injured—his foot was crushed by a transport of munitions—and hospitalized for several weeks. He returned to active duty in late 1916 to work in the meteorological service but never fully recovered from his injury and was demobilized in October 1917. As this indicates, he spent three years in the army, a commitment that deeply impressed Halévy. "It is provocative [*piquant*] to state," he wrote to Léon in 1915, "that he who demands immediate peace [that is, Alain] is he who, in voluntarily signing up, is the only one among us who performs more than his duty."[107]

Alain wrote extensively about the war in two publications. The first, *Mars ou la guerre jugée*, is a polemic against war written in early 1916 but not published until 1921.[108] The second, *Souvenirs de guerre*, was written later, published in 1937, and, as the title suggests, was a more personal, less polemical account.[109] Both advance Alain's pacifist agenda. And both remain engaging reflections about the play of passion and reason in wartime, and about the role of authority in military and civilian society.

Alain and Halévy shared a good deal. Both, not surprisingly, were appalled by the carnage. Alain saw a lot of this first-hand because of his service at the front; he wrote of how it would forever "stain" his memory.[110] "Regularly, that which is good is killed," he wrote to Halévy, "and that which is mediocre is conserved. I speak of infantrymen."[111] Halévy, of course, saw the frightening results of fighting as injured soldiers came to his hospital.

Halévy and Alain also shared disgust for the virulence and pervasiveness of war propaganda, and were shocked by how easily the so-called intellectual luminaries of France and other belligerent countries came to circulate horrific caricatures of other nations and other people. In the words of François Furet, "Their [Alain and Halévy's] commentaries form an oasis in the desert of ideas which masks the noise of propaganda."[112] We noted above Halévy's criticisms of this easy embrace of belligerent nationalism. Alain wrote similar passages, claiming, for example, that he would never pardon "the blustering of the *genre* of Barrès."[113] He spoke of warfare requiring that one do one's duty, but insisted that it was critical to avoid the emotional damage that hating the enemy inevitably brought in its train. "I refuse to hate all of a people, I insist on this idea, little agreeable as I understand it to be for those for whom war opens an access to fury which suffocates them. But for me, I feel solid and decided, without any hate. . . . One already has remarked that the danger, in this war, will come from passions poorly regulated. . . . Who knits some wool socks does a lot; who properly shods his horse, also does a lot. Prepare for the battle, but don't stir up your hate."[114]

Both Halévy and Alain participated in the war effort in a manner that kept them free from propagandistic enthusiasms and from direct government entanglements. Halévy resisted government appointments and therefore could observe the war, as he put it, "from below."[115] Alain refused to accept promotions "by instinct," because he feared such positions would compromise his freedom.[116] As he trenchantly put it in *Souvenirs de guerre*, "The temptation to be a just and humane leader is natural in an educated man; but it is necessary to know that power changes profoundly those who exercise it. . . . I permit myself to laugh at all those who disguise ambition with devotion."[117] "Free judgment," Alain wrote, was "the only resource against the mud and the blood."[118] Both Alain and Halévy continued their critical analyses of the war and, more broadly, both remained committed to philosophy, Halévy to his neo-Kantianism, Alain to a dedication to Descartes and Auguste Comte. It was exactly such a reasoned stance, they argued, that had been given up by the "intellectuals" who became propagandists for the nationalist cause.

Alain was eloquent about the emotions and passions stirred up by the war. He wrote about the pervasiveness of fear among the troops; about how the "marks of fear" forever surrounded the eyes of soldiers. "I believe that I carry these marks like glasses."[119] Alain argued that passions were the dominant force that propelled action, especially during war when man was, in Alain's words, "governable in his passions."[120] It was the duty of reason to justify or restrain the impulsive actions driven by passion; but too often,

reason failed to do so. In wartime, as he eloquently put it, "the reinforce-
ments of moral order are soon sent away."[121] What was needed was to encourage benign sentiments and to employ reason and will to counter the
aggressive passions—to counter the reign of heroism and to avoid the suppression of fear by "urgent action" that the dangerous fields of war encouraged and valorized.[122] Alain often returned to this theme of the passions
versus reason, to what he referred to as the tension between "passions and
interest."

Just as often, Alain faulted the political and educated leaders of the world
for failing in their duty to think hard enough about the evils and injustices
of the world, and for creating the wartime situations in which mechanical
passions ruled. "Human evils like war, abuse of power, absurd concentration
of wealth, are possible only by the blind belief of those who pass as educated."[123] When reason decided to support destructive passions, then blood-
shed would result, as happened in 1914. And the result was horrific. "War is
increasingly and incomparably the worst of all human ills, since it surpasses
at one and the same time the guarantees of free thought, the liberty of action,
[and] the security and welfare of the community."[124] Years later, in August
1934, to provide another example of Alain's contention that fanaticism and
hatred must be constrained by will and reason, Alain wrote to Halévy about
the economic and political problems facing France. At this time, he did not
believe that these problems would lead to a serious international conflict, nor
to a civil war, because calm reason was sufficiently strong to push back against
the fury of released passions. In Alain's opinion, the toxic mix of power,
interest, and weak reason was not present in 1934, but he feared for the future.
"These [current] wars of fools are small wars. The large War will be made by
reasonable men."[125] Alain believed that reason could all too easily give in to
fierce action. "It is by the faculty of the mind that man saves himself, but it
is by the faculty of the mind that man loses himself."[126]

Obviously, calm reason had not been strong enough in 1914 to forestall
the carnage. Aggressive passions were valorized, and the reign of patriotic
intoxication and fanaticism, with all its virulence, was the sad result. Alain
was particularly troubled during the battle of Verdun, as he recounted to
Élie's wife, Florence.

> One thing continues to astonish me. It is that the reasoners here
> (and everywhere) get angry when I speak of the value of human life
> at this time. One considers me only a woman saying: "It is a first

principle that during war one kills men." I have not come to accept that. I continue to do it [to serve in the army], and I conscientiously do it according to my métier, but I do not want to accept it and I do not understand the spirit that accepts it here. In my opinion, this cancels out all morality. How is one able to want the best for mankind, and admit at the same time that one works to kill them? . . . So I shall write against the war and against those who accept it.[127]

This was, in fact, exactly when Alain was writing *Mars ou la guerre jugée*, his most aggressive book against war.

It was at this same time that Alain laid out for Florence the main points of his philosophy.

1) There does not exist a people [as a group] among our neighbors who looks to conquer, burn, violate. This desire, if it exists among some of them, is not sufficient to unleash the war, which always results from an ensemble of bad circumstances that allow this possibility. And these circumstances can be changed by a half-dozen informed men. . . .

2) Passions are never transient. Interests are always transient. . . . I believe that war is a fact of passions, with this illusion common to all belligerents, that they are defending something that is more valuable than life.

3) In view of calming the passions as much as possible, I would like the disposition to sacrifice other people's lives rather than one's own . . . to be less honored. This is only just. . . .

4) I remain persuaded that this war will end, at best, by an arrangement that is as possible today as tomorrow, always difficult, always unacceptable for those who have spoken too much or promised too much, or have believed too much in their imagination.[128]

Halévy would have had few objections to this characterization of the relationship between the passions and reason. Just like Alain, Halévy wished for reasonable action to prevail; just like Alain, he saw that unconstrained passions were being encouraged and that sober reason was being pushed aside. This was one of the reasons, as we have seen, that Halévy was anxious to get the *Revue* back in circulation. "It is necessary to save intelligence,

European intelligence, from the peril that it courts of being annihilated under the bloody ruins."[129]

There were, however, some important differences in the responses of the two friends to the war. Halévy believed the Central Powers were responsible for the outbreak of the war, and he therefore accepted the necessity for France to continue the struggle until German military power had been destroyed. He even came to see such conflicts as a natural, if unfortunate, part of human history. As he put it in February 1915, "If war is the law of humanity, we accept war. If universal peace is our ideal, we say: down with war! Without reserve. But to believe that one will arrive at a universal peace by a 'crusade' [for peace], this is a pure chimera."[130] Alain, on the other hand, saw war as a result of the rational failure of the people of Europe, a failing that had led them to believe that war was inevitable and necessary. He railed against the civilians who believed that war was inevitable, arguing that it was this *belief* in inevitability that in fact made it so. He explained this to Florence in a letter in 1915.

> Concerning all those who say and believe that the war is a natural curse. When one believes it, it is true; when one no longer believes it, it is no longer true. It is a question therefore not of proofs, but of good will; and if the good will is lacking, one gets annoyed. Such is the way things work. . . .
>
> It was a necessity for England to make the neutrality of Belgium respected, as it was a necessity for German to pass through Belgium at the moment that it went to war. But the war itself was the effect, wanted or not wanted, of the opinion of those who, in all countries, had been saying for 40 years that war was inevitable. These are the savages. The rest, massacres, fires, violations, are the consequences of necessity, like a rock [on a hill] that rolls.[131]

Alain was especially critical of those who raced to declare war and who supported the continuation of war but who personally refused to fight. "The warriors in all the countries are always the idle class."[132]

Halévy agreed with Alain that the dispositions of the populations of Europe were in part responsible for the outbreak of the war. He was also attentive, however, to the actions of political and cultural leaders, and to the wider economic and military forces that led to the conflict. He was especially impressed with the dangerous power of popular Pan-Germanism and Pan-Slavism. As we shall see, his future volumes of *The History of the English People in the Nineteenth Century* (the so-called "epilogues" published in 1926 and 1932) would address this issue of the complex causes of the war.

The most significant difference between the two friends, however, was their opposed moral stances toward war. Alain remained in revolt against it, even as he participated in the actions of the French Army on the various fronts where he was stationed. In his mind, this separated him fundamentally from Élie, who he believed had too quickly accepted war as a normal part of human history. As Alain put it in a letter to Florence,

> [Élie] considers war as something as natural as marriage or hypothesis, while I cannot at all support it . . . and remain in obstinate protest against it. In the meantime, I shall work to understand what exterior and interior causes lead some men, who are neither mean nor violent, to accept it. This, it seems to me, will be the most pressing issue once peace returns. The more I have thought about it, the more I am persuaded that one is able to avoid war by small means applied with care, as one avoids household quarrels and, in general, all types of passionate follies. . . . I have avoided so many times the inevitable extravagances that passions bring, that I hold out great hope for my friends the people. Is this ridiculous? Whatever, if this is ridiculous, it is necessary to brave the ridiculous.[133]

Alain believed that the outbreak of war and the continuation of war to be the result of moral weakness, and indicated the unfortunate reign of weak reasoning. "I understand war as an effect of human weakness," he wrote in March 1919.[134]

Alain was an uncompromising moral idealist. Before the war, he had distanced himself from the *Revue* because he believed that it was failing to focus sufficiently on morality.[135] During the war, his correspondence with Élie and Florence Halévy was peppered with moral references, with his articulation of the centrality of moral issues, and with his uncompromising stance in the face of the given facts of the world.[136] "Morality is born at the moment where one subordinates Necessity as means to Liberty as end; morality destroys nothing, it gives a sense to that which is."[137] He was an idealist unwilling to compromise: "Truth is not able to be drawn from facts, but only from truth."[138] What this meant during the conflict was that any chance for peace must be enthusiastically embraced. "I prefer the most precarious peace," he wrote to Halévy in February 1915, "a precarious peace for ten years, twenty years, one hundred years, or one year, to a single minute of war. I think too much of each infantryman killed. . . . The fact of history is that decisions are never made in the presence of the cadavers"[139] His frustration was directed, especially, at civilian leaders and intellectuals who were not direct participants in the fighting. "I would not sacrifice the life of even one peasant for the satisfaction of esprit. I see that the civilians understand things otherwise, which is why I am bitter."[140]

Halévy, on the other hand, was a moral realist, who took cognizance of the weight of wider forces and long-term consequences, however unappealing, before deciding how it was appropriate to respond. To employ Max Weber's distinction, Halévy insisted that it was necessary to distinguish an "ethic of ultimate ends"—the desire for peace—from an "ethic of responsibility" that considered the effects of actions. And during World War I, Halévy argued, as we have seen, that realism forced one to conclude that a premature peace would not end the war; it would only postpone the defeat of Germany, the necessary condition of a lasting European peace. He also sadly concluded that warfare was a part of human experience, a part that, however abhorrent, could not be wished away. In the midst of war, Halévy believed there was no choice but to make war. He wrote the following to his mother in November 1914:

> If one does not wish, in order to end war, to confront war as a pacifist (and this is a very roundabout road), it is necessary to make war either as a vandal or as a sportsman; and the second method is better. It is necessary to consider war as an institution, which has its ceremony and its rules; it is necessary to strike as a brute, and not to hate one's enemy. It is extremely paradoxical; but you cannot escape from this conclusion if you reflect upon it, and you will remark that warriors are just. . . . We are, God have mercy, . . . forced to see it through to the end, not by our reason, not by our heroism, but by a fatality that pulls us along.[141]

A year later, Halévy had not changed his mind: "When war breaks out, all that which is not war is idiotic."[142] In 1917, he wrote: "The century has not yet come where humanity will find the means of developing itself without war and without revolutions."[143] In short, there was an acceptance that war must be viewed as an inevitable part of human change, and that the appropriate response is not moral railing against it but rather attempting to find the best path through it. "As I have said many times, this war will not end with a simple return to the status quo. . . . Unfortunately, it is not thus; and wars are probably, in the history of humanity, crises of growth of which the law escapes us."[144]

It is testimony to the strength of the friendship that these differences did not create a rupture between Halévy and Alain during the war. The frustrations were palpably expressed in their correspondence with others. Alain, for example, in 1915 wrote to his close friend Marie-Monique Morre Lambelin: "Concerning political things, I am not able to avoid irritation absolutely. Yesterday, I wrote again to Élie, who sustains with obstinacy, as does his wife, that governmental thesis [concerning the continuation of the war], and with a wealth and a cunningness of extraordinary arguments."[145] "I have a letter from Élie," he wrote a few weeks later, "incredibly foolish, with some ridiculous formulas: history does not appear to me thinkable without war; certainly I have been a little duped by these bad thinkers."[146] By December 1916, his impatience was reaching boiling point. "I have responded to Élie. As I spoke to him of peace, he responded to me: 'You understand nothing of this war.' They have a manner of pushing away opinions that are frightening. Where do they get this right? Why have I always come under the surveillance of two or three prigs, [Lucien] Herr, Élie, [Xavier] Léon, who lay in wait for inconvenient thoughts?"[147] Three days later, he was at his wits' end: "Élie is unbelievable and I don't write to him half of what I think."[148]

Halévy's frustration with Alain and other pacifists also grew as the war continued. Halévy believed that their reasoning could not dispel the grim reality of the situation that France and its citizens faced, and he feared that they might erode the ability of France to win the war. His impatience is evident in this April 1917 to Xavier Léon: "It is clear that the pacifists render themselves ridiculous in sending their motion to President Wilson, eight days before the president enters the battle. One time more, they demonstrate their incomprehension of the situation. The pacifists recognize that the facts are against them, but that, because the facts cannot be true against reason, one must continue to embrace reason against the facts."[149] The situation in which France found itself was in fact quite straightforward. War, Halévy argued, had been brought to France by the invasion of 1914. "I don't know why we are taking so much trouble to justify philosophically our cause. We defend *our existence*, and that is sufficient."[150]

## CHAPTER 8

# Post War

## (1918–1924)

Strongly as I believe in the necessity of dictatorship, with all its worse
[*sic*] implications, in time of war, I hope that war is now over, and
that the blessed day of thought and anarchy is dawning again
upon us.

— Élie Halévy to Bertrand Russell, 15 April 1919

Élie Halévy emerged from World War I relieved that the Allies had defeated
Germany and anxious to return to his scholarship on English history. He
also was concerned, however, with the economic strains, social instabilities,
popular frustrations, and ideological shrillness that the war had left in its
wake. Domestically, the war had led to new cynicism concerning the effectiveness of the institutions of the Republic. The quarrels among politicians
and the ideological divisions between political parties—seemingly endemic
to French political life—had, if anything, been exacerbated by the conflict.
French parliamentarianism, Halévy lamented, had become "essentially a parliamentarianism of paralysis."[1]

The loss of life during the war was nothing short of tragic. France had
mobilized eight million men—62.7 percent of all males between the ages of
eighteen and forty (20 percent of the population)—and had suffered the loss
of a higher proportion of its population that any other nation (approximately
1.4 million dead, three million disabled). It is telling that, even though France
had "won" the war and annexed Alsace-Lorraine from Germany, its population

was lower in 1919 than it had been in 1914 without Alsace-Lorraine (39.5 million in 1914 versus thirty-nine million in 1919).

The economic consequences of the war were also devastating for France. Much of the fighting on the Western Front had taken place on French territory, and the consequent damage was extensive. Industrial production at the end of the war was 60 percent of what it had been in 1914; it was not until 1924 that industrial productivity reached prewar levels. Moreover, extensive wartime spending created debt, currency instability, and inflation. The French prewar budget had been approximately five billion francs; by 1918 it was 190 billion francs, and to cover this, the French government borrowed extensively, went off the gold standard, and printed money. After the war, debt service amounted to seven billion francs a year, significantly more than the entire national budget before the war. Even more devastating was the resulting inflation, which was a disaster for many especially in the middle class. France faced a broad spectrum of economic problems, like all European countries, and it dealt with these poorly during the interwar period. Halévy concluded that France was no longer the uncontested great power it had been in 1914; it had become a second-rate power when compared to England, Germany, and the United States.[2]

Halévy also was shocked by the blossoming of anti-intellectualism and the new contempt for liberal and humanistic values. Robert Wohl reminds us that there were three different "generations of 1914" that emerged from the war in France, each with distinctive ideals and doctrines.[3] They nonetheless shared a great deal, including a belief that they were beneficiaries and victims of rapid change—rapid change associated with planes and automobiles, but most dramatically represented by the war itself. And they shared what Maurice Barrès characterized as "prejudices, a vocabulary, and objects of disdain."[4] This disdain was largely directed at the cultural and intellectual traditions of prewar France, including the faith in Enlightenment reason and in the institutions of the Republic. Reason was widely discounted in favor of energy, the irrational, and the unconscious. The Republic was dismissed and attacked as corrupt, ineffective in saving France from the political and economic problems that the nation so obviously faced. Many intellectuals between the wars were attracted to the antiliberal, antidemocratic movements on the Right and Left.[5] Halévy was appalled and, as we shall see, forcefully pushed back.

Halévy also viewed with trepidation the growing power and reach of national states and their bureaucracies, a continuation again of developments of the war years. Especially troubling, he believed, was how the new muscular states were mobilized by charismatic leaders, who were able to appeal to the public with promises of prosperity and power, and who now were able to manipulate public opinion with sophisticated appeals to radical nationalism —what he would come to call the "organization of enthusiasm." This was the distressing convergence he observed taking place in Italy in the early 1920s, in Russia following the dismantling of New Economic Policy in the late 1920s, and, of course, in Germany in the early 1930s. The result led to regimes that suppressed dissent internally and threatened aggression externally, a toxic mix that, Halévy believed, threatened the stability of Europe. These specific cases are the focus of Chapter 10, where we turn to Halévy's analysis of the era of tyrannies.

Finally, Halévy worried about similar war-related developments in the Western European democracies, especially as these intersected with the impatient expectations of various popular groups, and with the diplomatic and economic challenges left behind by the conflict. How were these countries, victorious but deeply scarred, to deal with the economic problems of inflation, depression, and uncertainty; with popular impatience with bourgeois politics; with the invigorated demands made by labor; and with the prospect of facing the radical nationalism of resurgent hostile powers? This chapter focuses on these domestic and international concerns, and on how they had an impact on Halévy's scholarship.

## Return to England and Scholarship

During the last year of the war, Halévy was anxious to return to his scholarly work, especially to his history of England. As he put it in a letter to his mother in August 1917, "To the degree that months follow months, and that I advance in age [he was forty-six years old at the time], I feel more than ever the necessity to take up again, as soon as possible, my large work [on the history of England]."[6] He wasted no time as the Armistice approached. In July 1918, Paul Mantoux wrote to him, encouraging him to come to England. "Your presence alone will permit us to take advantage, for the interest of France, of the excellent relations and authority you have here in England with the intellectual milieu, above all with those who are attached to the liberal tradition."[7] Halévy required no further encouragement, and in

November 1918, immediately after the signing of the Armistice, he and Florence sailed for England. He was charged by the French Commissariat à la propagande with the mission "to study the political and economic questions that are posed by the ending of the war, and notably the measures taken for 'reconstruction.'"[8]

Once settled, relatively uncomfortably because of the privations caused by the war, Halévy renewed his contacts of the past—with Graham Wallas, Alys Russell (estranged from Bertrand), the Whiteheads, Sir Frederick Pollock and his family, Ernest Baker, George Trevelyan, among others—and threw himself into work to provide the studies with which he was charged and to finish the scholarship that the war had put on hold. He wrote two articles on the English elections of 1919, another on the new British education law (the work of his friend H. A. L. Fisher, education minister in the cabinet of Lloyd George), and a short reflection on "the English people and Lloyd George."[9] At a conference in Oxford in September 1920, he presented a paper entitled "The Problem of Nationalities."[10] He returned to the British Library to do the final research for the second and third volumes of his *Histoire du peuple anglais au XIXe siècle*; these two volumes, covering the years 1815 to 1841, were published in 1923 and were quickly translated into English. He also began his inquiries into labor relations, socialism, and politics, attempting to judge the impact of the war on these important issues. This took him and Florence to Wales in April and May 1919, where they met workers and descended into a coal mine.[11] Élie's reflections resulted in articles on the Whitley Councils—industrial councils created in 1917 that were to include representatives of labor, industry, and the state—and, more generally, on the transformation of English socialism caused by the war.[12]

The rhythm of the Halévys' life returned to what it had been before the war, except for the unusually long stay in England in 1918–1919.[13] Each year, Élie and Florence would visit England during the spring, collecting documents for Élie's history of England and pursuing their research on contemporary issues. They met colleagues, saw friends, and Élie presented papers at conferences. His English-language skills were reported to be flawless.[14] In the summer, they would return to their home on the outskirts of Paris—the Maison Blanche in Sucy-en-Brie—where writing became a major focus. This usually was broken by a vacation trip to the Alps, and sometimes by a trip to Italy to visit Florence's family and/or an excursion to Greece or (as in 1932) to the Soviet Union. In the autumn and winter, the Halévys would return to Sucy, and Élie would teach his course in Paris at the École libre des sciences politiques, alternating, as before the war, between a course on the history of England and a course on the history of European socialism. In addition, of course, he continued to be closely connected with the direction of the *Revue de métaphysique et de morale*. This continued to be an influential journal, in part because the decimation by the war of the younger generation left older intellectuals like Halévy at the center of public cultural affairs.[15]

All of this might suggest that there was great continuity in Halévy's perspective before and after the war. In many ways, this was true. Much of Halévy's scholarly work was similar, focusing on the history of the English people and the history of European socialism. But there were significant changes in Halévy's perspective, as indicated by the early postwar writings mentioned above. These marked his new concerns about the evolution of democratic and liberal societies, and about the implication for modern societies of revolution and war. One may glimpse some of his new concerns in a short article that focused on the British statesman John Morley, written by Halévy for the first number of the *Revue* of 1918.[16] Halévy argued that Morley was the "last of the great Victorians" who stood for a generous liberalism that was serious, charitable, and capable of tolerance. Lamentably, Morley and his contemporaries had been replaced by British leaders of a younger generation who were both more defensive and more aggressive. Morley represented for Halévy the end of the reformist Benthamite tradition in England, and the transition from a nation devoted to peace and free-trade liberalism (1815–1860) to a nation driven by nationalism and empire (1879–1890). The article drew from his memories of England before World War I, when Halévy had experienced first-hand, during the Boer War, the turn of British public opinion to aggressive imperialism and hostility to France. It is an early indication of his changed views of England, considered in detail below.

Equally significant was Halévy's assessment of the state and socialism. His view of the spectrum of possible socialisms did not change during of the war, but Halévy did come to believe that the socialisms that would survive the conflict would be more authoritarian. To put it in the terms that he employed to discuss the tension at the heart of socialism: the "organizational" tendency of socialism was becoming more prominent at the expense of the "liberationist" side of socialism.[17] He had sensed such a change as early as July 1915, as indicated in a letter to Xavier Léon.

> The influence that the war is able to have on the destinies of socialism merits a study.

[The war is] probably unfavorable to the progress of the liberal forms of socialism (syndicalism, etc.), on the other hand it reinforces, significantly, state socialism. I see things in this manner, but others may see it differently, and the subject merits reflection.[18]

His view of the growth of the administrative and statist dimension of socialism would be strengthened by the end of the war as Halévy assessed the effect of the governmental changes introduced in all of the belligerent nations. He lamented that the war had increased the power of states over smaller associations and groups, and he worried that liberties would suffer. He expressed this clearly in 1918 in a letter to his English friend Graham Wallas, in which he responded to Wallas's longing for "organization": "What you and I yearn for after peace, is it really organization—whether theocratic or scientific matters little—that we yearn for, and not rather individualism, anarchism, or whatever you choose to call it? I mean the freedom to do what you like, read what you like, admire what you like, go travelling where you like. Organization indeed! We have that, since the war began, with a vengeance."[19]

## The Legacy of the War: The Problem of Nationalism

Halévy's concern with the growth of organization and administration was connected with a perception of the strengthening of a virulent nationalism. As we saw above, the outbreak of war had led to nationalist enthusiasms that Halévy resisted. He feared that rabid nationalism was eroding valuable international connections and, therefore, the possibility of serious intellectual interchange. In January 1918, he expressed this clearly in a letter to Xavier Léon.

When I tell you that I am less nationalist than ever, my preoccupations are much less political than intellectual. I ask that we not allow a religion of patriotism to be established, one that would be more exclusive, more tyrannical, more bloody than any church. I ask that there remain some intellectuals, some professors, some "mandarins" to conserve intact the storehouse of European culture. I ask that the French not forget the existence of Kant, of Hegel, or of Goethe; that they search out some Germans (republicans of Switzerland or southern Germany, etc.) with whom it is possible, without dishonor, to renew relations. We cannot spend the rest of our lives—which are beginning to shorten—on these idiotic questions of races, languages, and borders.[20]

Halévy's concern continued after the end of hostilities. To his friends, Halévy expressed his despair. "Concerning the future of the European mind," he wrote to Alfred Zimmern in August 1919, "I decline to say anything. I am just as shocked as you may be with the narrowness and bitterness of modern nationalism."[21] To Xavier Léon, he insisted on the need to organize support for internationalism and peace. "It is necessary . . . to work to renew the threads of European civilization; and for us, who are not, thank God, politicians, there is no task more urgent."[22]

Halévy, again as we saw above, was critical of intellectuals everywhere for giving in to the easy sentiment of nationalistic enthusiasm during the war. But in terms of its origins, he now expressed his opinion that German thinkers had made a greater contribution to this disturbing cultural phenomenon than the intellectuals of other countries. He had avoided attacking German intellectuals during the war, but at the end of 1918, his frustration spilled over in this letter to Léon:

> A new philosophy suddenly appears: the philosophy of the war of races—of nationalism (to employ the fashionable word although it is etymologically inadequate to the idea). And for this philosophy, modern Germany is particularly responsible. And in modern Germany, the class of professors, of university professors, is particularly responsible. When it sees its intellectuals condemned to a kind of moral quarantine by the people it has fought against, it is necessary for Germany to bear the weight of the intellectual crimes it has committed against reason and common sense. It is necessary, for scientific relations to be normally reestablished between nations, that the regime of Prussian university professors collapse just as the regime of the *Junkers* comes to collapse.[23]

What especially concerned Halévy was the lamentable silence of university professors after the war, at a time when other German intellectuals were signing counter-manifestos and trumpeting their humanitarian tendencies.[24] He hoped that Germans would rediscover the generous cultural traditions of their past. In the same letter in which he complained of German university professors, he pointed out: "There is no country in Europe which has had intellectuals more capable of intellectual cosmopolitanism, more denuded of nationalism, than Erasmus, Leibnitz, or Goethe, etc. etc."[25]

Halévy's perception of the dangerous growth of aggressive patriotism and nationalism was closely connected, after the war, with support of Woodrow Wilson's program of "self-determination," reduction of armaments, and the creation of the League of Nations. Halévy was critical of Wilson's embrace of the Monroe Doctrine but generally supportive of Wilson's agenda.[26] In 1918, he contrasted Wilson's vision of the world with the troubling perils of "Germanic nationalism," based on notions of race, and with Russian Bolshevism. Germany, he wrote in early 1919 when the new regime was facing the violence of left-wing extremists, needed "not an army, but a regular government."[27] He was more despairing of Russia. While there was no convincing guidance, according to Halévy, to justify claims that the Bolsheviks were persecuting dissidents, he nonetheless was critical of the unfolding of events, and critical of the leaders of the October Revolution.[28] "I see the Bolsheviks as grandiose fanatics, the Tartars of Marxism; they will conclude whatever peace with whomever, [and] promising who knows what, they will consider themselves tied by no promise, receiving money from all sides, [and] will make use of it as they wish. Moreover, it is necessary to beware of the impression this fanaticism can produce on the Latin imagination."[29] This did not mean that Halévy wished to intervene in the Russian Civil War. As he insisted to his mother, "That which I do not want, and on this *I am perfectly clear* [in italics and in English], is that we send French soldiers to reestablish the Tsarist regime."[30]

When Halévy turned to the situation in France, his major concerns were financial stability and the country's relationships with England and the United States. "In France," he wrote to his mother in 1919, "that which I dread is bankruptcy."[31] To Xavier Léon, he lamented: "Our financial situation is disastrous."[32] It was economic instability that, he feared, would lead to ideological extremism. "One asks me, not without anxiety, if it is necessary to worry about the contagion of bolshevism. I respond that, in normal conditions, there would be nothing to fear; that the structure of France, with its millions of small farmers, shields it, more than any other country in Europe, from a socialist revolution. But we are, as Italy, on the verge of bankruptcy; and revolutions have always closely followed bankruptcies."[33]

Halévy worried that the economic problems would continue if the government of France did not take reasonable action to stabilize the currency and to pay off its debts. Unfortunately, the government seemed intent to rely on reparations from Germany to stimulate the economy, a view that Halévy believed was naive. He reported to Léon in 1920 that he had read John Maynard Keynes's *The Economic Consequences of Peace* and agreed with the English economist's analysis and criticism of the demands for unspecified reparations from Germany.[34] "Sooner or later," he wrote to Léon in 1922, "it will be necessary to arrive at a settlement of all the international debts in the spirit of Keynes."[35]

Halévy also feared that strident French nationalism would isolate the country.[36] French political writers and leaders who insisted on annexations, he reasoned, were giving in to a simplistic nationalism that would alienate other liberal democracies and likely lead to new conflicts. "I protest with my last energy against the annexation of the region of the Saar," he wrote to Léon in January 1919. When there was talk of occupation of the Ruhr, Halévy expressed his disapproval.[37] Given such widespread annexationist sentiments, he thought it was nothing short of "bizarre that it is in Paris that one shouts most forcefully against the annexationist stirrings of Italy."[38]

Halévy considered his role to be an informed intermediary between the French and the English, a voice of reason that could correct mistaken perceptions of one nation by the other. His early articles about the English published in France were judicious analyses of the election of 1919 and of the changes and continuities of British political culture. The election, he pointed out, was significant because it expanded the suffrage to workers and women and because it was the first election to reveal the effects of the war.[39] It registered the impact of important changes in British politics and society: new forms of mobilization (mass meetings, and so on); impatience by the Irish republicans of Sinn Fein for independence; growing power of workers demanding reforms (some, like the eight-hour day for railway workers, granted by the government on the eve of the election); and the instability of traditional party politics (marked especially by the split of the Liberal Party between Asquith and Lloyd George). There was a new fermentation among the electorate, now impatient for change. "The democratic evolution of England that was so rapid before the war," he wrote, "had become even more rapid since the war, and the patriotic coalition of the parties, far from paralyzing the reforming action of the Radical Party or of the Workers Party, broke the resistance of the Tory Party to reforms."[40] In spite of this new political and social effervescence, however, the election of 1919 also demonstrated convincingly that the English people had great confidence in the parliamentary system. Moreover, they were satisfied with the leadership of Lloyd George, who promised peaceful resolution of the problems facing the country. "The world is in flames. In Flanders, in Lorraine, in Venice, in the Balkans, in Asia, bloody battles have changed the face of the world. Austria is dismembered. Revolution reigns in Petrograd, in Berlin, in Munich. A political man [Lloyd George] rises up, and promises to his country that here at least all the problems will be resolved legally according to the peaceful ways of traditional parliamentarianism."[41] While the world was in turmoil, Halévy was impressed with the great stability of the liberal political system of England.

Halévy implied that there were lessons to be learned by the French, who had emerged from the war too nationalistic and revanchist. In an article in 1920, he reminded the French that historically the English had emerged from armed conflicts favoring diplomatic moderation and European equilibrium.[42] This had favored French interests in earlier eras, when there were no vindictive actions against France—for example, by Castlereagh in 1814. It should not surprise the French, he suggested, that such moderation was again ascendant after World War I. In an article in 1921, he pointed out that there was nothing inevitable or necessarily enduring about a French-British union in opposition to Germany. There had been, he reminded his readers, a strong prewar movement in Britain to bring the "Teutonic races" together.[43] He was particularly concerned, as the months passed, that French illusions about England and the English might lead to French diplomatic isolation.

Halévy made clear his anxieties concerning the current policies of the French government in an important article published in 1923.[44] He was worried about the growing anti-French opinion in Britain, attributing this in part to the power of the British press and the limited intelligence of popular opinion.[45] But much of this anti-French sentiment, he argued, was the result of French missteps: the Anglophobia of the French press; the insensitivity of the French to the postwar economic problems faced by Britain; the threats by the French administration that it needed to occupy the Ruhr to force Germany to make reparations payments; in general, "the Machiavellianism" of the Quai d'Orsay. He was happy that France had succeeded in retaining its republican institutions, unlike many Continental nations in the interwar years, but he believed it was important for France to make clear to other nations that it had no desire to extend its territorial acquisitions beyond Alsace and Lorraine. This would require more restraint on the part of French politicians. He counseled French leaders to avoid alienating Britain and other liberal nations like the United States, and to work to keep France from being foolishly isolated. It also was necessary to redouble efforts to make the League of Nations an effective organization.

Halévy addressed related issues when he had the opportunity to talk about France to British audiences. When he was asked to give a lecture in October 1923 at the London School of Economics and Political Science, he used the occasion to counter what he considered to be mistaken perceptions about France that were current in England.[46] He focused on the arguments advanced by G. P. Gooch in his Creighton Lecture. Halévy argued that Gooch was wrong to claim that France had been taken over by revanchist nationalists in the years before 1914, incorrectly implying that the political culture of France did not differ significantly from Germany's in the lead-up to the declaration of war in 1914. Halévy pushed back. He began by reminding the audience that after the Franco-Prussian war of 1870–1871, France had established a constitutional democracy led by popularly elected politicians. Germany, on the other hand, was still ruled by a Kaiser who governed with ministers he appointed and dismissed at will. "As a matter of fact," he wrote, "though the German *Reichstag* was elected by manhood suffrage, the Government had not, until the very day when the war was declared in August 1914, accepted the notion of a responsible ministry."[47] Such domestic issues could not be rigidly separated from foreign policy. Even more important, according to Halévy, it was essential to avoid interpreting World War I as revenge for the war of 1870–1871 or as a renewal of some recurrent Franco-German enmity. He pointed to the intellectual and political rapprochement of France and Germany between 1879 and 1904. And he was especially at pains to stress that France was not itching to enter a war in 1914. Every French election from 1870 to the outbreak of the war, he pointed out, was a victory for the party of peace, not the party of war.

During these years, Halévy gave a lot of attention to the issue of the causes of the war, publishing in 1921 an article on prewar British-German tensions, and another in 1924 on the origins of the Entente.[48] These were early sketches of the arguments he provided in expanded form in the second volume of his "Epilogue," published in 1932. This and his last writings are analyzed in the following two chapters.

Halévy believed that both the French and the British should realize that President Wilson articulated one of the most reasonable international philosophies of the era. "I do not say that this man hides two angels' wings under his presidential jacket. But he gives voice to an idea—a fixed idea, if you wish—in this crowd of appetites."[49] Halévy referred to himself in March 1919 as "an obstinate Wilsonian," adding, "[I] think that this opposition [to Wilson] is very dangerous for us, that the *League of Nations* is the only diplomatic system that is able to tie together in a permanent way America and Europe, [and] that Wilson is, consequently, among the Americans, our true ally. . . . I am a very radical Wilsonian."[50]

This did not mean that he believed Wilsonian idea of self-determination would solve all problems. Quite the contrary: he reasoned that self-determination, though important, would almost inevitably lead to conflicts if it alone were the principle of international relations. National minorities, for example, could create instability by seeking assistance from their national brethren residing in other nation-states. In 1920, he presented his thoughts on "the problem of nationalities" at a Congress of Philosophy held at Oxford.[51] He argued that "the self-determination of people" was an attractive but utopian principle if not balanced with a consideration of "natural frontiers" and "European equilibrium." He concluded that, to be effective, the Society of Nations should rest, "not on a simple principle, but on a plurality of principles which ought to complement each other."[52] In unpublished essays written at the same time, Halévy concluded that these three principles had to be operative and kept in equilibrium.[53] Even when they were, however, it would be difficult to prevent strong nations from using force to extend their borders to gain control of valuable natural resources and/or to protect populations they considered constituent parts of their "nation." To believe that one principle could settle these conflicting interests was naive. "Utopia is the air that we breathe," he wrote. "Between the utopias of pacifism and the utopias of conquering, how are we to maintain an equilibrium that is in some ways miraculous?"[54]

In a third unpublished fragment, Halévy considered what he termed a "middle utopia" between "pure imperialism" and "pure federalism."[55] He argued that the chances of a "universal empire" similar to that of ancient Rome was not possible in the modern era, because nationalism had become too strong, and also because competing nationalisms had brought widespread feelings of insecurity. Moreover, while the Romans had shown respect for other civilizations, it was not likely that a modern powerful European nation like Germany—the obvious candidate for leadership of a modern European empire—would be similarly inclined. He reasoned that Germany would always be anxious about its power and security, and would always insist on dominance. "It is a nation that wishes to grow at the expense of other nations, without ever losing consciousness of the fact that it would be enough for some historical accident to intervene for the situation to be reversed, [and] for these nations currently menaced in their integrity by Germany, to become in their turn menacing to the integrity of the German nation."[56] A federal organization without any strength was equally unrealistic. What was needed, Halévy suggested, was a "historic power" capable of imposing respect for decisions on the nations of Europe; a power that was not "a conquering and dominating nation." After rejecting the idea that the pope might fulfill such a role, he proposed the creation of a Parliament of Nations. It would be a federal organization modeled on the organization created to represent the British colonies. It would meet in England and also rely on England and its naval power to execute its decisions. This proposal clearly demonstrates Halévy's high regard for the prudence and tolerance of the English. Nonetheless, one suspects that he never made the proposal public because he recognized how unrealistic it was. In the extant fragment, he characterized the proposal as "a utopia." In the isolation of his study, however, he could imagine that it was "a utopia of which it was necessary to run the risk."[57]

Such musings are evidence of Halévy's attempt to imagine a strategy to contain aggressive nationalism. Another way was to encourage cosmopolitanism. The most dramatic example of this was the decision of the editors of the *Revue de métaphysique et de morale* to bring Albert Einstein to Paris for an international conference. Einstein was, of course, German. But he was a committed pacifist and arguably the most famous scientist in the world. To bring this about, the editors of the *Revue* worked with Paul Langevin, an important early proponent of relativity in France. Langevin had taught courses, given lectures, and published articles on relativity before the war. Together, they brought Einstein to Paris for a meeting on 6 April 1922 with French philosophers. Xavier Léon made the opening introductory remarks, suggesting that Einstein's project was similar to that of Henri Poincaré's.[58]

Philosophically, the meeting at the Société français de philosophie, where Einstein presented his theory of relativity, and where Henri Bergson, Léon Brunschvicg, Émile Meyerson,[59] and others responded, probably misfired, as each presented or re-presented his philosophical stance, and therefore largely talked past the others.[60] But as a move to counter the exclusive nationalism in both France and Germany it was an important step. Halévy and his compatriots at the *Revue* saw the visit as the opportunity to reestablish ties between French and German academics. Einstein came to view his visit in a similar manner, though initially he had refused the invitation because he was upset that his German colleagues were still excluded from French academic

life. But, in part because of the intervention of Walter Rathenau, foreign
minister of the Weimar Republic, he came to view the visit as a service to
European relations.[61] There were some French objections to Einstein's visit
by hyper-nationalists of Action française, but in general the popular press
viewed it in a positive light. Halévy and Léon viewed it as an important step
toward invigorating European cosmopolitanism.

## The Legacy of the War: The State and Socialism

The growth of nationalism after World War I, and the concurrent expansion
of economic and administrative organization "from above," worried Halévy.
It had the potential of suffocating initiative and threatening the autonomy of
individuals. Halevy was equally troubled, however, by calls for an exaggerated
privatization of activities, and for the aggressive decentralization of power at
the expense of the state. Jean-Fabien Spitz has emphasized in his recent scholarship the importance of a political tradition in France that insisted the state
was the critical institution for the protection of individuals facing the power
of individuals and private groups.[62] This was a tradition, of course, that
extended back to those theorists during the Old Regime who argued that the
only institution capable of restraining the power of nobles and of other corporate interests was the state—the so-called *thèse d'état*. During the nineteenth century, writers like Louis Blanc, Charles Dupont-White, and Émile
Durkheim also supported the intrusion of the state against private interests
but based their arguments on more sophisticated analyses of the growing
complexity of societies and, therefore, the growing need for a regulatory
framework to constrain the selfish interests of individuals and powerful
groups. In short, they argued that there was not *necessarily* a conflict between
the growth of the state and individual liberty; indeed, the state performed an
essential role of protecting individual liberty.

Halévy frequently made statements that supported this role of the state.
For example, in a letter to Célestin Bouglé in 1902, he worried about the
"despotisms of the group" and looked to the state to protect citizens against
this.

> From full and entire liberty is born all inequalities, all the despotisms
> of the group—clerical or industrial [and these will continue to exist]

until the day when the weak invent the State to protect themselves against their masters. . . .

*Liberalism* . . . admits the necessity of the state, but acknowledges that the state is able to become tyrannical, and that it is necessary to constitute the State in conditions such that, remaining effective, it is constantly prevented from becoming tyrannical. . . . I believe that the state, *in its essence*, is not tyrannical; it is, *essentially*, the organ for the defense of the whole society against particular societies, of all individuals against all the groups. It ceases to respond to its essence when it becomes the organ of defense of groups and of particular societies. But when it fills its function, when it works to fight against the preponderance of particular societies and groups frightened of its action . . . [it becomes] the sole means that is in our power to defend liberty.[63]

After World War I, Halévy remained philosophically committed to this "liberal" stance, but he lamented the growth of state power and complained that the result of state intervention was more likely suffocating than liberating. While he did not question the importance of national administrations, he had become more critical of the excessively bureaucratized state.

This was closely connected with Halévy's changed assessment of socialism. Before the Great War, as we have seen, Halévy had an ambivalent relationship to socialism. Depending on which socialist movements around which (or against which) he was positioning himself, he was more or less inclined to be sympathetic. He admired how the writings of socialists analyzed the concentration of wealth and recurrent crises of overproduction. He was sympathetic to their calls for greater equality and their exposure of the injustices of industrialization. He respected the moral fervor of their demands for reform; and he responded warmly to the critical and emancipatory elements within some strains of socialist thought—many of which had their origins in early French socialism. He was favorably disposed to state intervention to redistribute wealth, and to what he referred to (in his first lecture on the history of socialism in 1902) as "administrative collectivism."[64]

Nonetheless, Halévy refused to call himself a socialist and insisted that he was a liberal.[65] In part, this was because he believed that many socialists focused too exclusively on material interests and on a limited range of human sentiments. Other socialists, he charged, embraced an unduly reductive sociological perspective. He judged these too narrow to capture the complexity of human action; they offended his neo-Kantian view of human rationality, human nature, and human motivation. More important, he refused to call himself a socialist because he was critical of the close connection of pre–World War I French socialism with revolutionary Marxism and revolutionary syndicalism. He disliked their demands for radical change through revolution and violence. Finally, he refused to call himself a socialist because there were organizational elements within the socialist tradition that he found disturbing. Nonetheless, he remained ambivalent, writing to Bouglé in 1913, "I recognize that socialism contains the secret of the future. But I cannot decipher this secret, and I am not able to say if socialism will conduct us to a universalized version of the Swiss republic or to European Caesarism."[66] I believe Halévy should be characterized, during this period of his life, as a "socialist liberal."[67]

After the Great War, Halévy concluded that socialism was implicated in the advance of Caesarism; that is, in the "tyranny" that was characteristic of many interwar European societies. He had noted in 1895 that there was a tension at the heart of European socialism between liberation and organization.[68] By 1936, he argued that this dichotomy was central, and that lamentably the organizational strain had triumphed.[69] This shift in his thinking began during the war and became a settled aspect of his thought after he had analyzed the social question in England in 1919–1922 and the transformation of labor that this involved.[70] It was at this time that Halévy came to the conclusion that the constructive, liberating side of socialism was in the process of being overwhelmed by the statist, organizational side.

The change in his thinking was associated with his concern over the dialectical interplay of nationalism with the administrative and organizational imperatives of war. Statist nationalism was mandated by governments during the war, but it continued to be embraced after the war by postwar administrations, by industrial executives, and by the leaders of labor organizations, responding to the transformation of international dynamics and to new dangers of revolution. And according to Halévy it also came to be embraced by workers, who gave up syndical goals for the promise of higher wages, shorter working hours, and job security. This transition in his thought was intimately connected with his growing pessimism, something that is examined in more detail in the next two chapters.

Halévy worried about the growth of the administrative and statist dimension of socialism early in the war, as indicated in a letter, noted above, that he wrote to Xavier Léon in July 1915.[71] As the conflict dragged on, his

concern became more focused. Halévy lamented that the war had increased
the power of state bureaucracies and administrations, and he worried about
the long-term effects. While this seemed to be true everywhere, he was especially concerned that it was true even in England, the land of Manchester
Liberalism and moderate socialism. He analyzed this English transition carefully in two articles and an address in 1919–1922.[72] It is here, I believe, that
Halévy first presented his critical assessment of moderate socialism.

The first article, "La politique de paix sociale en Angleterre," published
in 1919, broadly analyzed the reconstruction after the war, by which Halévy
meant the rebuilding of the social edifice that took into consideration the
disruptions of the war, but also the insights that were gained during the
war—insights like the effectiveness of the "appeal to the collaboration of
the classes" and "the growing confidence in the efficacy of interventions by
the state."[73] He focused especially on the efforts of the government to facilitate the improvement of relations between employers and workers. The war,
of course, had led to urgent needs concerning manpower and production,
and the result was a marked increase in the directive and coordinating role of
the state. In Halévy's words, "Now the chief consumer of the nation, the
state set itself up as the final arbiter of production and distribution."[74] It
intervened to control production of essential items, to ration raw materials,
to set minimum wages in some industries, and to arbitrate disputes between
management and workers. And this activity, combined with the dramatic
increase of wartime production, led to new thinking about the relations of
state, industry, and labor. It "spawned a multitude of more or less utopian
plans to bring about social peace by means of the joint association [*le syndicat
mixte*] within which employers and workers in the same industry would frat-
ernize. . . . Thus, in the second year of the war, the imagination of the
system-makers, dormant at first, came to life."[75]

There was still opposition to the high degree of state intervention by
democratic socialists, syndicalists, and Guild socialists. Democratic socialists
demanded more guarantees for the workers. Syndicalists and Guild socialists
called for industrial organization that would give workers and their committees more control on the shop floor and over the distribution of profits. It
was, Halévy noted, the old tension "which had repeatedly cropped up in the
world of labor for a half-century, between the 'anarchists' and the 'authoritar-
ians,' between the 'federalists' and the 'centralizers.' "[76] A compromise was
worked out in 1917 by the government committee, created in March 1916,
that was chaired by J. H. Whitley. It specified that each industry would have

a national industrial council to set policy composed of representatives of labor, industry, and the state. Halévy's article in 1919 was primarily devoted to assessing how these councils had functioned in the two years since their inception in 1917.

Halévy's assessment was mixed. Large established unions had no need for these new joint industrial councils, because they had already set up conciliation boards with management. Some of the new large unions welcomed the creation of these councils, but the smaller craft unions embraced or resisted depending on their differing needs and perspectives. Also difficult was the setting up of Whitley Councils among employees in public service. Moreover, the Whitley Councils had to compete, in some industries, with trade boards that were created by an act passed in 1918. Most discouraging to those pushing the creation of these councils, however, was the fact that the number of workers represented remained relatively small—roughly three million workers out of sixteen million was Halévy's optimistic estimate. The creation of the Whitley Councils was important, however, because, in Halévy's opinion, "it mark[ed] the moment when management as a whole and the state itself, after long years of opposition, specifically concurred in the principle of this working-class policy." What was this policy? To have "wages and, in general, all working conditions regulated by collective agreements, and permanently protected by joint committees of employers and workers."[77] This was important, Halévy reasoned, because workers were in a position of political strength. He wrote to his brother, Daniel, in March 1919 that in England "all take orders from the working class," something that was true even for leaders of the unions.[78]

Did these councils, therefore, create a new industrial system? Halévy thought not. When he examined the details of the activities of the councils, obviously limited given the short time of their existence, Halévy judged as nil their ability to permanently resolve divisive class interests. "In fact, when employers and workers come together in an *Industrial Council,* there is a misunderstanding between them. Not to understand its nature is to live in a dream world."[79] Workers, Halévy claimed, hoped the councils would gain for them not just higher wages and better working conditions but also participation in industrial operations; that is, they wished to have some say in the marketing of products and the distribution of profits. Employers, on the other hand, wished to resist such moves and even to strengthen their authority.

There had been progress on the wage front, according to Halévy, before and during the war. He described this progress in terms similar to those he

used in 1906 to describe the "distribution of wealth." But what, he asked
rhetorically, did this imply?

> Do we see in the profits of capital—the truly industrial factor on
> which Ricardo, as well as Karl Marx, concentrated all his
> attention—the benefit taken by the employer from the worker,
> whose labor he has been able to render more productive without
> proportionally increasing the remuneration of that labor? If so, then
> it is necessary to say that all the syndicalist customs that the English
> worker has been able, progressively, to impose on the employer in
> view of improving his economic situation, imply a real beginning of
> *joint control.* It is not yet a system of "industrial democracy," but a
> mixed system in which the aristocratic element steadily retreats
> before the invasions of the democratic element. And, in some firms
> where labor organization has been perfected, one has the impression
> at times of an almost totally realized industrial democracy. . . .
>
> Or, on the other hand, do we see the commercial factor, that
> is, the profit taken by the capitalist not from the producer he has
> hired and to whom he pays a low price for his labor, but rather the
> profit taken from the consumer who he succeeds in making pay
> more for his products than the cost of their production?[80]

In both cases, the pay of workers would go up, and the tensions between
labor and management would continue. But the contrast marks the different
directions desired by workers and management. "The workers talk about
participation in the management of the business. The employers reply by
talking about participation in profits and concede to the workers, in the most
favorable cases, only a bastard form of *joint control*."[81]

Halévy suggested that the Whitley Councils could move in either direction, but that the direction favoring management was the more likely. This
was evident in the arrangements of the first councils. These tended to be
structured around keeping management in place and raising the prices of
finished products to offset increases in wages and profits. It was the sort
of cooperation between management and labor that management tended to
support, presenting it as designed to work to the advantage of both parties as
long as the finished products could be sold. The success of such agreements
depended on markets, of course, and they were often accompanied by calls
for protectionist legislation that would assure domination of the domestic

market. The logic of these arrangements, as Halévy pointed out, was an implicit renunciation of any notion that workers of the world would unite to eliminate the profits of the "idle class." And because of this, it was perhaps not a surprise that many socialists rejected such arrangements. Their notion of what the councils should attain was predicated on notions of workers asserting more control over management decisions, including marketing and price; and on this front, they were frustrated.

Halévy was also concerned that while national and district councils were set up, there were in fact very few committees on the shop floor—that is, committees in which workers would have predominant influence. Even the big unions were not strongly in favor of such local committees, as they potentially would compete with the centralized administration of the unions. Halévy summarized the result: "Distrusted by employers and unions alike, the *Works Committees* have made only modest progress. As a result, the idea of a system of *joint control* has suffered. . . . I do not foresee exactly an active revolt [by workers] against the industrial council, but rather a growing skepticism until the time when the institution, insofar as it differs from a simple *Conciliation Board*, becomes obsolete."[82]

What in fact occurred in England, however, was not the widespread creation of Whitley Councils but rather the creation of a National Industrial Council during the crisis of 1919. This did not assume that the class struggle could be transcended, and for this Halévy gave the new council high marks. It was, in essence, a national conciliation board for negotiation when disputes between employers and workers led to an impasse. This was a moderate solution that Halévy favored. He implied this in a letter to Xavier Léon following his visit to mines in Wales in April 1919. He reported positively that the syndicats in Wales were more like English labor unions, and not like the more revolutionary French syndicats of the Confédération Générale du Travail. He sounded hopeful that in all areas of Britain, except Ireland, "the experience of democratic socialism" would likely arise, not "without troubles, but with the minimum of disorders."[83]

Halévy concluded the 1919 essay on a relatively optimistic note, arguing that such a national council, acting as a conciliation board, was the characteristic English way of proceeding. It accepted the existence of the class struggle, but confronted this with an institution that would encourage discussion and compromise. There was nothing like it in continental European countries, where the class struggle was more contentious. Halévy feared that on the continent class tensions would lead to violence: either "crushing the working-class insurrection in blood or . . . resolving the social question by the dictatorship of the proletariat." But, this was "continental language, not British language. The English method and language are the method and language of parliamentarianism."[84]

When Halévy returned to the issue of labor in England in March 1921, in an address to the *Comité national d'études politiques et sociales*, he again commended the English for avoiding the rhetoric and action of revolution, but the tone of the essay was much more pessimistic. The English would avoid revolution, he reasoned, because of political and cultural traditions, and because both strains of English socialism opposed it. Fabian socialists like Sydney and Beatrice Webb understood "industrial democracy" to mean a system in which industries were "subject to the government of a democratic state." Guild socialists like G. D. H. Cole and S. G. Hobson did not call for a takeover by the state, but instead the establishment of worker control of industrial enterprises. Halévy referred to Guild socialists as "moderate syndicalists" to distinguish them from revolutionary syndicalists in France, arguing that, unlike their French counterparts, they called for a nonrevolutionary transition and for a number of functions to be assigned to the democratic state.[85]

Halévy again discussed the creation of the Whitley Councils, and again pointed out that the shop floor "works committees" were few in number and not organized in a manner to advance the program of worker control. He came to the conclusion that the Whitley Councils that existed functioned as traditional conciliation boards, and indicated "the recognition of trade unions by the state in England."[86] But, critically, they did not initiate worker control. The actions of the large powerful unions went in a similar direction: there was a push in 1919 for worker control, especially among miners, but ultimately it fizzled.

What was new in this article was Halévy's increased pessimism concerning working-class influence on the councils and, closely tied to this, his changed assessment of the demands and goals of workers. While previously he had assumed that workers would continue to embrace the syndicalist goal of worker control, he now concluded that workers were more interested in higher wages, shorter working hours, and job security.

> I predict, among the working class, the decline of this great movement of propaganda for worker control, because it does not correspond perhaps to the profound needs of the proletariat in large-scale industry.

What the working class demands is not participation in the chances of gain, and with them the risks of loss, both inseparable from the management of a large enterprise. The working class is eager for security; workers want a stable wage and guarantees against unemployment.[87]

"I do not see, in all this business," he wrote, "a beginning of what I have earlier called worker control."[88] In short, Halévy came to the conclusion that the appeal of Guild socialism among workers had been ephemeral, existing from the early years of the twentieth century to about 1920.

A year later, in 1922, Halévy again wrote about the state of the social question in England, and the conclusion was even more pessimistic. In part, this was because he saw working-class poverty and frustrations growing, and could see no way that their demands could be met. In April 1921, he wrote to Xavier Léon that "the situation for workers here is serious."

It seems beyond doubt that workers are marching to their defeat. Working class leaders take this into account and only reluctantly give the order to go into battle. It is necessary that things finish in this manner; but one cannot fail to sympathize with these poor devils who had been promised, in order to prevent them making revolution during the war, the earthly paradise after the peace, but who are now denied that which one is not able to give them, and who go quite simply to die of starvation.[89]

As before, in 1922 he summarized how the war had led to state monopolization of British commerce: it "decided what exports and imports could be allowed; it restricted civilian consumption; it operated all the coal mines; it ran all the railways and the entire merchant fleet; it manufactured munitions and controlled all the industries that affected the conduct of the war in any degree."[90] The question facing the English after the war, he suggested, was what would change or remain the same now that the imperatives of war no longer weighed on the nation. Halévy pointed out that four years earlier, in 1918, most people assumed that many of the wartime changes would be permanent. This was supported by the program of state control publicized by Lord Haldane and by Fabian socialists like the Webbs. Moreover, laws were passed in Parliament in 1919 to address the issues of housing, utilities, transportation, and energy. There was opposition by Guild socialists like

G.D.H. Cole who called for worker control of industries, not state control; and there was some opposition by the owners of industries, who felt threatened by both the Fabian socialists and the Guild socialists. Ultimately, however, the way things worked out frustrated the hopes of socialists of both varieties. Halévy reasoned that this was due to a number of factors. One was the conflicting demands of Fabian and Guild socialists.

> Bureaucratic collectivism and *Guild Socialism* were very far from reinforcing each other to bring about the realization of a system in which, beginning with the mines and the railways, the political state and the trade union would share the management of industry between them. On the contrary, as it happened, they canceled each other out. Capitalism, with the help of the government, played them off against each other, and very cleverly used the *Guild Socialism* of Mr. Cole to escape the bureaucratic collectivism of the Webbs.[91]

Another essential player in this development, as this quotation indicates, was the government. Prime Minister Lloyd George, according to Halévy, progressively reduced his support for socialist reform as the militancy of workers decreased in 1919. "The problem for him and is associates," Halévy wrote, "was no longer how to obtain the necessary powers to nationalize the railways dictatorially. The problem was to liquidate as quickly as possible the embarrassing question of nationalization by returning to the normal prewar system."[92]

Also critical in this rollback of socialist advance, according to Halévy, was the action of the leaders of the Labour Party. No longer were they advocates of collectivization. Rather, they pushed for higher pay and better conditions for workers. They dropped the fight for joint control of management, thereby accepting that capitalists and the state would be left in control. Even though there was a notable strengthening of working-class organizations, working-class leaders were becoming more moderate in their demands. "One cannot say that the recent liquidation of the laws that brought all the industry and commerce of the kingdom under national control was accomplished over the resistance of trade-unionist and Labourite leadership. It was done with the connivance—let us go further and say with the collaboration—of this leadership."[93]

Finally, echoing the point he had made in his speech of 1921, he pointed out that workers accepted these changes without significant protest. They too seemed content to trade away decision-making power for promises of higher pay, better conditions, and more security. In short, whatever socialist rhetoric remained among workers and Labour leaders, it was belied by moderate action. Halévy pointed here to an important generational shift in the cultural interests among Labour activists. He noted that the famous Fabian socialists were now in their sixties and that the famous Guild socialists were in their thirties; younger militants, in their twenties, were drawn to neither, and instead were enamored of Sigmund Freud and Bertrand Russell—that is, psychoanalysis and individualism. Socialism of either the Guild or Fabian variety was losing favor, even as the Labour Party continued to grow.

All of these factors—the growth of state bureaucracies during the war; the centralization of political and economic decision-making; the acceptance of this by Labour Party leaders; the post-war failure of plans for the nationalization of industries; the actions of government leaders like Lloyd-George; the "collaboration" of Labour leaders; the post-war decline of working-class demands for "worker control" in exchange for higher wages and security—led to change. All of these were important elements in Halévy's assessment of the fate of British socialism after the war.

It is useful, in assessing Halévy's new perspective, to compare his post-war stance with the one he had taken in his 1906 article on the distribution of wealth.[71] Halévy had argued in this article that the market was not "natural," but was rather an institution that gained its legitimacy by its popular acceptance. The market, in short, was a system of conventions that regulated economic exchange, and, he further argued, these conventions were a result of decisions made by associations of humans. As such, new conventions about economic relations could be conceptualized and institutionalized. The desired method of making these decisions about the market, according to Halévy, was dialogue and cooperation among producers; in essence, an extension into the economic arena of the political process of deliberation and compromise that had been introduced into politics by the French Revolution. The ideal organization of the economy would be to make it an arena for judgment, moderation, and cooperation, including the active participation of "associations of producers." One of the main reasons that inequities still existed in France after 1848, he suggested in this article, was that the people, including workers, accepted "aristocratism;" that is, they accepted hierarchy and inequality. He hoped that a peaceful process for progressive economic change would be found acceptable as workers came to reject the hierarchical view that had such power in the middle of the nineteenth century. Halévy remained concerned that the class divisions of modern industrial societies could disrupt this process, and that conflict would develop. But, given the proper context—England offered the model—a peaceful resolution of what he came to call "the social problem" was possible.[95]

After the war, Halévy concluded that the changes introduced by the conflict, as enumerated above, had undermined the chances for such a peaceful process unless it was inextricably tied to nationalism.[96] Halévy retained some sympathy for non-authoritarian socialism after the war (see, for example, his article on Sismondi, published in 1933).[97] But, the war had eliminated the tension within socialism between the liberationist and organizational strains in favor of the *étatiste* version. In 1934, he characterized his postwar disappointment with socialist parties in the west as "the bitterness of disappointed expectations."[98] He believed, in short, that only state socialism remained a viable option, and despaired that there was no longer much hope for a socialist "redistribution of wealth" through negotiation and compromise that was not directed by the centralized state. Workers would continue to press for higher pay and better working conditions, but any hope for their participation in formulating policy or in the management of industry had been jettisoned; negotiation and compromise seemed less and less likely. Halévy's consistent assumption about workers after this date was that their goals were confined to higher wages, shorter hours, and better conditions of work. His conclusion after 1922 was that moderate syndicalism or Guild Socialism was not possible. Why? As he wrote in 1934: "I believe that it is the psychology of workers that accounts for the failure. They want better conditions, higher salaries, fewer hours of work. But the responsibilities of the direction of affairs frightens them; they willingly leave these to the captains of industry."[99]

Moreover, by accepting the control of industry by management, with the collusion of the leaders of the Labour Party and the state, the force of nationalism was reinforced. This was the trajectory that would increasingly worry Halévy. The new labor-management understanding was intimately interrelated with the reinforcement of protectionism and nationalism. Therefore, all forces seemed to converge for a strengthening of the state, now viewed as necessary for raising tariffs to protect domestic sales, for conquering new foreign markets, for the profits of industrial investors and managers, and for the wages of workers.

This assessment was a central element of Halévy's growing post-war pessimism and fatalism. Fifty years ago, R. K. Webb, the historian of England

and the translator into English of *The Era of Tyrannies*, argued that these "three articles . . . document an important biographical fact—the dashing of Halévy's English hope."[100] I think that this is correct. I would only add that a central element of this was that they document the dashing of Halévy's hopes for the influence of a non-authoritarian form of socialism—for the moral critique and working-class perspective that he had believed, before the war, producers and their associations would contribute to dialogues concerning the distribution of wealth. His view of socialism, subsequently, stressed its "organizational and hierarchical" nature.

This is confirmed by his later writings. In a review of G. D. H. Cole's *Workshop Organization*, published in 1923, Halévy stated that the syndicalism of the Shop Steward Movement in England was only "a transitory episode in the history of syndical organizations."[101] In a 1926 review of Cole's *Organized Labour: An Introduction to Trade Unionism*, he pointed out that while in 1918 Cole had been optimistic about the success of worker control of industry proposed by Guild Socialists, by 1924 he had come to the conclusion that syndicalism in England was declining.[102] Halévy even began to see signs of this conservative turn of British labor taking place before the war. In the first volume of the *épilogue* to his *Histoire du peuple anglais au XIXe siècle* (covering the years 1895–1905), published in 1926, Halévy discussed the conservatism of British labor, noting how many workers were happy to accept a system, "dangerous for the consumer," that would tie their wages to the profits of employers.[103] Six year later, in 1932, he noted that in the years before the Great War some labor organizations were preparing for class war, but that in general labor unrest in England during this era "constituted so many victories for *étatisme*."[104] As the years passed, Halévy would become even more categorical about the connection of socialism with the growth of centralized state power. These would become closely associated with his perception of other troubling developments: the erosion of transnational intellectual exchanges, the growth of selfish economic interests, the emergence of charismatic strongmen, and the expansion of thought control by the state—what he famously termed "the organization of enthusiasm." These are the focus of the following two chapters.

## Halévy and Alain Once More

As Halévy became more pessimistic about the prospects of moderate socialism, and more concerned about the growth of state power, it is useful to contrast his thought with that of his friend Alain. As we have seen, there was a strain in their relationship caused by their differing stances on the war. They, nonetheless, continued to share a great deal, not least concerning the changing nature of the economy and the appropriate role of workers and their organizations in relationship to these changes.

Alain had commented very positively before World War I on Halévy's 1906 article on the distribution of wealth. He agreed with Halévy that the market was not "natural," but was rather an institution that gained its legitimacy by its popular acceptance. The market, in short, was a system of conventions that regulated economic exchange, and these conventions were a result of decisions made by associations of humans. As such, new conventions about economic relations could be conceptualized and institutionalized. The desired method of making these decisions about the market, according to both Halévy and Alain, was dialogue and cooperation among producers; in essence, this was viewed as an extension to the economic arena of the political process of deliberation and compromise introduced by the French Revolution.[105] The ideal organization of the economy would be to make it an arena for judgment, moderation, and cooperation. Halévy, however, was concerned that the class divisions of modern industrial societies would not permit this peaceful process, and that conflict would develop. Alain was more optimistic, always insisting that will and reasoned judgment could, and should, prevail. He was also less pessimistic about the growth of administration and organization, and less worried about the prospect of class conflict.

While Halévy was becoming more pessimistic, Alain continued to write about the importance of will and justice in all areas of human life, including in the economic arena.[106] He rejected all fatalism concerning the conditions of the market, just as during the war he had rejected Halévy's "fatalism" concerning the necessity of continuing the war. In his *Propos*, for example, Alain wrote the following about striking workers: "What, then, do they [workers] want? No longer to be the tools or the means, but to be ends. That the just salary be defined, not by the price of work in the market, but as the condition of a human life, where will be counted all the needs, all the leisure that a man needs; the care if he is sick; the rest if he is fatigued or old. Understand by that that there are some salaries that the employer has no right to offer, and that the worker has no right to accept."[107] Again, Alain's hopeful idealism crossed with Halévy's less roseate assessment of industrial reality.

## *History of the English People in the Nineteenth Century,*
## Volumes 2 and 3 (1923)

Halévy was primarily identified by the public, and primarily identified by himself, as a historian of nineteenth-century England. Not surprisingly, therefore, it was to his multi-volume history of England to which he was anxious to return after the war. While he worked on his articles and lectures about nationalism, about the social question, and about the relationship of workers to the state, he was also completing two new volumes of his magisterial history. These new volumes of *Histoire du peuple anglais au XIXe siècle*, which covered the years from 1815 to 1841, were published in 1923.[108]

Any brief summary of a history that extends over 600 pages is unlikely to do justice to the range of topics covered and the detail and subtlety of the portraits and analyses. This is certainly true when confronting Halévy's two volumes. As with the previous volume *L'Angleterre en 1815* (published in 1912), these new volumes cover many subjects, though there is more attention than in the previous volume to the sequence of events, to the internal struggles within and between political parties, and to the reform of government institutions. There are descriptions of leaders and luminaries, but more broadly the focus is on the people of Britain; their economic struggles, their political and social dispositions, their patriotism, their national peculiarities. Not surprisingly, Halévy touched on general issues that remained at the center of his thought: the importance of philosophical traditions; the issues of liberty and social justice; the tensions among these and, more broadly, the manner in which these developed in Great Britain.[109]

Halévy noted in the "preface" of volume 2 that the war had changed his view of some things. Before the war, for example, he had been charmed by the foreign policy of George Canning; now, he preferred the more conservative policy Robert Peel.

> If we had lived during the era of Canning, it is probable that
> . . . we would have rejoiced to see him so successfully dividing,
> teasing, and flouting the reactionary, mediocre, and mean govern-
> ments, objects of scorn and of hatred for all generous hearts. And
> even if we had written ten years ago [before World War I], perhaps
> we would have pardoned Canning many of his adventurous actions,

which continually led him to the brink of war. An entire phraseology
was at our disposal then, very plausible, to explain that in many
cases war is progress, movement, and life. But we have, in the interval, learned to know war. We now feel an instinctive distrust for a
statesman who made a career of diplomatic difficulties, and whose
career shone most brightly when world affairs were most troubled.
. . . We would not be able to resist the pleasure of citing, when we
encountered them [Canningites] . . . : "Men delude themselves
when they believe that a war consists entirely of a declaration, a
battle, a victory, a triumph. The survivors think not of the widows
and orphans of the husbands and fathers who have fallen on the
field of battle."[110]

After World War I, having seen war, Halévy carried a far more favorable
attitude toward all things that were in the interest of peace. As a consequence,
he now judged Peel more reasonable than Canning, "a far more resolute
friend of peace."[111]

Volume 2, which covers the years 1815–1830, begins with an analysis of
the fiscal and economic problems following Waterloo and the Congress of
Vienna, and it concludes with the death of King George IV and the beginning of the reign of William IV. The extensive treatment of the issue of
post-Vienna government finances suggests that Halévy had become more
sensitized to fiscal issues because of the economic problems of post-Versailles
Europe, much on everyone's mind when the volume was published in 1923.
The early chapters focus on how the various political parties and national
leaders addressed the issue of the national debt that burdened England as
a consequence of the high costs of fighting the revolutionary wars against
France.

The other issue given prominence in this volume, one related in obvious
ways to the issue of the national debt, was the succession of economic crises
in 1816, 1819, and 1825. The textile centers in the north and center of the
country were especially hard hit, and the result was significant labor unrest
and government repression, most famously the confrontation at Spa Fields
on December 2, 1816, and the St. Peter's Field Massacre ("Peterloo") on
August 16, 1819. Halévy argued that these outbreaks of working-class activism
were class rebellions driven by economic discontent. Workers, especially in
the textile centers, were paid low wages and faced a high cost of living. During the trade depressions created by the periodic cycles of overproduction,

they faced severe conditions and, in Halévy's own words, "found themselves reduced to starvation."[112] The middle and upper classes, on the other hand, obviously more comfortably off and less threatened economically, were shocked at the massive scale of working-class action, and terrified by what seemed like anticipations of a French-style revolution. The political class responded with bills that suspended Habeas Corpus and that restricted free press and the right of assembly.

Halévy also devoted many pages to analyzing the convergence and divergence of the issues of tax reform, franchise reform, and tariff and custom reform. There were periods when the campaign for the reduction of taxes was joined by those favoring the extension of the franchise and the elimination or reform of the Corn Laws; this was true, for example, when workers and progressive manufactures closed ranks against the landed class during the economic crisis in textiles in early 1819. At other times, however, supporters of these various causes diverged; for example, when Radicals called for suffrage reform and free trade, but faced the opposition of manufacturers who joined with the landed class to keep the suffrage restricted and the Corn Laws in place.

Other issues cut across these political and economic developments: most notably, religious reform and foreign policy. On January 19, 1821, Castlereagh laid down for the first time in a public document the principle that was the touchstone during this era of English relationships with other countries: the policy of non-intervention in foreign disputes. The principle was generally accepted by subsequent leaders like Canning and Wellington, though Canning was more willing to threaten military action. On the religious front, it was during Wellington's term as Prime Minister (1828–1830) that the Test and Corporation Act was repealed (1828), eliminating the legal restrictions on non-Anglican Protestants, and that Catholic Emancipation was instituted (1829), allowing Catholics to be elected to Parliament.

Volume Three covers the years 1830–1841. It focuses on the Liberal ascendancy: of the governments led by Charles Grey (1830–1834) and William Lamb, 2nd Viscount Melbourne (1834 and 1835–1841). Little attention is given to the personal lives of these leaders, or of other important figures, beyond their professional actions. There is nothing, for example, about Melbourne's problematic personal life. The focus in on the maneuverings of the various parties and their leaders to pass or impede important reform bills: the Parliamentary Reform of 1832 that extended suffrage; the Emancipation Act of 1833 that abolished slavery throughout the British Empire; the Factory Act of 1833 that restricted the work week of children under 13 years to 48 hours; the Poor Law of 1834 that established the controversial workhouses. Halévy analyzed the waxing-and-waning of religious influence, noting that, building on the reforms of the late 1820s, there were secular advances, such as making the admission to the University of London free of religious allegiance, and also the establishment of a civil registry of marriages that allowed non-Anglican Protestants more freedom (both enacted in 1836). But, he also points out that there was continued religious influence, in the retention of the requirement of Anglican adherence for entry into the universities of Oxford and Cambridge, and in the Evangelical spirit that animated Anti-Corn-Law meetings, which Halévy believed mirrored the enthusiasm of Methodist meetings during the eighteenth century.

The volume ends with an extended discussion of the Chartist movement and the agitation to eliminate the Corn Law tariffs. Drawing from his previous work on Philosophical Radicalism, he emphasized the importance of Utilitarian philosophy for both movements, though in different ways. Bentham's philosophy, he reminds the reader, had two distinct aspects. The first aspect was the idea that society was in part the creation of the legislator, who represented an activist state that imposed positive law. Utilitarian philosophy, he writes, was "an authoritarian doctrine which looks to the conscientious intervention and a scientific sort of government to realize the harmony of interests."[113] The second aspect was the idea that society was considered "a spontaneous product of the wills of individuals, beyond all constraint of the state."[114] Cobden and his free-trade supporters in the Anti-Corn-Law League favored the second aspect, because they, like Bentham, believed that the state should not intervene in the economy with mercantilist restrictions; however, unlike Bentham, they disliked state intervention in all its forms. The Chartists were drawn to the first aspect of Benthamism, because they demanded state action to provide popular education and to protect workers by such mandates as a minimum wage. Leaders of the Chartist movement also demanded political reform, and some of them, disciples of the co-operative socialism of Robert Owen, proposed further social reform. Halévy points out, however, that popular Chartism generally was restricted to the economic needs of workers, which made them susceptible to the appeal of Anti-Corn-Law activists who claimed that free trade would reduce the cost of food. Though the Corn Laws would not be repealed until five years after Melbourne's government had fallen, and five years after the close of this volume, Halévy was explaining the positions of the forces which would lead in 1846 to the elimination of the grain tariffs that had benefited landowners.

Halévy seemed to imply that the Manchester Philosophy of free trade and limited government was prevailing over the Westminster Philosophy that celebrated the benevolent intrusion of the state. He showed that the mercantilist restrictions cherished by the trading and maritime interests and the protectionist restrictions favored by the landed interest were giving way before the interests of the manufacturing and working classes, groups that would benefit from the lower food costs brought about by the free trade of grain. On the other hand, Halévy did not ignore government-initiated reforms, like the Irish Church Reform Bill (1833), the commutation of the tithe (1836), and the Dissenters' Marriage Bill (also 1836). Such laws, along with the other important government-sponsored reforms enumerated above, indicate that the state was intervening to provide a regulative framework for industry, labor, police, transportation, and religion.

These volumes demonstrate the consistency of Halévy's argument about the distinctiveness of England and English culture. As in his previous scholarship, he pointed to an English character that demonstrated the intertwining of individualism and moralism—the latter strongly resting on the legacy of Evangelical Protestant Christianity. It was this combination of individualism and moralism that, in Halévy's opinion, explained the reasonableness of English political culture. And this, when combined with Utilitarian Radicalism, was what explained the manner in which, during the early years of the nineteenth century, English politicians and political thinkers began to imagine ways in which the state should intervene to remedy the inadequacies of this individualistic approach. The results were limited before the Victorian era, of course, but it was during this earlier era that the first steps were taken for the state provision of essential services, for the funding of public schools, for the protection of workers. It would take the strengthening of labor organizations and the sociological revolution of the late nineteenth century to push such reforms ahead in a comprehensive way, but they were built on the reforms introduced in this period. Halévy made them the center of his history.

## CHAPTER 9

# "The World Crisis"
# Reconsidered

## (1924–1932)

As long as we have not developed a fanaticism of humanity powerful
enough to counter-balance or to absorb our fanaticisms of nationality, we cannot blame our state leaders for our own sins. We search
sooner for reasons to excuse them when, in the event, they feel themselves forced to cede to the pressure of our fanatical and disinterested
emotions.

—Élie Halévy, "The World Crisis (1914–1918)"

Halévy decided in 1923, following the publication of the second and third
volumes of his *History of the English People in the Nineteenth Century*, to write
an "epilogue" to his history of the nineteenth century before completing the
volumes on the Victorian Age. This epilogue was published in two volumes:
*The Imperialists in Power (1895–1905)*, published in 1926, and *Towards Social
Democracy and Towards War (1905–1914)*, published in 1932.[1] He also presented a series of lectures on the war at Oxford in 1929.[2] This chapter focuses
on Halévy's analyses of the forces leading to World War I and the transformation of European culture that ensued.

Halévy also continued to be attentive to postwar European issues, focusing especially on the rise of Fascism in Italy, the evolution of Bolshevism in
Russia, and the coming to power of Nazism in Germany. He concluded that

these regimes had similar features and were able to thrive because of the radically changes circumstances created by World War I. Halévy came to believe that these tyrannical regimes, combined with the transformed world out of which they had emerged, presented daunting challenges for liberal democracies. How, he wondered, could democracies resist totalitarian regimes without themselves becoming tyrannical? He was not optimistic. He feared that liberal democracies, facing the new era created by war and revolution, and inhabiting a world order populated by charismatic leaders able to "organize enthusiasm," would be forced, if they were to survive at all, to change in unfortunate ways. These issues were the focus of his reading and lectures during the 1930s, and they provided the backbone of his famous essay in 1936 "The Era of Tyrannies." These issues are examined in the next chapter.

### History of the English People in the Nineteenth Century, Epilogue, Volume 1: The Imperialists in Power (1895–1905) (1926)

The decision by Halévy to focus on British history in the years leading up to World War I involved a return to a consideration of empire, a topic, as we have seen, that had already received his attention, most notably in his short book *L'Angleterre et son Empire*, published in 1905.[3] In that book, he noted the growth of British interest in empire during the second half of the nineteenth century and argued that it represented a move away from the free-trade and commercial focus of the previous decades. This corresponded, he pointed out, with a qualification of the noninterventionist "balance of powers" orientation that England had adopted earlier in the century and represented a move toward forming alliances with other nations for national security.

Imperialism was the most important dimension of this new configuration. It was supported because it was believed to provide economic benefits: new markets for goods not sold at home; arenas for the investment of surplus capital; the assurance of access to natural resources. In addition, it was supported for cultural reasons: the so-called civilizing mission of transporting superior institutions and ways of life to less advanced areas. And it was supported, finally, because it was believed to provide national strength vis-à-vis the other great powers. Halévy maintained that it was this combination of economic self-interest, nationalistic passions, and the lofty ideals of the "white man's burden" that recommended empire to the English people. Disraeli, he suggested, "invented imperialism" during his administration between 1874 and 1880. But it was under the subsequent political leadership of Gladstone and Salisbury that England expanded its reach with a more aggressive form of imperialism. And it enjoyed its true flourishing during the leadership of Joseph Chamberlain, who appealed to the enthusiasm for empire to undergird his own political popularity. The power of the attraction of empire was demonstrated by the fact that, even though some colonies were not economically beneficial, they remained popular.

Halévy had been attentive in his book of 1905 to the effect imperialism had on British mores.[4] Like Alexis de Tocqueville, who had celebrated the potential link between French colonial action in Algeria and the growth of "virtue" and patriotism among French citizens, Halévy was impressed by the link between British imperialism and a change in British mores. While Tocqueville was positively impressed, however, Halévy believed the effect was negative. He believed that empire was contributing to the rise of a disturbing nationalism and, at the same time, eroding the work ethic for which the British were justly celebrated. "By the expansion over non-industrialized territories, does not England tend to become a nation no longer composed of industrial workers but of capitalists and administrators; no longer of men who work but of men who, in order to live, take a portion of the work of others? But, is it not from this idleness, to which the exercise of the functions of command condemn them, that superior races degenerate?"[5] Moreover, the fact that the English denied civil liberties to colonial populations was a fundamental violation of a basic national principle, a qualification of one of the superior ideals associated with the nation.

Halévy's correspondence and subsequent published works provide a consistent criticism of the growing enthusiasm for empire during the late nineteenth and early twentieth centuries among the general British population and among its political leaders. He lamented to his friend Célestin Bouglé, for example, that the virus of colonization seemed impervious to democratic forces.[6] In his 1918 article "Les souvenirs de Lord Morley," he noted the transition of England from a country devoted to liberty to a country enamored of increased nationalism and a new enthusiasm for empire.[7] It was, however, in the volumes of the history of the English people published in 1926 and 1932—in the epilogue volumes to his *History of the English People in the Nineteenth Century* that dealt with the period 1895–1914—that the focus on empire became central. Halévy analyzed empire in terms of its relationship to British world power, and also in relationship to internal cultural and political changes the country was undergoing. On both fronts, empire was inextricably connected with the run-up to the war in 1914.

There is no evidence that Halévy gave as much attention to the French Empire. The one significant exception was his expressions of discomfort during a trip to Tunisia and Algeria in the spring of 1897, discussed above. His correspondence indicates that he was shocked both by the poor conditions of the indigenous population and the brutality of the French. "Above all, I have been overtaken by a disgust, impossible to overcome, of the proceedings of the colons vis-à-vis the colonized."[8] But he also had nothing complimentary to say about the indigenous people and earlier settlers in the region. "It is a very mediocre civilization that we have demolished by entering here. . . . But it is a very lamentable civilization that we have put in its place. . . . I fear that this is above all the fault of the French 'colons.' "[9] Implicit in Halévy's comments is the not uncommon assumption of the superiority of French civilization, joined, however, by a lament that the French colonial population and administration was not representative of this, and not able to impose this on the indigenous population in North Africa. "We reproach the Arabs for having too much originality, and for not assimilating to our civilization. All this would be possible, if we had a little political genius. But we do not. We have the genius for political chaos, which is not the same thing."[10] These comments indicate a concern with the well-being of the indigenous population of North Africa and a belief that no improvement would be brought about through imperial conquest and settlement. Halévy suggested, in another letter to Bouglé in 1913, that aid for the Algerian people should be on the agenda of the Ligue des Droits de l'Homme.[11]

The first volume of his epilogue focused on empire, but it also explored, like the earlier volumes, a wide range of issues. Halévy gave special attention to how local and national leaders reflected wider public debates about internal problems and international affairs. He pointed to changes within continuities: how, for example, in this period, as in earlier ones, lords and gentry enjoyed political power, but how their wealth now frequently came, not from land, but from industry, business, and investment.[12] And, as always, behind the detailed account of events, there is his concern for the stability, liberty, solidarity—but also the inequality—that Halévy believed was a central feature of English society. What is striking, especially if one reads these volumes after those dealing with the earlier years of the nineteenth century, is how much more troubled he had become about the direction of change.[13]

Eighteen ninety-five marked the end of a half century of Liberal political dominance and the rise to power of the Conservatives and "Unionists," of Lord Salisbury and Joseph Chamberlain.[14] This corresponded chronologically, Halévy suggested, with the growth of socialism and with a significant shift in British cultural attitudes, including enthusiasm for empire, which in turn affected the trade and foreign policy of the nation.

The rise of socialism was marked by the growth of unions demanding legislation protecting workers, and by the emergence of important intellectual figures calling for socialist reforms. These would bear fruit, but only following a difficult period for militant labor in the late 1890s, symbolized by the failure of the strikes by engineers and Welsh miners in 1897 and by unpropitious legal decisions that made unions financially liable for the actions of individual union members. In spite of these setbacks, however, the era saw the growth of working-class organizations and parties, the election of Labour politicians in the early years of the new century, and the passage of social legislation, beginning with accident protection for workers in 1897. The passage of social legislation would accelerate after the Liberals regained power following the elections of 1906. Halévy remained impressed with the moderate nature of British socialism, especially in contrast to contemporaneous developments on the Continent. "When the spirit of Continental revolution reaches England," he wrote, "it acts like a shell that explodes in a ploughed field and does no damage."[15] But he nonetheless worried about the long-term implications, writing that in England "an alliance has been concluded between the intellectuals and the proletariat. In all countries, such an alliance is dangerous for the bourgeois order."[16]

The cultural change England underwent during this decade was arguably even more important. It was marked by the growth of popular religious indifference; by a decline of economic individualism and of the "appetite for work"; and by the rise of a Kiplingesque moral code that was chaste, brutal, heroic, and childlike. These, as we shall see, cohered nicely with the rise of imperialism, about which more below. Halévy referred to the cultural change as the rise of "decadence," though he remained impressed with the elements of continuity in British culture that he had noted in his earlier volumes of the history of England: the instinctive groping for practical solutions, the mutual tolerance, and the willingness to compromise.[17] But the change was significant, for it was related to a loss of confidence, a perception that other nations, like Germany and the United States, were progressing more rapidly than England, which, in turn, reinforced a domestic perception that England was beginning to fall behind.

The fear of national decline prompted education reform, which led to tensions between denominational religious schools and secular schools, all brought under heightened central government control by the education bill of 1902. It was also related to the decline in "high culture," in the influence of utilitarianism, and in the "morality of self-interest." There was new attention given to German philosophical thought (Thomas Hill Green); to theories that recognized the state as the repository of moral traditions (Bernard Bosanquet); to theories that insisted that individual interests should be subordinated to the interests of the state (Benjamin Kidd); and to theories that looked to Darwinian struggle as the template for understanding human affairs (Rudyard Kipling).

Closely related to this cultural shift, according to Halévy, was a new enthusiasm for empire. The broad support of imperialism, he suggested, resulted from the anxiety concerning the potential decline of the country mixed with robust strains of commercial greed and idealism.[18] Empire expressed the former because, he argued, it was assumed that it would help strengthen the English economy in this era of increasing competition, by establishing control of new markets and new sources of raw materials. At the same time, empire allowed the outpouring of a curious idealism, because it was assumed that it would bring to less developed peoples the advantages of British institutions, industrial know-how, and culture—the improvements of "civilization" realized as a result of the white man's burden. One indication of this cultural shift was the attack on free-trade doctrines by Chamberlain and others, accompanied with calls for the establishment of "export bounties" and/or tariffs to protect British industries and goods. Another sign was the new bellicosity of the British media and British culture: broad support for the Americans during the Spanish-American War (1898); nationalistic enthusiasm during the Fashoda Incident between France and Britain in East Africa (1898–1899); "a fit of patriotic frenzy" during the Boer War (1899–1902).[19]

Moreover, this strong support for empire was true not just in the ranks of Conservatives but rather reached across the political spectrum. Most Liberal leaders—Lord Rosebery, Edward Grey, Henry Asquith—supported empire, as did Fabian socialists like George Bernard Shaw and Sidney and Beatrice Webb. The latter socialists opposed, in a manner that clearly irritated Halévy, the "the right of small people to determine their own governments."[20] Even radical Liberals like David Lloyd George, who opposed the Boer War, attacked the gold mine profit makers, and appealed to British humanitarianism, did not insist on Boer independence. Empire, in short, had broad support. By the late 1890s, Halévy wrote, "a wave of imperialism swept over the country, and . . . hatred of the foreigner—of the Germans, of the Russians, of the French—prevailed over hatred of the domestic enemy, the hatred of race prevailed over the hatred of class."[21] The few surviving stalwarts of Gladstonian orthodoxy, committed to free trade and peace, were, in Halévy's words, left with "the bitter and proud satisfaction of feeling themselves an elite group, lost in the midst of a mob of lunatics."[22]

It was the same sense of national "decadence" and vulnerability that led British leaders to pursue a new foreign policy, one no longer based on "splendid isolation." There was a new sense that England needed allies, which led to attempts at the turn of the century to establish a Pan-Teutonic rapprochement with Germany, but which ultimately led in 1904 to the Entente Cordiale with France. And it led to the broad-based support of strong national defense, which translated into huge increases of appropriations for the navy. Joseph Chamberlain was particularly adept at exploiting the warlike passions of democracy for the support of empire and military growth, but few British political leaders or cultural figures were immune.

## "The World Crisis (1914–1918): An Interpretation" (1929)

After the appearance of the first volume of the epilogue in 1926, Halévy turned his attention to the second volume, which was to focus on the origins of the war. His preparation of the second volume of the epilogue was facilitated by his being named, in 1928, to the commission of historians formed by the French Ministry of Foreign Affairs to publish the secret diplomatic documents of the immediate prewar period. He worked with French colleagues like Charles Appuhn, Pierre Renouvin, and Sebastien Charléty, and also with G. P. Gooch and Sir George Aston in England.[23] He published an account of the work of the commission in an article in 1929.[24]

The broader context was also important, however. Halévy was anxious about the convulsions rocking contemporary Europe, and his lectures and scholarship turned increasingly to these: the origins and effects of the war; the emergence of authoritarian rulers in Italy and Germany; the changes in the Soviet Union as Stalin took power and the New Economic Policy was dismantled. This also was a period of strikes in England, and his thinking about issues leading up to the war was no doubt influenced by his witness of these strikes in 1926.[25] Sympathetic to the demands of workers, and recognizing the miserable conditions of miners, Halévy nonetheless lamented the social costs of the strikes.

In 1929, Halévy was invited by the University of Oxford to be the Rhodes Memorial Lecturer. He delivered three lectures, published under the title "The World Crisis of 1914–1918: An Interpretation." The lectures were a resounding success and secured Halévy's reputation in England. They provided a trenchant analysis of the underlying forces that had led to the outbreak of the war, and of the forces, unleashed by the war, that continued to have an impact on postwar Europe. There were three lectures: toward revolution; toward war; and war and revolution. They made the case that war and revolution were essentially intertwined in Europe between October 1912 (the beginning of the first Balkan War) and August 1920 (the date at which the last postwar treaty was signed). They registered Halévy's growing pessimism.

The essential element in this connection of war and revolution was the widespread desire of people for national liberation and national grandeur. Halévy disputed the thesis that the main cause of war was economic conflict, suggesting that the international ties between capitalist enterprises made most industrial leaders desire peace. He also pushed back against the argument that specific decisions by national leaders in the weeks before the war were the main cause of the outbreak of hostilities. He referred to these immediate decisions as "pills to cure an earthquake" and insisted that these were less important than "the collective feelings and movements of public opinion, which, in the early years of the twentieth century, made for strife." The most important of these was nationalism, which had led to "the earthquake itself."[26] Not only was this nationalism a powerful force that had undergirded imperial expansion by established European countries, as mentioned above; nationalism also came in the form of a new ideological enthusiasm for national or colonial liberation.

This latter "revolutionary principle of nationality" spread rapidly after the Russo-Japanese War of 1905–1906, according to Halévy. In his words, it "sent a thrill through the whole Asiatic continent. It now appeared that the Europeans were not the demigods they believed themselves to be, and had so long, by armed pressure, compelled the whole non-European world to believe."[27] In the years after the 1905 Revolution, the ideal of revolutionary nationalism, combined with a militant liberalism, spread first to China, India, Persia, and Turkey, and then to southeast Europe, where it led to the crisis of the Austro-Hungarian Empire and to the Balkan Wars. Halévy argued that World War I grew out of these conflicts in the Balkans.

The Great War was a war for the liberty of the people from its inception: not from the day when German armies violated the neutrality of Belgium—this was only an incident in the course of a war that had already begun—but from the day when, with the murder of Archduke Franz Ferdinand, the insurrection of the southern Slavs began. . . .

We should ask, not *who*, but *what* was responsible for the three declarations of war; and the answer should be: "The rotten condition of the Austro-Hungarian Empire, the fact that the revolutionary principle of nationality was at work within its limits, and that it was about to break up into a number of independent States." If so formidable an event as the dismemberment of Austria occurred, nothing short of a miracle could prevent its developing into a general war. European diplomacy did not work the miracle. And there was war.[28]

In central and eastern Europe, the rise of nationalism in the early years of the century had also inflamed Pan-German and Pan-Slav passions. It was this nationalism and these passions, more than economic competition or the machinations of national leaders, Halévy argued, that had led to war. The war itself, of course, exacerbated these nationalistic passions, something Halévy himself had experienced in France.

The other factor that transformed the nature of the conflict, and led to the problems facing postwar Europe, was revolution, especially the form this took in Russia in 1917. According to Halévy, conflicts between socioeconomic classes were not annihilated by the war, even if they were overwhelmed by nationalism in 1914. Class tensions were only briefly submerged. Before the war, economic inequality and elite indifference had led to class antagonisms. Halévy characterized the situation in the newly industrialized districts of Europe in the following way: "There, huge masses of suddenly congregated wage-earners faced minorities of arrogant task-masters, monopolizers of wealth, upstarts of industry."[29] This led to the popularity of various socialisms. In Germany—the most highly industrialized Continental nation, though one with "a political regime of feudalism and absolutism" the dominant strain of socialism took form within the Social Democratic Party. This party was doctrinally Marxist and revolutionary but programmatically pragmatic and moderate; it played "a clever and successful game, constantly making new recruits, constantly teaching them patience at the same time as hope, pursuing a policy not so much of revolutionary action as of revolutionary expectation, a policy of waiting."[30] The centers of the "revolutionary spirit" of European socialism were France and Russia, not Germany. In France, there emerged two radical movements, which sometimes coincided: first, revolutionary syndicalism, which called for the "direct action" of the general strike to put workers in control of workshops and factories; and, second, revolutionary Hervéism, which called for a violent coup de main by soldiers against the state in the event of a declaration of war. In Russia, the revolutionary spirit was carried by the Bolsheviks, who called for a Marxist-inspired revolution, and by the Social Revolutionaries, who appealed to traditional institutions like the village *mir* but also condoned terrorism and the wholesale assassination of government officials. Halévy judged these and other European socialist movements to have been serious threats to peace in the prewar years. "No responsible statesman," he wrote, "would have said, at the beginning of 1914, that he felt safe against the perils of some kind of revolutionary outburst."[31] Nonetheless, they did not lead Europe to revolution or conflict; nationalism did.

When these "class against class" forces reemerged during the war in Russia, however, they were of the most revolutionary variety—a revolutionary syndicalist-like militancy against capitalism combined with a Hervé-like pacifism against the war. These, Halévy argued, were instrumental in the toppling of the government of the tsar in the Revolution of March 1917, and this, in turn, created the chaos that allowed the Bolsheviks to take power through the coup of October 1917. The Russian revolutionary leaders did not ignore the nationalism. They reimposed state control of the economy during the period of the Civil War and also reinforced nationalist sentiments in the population. Revolution and nationalism were mutually reinforcing. The Russian Revolution, Halévy concluded, "had acted as a solvent of imperialism for the benefit, not so much of Communism, or even of socialism, as of nationality."[32] The Bolshevik victory also strongly influenced radical movements in other parts of Europe.

It was the combination of nationalism and state socialism that troubled Halévy. He believed that the war had transformed Europe irrevocably. He was one of the first to observe how much discontinuity the war had brought about. There were postwar continuities with prewar forces, but the pre-1914 world was gone forever. As the title of his lectures indicated, Halévy believed the war years 1914–1918 marked a "world crisis." To make this point, he rehearsed his argument about how the war brought about increased control of industry from above—that is, a form of "state socialism" that conformed to the desires of some prewar socialists, but at the expense of the hopes of others—syndicalists and Guild socialists—who desired working-class control. And he emphasized that this was frequently combined with a new fervent nationalism. Even the entry into the war of the United States in 1917—applauded by Halévy for making "the victory of the Allies a decisive victory"[33]—strengthened the forces of nationalism, because it was carried out under the ideological umbrella of Woodrow Wilson's ideal of national "self-determination."

Halévy judged that the end of the war had not brought about a waning of "national fanaticism." Instead, it was proving to be "more formidable than the fanaticism of humanity" or of the "fanaticism of class."[34] The popular enthusiasm associated with assertive nationalism was the root cause of the conflict, and he worried that it remained a central problem. "As long as we have not developed a fanaticism of humanity powerful enough to counterbalance or to absorb our fanaticisms of nationality, we cannot blame our state leaders for our own sins. We search sooner for reasons to excuse them when, in the event, they feel themselves forced to cede to the pressure of our fanatical and disinterested emotions."[35] This did not mean that Halévy denied the importance of economic and imperial tensions. These clearly were significant historical developments, as his analysis in the epilogue volumes of his *History of the English People* confirmed. But, in his mind, as emphasized in his famous lectures of 1929, it was the popular enthusiasms for national grandeur and national independence that were the key developments that caused the outbreak of the war. Not only had fanatical nationalism led to the carnage of 1914–1918, it was again threatening the peace of Europe in the late 1920s.

### *History of the English People in the Nineteenth Century, Epilogue, Volume 2: Towards Social Democracy and Towards War (1905–1914)*

Halévy focused explicitly on the origins of the war in the second volume of the so-called epilogue to his history of the English people during the nineteenth century, published in 1932 (and quickly translated into English).[36] It was entitled *Vers la démocratie sociale et vers la guerre (1905–1914)*, and, as the title suggests, the main framework of the book was to show how both Unionists and Liberals, even as they pushed through important social legislation, pursued a military policy devoted to empire and national defense. They voted credits for the expansion of the navy and supported extending the reach of the British Empire. The pursuit of these policies was, in Halévy's opinion, most surprising for the Liberals, who historically had been attached to the Gladstonian traditions of free trade, anti-imperialism, and hostility to the state and militarism. Once returned to power following the elections of 1906, however, they found themselves administering a vast empire, responding to working-class demands for state-directed reforms, and supporting the piling up of armaments. It is this history, and its relationship to the outbreak of war in 1914, that is at the center of Halévy's concerns in this new volume.

Because Halévy wished this to be a comprehensive history of the English people, he gave space to many issues. He discussed in detail, for example, both the "feminist revolt" and the issue of Irish independence.[37] The biggest *internal* issue, however, and the one to which Halévy gave the most detailed consideration, was the rise of labor and the manner in which the political leaders and parties chose to deal with working-class demands. Halévy argued that Marx had been accurate in predicting the decline of unskilled labor. "Sooner or later the competition of the machine must put an end to the workshop without machinery and to domestic industry. . . . The atrocious suffering of such labor will be sufficient to render its continuation impossible."[38] This did not lead England to revolution, however; nor is there any indication that Halévy lamented the fact that Britain did not descend into Marxian class war. Quite to the contrary, he remained complimentary of English moderation and pragmatism, and implied that he approved the legislation that promised to give assistance to disadvantaged workers. It was important, he wrote, that legislation be passed "to facilitate the transition from the regime of domestic labor to the regime of the factory equipped with automatic machines" and that employers, who were in actual contact with their workers, be made responsible for the welfare of workers.[39] He commented favorably on proposals for a graduated income tax to "remedy the inequality of wealth," and more generally "to use public finances" to provide assistance to the poor.[40] Bernard Shaw, he pointed out approvingly, had attacked the hypocrisy of a liberalism that accepted poverty as inevitable. Halévy remained committed to the redistribution of wealth that he had outlined in his article of 1906.[41]

There was important social legislation passed in Britain during these years, of course. Halévy argued that this was largely because of the demands and pressure brought to bear on Unionist and Liberal leaders by working-class activists and socialist intellectuals. In Halévy's words, when it came to passage of social legislation, the political leaders were "resigned more than enthusiastic."[42] Halévy seems little surprised by the extent of this spirit of resignation, noting that even the representatives of labor who rose into the ranks of government often came to identify with the possessing classes. "Some men of humblest origin were raised to political power on a program of war against the power of wealth, and, as ministers, if they became ministers, came to occupy in England a position that permitted them to put on a good show in a society based on the inequality of wealth which they denounced."[43] The result was a moderation of fervor on the part of working-class representatives. Lamentably, society, though "democratic in form," remained "plutocratic in fact."[44]

This did not diminish the demands of workers and their advocates, however, which grew more intense because of a combination of cultural and economic change. On the economic front, there was, in fact, contrary to Marx's prediction, no immiseration of the working class. But there *was* a growing discontent among workers concerning the disparities of wealth in society. Moreover, in the decade before the war the price of commodities was rising more quickly than wages, and this led predictably to working-class disaffection. The issue of inequality, Halévy suggested, was becoming more widely recognized, not just because of the behavior of the rich, but also because of publications that highlighted the disparity of wages and of the distribution of wealth. Halévy noted that analysts in 1905 had made it clear to the public that one-half of the total income of the United Kingdom was in the hands of one-ninth of the population, and that more than one-third of the total was in the hands of one-thirtieth of the population. These statistics led to broad support for legislation reforming income and inheritance taxes, and for introducing social legislation to protect the underclass.[45]

Equally significant, however, was the cultural element. Halévy insisted that this was as important as stark economic inequities for explaining why such a flurry of social legislation was passed in the years before the outbreak of the war. He characterized this cultural shift as nothing short of a moral revolt: a revolt by a lower class that no longer viewed itself as responsible for its poverty; and a revolt by an upper class that increasingly flaunted its wealth and power. Among both groups, the restraints connected with "the Protestant ethic" were becoming weaker. "The causes of the revolt which was now gathering strength is of a moral order. We are witnessing the decay of that Puritan asceticism which made the proletariat ashamed of its poverty as of a crime for which it was responsible, and which led the wealthy to regard its own enrichment, by work and saving, as the fulfillment of a duty. The wealthy now wanted to enjoy, to display its luxury; and the intellectual and working-class revolt is a response to this ostentation."[46]

The attempt to pass social reforms was at first frustrated by the Conservative opposition in the House of Lords. But once this was neutralized during the constitutional crisis of 1909–1911, there was passage into law of an impressive group of reforms: insurance against accidents and sickness (1906); an eight-hour day for miners (1908); old age pensions (1908); minimum wages for miners (1909); labor exchanges (1909); progressive taxation (1909); national insurance against sickness and unemployment (1911). These reforms did not exhaust the demands of workers, however. In fact, many workers in the years before the outbreak of war experienced a decline in real wages, and the result was an increase in working-class agitation. There were new strikes between June 1911 and May 1912, and another wave of strikes in 1913–1914. There was also, however, Halévy pointed out, more collective bargaining within the framework established by Parliament. The Board of Trade and the conciliation boards were becoming more effective, indicating that many workers were more accepting of the new order than the flurry of strikes might suggest. Even in the years 1910–1912, when revolutionary syndicalism was so vocal, Halévy suggested that cooperation between the trade unions and the government had become closer.[47]

The combination of these changes, in turn, led to new dispositions, new political alignments, and new concerns. On the one hand, there was a conservative reaction, one with which Halévy clearly had little patience. In a passage that is uncharacteristically charged with evaluative emotion, he expressed his impatience with those he called "the clubmen": "One knows these men who, very ignorant of public affairs, curse every day, as they smoke their fat cigars, against the tragedy of the era and against what they call the vulgarity of democratic *moeurs*."[48] More significantly, Halévy believed that the cultural and legislative changes of these years transformed Britain in ways that were not entirely positive, however necessary and justified these changes were in addressing social needs. His concern was that the new commitments of the government had altered the relationship between society (including its political representatives) and government (including its bureaucracy). He was worried about the emergence of what we would term the "administrative state": "There has been a singular reversal from the point of view of the history of British institutions. Formerly the English had prided themselves on having created the representative system in order to control bureaucratic power and to restrict its vague desire for action. Now, they are setting up a new bureau-cracy to control their representative assemblies and compel these assemblies to act."[49] This organizational-bureaucratic dimension of the changes intro-duced in Britain before the war was given a higher visibility in the writings Halévy produced after World War I than in his earlier works. This is not surprising. It corresponded with his heightened awareness of the importance of similar, but even more dramatic, administrative changes introduced during the war. And all of these were inextricably intertwined with his new sensitiv-ity to the convergence of nationalism and bureaucratic growth that, in his mind, undermined the prospects for liberty. These changes were also con-nected to his new assessment of socialism, as we saw in detail in the last chapter.

Another focus of the volume of 1932, extending here the analysis pro-vided in the volume published in 1926, was the importance of empire. Empire, as we have seen, was discussed in Halévy's 1905 book *L'Angleterre et son Empire*, and it was a centerpiece of the first volume of the epilogue. But in 1932 there were new elements that Halévy chose to emphasize, in particular those connected with the conflicts to which all empires seemed to give rise. These included, obviously, the rivalries between and among imperial powers. But equally and perhaps more important were the tensions between and among the indigenous peoples within the empires. Returning to a theme of his 1929 lectures on "the world crisis," Halévy now emphasized how these nationalistic forces often led to overlapping conflicts. They took the form of the colonized against the colonizers, often entailing revolts against Western domination. But they also took the form of rebellions and wars between and among the emerging national groups within empires. As peoples became newly conscious of their cohesiveness and their strength, their impatience with rule by imperial powers was joined with impatience with the potential domination by other emerging national groups. Halévy referred specifically to the nationalist revolts in Egypt, in Bengal, and in what became Turkey.[50] And, of course, he analyzed extensively the various nationalist rebellions and wars in the Balkans—the struggles by national groups against Ottoman and Austrian rule, but also the struggles among the emerging "nations." It was these nationalist revolts, especially those in southeastern Europe, and the manner in which they engaged the nationalistic passions of the major Euro-pean powers, that led to war in 1914.[51]

Halévy devoted many pages of this final volume to the foreign policy of Britain and to the sequence of events leading up to this end of the "epilogue" of the nineteenth century. There is careful analysis of the transformation of international relations under Wilhelm II, and of the sequence of events that marked the new century as it headed for war: the Tangier episode (1905); the Conference of Algeciras (1906); the Russian-English Convention (1907) concerning Tibet, Afghanistan, and Persia; the Young Turk revolution (1908); the Austrian annexation of Bosnia-Herzegovina (1908); the Agadir crisis (1911); and, of course, the assassination of Franz Ferdinand and the descent into war. These events were, in essence, the opening acts of the new century that Halévy viewed with such misgivings.

Halévy made no argument that there was a single "cause" of the war. One contributing factor was clearly the arms race. Halévy carefully analyzed the reorganization of the British Army under Haldane and the reorganization of the navy under Fisher. He provided an extensive discussion of the naval race between Britain and Germany, "At every turn," he wrote at one point, "we are brought back to the struggle between the two navies."[52] But a good part of the momentum for naval construction was the toxic combination of nationalist fanaticism and economic interest, an economic interest that involved a broad swath of society, because any slowdown would entail not only loss of revenue for the investors and the industry but also the loss of jobs. There was, that is, a close mutually supporting interrelationship between the government, the military, the private shipbuilding industry, and labor.[53] There was no phrase like the one coined by Dwight D. Eisenhower—"the military-industrial complex"—but Halévy clearly charted the emergence of just such a coalition of interests.

Did, therefore, capitalism lead to war? Halévy undertook a careful examination of this argument and found it to be part true and part false. It was part true to the extent that capitalism did often lead to money and merchandise looking for foreign opportunities and foreign markets, and this could easily lead to conflict with the capitalist interests of other countries. It was part false, however, because many industrialists were in favor of industrial cooperation in some areas. Halévy noted the example of the exploitation of mineral wealth in North Africa, which had led to cooperation among various European powers.[54]

Ultimately, it was nationalism across the Continent that was responsible for the outbreak of hostilities in 1914. This nationalistic virus was especially inflamed in southeastern Europe, where groups wished to achieve political autonomy. This entailed revolt against the Ottomans, the Austrians, and other emerging nations. But the nationalist virus was powerful everywhere in

Europe. Even the strikes of 1913–1914 in Britain were no impediment to this, because they were not in any way a revolt against patriotism in the name of class loyalty or a revolt animated by a conviction that it was necessary to abolish capitalism. The strikes were in the pursuit of more restricted objectives like the increase of wages and the reduction of hours in the work week.[55] Nationalism remained a powerful force in England, as it was across Europe, and more than anything else, this is what led to war in 1914.

CHAPTER 10

# The Era of Tyrannies

## (1932–1937)

What to do? . . . It would not be so grave if one could return to the
state of things when we were twenty years old [in 1890]. Then, all
the world armed. . . . But at that time, Europe was politically and
socially stable. It is very different today. What will be the *external*
repercussions of the internal disequilibrium?
                    —Élie Halévy to Xavier Léon, 4 June 1934

We traverse the era of tyrannies. And what gives strength to these
regimes is that they are aided, in what remains of the democratic
countries, by the secret sympathy of the conservative parties, on the
one hand, and, on the other, by the pacifism of the popular parties.
                    —Élie Halévy to René Berthelot, 8 August 1935

The mid-1930s were difficult years for France. The Great Depression, which
began in other parts of Europe in 1929, hit France in 1932 and ultimately
weighed more heavily there than anywhere else. French political leaders dealt
ineffectively with major economic and fiscal issues, which prolonged the crisis. There was no strong support for a Keynesian policy of stimulation before
1936, and successive French governments followed a policy of deflationary
austerity: as the economy slowed and tax revenues declined, expenditures
were cut, aggravating the downward spiral. When England and the United
States devalued their currencies in 1931 and 1933, respectively, France could

have (and, most would argue, should have) followed suit. Devaluation was postponed until 1936, and the result was that French exports remained relatively expensive and uncompetitive on international markets. Exports dropped by two-thirds between 1928 and 1933. As prices fell, peasants, small businessmen, and shopkeepers experienced especially serious suffering after 1932, and modern businesses that did not adjust quickly also faced dramatic losses. It is telling that the French economy did better in 1929 than during any subsequent year before 1950. France was the only major industrial power whose level of production in 1939, at the outbreak of World War II, was still lower than it had been in 1929.

The instability of the economy was reflected in the turbulence of politics. Left-leaning governments in 1932–1934 (the "Cartel des Gauches" led by Édouard Herriot) and 1936–1938 (the "Popular Front" led at first by Léon Blum) faced opposition from the financial and economic elite (*le mur d'argent*), temporized, and failed to introduce fiscal and economic policies appropriate to the crisis. These governments of left-leaning Radicals and Socialists alternated with the right-leaning governments led by Gaston Doumergue, Pierre-Étienne Flandin, Pierre Laval, and others. These tended to follow the traditional conservative economic policy of austerity (as did the Cartel des Gauches), which, not surprisingly, alienated labor and the Left. The economic problems associated with the Depression undermined political stability; there were no fewer than eleven governments between 1932 and 1936.[1]

Economic frustration and government ineffectiveness spilled over into political anger and provided fertile ground for rumors of government corruption. Political parties in the moderate middle lost support to the right-wing Leagues and left-wing Communists. The most dramatic breakdown of propriety and peace was the Stavisky Scandal of 1934, a financial scandal that became a political one and led to the antiparliamentary riots of 6 February 1934 in Paris. The police responded with the use of live ammunition that killed fourteen demonstrators and injured fifteen hundred—the highest number of casualties in Paris between the suppression of the Paris Commune in 1871 and the liberation of the city at the end of World War II in 1944. The result of the demonstration and repression was widespread shock. It led to another government crisis (Édouard Daladier resigned after having been in power for less than two weeks) and marked the beginning of what Julian Jackson has called "a French civil war lasting until 1944."[2] Political parties that worked within the electoral system were outflanked by radical groups on the Right and Left that recommended violence and attacked the culture and institutions of the Republic. Robert Paxton states that French politics in the years after 1934 faced a "crippling polarization."[3]

One of the most dramatic episodes was the angry physical attack on 13 February 1936, of the socialist leader Léon Blum (sixty-four years old at the time) and Georges Monnet and his wife by a group of anti-Semites and royalists on the boulevard Saint-Germain. Blum was left bloodied and hospitalized but survived to become the leader of the Popular Front government three months later. This rise to power of the unified Left speaks to the popularity of republican institutions in France, even in this difficult period. Nonetheless, Blum was in power for only thirteen months, and the vigor of antirepublican movements was undiminished.[4] The shrillness of voices on the radical Right continued.[5]

The early 1930s also brought, of course, international crises. François Goguel has argued that the fall of Édouard Herriot's cabinet in December 1932 marked the end of hopes for European reconciliation, a hope that had emerged in the mid-1920s with the Locarno Treaties and with Germany's entry into the League of Nations.[6] Other historians would cite, as the critical date, Hitler's appointment as Chancellor in January 1933. But the crucial point is that everyone, or at least everyone who cared to look, recognized that a new era had opened. Many continued to hope that some reconciliation of differences between France and Germany was possible, but as the years passed, with the remilitarization of the Rhineland (March 1936), the Austrian *Anschluss* (March 1938), the Munich agreement (September 1938), the German occupation of the Sudetenland (October 1938), and finally the occupation of the rest of Czechoslovakia (March 1939), fewer and fewer retained any hope that a military confrontation between France and Germany could be avoided. After Munich, polls indicated that 70 percent of the French people favored resisting further German demands; after Germany occupied Prague, 45 percent believed war would occur before the end of the year.[7] Halévy, as we shall see, came to this conclusion earlier than many of his contemporaries. While in the years after World War I he had had a favorable attitude toward all things that were in the interests of peace, when he weighed the dangers of Fascism and Nazism in the early 1930s he came to the conclusion that peace was no longer a likely option, and that even if it was, the result would probably be worse than war.

The early 1930s also brought new aggressive intellectual attacks on "bourgeois" prudence and philosophical moderation. Paul Nizan's *Les chiens de garde* was first published in 1932, with its unapologetic attack on previous

French cultural movements and intellectuals, singling out for special denunciation Halévy's friend and associate Léon Brunschvicg. Also in 1932, the left-Catholic Emmanuel Mounier founded *Esprit*. Though not as aggressively strident or as politically radical as Nizan, Mounier shared with him an attachment to absolute commitment, and he too opposed the tradition of republican individualism and what he called the false abstractions of "the ideology of 1789." In the previous year, 1931, Jean-Pierre Maxence had taken over the *Revue française*, and with the help of Thierry Maulnier and Robert Brasillach turned it into an antipolitical review that called for the "primacy of the spiritual." As David L. Schalk has pointed out, after 1932 everyone was attacking materialism and formalism, and trumpeting the need for "engagement." Nineteen-thirty-two, he suggests, was a year of "cruel reawakening" that should be marked off from the late 1920s, a time that seemed in retrospect "years of illusion."[8]

"Engagement" could signify any move to more active involvement, however, and in this restricted sense the term is appropriate for the interventions of Halévy in the era of the Dreyfus Affair and, again, during the 1930s. He, too, became "engaged" during these periods of political crisis in France. But his humanist engagement in defense of the Republic was fundamentally different from the spiritualist orientation of Mounier and Maxence, and different as well from the criticisms of "natural law," "human nature," and epistemology (all important for Halévy and his friends) that animated Nizan.[9] During the interwar years, there emerged a lacuna between the Kantian rationalism of Halévy and his associates, on the one hand, and, on the other, the broadly defined "generation of 1914." The divide became even more pronounced as phenomenology and existentialism became the new intellectual fascination of French intellectuals after World War II. Martin Heidegger's move to ontology, already important in Germany before the war, became a central assumption for Jean-Paul Sartre, Emmanuel Levinas, and others of their generation during and after the war. The epistemological orientation of the neo-Kantians, with its embrace of reasoned republican politics, was left far behind.

## The Future of Europe

Halévy was overwhelmed with work during the 1930s. He was attempting to finish another volume of his *Histoire du peuple anglais* devoted to the Victorian Age. Once this volume was completed, he contemplated taking a break of two years to edit and organize his extensive notes on the history of European socialism—a reorganization and rewriting that, unfortunately, was never realized. And he was occupied with duties related to the *Revue de métaphysique et de morale*, which increased significantly because of the serious medical problems of Xavier Léon, who died in 1935. The weight of organizational and editorial work fell on Halévy's shoulders. Halévy was also frequently approached to give lectures and participate in conferences, though he attempted to keep these to a minimum. As he related to Xavier's widow, Gabrielle, in June 1937, the weight of obligations was heavy. "Honestly, during the last year, I have done too much for my strength, and my personal work has suffered as a consequence."[10]

Much of the heaviness of Halévy's attitude, however, was due to the state of affairs in Europe. Halévy's actions and publications during the early 1930s indicate increasing anxiety, as the economic crisis worsened, aggressive nationalism spread, and European democracies faced growing threats. In 1931, for example, Halévy discussed in his correspondence the economic problems facing Europe, suggesting that the inevitable crisis of overproduction, like the one that Europe was facing, was a consequence of capitalists searching for markets and profits in more areas of the world. He noted that France "suffer[ed] less than other countries, because it is more behind, less industrialized." But, the economic difficulties were becoming more widespread everywhere and, unfortunately, "given the scale of these problems, MacDonald and Briand, Pierre Laval and Mussolini are nothing but ridiculous puppets."[11]

In February 1932, he made a presentation at the Nouvelle école de la paix focusing on how to move toward a durable peace in Europe.[12] In it, he expressed his well-known respect for English moderation, pointing out that England continued to be a country that valued political liberalism and freedom of expression, largely because the overwhelming majority of English people agreed that fundamental policy differences should not lead to civil war. He spoke with great respect of British optimism, and of what he called the cultural "amalgam, alloy, synthesis" that made up "English equilibrium," that "mélange of intellectual confusion and practical confidence, of modesty and pride, of sincere internationalism and exclusive nationalism."[13]

But the main pitch he made in the address was to challenge political leaders in England and France to solidify the alliance between the two nations. In the current troubling context, he argued, this alliance was at the center of all hopes for European peace. Unfortunately, there were significant areas of tension. Many in England, for example, had put aside their hate for Germany, which had been intense during World War I, and concomitantly were frustrated with the belligerent stance the French government continued to take vis-à-vis Germany. Halévy suggested that the change of British opinion was related to the fact that Germany was no longer seen as challenging Britain on the high seas. He worried that a serious discord between England and France was developing and argued that both countries needed to adjust their positions to strengthen the alliance.

There were three specific areas of difference between the allies that Halévy believed needed to be resolved. The first was reparations. On this issue, he firmly took the British side. He argued that the French were being unreasonable to expect reparations to solve the debt problems that were a consequence of the war; moreover, it led to understandable German resentment. It was necessary, he reasoned, to resolve the issue of war debt without continuing to punish Germany.

The second issue was disarmament. Halévy claimed that the argument in favor of disarmament rested on the naive belief that the security of nations could be provided by the international community through the League of Nations, which had the power of punishing aggressors with economic sanctions and/or with military intervention. Unfortunately, the League had not shown itself willing or able to do either. When Japan invaded and subsequently annexed the province of Manchuria in 1931–1932, for example, the international organization did not act. Halévy was also unimpressed with the Kellogg-Briand pact of 1928 that had condemned military actions for the resolution of international disputes. The signatory nations, he pointed out, had outlined no recourse beyond rhetorical condemnation in the event of a violation of the terms of the treaty. Finally, he pointed out that while England had supported, or had remained largely silent, during the discussion of these agreements, it had never mentioned that the logic of such agreements was that similar moves toward disarmament should be made on the naval front. The British, of course, would resist any such move, and would insist that they should continue to enjoy "the domination of the seas."[14] Halévy did not recommend naval disarmament, but he thought a forthright recognition of the difference was needed and suggested that it was dangerous to push the democracies toward disarmament of their land forces.

The third issue was the call for revision of the territorial clauses of the peace treaties of 1919, an idea that he feared was growing in popularity in England. He suggested that discussions of border modifications raised concerns about the security of the "successor" states Yugoslavia, Czechoslovakia, and Poland. "What is the solidity of these new states? Will they not soon be menaced in their integrity, perhaps in their existence, by a Germany which will not for long remain disarmed? Will it then be the case that respect for the treaties, and that concern for the independence of people, will lead the English to take up arms against Germany?"[15] Halévy did not doubt that there were unpleasant aspects of these treaties, but he strongly believed that Germany should be given no hopes that changes might be forthcoming. Any such hopes—even false ones—would "inflame German chauvinism": "It is necessary, if one truly places the concern for the peace and justice of Europe above everything else, to insist on the sacred character of the treaties of 1919, [and] if one revises them, with regret, and as little as possible, on such-and-such point of detail, to always do so in a manner that does not place in peril the major elements of the treaty."[16]

Halévy also had some harsh words for the French. In addition to criticizing French rigidity on reparations, he suggested that the attempt to rapidly expand the size of the navy was unnecessary as long as the French-English alliance remained in place. Given domestic problems (obviously alluding here to the economic problems France was beginning to face), he wrote: "It is on the seas above all that our ambitions are able to be disproportionate with our politics."[17] He also was irritated that some politicians insisted that the "natural frontier" of France was the Rhine River. Such nonsense, he pointed out, could only succeed in reviving "the vision of an incurably Napoleonic France."[18]

Halévy ended on a somber note ("our situation is grave," he wrote), but he refused to give in to despair. He recognized that individuals were often impotent before large forces, but he disagreed with the pessimism of French intellectuals like his friend Alain, who adopted a stance of resignation before fate. Halévy claimed, instead, that "man is able to triumph over the appearance of fatality if he knows to acquire the will and technique of peace."[19]

A little over a year later, in April 1933, Halévy had a heated public exchange with his contemporary and friend Théodore Ruyssen[20] at a meeting of the Société français de philosophie.[21] The exchange was about nationalism. Ruyssen supported a form of juridical idealism that insisted on the importance of minority rights protected by international communities like the League of Nations. Halévy expressed skepticism that this was sufficient, arguing that the new regimes of Mussolini and Hitler would ignore international rules that attempted to limit their power. "In the twentieth century, what are the new phenomena? It is, for ten years Mussolini, and it is Hitler. One speaks to us of the rights of minorities, guaranteed by a super community of States, the League of Nations. However, the degree to which one obeys is the degree to which one limits the sovereignty of states. But do states accept this limitation?"[22] Halévy implied that Mussolini and Hitler clearly would not countenance such a limitation. In the dialogue, Ruyssen and Dominique Parodi[23] pointed to principles—respect for minority rights and federalism (Ruyssen) and universal moral principles (Parodi)—principles for which Halévy had deep respect. But he insisted that the current historical context impelled one to recognize that the central issue to be faced was the power of unreasonable nationalist sentiments. "For twenty or thirty years, each time that I have encountered a Belgian, and our conversation has moved to the conflict that divides the Flemings and the Walloons, I have asked my interlocutor why the Belgians don't adopt the Swiss model, why don't they federalize their country, with the people of each province becoming free to speak the language that they wish? But no, I have always felt that I had hit an implacable fanaticism. Two nationalisms collide, and between them all conciliation seems impossible."[24]

Things did not improve, of course. Looking back in 1937, Halévy recognized that the uprising of 6 February 1934 was a disturbing watershed. "It is from the uprising of the 6 of February 1934 that all our misfortunes date."[25] But his correspondence also noted the Italian invasion of Ethiopia; the outbreak of the Spanish Civil War; the threatening stance of Germany against Czechoslovakia. By early 1937, Halévy was complaining that the combination of crises was making him dizzy ["crée une vague impression de malaise"].[26]

The depth of his anxiety for the stability of Europe led to a marked political-intellectual divergence with his brother, Daniel, who, in the interwar years, devoted his attention to writing essays and to editing a prestigious collection of novels and essays—the "cahiers verts"—for the publishing house Grasset. As Sébastien Laurent points out in his recent biography of Daniel Halévy, the themes of his writings remained very much the same as those before World War I: defense of classicism against the new literature; an attachment to ancienne France. What changed was his move toward the political right wing, closer to Maurice Barrès's cult of the soil and the dead. Most striking about Daniel Halévy's writings of these years is what was missing. There was no political analysis of Fascism or Nazism; no description of racism and/or anti-Semitism. While Élie was writing about the dangers confronting liberal democracies, Daniel was becoming more critical of liberal democracies.[27] They were moving further and further apart ideologically. In July 1931, Élie wrote to Daniel about the latter's new book, *Décadence de la liberté*: "You are always a member of the center left of the extreme-right, which leaves the reader a bit perplexed. And this 'decadence of liberty,' one wonders—I wonder myself—if you don't experience a sensual pleasure in describing it, finally to persuade us that there is no point defending what remains of it. What good does it do to save one's head if one has already been decapitated?"[28]

## The Soviet Union, Italy, and Germany

While his professional reputation was based on his books devoted to English history and on his lectures about the history of European socialism, Halévy also devoted a great deal of time after World War I to studying the changes taking place in Russia, Italy, and Germany. He prepared lectures on postwar changes in these countries, focusing especially on the rise of authoritarian movements and leaders. The notes to these lectures indicate that he was introducing new elements into his analysis of postwar Europe.[29] He seemed to be particularly interested in the socio-economic changes that resulted when Communist and Fascist leaders took control, and how they successfully organized and channeled the nationalistic enthusiasm that the war had exacerbated.

The most fully developed part of Halévy's analysis was devoted to the changes introduced by the Soviet leaders following the Bolshevik Revolution. Halévy's lecture outlines divided Soviet history into five eras: a preamble focusing on the Soviet regime and the dictatorship of the proletariat and then four sections covering the "evolution of the regime between 1917 and 1928." The first period was entitled "systematic anarchy" (7 November 1917 to 3 March 1918); the second, "war Communism" (March 1918 to 1921); the third, the "New Economic Policy" (NEP) (1921–1928); and the fourth, the period of return to "integral communism," tyranny, and authoritarianism (after 1928).[30] In his correspondence, when Halévy referred to Russia and the Russian people, he was generally dismissive.[31] He was more interested in the actions and ideological orientation of the Bolshevik leadership.

The history he conceived is a familiar one. He mentioned the painful losses entailed by the Treaty of Brest-Litovsk in March 1918, the outbreak of the Civil War, and the remilitarization of Russia under Trotsky. Economic problems quickly led to the requisition of grain to provision the cities, to the increasing control by the Party of factories and cooperatives, and to the nationalization of land. This allowed the regime to consolidate its control and permitted it "to resist all anti-Soviet attacks."[32] Halévy then provided a brief discussion of Lenin's hope to extend the Revolution beyond the borders of Russia, a hope that was frustrated by the failure of revolution in Germany and Austria, the check of the Béla Kun regime in Hungary, and the victory of the Polish armies led by Pilsudski. Following these checks, Lenin implemented the NEP, which Halévy characterized as "a strategic retreat . . . provisional and partial": "One had given freedom to retail trade, but the development of this commerce was in fact paralyzed by the prodigious extension of the cooperatives. Large-scale commerce remained under strict [state] control. Finally and above all, the monopoly of foreign commerce and the collective property of industrial enterprises was maintained. These were sufficient to limit the concessions to capitalism and to conserve the principles of communism."[33] Halévy then discussed the rise to power of Stalin following Lenin's death in January 1924, and the turn to collectivization under the five-year plans in 1928. He noted the heavy costs of this, but also the economic growth that it initiated. He explained the success of the Bolshevik experiment by the enthusiasm of the Russian people, but also by the strength of the Party, and by use of state terror against any opposition. "The Russian communist party resembles a collective version of the rule of Peter the Great: it works to modernize, to industrialize, to Westernize Russia—not only European Russia but Asian Russia—by the same violent methods that Peter the Great had already employed."[34]

The archive containing Haléry's notes and papers includes numerous pamphlets and newspaper clippings related to changes in the Soviet Union. One from early 1920 describes an interview with Lenin that raised the issue of the famous Twenty-One Points. The interviewer asked Lenin when the present period of "dictatorship of the proletariat" would be replaced by a regime of freedom for unions, press, and individuals. Lenin was reported to have replied: "We have never spoken of liberty. We exercise the dictatorship of the proletariat in the name of a minority because the peasant class in Russia is not proletarian, and is not yet with us. We shall exercise the dictatorship over them until they submit. Gradually their psychology is changing. Our difficulty is that we have no industrial products with which to pay the peasants for the produce which we requisition from them. We therefore have to continue printing paper money, which is nothing more than a promise of payment in kind. I estimate the dictatorship will last about 40 years."[35] There are extensive notes from Lydia Bach's *Moscou: Ville rouge*, William Henry Chamberlin's *The Russian Revolution*, and Alexander Meyendorff's *The Background of the Russian Revolution*.[36]

The Halévys visited the USSR briefly in September 1932. Élie never published anything related to this trip, but his notes and correspondence indicate his disapproval of the nature of the Bolshevik regime.[37] Two years later, he wrote a letter to Étienne Mantoux that expressed his reservations concerning Soviet Communism. Mantoux was considering a commitment to Communism. Halévy vigorously pressed him to ask himself why he would wish to take such a step. If it was because Mantoux believed it would lead to positive practical results, then he agreed that it was an understandable move. If, however, it was simply to take "the most intransigent attitude" that "is the best . . . for disengaging you from all responsibility with regard to a society," then he counseled against it. He suggested that Mantoux look, not to the Soviet Union, but toward Scandinavia and Holland for reforms that would truly help the popular classes.[38] The letter indicates his very pragmatic stance concerning social reform, and his opposition to the particulars of the Soviet model.

His letter to Mantoux also shows how favorably inclined Halévy remained toward progressive social reform. As we shall see below, he believed one needed to assess soberly the historical conditions that European societies faced in the postwar era, and to avoid idealized views of egalitarian socialist societies. He was disturbed that the Left in Western Europe during the early 1930s was infatuated with the Soviet Union. Moreover, he did not believe, as did Léon Blum, that history was inevitably leading to liberal socialism. Utopian protest was foolish, he argued, however strongly motivated by moral ideals. Equally naive were assumptions about the inevitable progress of history. It was necessary to face problems with realistic expectations, and to consider carefully the practical consequences of one's actions. Not unlike his objections to Alain's pacifism during the war, Halévy recommended—to use Max Weber's famous distinction—an "ethic of responsibility" over an "ethic of ultimate ends."

Halévy's analysis of Italy reads like a modern textbook account.[39] Halévy discussed the serious economic problems Italy confronted after the war, as well as the ineffectiveness of the government of Giolitti. He recounted the early history of Mussolini during his syndical and socialist years, and his turn to Fascism after the war. In his Oxford lecture of 1929, he mentioned the early revolutionary stance of Mussolini, and subsequently told his mother how this portion of his presentation had surprised the audience.[40] He described the October 1922 "March on Rome," the vacillation of the king, the refusal of the army to intervene, and the offer of the post of prime minister to Mussolini. Turning to the programs of the new regime, Halévy mentioned that Mussolini had preached an antidemocratic, antiparliamentary discourse in 1921, but that when he gained power he initially imposed a policy of liberal economics, specifically designed to combat the socialists. Little by little, however, Mussolini imposed a corporate system that "conform[ed] to the Hegelian conception of a strong state, in which force is employed for the good of the people and which integrates all national activities."[41] Progressively Il Duce became the head of the entire system. In sum, he "organized enthusiasm" and became a tyrant.[42]

Halévy's opposition to Italian Fascism became more and more personal. Halévy and his brother provided lodging and support to Italian intellectuals fleeing Fascist Italy. Gaetano Salvemini took refuge with Élie in 1924. He was followed by Giuseppe Prezzolini and Curzio Malaparte, both of whom were published by Daniel Halévy in his "cahiers verts" series. Both spent time at Daniel's residence in Paris on the quai de l'Horloge. Élie also became friends with Carlo Rosselli, a leader of the Italian anti-Fascist movement in France, and his brother Nello. They were both assassinated in Bagnoles-de-l'Orne on 9 June 1937, by extreme right-wing French assassins of the Cagoule, working at the instigation of the Italian government of Mussolini. Halévy was in England at the time and was devastated when he received news of their deaths.[43]

The nightmare of developments in Italy paled, however, in comparison with those in Germany. Halévy's account of German developments after World War I emphasized the establishment of the parliamentary system of the Weimar Republic (in spite of the Kapp putsch attempt in Berlin in 1920 and the Hitler putsch attempt in Munich in 1923), and Halévy analyzed the growth of the strength of the state and of industry at the expense of labor. He explained the disaster of Hitler's rise to power by the economic crisis of the Great Depression, which began in 1929, by the machinations of conservative politicians like Franz Von Papen, who orchestrated Hitler's appointment as Chancellor, and by the resurgent nationalism of the German people. He described Hitler as "a fanatic, a visionary whose deep convictions have never changed."[44]

His correspondence leaves no doubt that Halévy viewed the rise to power of Hitler as catastrophic for the peace of Europe. He related in a letter to

Léon how shocked he was when, working in the library at the Athenaeum in London on 3 May 1933, he looked up to see the Nazi flag displayed on the front of the German Embassy next door. "This sinister spectacle demoralized me for the remainder of the morning."[45] Halévy forced himself to recognize the shocking fact that Germany would rearm for war. Two weeks after seeing the unfurling of the Nazi flag in London, he again wrote to Léon. "I do not complain; all that which earns time before the beginning of the next war is that much earned for civilization; and besides whatever is the intensity of the passions to make war, it is still necessary to have arms; and Germany does not have them. It therefore turns its passions against the Jews, whom the Germans have entirely disarmed. It is in 5 or 6 years, when the equilibrium of forces will be reestablished between Germany and its enemies, be it by rearmament of the former or disarmament of the latter, that the situation will become critical,"[46] A week later, he mentioned the "anti-Jewish atrocities" of the German government.[47]

## Socialism and Democracy

The publications Halévy penned in the early 1930s also remained attentive to the issue of socialism. In 1933, he published a short book on Sismondi, and what is impressive is how consistent Halévy remained in terms of his assessment of the positive and negative potentials of socialism. The introduction by Halévy presented a very sympathetic picture of Sismondi (1773–1842) as he confronted the issue of the economic and social problems unleashed by emerging industrialization. While Sismondi in his first publications of 1801 and 1803 had subscribed to a straightforward apology for the unalloyed benefits of the market, by 1818 he had become more critical. Industrialization brought both wealth and misery, he claimed in his *Nouveaux principes d'économie politique* (1819). He challenged a stark Smithian model, arguing that unregulated production dangerously intensified social and economic inequalities. "One nation alone [England]," Sismondi wrote,

> unceasingly shows the contrast of its obvious wealth with the frightful misery of a tenth of its population, reduced to live on public charity. But that nation, so worthy of imitation in so many ways, so dazzling even in her faults, has seduced by its example all the statesmen of the continent. And if these reflections are no longer able to

be useful, at least I shall consider that I have served humanity and my compatriots by showing the dangers of the course she is taking, and by establishing, through her own experience, that basing all political economy on the principle of unlimited competition is to justify the efforts of each individual against society and to sacrifice the interest of humanity to the simultaneous action of all forms of industrial greed.[48]

Halévy was obviously sympathetic to this position, as he was to the attack by Sismondi on the abstractions of the social sciences, and in particular his negative assessment of the theories of the early classical economists. Reality was more complicated than these models indicated. Sismondi, Halévy wrote, "insisted on the complex nature of the subject of social science, [and] being complex, it is variable: hence one can vary them at will, within the limits of what experience shows to be possible."[49]

Sismondi argued that the orthodox theories of the English economists were wrong on two fronts. First, unfettered competition did not benefit everyone, because it led to an inequitable concentration of wealth. Second, such competition led to instability because the increased volume of goods produced would eventually have difficulty finding consumers, leading to "crises of overproduction." What was needed was to manage society so that the general interest would be served. How was this to be brought about? Sismondi recommended giving workers freedom to form groups so that, by uniting their individual weaknesses, they would be able to resist the oppression of the owners of industry. He recommended passing legislation to protect children and to limit the length of the workday for adults. And he recommended moving toward a system by which workers were provided guarantees by their employers against risk and unemployment. Sismondi wanted, in Halévy's words, "economic growth, not paralyzed but regulated by law."[50] Sismondi subsequently expressed sympathy for the uprising of the Lyon silk workers in 1834. He was inclined to believe that the state could intervene to limit production and prevent it from outstripping demand— that is, to avoid the crises of overproduction that inevitably would arise if the market were unregulated.[51] He was not supportive, however, of Swiss democrats who pushed for centralization, so it remains somewhat unclear *how* the "regulation" of the market was to be brought about. It was to be effected, it seems, by a new legal framework resulting from political intervention and a new contractual framework resulting from negotiations between workers and employers.

The positive manner in which Halévy presented Sismondi's theories in 1933 indicates how favorably inclined he remained to the libertarian side of socialism. And it shows how consistent was his criticism of classical economic theories that assumed that the market was "natural," and that the laws of the market were immutable. Like Sismondi, Halévy continued to insist that the rules of economic interchange, and hence the rules that determined the distribution of the benefits of industrialization, were negotiable. Given the changes introduced by industrialization, which brought new class divisions, one could discern the "laws" upon which extant society operated and "the effect of the operation of those laws on the happiness of the individuals who are members of this society." Critically, however, changes could be made. When the effects of the operation of these "laws" is not positive, then "one must find out, on the basis of experience, how it is possible to modify relationships that have nothing immutable about them. This is the art of politics."[52]

The "art of politics" could, of course, lead in various directions, some better than others. Halévy clearly favored the type of adjustments that Sismondi recommended: the redistribution of wealth, the encouragement of arenas where negotiation—political and economic—could take place. But he worried about the authoritarian manner in which some changes had been introduced and the effects of these changes on social relations. In the socialist world, for example, there were disturbing directions in which reforms had come "from above" in ways that reduced the power of workers to make decisions about issues that directly affected them, and in ways that increased the power of bureaucrats and the state at the expense of other groups.

As we saw above, his assessment of changes in postwar England led Halévy to the conclusion that changes introduced by the war, and supported by most groups (including workers), were moving the country toward the type of authoritarian socialism that he disliked. He had concluded that syndical, liberal socialism was unsustainable; étatisme was the order of the day. This was clearly articulated in an address he gave at Chatham House in London on 24 April 1934.[53] He framed his analysis by highlighting what he characterized as the four defeats of British Labour since the end of the war. The first "defeat" recounted the history of the Whitley Councils as told in his writings of 1919–1922: how labor, encouraged by the state, had traded its demands for workplace influence and its commitment to class solidarity for guarantees of higher wages and increased job security. The second defeat of

Labour occurred on the political front after Ramsay MacDonald became prime minister in 1923. He was quickly removed from office after he had succeeded in getting the French out of the Ruhr. The third defeat was on the labor front in this same period. When the French occupation of the Ruhr came to an end in 1925, the price of coal fell precipitously, and this led to a conflict between coal owners and miners, with calls by the latter for national-ization and reorganization of the collieries. The strike that took place in 1925 was a complete failure for labor, leading to a new Trade Union Bill that was more reactionary than any since 1871. The fourth defeat, finally, took place in 1929, when MacDonald again led some socialists in a conservative direc-tion when faced with the economic crisis of the Great Depression. Together, these added up to a failure of liberal socialism in Britain.

There were still, during these years, arguments by syndicalists in France, Italy, and Spain that called for the elimination of the state; and there was also the influence of Guild socialism in England, a movement that called for a compromise between radical syndicalism and etatism. In Halévy's opinion, however, after the war the only type of socialism that remained robust was the strain calling for state control, for nationalization. He suggested that there were several reasons for the failure of liberal social-ism, but that one of the most important was that the electors of the Labour Party were not committed to socialist reform. They wanted higher wages, shorter hours, and better conditions of work, what Halévy referred to as "fiscalism," to distinguish it from socialism. "The system consists in allow-ing the profit-making system to go on, but to take money from the pocket of the profit owners and put it into the pocket of the workers."[54] This was inextricably intertwined with, and indeed expressive of, the fact that most workers (a group that obviously overlapped with electors of the Labour Party) were not committed to the ideals proposed by socialist leaders. Guild socialists failed because workers, in Halévy's words, "do not wish to have the responsibility of bossing the trade. They wanted better conditions of life, higher wages, shorter hours, but they did not want the responsibility of leadership."[55] As his previous analyses had suggested, Halévy believed workers were not interested in pressing for syndicalist control of produc-tion, or even for some corporatist form of joint management. They were happy to receive, instead, bread-and-butter improvements in pay and work-ing conditions. This lack of working-class support for syndical ideals was joined by a lack of commitment on the part of their leaders. "I am afraid that rather than socialistic in spirit they [British Labour leaders] are whiggish, eager to protect the individual against the state, not to make the state strong against the capitalists."[56]

Halévy concluded this essay by highlighting his claim that there was a fundamental tension at the heart of socialism—"on the one hand, liberty, and on the other, organization."[57] But, even more starkly than previously, he now suggested that this conflict *within* socialism, one that was especially pronounced among socialist leaders, contributed to the failure of socialism. One demonstration of this was the tension at the heart of the program of British workers and their leaders that called for a continued commitment to free trade, while at the same time supporting protectionism for certain industries to hold up profits and save jobs. In Halévy's opinion, this confused stance, which implicitly included support of a protectionism that would guarantee the profits of industrialists, showed how far British labor had strayed from the socialist ideal of working-class solidarity. Moreover, it was a stance that easily cohered with nationalism and militarism.

## "The Era of Tyrannies" (1936)

The presentation by Halévy at the Société française de philosophie in November 1936—his famous discussion of the era of tyrannies—generated a robust discussion that was subsequently published. The exchange indicates how his previous analyses cohered into a stark assessment of the state of Europe. His argument was that World War I had led to deep structural and cultural changes in Europe that marked the beginning of a new era.

> The era of tyrannies dates from August 1914, that is, from the time when the belligerent nations adopted a regime that can be defined as follows:
>
> (a) In the economic sphere, greatly extended state control of all means of production, distribution, and exchange;—and, at the same time, an appeal by the governments to the leaders of workers' organizations to help them in implementing this state control—hence syndicalism and corporatism along with *étatisme*.
>
> (b) In the intellectual sphere, state control of thought, taking two forms: one negative, through the suppression of all expressions of opinion judged unfavorable to the national interest; the other positive, through what we shall call the organization of enthusiasm.[58]

Halévy concluded his 1936 discussion arguing that if war broke out again in Europe—with the democracies facing the tyrannical regimes in Germany and Italy—the statist consolidation of power in the democracies would increase. It would, in his words, "consolidate the 'tyrannical' idea in Europe."[59] "If war begins again, and if the democracies are forced to adopt a totalitarian regime in order to save themselves from destruction, will there not be a generalization of tyranny, a strengthening and spreading of this form of government?"[60] Halévy could not see how liberal regimes could survive another such cataclysm.

Halévy explained that he had chosen the term "tyranny" rather than "dictatorship" because the latter referred to authoritarian regimes that were temporary, and that therefore left "intact in the long run a regime of liberty which, in spite of everything, is considered normal." He argued that the concept of "tyranny" better fit the current state of European affairs because, however objectionable, it in his words "implies a normal form of government, which the scientific observer of societies must range alongside other normal forms—monarchy, aristocracy, and democracy."[61] He wished to stress that he saw the new authoritarian regimes as permanent fixtures of post–World War I Europe.

World War I marked the beginning of a conflict from which, Halévy reasoned, there could be no positive exit. The least acceptable outcome would have been a German victory in the war, because this would have meant the ascendancy of Prussian militarism and of chauvinistic nationalism. But the victory over Germany in 1918 had not resulted in peaceful intrastate relations among the major powers. Rather, it had led to European-wide instability, an instability that existed between states and within states, transformed by the war.

The most troubling of these internal transformations took place when states collapsed under the pressure of war and/or subsequent crises. This was Halévy's explanation of the rise to power of the Bolsheviks in 1917 and the Italian Fascists in 1922. In Russia, it was the war that brought about the collapse. "Because of the anarchical collapse, because of the complete disappearance of the state, a group of armed men, moved by a common faith, decreed that they were the state: in this form Bolshevism, is literally, a 'fascism.'"[62] And because they found themselves fighting for the survival of the new regime [during the Civil War], "they returned, by the force of things, to a kind of patriotism at once territorial and ideological; and their tyranny, for anyone who looks at it from the ideological point of view, ends up looking very like the German and Italian tyranny."[63]

A similar loss of the ability of the state to provide order also led to the rise to power of Mussolini and the Fascists in Italy. "There was anarchy, in 1920, the year of the occupation of the factories. It was then that Giolitti gave arms to Mussolini and to his Fascists to police the country, because one was not able to depend on the army. But it was two years later, when Mussolini seized power, that disorder, in part thanks to him, had ceased. What carried him forward was the memory of the fear felt in 1920, and the persistent sentiment that they had been saved from the inability of the parties of order to maintain order by parliamentary methods."[64]

In short, Halévy came to believe that the war and its aftermath created the chaos that, in turn, led to widespread loss of confidence in parliamentary governments. This crisis of popularity, combined with the extraordinary power that centralized governmental administrations had amassed during the conflict, resulted in the rise to power of tyrannical leaders. The Russian Bolsheviks on the Left took advantage of the crisis in 1917–1920; the Italian Fascists on the Right took advantage of the crisis in 1920–1922. The authoritarian nature of the regimes created was notably similar, according to Halévy, though he recognized that their ideological frameworks were radically different. A similar domestic crisis in Germany led to Hitler. The readings and lecture notes of Halévy during these years indicate how carefully he attended to the rise to power of Mussolini and Hitler, and to the changes taking place in the Soviet Union, especially after the death of Lenin. In sum, he believed that the war had paved the way for authoritarian etatism, for an era of tyrannies, in which states led by authoritarian leaders increasingly controlled politics, the economy, and public opinion.

The crisis was felt even in the nation-states of Western and Central Europe, though here the parliamentary regimes held on, at least in the short term. Unfortunately, the peace treaties at the end of World War I had not led to a common program of defense among former allies. It had not come to a reasonable settlement about reparations, to mention one issue that led to continuous discord. Moreover, the new nation-states created after the war were not stable. Halévy feared the emergence of disputes over borders, which he believed would inevitably come to involve all of the major powers. Just as troubling—indeed, more troubling—in Halévy's estimation were the internal changes in these parliamentary regimes. During the war, states had taken control of the economy—of production, of distribution, and often of exchange. And the war had also led to censorship, to the growth of chauvinistic popular movements, and to a strengthening of nationalism and to conformism among elites. Together, these changes opened a path for the rise of tyranny.

Theoretically, Halévy agreed that it was possible to imagine a democratic socialism, one that was authoritarian in the economic sphere but liberal in the political and intellectual spheres.[65] He was convinced, however, that the historical conditions would not allow such regimes to develop. Socialism in postwar Europe would be authoritarian. This was closely connected with Halévy's conviction, examined above, that moderate socialism had disappeared as an option, and that workers and their leaders were now throwing their support behind a strong state. This was true even in traditionally stable and moderate nations like England. By 1936, Halévy had become even more categorical in presenting this view. In "L'Angleterre: Grandeur, décadence et résistance du libéralisme en Angleterre," published in 1936, the same year as his famous address on tyranny, he still held out some hope that British parliamentarianism would restrain the worst excesses of authoritarianism, but now he characterized prewar trade unions as demanding "la tyrannie syndicale," and posited that after the war there was a conflation of guild socialism and statism.[66] In "L'ère des tyrannies," Halévy advanced a similar argument. He still mentioned the difference between Guild socialists and Fabian socialists, but he judged them all as originating from, and tending toward, the same framework of state control.[67] "In the economic sphere . . . the prewar socialists demanded state control of all means of production, distribution and exchange. But this state control, in large measure, was brought about by the war, for reasons that the socialists had certainly not foreseen. If one goes back, before the war, for about a quarter century, the socialist program—if you wish, the Guesdist program—called purely and simply, as though this was sufficient to resolve the social question, for nationalization, for state control of the main branches of industry, starting with the railways."[68] He immediately followed this by mentioning the importance of syndicalism but characterized it as a "utopia," clearly indicating the shift that had taken place in his thinking about socialism.[69] Before the war, he had looked sympathetically on workers and their organizations who wished to be engage in negotiations about the economy. He still nods weakly in this direction in 1936.

> In 1914 the syndicalist movement had already been in existence for
> a number of years; too full of distrust for the state to accept this
> solution [of nationalization]. It called for the general syndicalization

of industry, without any intervention by the state, and the absorption of all bureaucracy into the syndicalist organization; in other words, the radical suppression of the state. Among the English, however—moderate people even in their utopias—a mixed doctrine was elaborated, one that looked to establish a kind of compromise between the radical syndicalism of the French, Italians, and Spaniards, and a kind of *étatisme*. What were the legitimate functions of the democratic state? What were those of the syndicalist corporations? Such were the questions the Guild Socialists discussed among themselves.[70]

During the war, Halévy now argued, syndicalists were brought into the government to jointly work toward the nationalization of industry. And this brought about—in what was the critical turn in Halévy's assessment of the Guild socialists and what they stood for—an identification of their program with state socialism. "But, scarcely had the war begun, and because of the war, we see . . . an appeal by the governments to the leaders of workers' organizations to help them in implementing their work of establishing state control. Hence, syndicalism and corporatism at the same time as *étatisme*."[71]

That Halévy had become pessimistic—even dismissive—of moderate socialism is also evident in his response to Célestin Bouglé's intervention in the debate that "L'ère des tyrannies" initiated. Halévy had suggested in the original essay that the French coup d'état of 1851 was a "reaction against socialist anarchy." Bouglé objected to this characterization, pointing out that Louis Blanc and others had proposed democratic socialism, not anarchy. Halévy rather weakly responded that what he meant was "reaction against the fear of anarchy," and that this was essentially the same thing. This response indicates that he now believed the crisis of the Second Republic was caused by Blanc and his associates, a perspective that it is difficult to imagine him supporting earlier in his life. He depicted Blanc as a dangerous authoritarian who opposed a virtuous liberalism, and suggested that Proudhon and Michelet were accurate when they attacked Blanc. "They denounced Louis Blanc for his glorification of Terrorism, the Committee of Public Safety, and Robespierre, a stance that he [Blanc] opposed, as a disciple of Rousseau and an incorruptible, to republicans without morality who, on the basis of Voltairean liberalism, were leading France to domination by the clergy and to Caesarism. Have they been proven wrong?"[72] There were similar dismissals of Blanc in Halévy's correspondence. In August 1936, for example, in the context of a discussion of the Popular Front, Halévy wrote to Meyendorff: "You interpret correctly Tocqueville and Louis Blanc. Tocqueville correctly saw the nature of the problem [of socialism in 1848]; and again it appears suddenly before our eyes. The nationalism of Louis Blanc and the socialists of his school, enemies of the flat regime of Louis Philippe, passes all limits of belief."[73]

Another indication of how thoroughly Halévy had come to reject any idea of a positively functioning Guild-like socialism was his response to Charles Appuhn in "Appendice II" to "L'ère des tyrannies": "I should rather speak of unionist anarchy to designate the paralyzing effect imposed by workers on the discipline of production when they feel themselves more or less masters of the factory. To react against this anarchy, appeal is made to the state 'to maintain order,' as Appuhn put it, but not, as he put it less happily, to maintain 'respect for persons' and 'freedom of labor.'"[74] This indicates, again, how much Halévy's faith in workers and their associations had declined. Now, Halévy suggested, worker control could only lead to "anarchy" or, in reaction to this, to a corporatism that was in fact only "state control of the economy." There seemed no space in his assessment for workers to participate in industrial management. It was either "anarchy" or "totalitarianism."

In sum, Halévy had come to view all socialisms as authoritarian, as "moving towards a kind of nationalism."[75] Authoritarianism was no longer viewed as a defining element of one strain of socialism (his view before the war). It was not presented as an unfortunate aberration of what was most valuable in the socialist tradition (his former view). It was now presented as *the* central part of its heritage. Halévy mentioned in passing that Roosevelt's New Deal might move toward a corporatism "without suppressing freedom." But the situation in Europe would not allow this. In Europe, even democratic governments, now facing a likely future of armed struggle against fascism or Bolshevism, would need "to adopt, in order to save themselves from destruction, a totalitarian regime."[76] The essence of socialism in Europe was inevitably forced to become authoritarian, because of internal developments within the movement itself and because of the unique historical conditions created in Europe by the war. "Every socialist government coming to power is condemned to employ a complicated scholastics to explain how it ought to proceed when, professing a doctrine of complete socialism, it takes power in a non-socialist society."[77]

Halévy's conviction that there had been an eclipse of moderate socialism was an important element in his growing pessimism about the future of

Europe. There were, of course, the other important elements mentioned above. As we have seen, Halévy was unhappy with the erosion of transnational intellectual exchanges, a central lament of his wartime correspondence, and one that he continued to express after the war. He also was dismayed by the growth of selfish economic interests, an important theme of the postwar volumes of his *Histoire du peuple anglais au XIXe siècle* (where, to offer one example, he pointed to the mutually supporting economic interrelationship in England before the war of the government, the military, the private shipbuilding industry, and labor).[78] And, again as we have seen, he was appalled by the growth of nationalist fanaticism; that is, the embrace of a nationalism unmediated by reflection and untempered by reason.[79] Finally, he viewed with trepidation the economic situation that European countries, especially France, faced.[80] If you combine these troubling developments with the emergence of charismatic strongmen and the expansion of thought control by the state—what Halévy famously termed "the organization of enthusiasm"—then you have the baleful mix so trenchantly criticized in "The Era of Tyrannies."[81]

## Halévy's Pessimism

In the mid-1930s, Halévy also turned, with some relief, to his work on the history of Victorian England. "You know my monotonous existence," he wrote to Léon in April 1934. "I plunge myself into the atmosphere of 1850. Not without pleasure; because the atmosphere of 1934 scarcely pleases me."[82] Two months later he again expressed his despair concerning the state of European affairs. "What to do? . . . It would not be so grave if one was able to return to the state of things when we were twenty years old. Then, all the world armed. . . . But at that time, Europe was politically and socially stable. It is very different today. What will be the *external* repercussions of the internal disequilibrium?"[83] He retreated into his scholarship. "I am again thrown into the current of English history of about a century ago. I sense that I am anachronistic, but not unhappy for that. Because I am not a child of war; and the century that begins under my eyes since my childhood astonishes me but does not enchant me."[84]

Halévy's pessimism grew as the months passed. In September 1936, Alain wrote to Florence that "Élie astonishes me with the constancy of his despair."[85] In one of his last letters, to René Berthelot, Halévy complained of the continuing financial and economic mess that France was enduring, and also of the peculiar response by France and England to the dangers presented by Mussolini and Hitler. "Moreover, don't believe that England, even at midday, will see the sun. It is a strange situation . . . in the two countries. The left wing raises its fist against the two tyrants, but are for peace at any price; the right wing is always ready to arm, but have a fear of communism that throws them into the arms of their worst enemies."[86] Two months later, in a letter to Raymond Aron, Halévy addressed his concerns about the French economy. The Popular Front had reduced the workweek in factories to forty hours, a positive step for workers. Unfortunately, this had led to a drop in production at just the moment when the stimulus program of the Popular Front was creating more demand. The result was that French producers were not able to satisfy demand. Moreover, at the same time, there were laws passed to protect small businesses against the modernization of large industry. Halévy was concerned. "At the same time that the reduction of the number of hours of work and the diminution of the output of work impoverishes the nation, one unanimously votes extraordinary laws against large low-cost stores [magasins à prix unique], [and] against the introduction of machines in the factories that manufacture shoes and produce flour. These laws are to please small business people of the middle class [petites gens de la classe moyenne]. So there is a conspiracy of the middle classes and the proletariat against the intensification of production."[87] The result, he feared, would be continued economic stagnation.

The domestic and international problems were growing, and in the year before his death in August 1937, Halévy was more and more in despair. He looked, without great hope, for a revival of popular sanity.

> Is it therefore necessary that our political leaders wait passively for these collective and anonymous forces to impose themselves again, and that a new war, a new revolution—in the manner of an inundation or of an earthquake—submerging and shaking the world? Briefly, does my interpretation of history imply the failure of all politics? Rather, it signifies, if you want truly to understand me, that the responsibility of the horrors which torment humanity should be transferred from political leaders to the common people, that is to say to ourselves. . . . [It is necessary] for us to substitute the spirit of compromise for the spirit of fanaticism.[88]

## Halévy's Death (1937)

Halévy's health deteriorated in 1937. During the spring, while in London, he experienced chest pains that led to a consultation with a cardiologist. The diagnosis was pessimistic.[89] Halévy remained very busy, however, even when he returned to France. On the first day of July, he was interviewed on Radio Paris about English-French relations before World War I. At the end of the month, he assisted at the opening of the ninth International Conference of Philosophy at the Sorbonne. But in August his health declined quickly, and on the night of 20–21 August he died at his home in Sucy-en-Brie of a myocardial infarction, or heart attack.

Friends were shocked at the suddenness of Halévy's death. Condolences were sent to his widow, Florence,[90] and in the weeks and months that followed celebratory remembrances were published in journals in France and England.[91] Very quickly, Florence joined with friends and colleagues to plan for the appearance of Halévy's unpublished works. We have examined the most important of these above: *L'ère des tyrannies*, published in 1938, and *Histoire du socialisme européen*, published in 1948. In addition, the unedited passages and notes for another volume of his *Histoire du peuple anglais*, brought together and supplemented by Paul Vaucher, was published in 1946. It is testimony to the immense respect Halévy enjoyed that these works saw the light of day.

# Conclusion

The historian who would neglect the history of doctrines where doctrines are tied up with events would commit a grave error. That said . . . I am far from thinking that one can reduce history to the history of doctrines.

—Élie Halévy, "L'ère des tyrannies," 1936

The history of Élie Halévy shows the mark of his philosophical formation, because it is enlightened by the grand ideas that are confronted, combined, or opposed in each époque. The history of Élie Halévy is the politics of the past, reconstituted in function of the value of the ideas embraced and of the men who carry them into combat without having full knowledge of their significance or the consequences of their acts.

—Raymond Aron, "L'itinéraire intellectuel d'Élie Halévy"

By the time he had completed his study of England, Halévy had arrived empirically at an implicit philosophical definition of liberty, together with an objective and general conception of the sort of political and social environment in which liberty was possible.

—Charles C. Gillispie, "The Work of Élie Halévy"

The outpouring of homage to Halévy after his death in 1937 testifies to the depth and breadth of his scholarly achievements. British scholars lauded the sympathetic observer of their country and the magisterial volumes that he had devoted to its history. French scholars remembered the penetrating intelligence of their colleague, the brilliant lecturer, the incisive critic, the politically engaged defender of the Republic. Commentators complimented the prescience of his analysis of totalitarianism "tyranny" and the sophistication of his methodologies. Subsequent historians and political theorists, however, have challenged some of Halévy's conclusions. This final chapter focuses first on the distinctiveness of his methodology and then turns to a brief consideration of these scholarly assessments. It concludes with the claim that Halévy should be seen as a participant in the tradition of French liberalism.

## Methodology

Methodologically, Halévy wrote histories that were combinations of what today would be labeled intellectual history, cultural history, political history, and socioeconomic history, with inclusion of a strong dose of foreign policy. At their core was often a teasing out of an internal conflict within a national culture or system of thought: the tension in Plato's *Dialogues* between the "regressive" and "progressive" dialectic;[1] the conflict in Utilitarian doctrine between the "natural harmony of interests" and the "artificial harmony of interests";[2] the incompatibility in socialist theories of emancipatory and authoritarian tendencies.[3] This logical/philosophical analysis—a legacy of Halévy's philosophical training—did not lead to simplistic categorization of thinkers or movements, however. Halévy was sensitive to the nuance of thought and categories; he recognized that classification could be distorting. When considering what Bentham took from Hume, for example, he began with an analysis of Hume's doctrine, describing it as a complex combination of "skepticism," "associationism," "rationalism," and "naturalism."[4] "It is interesting to note," he wrote, "that, in the writings of Hume, precisely because his thought is complex and defies simple solutions, one finds the birthplace of diverse interpretations that were able to be, and effectively went on to be, proposed by utilitarianism."[5] The ambiguities and complexities of a thinker's philosophy could be an important source of subsequent differences of interpretations.

Just as important as this careful analysis of the complex nature of philosophical positions, however, was the manner in which doctrines were received and applied. Halévy was particularly sensitive to the paradoxes that resulted from the reception and development of ideas, and impressed with how the same theories were appropriated and applied in radically discrepant ways. He believed that it was essential to understand the relationship of doctrines to the individuals who mobilized them, and to consider how doctrines influenced, and were influenced by, wider historical forces—economic, political, social, and cultural. He was concerned with how theories were embodied in institutions, and how they informed the general beliefs and mores of a society. To put it another way, Halévy was interested in systems of thought but did not present them as direct or unmediated causes of large historical movements. Doctrines were always part of complex constellations that pointed to chronological and geographic specificities, and to the peculiarities of individuals and national cultures. The frameworks for understanding this were more historical than philosophical.

It is also important to recognize that the inherent power of an idea was not, at the end of the day, what was important for Halévy. Theories of intrinsic clarity and philosophic sophistication could lead to unfortunate movements; weak ideas could lead to impressive positive developments. The historian's task was to determine how ideas and doctrines were articulated, understood, received, applied, and passed on. The internal logic of a constellation of ideas might help the historian understand the potential for various subsequent developments, but it was the nature of these developments that was important. "Imperialism" and "nationalism," for example, were not intrinsically attractive to Halévy, nor were they particularly complex or sophisticated, but their popularity and significance in the late nineteenth century were undeniable. As a consequence, he made them a central focus of his analyses of British politics and European history in the decades surrounding World War I, as analyzed in my Chapter 9.

The first example of Halévy's distinctive historical-philosophical approach was his analysis of Benthamism and "philosophical radicalism." As mentioned in Chapter 3, Halévy insisted that Bentham's thought contained an internal contradiction between "the natural harmony of interests," crucial for his Smithian theory of the economy, and "the artificial harmony of interests," central to his theories of civil and penal law. Having outlined this internal contradiction, he traced how each central principle was taken in divergent directions by figures in the wider movement of philosophical radicalism. Those who emphasized the natural harmony of interests and applied it to the economy hoped to reduce the actions of the government in economic policy. Richard Cobden represented this orientation; probably its greatest success was the elimination of the Corn Laws in 1846. Those who applied the natural harmony of interests to the economy *and* to government (thereby breaking with Bentham's theory of law)—Thomas Hodgskin is an example—pursued an anarchist or libertarian policy. On the other hand, those who emphasized the artificial harmony of interests and applied it to politics followed Bentham and James Mill's faith in bureaucratic paternalism and political activism. Those who applied it to government *and* to the economy (thereby breaking with Bentham's laissez-faire economic theory) supported policies closer to the socialisms of the Saint-Simonians and Robert Owen. The central issues that Halévy highlighted in his analysis were old chestnuts—still very much with us—concerning how much a society should privilege spontaneous free choice and how much, in the pursuit of equity and justice, it should look to administration and the state. His history showed that Utilitarianism in England had a broad and complex legacy, and his analytical framework was imploring his readers to recognize and confront this complexity.[6]

As this suggests, when Halévy turned to the wider frameworks within which doctrines unfolded, he tended to highlight the importance of different individuals and the variety of directions in which they moved. He refused to believe that a doctrine had only one correct meaning. Rather, doctrines attracted various protagonists and were likely to have different meanings in different national contexts and different historical eras. Halévy was sensitive to the meanings carried by concepts at a given time and place, and he was especially intrigued by how these changed over time. This diachronic sensitivity was especially evident in his contributions to Lalande's *Vocabulaire technique et critique de la philosophie*, where Halévy analyzed the development of terms like "individualism," "liberalism," and "socialism." His histories scrupulously avoided anachronism.

The historical perspective Halévy took was also comparative; his approach was (to employ the now fashionable term) "transnational." He wished to uncover the interrelatedness of the historical movements in various nation-states and to highlight the peculiarities of each. One of the main issues that organized his volumes on English history, for example, was why this country had been, during the decades after the Glorious Revolution and especially during the revolutionary era of the late eighteenth and early nineteenth centuries, free of revolution and violent crises. To answer this question, Halévy provided careful investigations of the political and economic spheres but came to insist on the peculiarities of British culture.[7] Central here, as shown in Chapter 6, was not just Utilitarianism but also evangelical Protestantism, especially Methodism. Halévy argued that these seemingly contrary movements, based as they were on different and even hostile metaphysical principles, in fact converged in their recommendation of similar forms of personal behavior and social comportment. They both discounted short-term pleasures in hopes of achieving future rewards and recommended a "reasoning, calculating, and prosaic morality" that emphasized personal responsibility.[8]

There is an intriguing comparison, on this front, with the contemporaneous theories of Max Weber. Weber was also intrigued by the power of religious culture, and in 1904–1905 advanced his famous thesis that there was an "elective affinity" between the ascetic rigors of Calvinist Protestantism and the self-denying acquisitive drive that characterized early capitalism.[9] Both Calvinists and capitalists believed that there was a disciplined obligation to work. Halévy, of course, emphasized not the economic but the political consequences of Protestantism, and he analyzed the importance not of Calvinism but of Methodism. However, Halévy and Weber shared the view that religion was more than a dependent variable explained by economic development, as Friedrich Engels and crude Marxists would have it. Halévy and Weber believed that Protestantism had left psychological and behavioral residues, and that it remained a central cultural influence in secular movements of the modern industrial age. In their opinion, it was crucial to weigh its importance if one wished to understand economic, social, and political behavior.

His comparative orientation also led Halévy to distinguish what was singular about France's culture and politics. Deeply committed to the constitutional system of the Third Republic—he frequently referred positively to the "constitution of 1875"—he was not happy with its political leaders, nor with the political culture that alternated between inattentiveness and revolutionary impatience. He worried about the principled bickering among French politicians, the constant maneuverings of the political elites, the ideological stridency and "disastrous eloquence" that prevented compromise and often led to "parliamentary paralysis."[10] He worried about the ease with which popular crowds could be mobilized by demagogic spokesmen spouting dubious ideas, and he was troubled by the propensity of radical groups on the Right and Left to call for violence and "revision" of the Republic. This was the main reason he insisted that he was a liberal. In terms of his doctrinal sympathies, Halévy was between the Radicals and the Socialists. He distrusted both parties, however, though for different reasons. Some among the Radicals, he suggested, were looking to profit from the Republic rather than to serve it. The Socialists were little better; either they were in tacit collusion with the Radicals, or alternately prisoners of a rhetoric of socialist revolution. Before World War I, though strongly in favor of progressive economic reform, he pushed back against syndicalists of the Confédération Générale du Travail and against socialists of the Section Française de l'Internationale Ouvrière who were committed to revolution. Even Jean Jaurès, who supported the Republic, could not resist revolutionary rhetoric. After the war, the tone on the Left did not improve. Members of the French Communist Party embraced Third International Marxist-Leninism; leaders of the Socialist Party like Léon Blum struggled to avoid being outflanked on their Left, and consequently made ambiguous statements about the need for revolution. Most historians view Jaurès and Blum as pillars of French socialist reformism; Halévy was not convinced.

This is all the more surprising because Halévy had an intense interest in the emergence and development of European socialism. And, like his analyses of other doctrines and movements, as we saw in Chapter 5, Halévy's approach to socialism was multilayered and comparative. He was interested in the theories of individual socialists, the contexts within which these theories emerged, the impact of their ideas on socialist movements, and the wider juridical, economic, and political consequences. His analysis of the thought of Saint-Simon and the Saint-Simonians, to mention one example, was incisive in its textual analysis, but it also traced the influence of their ideas on radically different movements, from the revolutionary Left (Louis Blanc and Karl Marx) to the authoritarian Right (Louis Napoleon and Bismarck).[11] As we saw in Chapter 8, when Halévy assessed the historical forces that during World War I had begun to operate on the internal tensions within European socialism—the conflict at its heart between its emancipatory and organizational impulses—he came to the conclusion that socialism was assuming a new, more authoritarian face.

Raymond Aron suggested that Halévy should be seen as the descendant of Montesquieu and Tocqueville.[12] This is appropriate, as each married intellectual history with political history, and each employed a comparative framework that insisted on the importance of national traditions. But there were important differences, in part reflecting the very different epochs in which they lived. Of the three, Halévy was the most interested in economic issues, not so surprising given the importance of industrialization in his era. His volumes on nineteenth-century English history included long sections devoted to economic development and many pages about the growth of the industrial working class and the problems this class confronted. Halévy was also the least sociological of the three. He accepted that social forces were extremely important but rejected the view that these were more important than individuals and culture. He was not attracted to arguments that climate

was influential on political organization, nor to notions of collective conscience. Perhaps it was the rise of the *discipline* of sociology during his lifetime
that led Halévy to consider carefully its reductionist propensity.[13] As we saw
in Chapter 2, he resisted Durkheim's tendency to discount the contributions
of philosophy and psychology in favor of sociology, and rejected the subordination of questions of morality to collective social relations. Among the sociologists of his era, Halévy was closer to Gabriel Tarde, who defended morality
and individualism, though Halévy pushed back against the political and
social conservatism of Tarde and believed him to be deaf to historical nuance
and specificity.

## Influence of Halévy's Scholarship

Halévy's legacy is mixed. He is recognized as one of the great—perhaps the
greatest—historian in the French liberal tradition. During his lifetime, he
was almost universally acclaimed by British historians and political theorists,
and also came to receive posthumous applause for raising the alarm about
the rise of tyrannical regimes—what came to be called "totalitarianism." Subsequent scholarly assessment has been more mixed, though generally positive.
Following is a brief consideration of some of the controversies surrounding
Halévy's different works.

### La Formation du Radicalisme Philosophique

The deepest influence of Halévy's oeuvre has been on British history, the
focus of so much of Halévy's own scholarship. First came *La formation du
radicalisme philosophique*, the third volume of which was published in 1904
when Halévy was only thirty-four years old. The reaction among British
scholars was almost universally complimentary during the six decades following publication;[14] subsequently there has been significant pushback against
some of his generalizations. Few have doubted the enormous contribution
his volumes made at the time of their publication. Halévy established a path-
breaking chronology of Bentham's writings, many of them never before published or cited. He linked Bentham's writings to a wide cast of philosophers
and political economists. He synthesized an enormous amount of disparate
material. Charles Gillispie, writing in 1950, could still claim that Halévy had
accomplished "a too rare feat . . . . he has added to historical literature a

secondary work so perceptive and so clear that it provides the reader more illumination on its subject than a study of the sources would do."[15] Talcott Parsons in 1968 characterized Halévy's study as the "virtually definitive analysis of Utilitarianism."[16]

Scholarship of the past fifty years, however, perhaps not surprisingly, has led to calls for qualification of some of Halévy's claims. This has been the result, in part, of the extensive research, ongoing, for the new edition of Bentham's oeuvre,[17] but also of new scholarship on the wider history of Utilitarianism.[18] William Thomas has argued that Halévy exaggerated the influence of abstract philosophical issues among the early philosophical radicals, and that this should be balanced with more attention given to their interest in practical political issues.[19] Thomas, nonetheless, has referred to *La formation du radicalisme philosophique* as "a still unsurpassed classic."[20] Frederick Rosen, one of the editors of *The Collected Works of Jeremy Bentham*, is a harsher critic. He has argued that Bentham was more committed to constitutional democracy in his earlier writings than Halévy allowed. While Halévy emphasized a shift in Bentham's position on constitutionalism and politics due to the influence of the French Revolution and, after 1808, of James Mill, Rosen has claimed that there was more continuity. He also has argued that Halévy was mistaken when he insisted that there was a theoretical conflict between Bentham's economic and legal theories.[21] Others, like Jean Pierre Dupuy, have raised philosophical objections, more resonant of recent debates about John Rawls's philosophy than of the history of British Utilitarianism.[22]

Most scholars, however, continue to be generous in their assessments of the contributions Halévy made, suggesting revision, not replacement, of his theoretical framework. H. S. Jones recently called *La formation du radicalisme philosophique* "a classic work."[23] Nonetheless, given the numerous thinkers and diverse doctrines now included under the broad label "Utilitarianism"— Bentham, John Stuart Mill, Henry Sidgwick, to name just a few of the luminaries—it seems fair to conclude, as has Stefan Collini, that Halévy "may have accepted rather too readily the exaggeration of both the homogeneity and the influence of the Philosophic Radicals."[24] It seems highly unlikely that any characterization of *the* nature of the movement will enjoy universal assent anytime soon.[25]

### *Evangelical Protestantism and the "Halévy Thesis"*

The "Halévy thesis" concerning the importance of evangelical Protestantism, especially Methodism, in modern British culture also has received widespread attention, much of it positive, though with some resistance from labor historians like E. P. Thompson and Eric Hobsbawm, and from recent historians who look to other institutions and other aspects of culture to explain British stability. Halévy's thesis, as we have seen, is that Methodism in the late 1730s reawakened a deep but latent Protestant fervor that had gone largely dormant. Part of the reawakening was due to the social turmoil caused by industrial overproduction and also to political turmoil that led to the fall of Walpole in 1742. The other part that explains the rise of Methodism, according to Halévy, was the newly embraced doctrine of instantaneous conversion (picked up from German-speaking Moravian Brethren) and the newly acquired revivalist techniques (picked up from Welsh Nonconformists). He claimed that George Whitefield and the Wesleys were able to channel political and economic discontent into Methodism, an evangelical movement that retained a conservative stance vis-à-vis the state and a hierarchical view of church organization. The Halévy thesis is, in essence, that this religiously enthusiastic but socially conservative movement became foundational for English popular culture, and as such helps explain the stability of Britain during the revolutionary era and through the nineteenth century.

It is a thesis that has encouraged a debate that J. D. Walsh characterized in 1974 as one that "fizzes, jumps, and occasionally explodes."[26] Walsh himself focused on the issue of Puritan religious sensibility, suggesting that Halévy was on to something when he argued that Methodism rested on a sense of moral duty and feeling of sin that was common among Puritans, a sensibility that responded positively to the doctrine of grace so enthusiastically preached by the Methodists. Walsh also suggested, however, that Halévy probably did not make enough of "the positive, symbiotic relationship between declining Nonconformity and rising Methodism"—that is, the manner in which Methodism at first absorbed a considerable number of nonconformists into its societies before, at a later stage, it infused the movement of Protestant Dissent, broadly considered, with new enthusiasm.[27] He also suggested that Halévy exaggerated the speed with which Methodism spread, underestimating the importance of, in his words, "its army of lay preachers, crude but fervent."[28]

The thrust of these qualifications is that, in order to explain the nonrevolutionary temper of the English, attention should also be given to variables besides evangelical Methodism. Perhaps, as Christopher Hill has suggested, Methodism was like Puritanism, in that it appealed to the "industrious sort of people" because of its glorification or thrift and work—that is, because of its asceticism.[29] Or, perhaps, as Michael Walzer has suggested, Methodism was simply another form of group association that appealed because it compensated for the loss of community that industrialization inevitably brought in its train.[30] Or, perhaps, as recent scholarship has suggested, British stability has more to do with the highly aristocratic and Anglican dimensions of English culture than with evangelicalism of the popular classes or, for that matter, with nonconformity.

Walsh also emphasized the socially radical nature of some early Methodist preaching, a perspective that is shared by British labor historians who have objected to the broad sweep of Halévy's thesis. Historians like E. P. Thompson[31] and Eric Hobsbawm[32] have emphasized the disruptive, anti-aristocratic attacks of the rich and powerful by Methodist preachers—the glorification of the "godly poor" and the denunciation of the "ungodly rich"—and have insisted that this side of evangelical Methodism fed into working-class radicalism. This is now widely accepted by historians of British labor. Historians recognize that while one side of Methodism encouraged obedience to hierarchy, another side acted as a solvent on patriarchal deference.

This still leaves to one side, however, the larger issue of British stability, and of how important working-class culture (with full recognition of its religious dimension) was for any satisfactory explanation of this. Halévy argued that the crisis of the late 1730s did not lead to social revolution because, in part, there was no radical bourgeoisie to lead popular discontent. And he argued in subsequent volumes of his history of nineteenth-century England that this conservative cultural mix remained central as it spread into the middle classes by means of the activities of voluntary associations. Recent scholarship has tended to view the religion and culture of the working class as an autonomous arena, however, and, when considering the issue of British stability, to emphasize not the working class or the middle class but the permanence of British institutions and the strength of aristocratic norms and class power.[33]

## "L'Ère des Tyrannies"

Halévy is widely recognized as being among the first to recognize that radical left-wing and radical right-wing movements during the interwar years had important similarities. There were objections raised at the time by those on the Left, even though he recognized the importance of the differing ideological orientations and contrasting goals of Fascists and Communists. When

Halévy first presented his thesis to a gathering of the Société français de philosophie in November 1936, his friend Célestin Bouglé disagreed with the emphasis on the authoritarian side of socialism, arguing that it discounted the emancipatory side. In the months after Halévy's death, however, Bouglé moved closer to his analysis. The debate over the heuristic value of categories like "totalitarianism" has waxed and waned as contexts changed; the debate continues in the present, though the category has enjoyed a renewed popularity since the end of the Cold War in 1989 and the implosion of the Soviet Empire in 1991.

In the case of Halévy, as seen in Chapter 10, the view that European liberal democratic regimes would be forced to embrace authoritarianism was closely tied to his post–World War I pessimism. This has led some to charge that he exaggerated the dangers to liberal democracy. Raymond Aron, for example, pointed out that, contrary to Halévy's prediction, not all liberal democratic regimes facing fascist tyranny in the interwar years became, in their turn, tyrannical.[34] They were more resilient than Halévy allowed, more able to mobilize for defense without becoming as authoritarian as the regimes against which they mobilized. The logic of Aron's point is persuasive: the historical trials that liberal democratic regimes faced did not fatally commit them to tyranny. By the late 1930s, the pessimism felt by Halévy led him to emphasize general forces—cultural, institutional, and economic—that too radically discounted the ability of people to make their own history. His pessimism, in sum, kept him from viewing positive ways that European liberal democracies could move ahead.

This is closely tied to another criticism. Halévy, as we have seen, argued that the changes introduced during World War I, including the increased power of states and the new prudential attitude of the working class, made the survival of liberal socialism and moderate syndicalism impossible. He insisted that the authoritarian side of socialism had prevailed, and that liberal socialism had disappeared as a viable option for European societies. Subsequent history has demonstrated, however, that liberal or reformist socialism was not as fragile as Halévy concluded. Since the end of World War II, there have been periods of robust social democracy in Europe. Western and northern European democracies introduced extensive social welfare programs while avoiding the distressing dictatorial rule and "organization of enthusiasm" that Halévy believed were their necessary concomitants. There has been, in short, a greater variety of regimes than he assumed was possible.

There is also room to question Halévy's account of the rise of totalitarian movements. The account Halévy gave emphasized many of the elements that scholars still insist were important: the frustrations resulting from World War I; the economic crises of the postwar inflation and the Great Depression; the contempt for liberal and humanistic values; the popular impatience with liberal and socialist "bourgeois" politicians. Recent scholars would wish to emphasize, in addition, the rise of mass politics and anti-intellectualism. They also look at the role played by conservative politicians in Italy and Germany, politicians who were instrumental in opening the door for Mussolini and Hitler to assume national leadership.[35]

## Histoire du Socialisme Européen

His post–World War I pessimism led Halévy to adjust his analysis of European socialism, in ways described in the chapters above.[36] One of the most puzzling issues concerning his analysis of socialism both before and after the war was his tendency to ignore the reform socialist tradition in his own country. It is curious that Halévy did not devote more attention to the varieties of socialism in France that rejected the revolutionary and deterministic views of Second or Third International Marxism, and also rejected the violent orientation of French revolutionary syndicalism. He weighed the importance of syndicalism in France, of course, and noted that syndicalism in Britain took a less revolutionary form than on the Continent. He largely ignored, however, reform socialists like Benoît Malon and Georges Renard, editors of the *Revue socialiste*, a journal created in 1885.[37] He also seems not to have considered important the views of Charles Gide and others of l'école de Nîmes who recommended social solidarity and cooperative institutions, nor the recommendations of Bouglé, who ran the Centre de documentation sociale and championed "industrial democracy" and republican citizenship.[38] All of these figures favored working within the institutional structure of the Republic to bring about progressive social and economic reform. This was a robust moderate socialist tradition—variously labeled "reformist," "moral," or "idealist." It was "reformist" because it insisted that the democratic institutions of the Third Republic were a precondition for socioeconomic reform and socialist progress. It was "moral" because it rested less on Marxist notions of the inevitable unfolding of history than on a belief that action would result from a sense of outrage at injustices confronted. It was "idealist" because it was not entirely grounded in the present but rather imagined a better future based on human rights and justice.[39] Halévy did not give these much attention. He also was quick to emphasize the revolutionary rhetoric of socialist luminaries like Jaurès and Blum, while ignoring their programs of reform and their acceptance of the importance of liberal democratic institutions. Most scholars see them, instead, as central figures of French reform socialism.

It is also curious that Halévy, given his sympathy for moderate late nineteenth-century socialism, did not give more attention to the New Liberals in England.[40] This group of intellectuals—most notably John A. Hobson, Leonard Hobhouse, John Lawrence Hammond, and Barbara Hammond— were advocates of a socialist liberalism that rejected both the laissez-faire doctrines of classical liberals and the state-directed collectivism of Fabian socialists like Sidney and Beatrice Webb and George Bernard Shaw. The New Liberals boldly confronted the inequities of English society (especially those related to traditional land ownership) and responded to the dislocations caused by industrialization with proposals for social and tax reform. They provided much of the intellectual justification for the welfare-state legislation introduced in England in the years immediately before World War I: old age pensions, health and unemployment insurance, minimum wages, labor exchanges, school meals, and progressive taxation.

The explanation for the resistance Halévy showed, I believe, is that he did not share the idealist conception of society and historical development that New Liberals were attracted to. Hobhouse, for example, embraced an "organic" and "harmonious" conception of society that registered the influence of T .H. Green and his idealist philosophy. Hobhouse believed that liberty for self-development was a constituent element of the common good, a point of view that entailed the avoidance of confronting the issue of how to arbitrate competitive interests, of how to imagine how incommensurable differences were to be negotiated. The ideal of the common good obscured the actuality of political conflict.[41] Halévy's conception of society assumed more conflict, both economic and political. Halévy believed that the instantiation of liberty for self-development was important, but he did not assume that this conformed in all cases with the common good. He took the presence of competing individual and class interests as a given, and believed that the goal of effective policy was to find a means to allow for negotiation and compromise. Another way of stating this is to suggest that Halévy's Kantianism was resistant to the Hegelian-inspired idealism of T. H. Green and his successors.

This also helps explain the close relationship Halévy had with Graham Wallas. Like Halévy, Wallas was interested in the complex nature of human conflicts.[42] He was not drawn to idealistic assumptions that there was a natural growth of social responsibility and altruistic sentiments. Both Wallas and Halévy wished to move in the direction of encouraging the growth of "egalitarian" culture among the general population, and both were sensitive to the danger of state power and to the effective, but dangerous, use of media by those who wished to "organize enthusiasm."

## French Liberalism

Subsequent scholarship has supplemented, and at times replaced, Halévy's contributions to our understanding of British Utilitarianism and Methodism, European socialism, and the radical movements of the interwar years. None of this is surprising, given that Halévy died more than eighty years ago, and much of his scholarship is more than a hundred years old. Any reasonable person—and Halévy was more reasonable than most—would expect subsequent scholarship to offer corrections and provide new insights. The previous section has attempted to situate Halévy's scholarship in a few of these scholarly contexts.

The broader historical context in which Halévy himself should be placed, however, is not sufficiently highlighted by the subsequent controversies concerning his own scholarship. Rather, he should be seen as a participant in the tradition of French liberal republicanism. Halévy's years (1870–1937) are almost identical to those of the French Third Republic. He did not live to see the sad end of the Republic in 1940, but he did see many of the dangers that led to its demise. His response was to double down on his liberal credentials. He was an extraordinarily impressive participant in the French liberal tradition.[43] This tradition assumed a distinctive form during the French Revolution, and subsequent French liberals, like Halévy, should be seen as its descendants.

The history of French liberalism is undergoing a renaissance. For much of the twentieth century it was viewed with disdain, as insufficiently "engaged," as too tentative in its demands for social reform, as unduly optimistic concerning the progress of reason and science. Scholarship during the past three decades has challenged these views, though it is notable that there is still, to the best of my knowledge, no general history of French liberalism that goes past the consolidation of the Third Republic in the late 1870s. Part of the ongoing reassessment has been the consequence of the decline of *marxisant* frameworks of analysis following 1968, reinforced by the decline of the radical Left following the end of the Cold War. Another element contributing to this reassessment has been the emergence of more nuanced definitions of "liberalism," ones that are not limited to legal (civil liberties), political (constitutionalism), and/or economic (free trade) dimensions. Scholars are insisting that conceptions of science, of religion, of the role of the state, of solidarity, of sociability, of mores of identity, of gender, and of the self must also be taken into consideration.

The recent analyses of the various strains of French liberalism during the early nineteenth century have demonstrated that most French liberals, in contrast to their Anglo-American counterparts, did not assume that it was sufficient to establish a regime of absolute rights and constitutionalism. This was in large part because French liberalism emerged during the turmoil of the French Revolution and subsequently retained many of the concerns that defined early liberal attempts to traverse the illiberal circumstances of this era. They were acutely sensitive to and troubled by the way in which revolutionary upheaval had become a breeding ground for unruly political emotions, allowing the worst drives of human nature to develop and become more widespread. Social and political institutions, habits, moeurs that generally restrain desires and instincts had been weakened. They believed that it was necessary to find institutions and arenas of sociability that would revitalize positive sentiments, encourage moral action, and foster civic commitment.

As this indicates, early French liberals were ambivalent toward the revolutionary heritage. They opposed the absolutism of the Old Regime but also opposed the left-wing absolutism associated with the Terror. They were in favor of civil liberties and popular sovereignty but believed the latter must be constrained by political institutions and civic mores. Constitutional guarantees were essential, with the separation and balance of power, but early nineteenth-century liberals were not necessarily committed to either a monarchy or a republic. Which one was favored depended on the competing forces that needed to be kept at bay. Liberals wished to keep both absolutists and violent revolutionaries from regaining power. They worried about the resurgent power of traditional elites but also worried about the proclivity of the French for insurgencies and *coups de force*. Representative democracy was their preferred constitutional system, but one with a restricted franchise.

French liberals argued that liberty was not reducible to sovereignty. They embraced popular sovereignty because they believed that liberal freedoms were inextricably bound up with popular government. But they did not trust the daily impulses of the masses, who could be misled to believe that revolutionary regeneration was a simple process and/or that a charismatic leader could quickly initiate a miraculous "regeneration" of society. To protect against this, liberals wished to restrict the franchise and separate and balance power. Their view of sovereignty was that it must be divided. Institutions must be constructed to incorporate equilibrium and avoid the concentration of power. They were "pluralists" in the sense that they resisted the revolutionary mentality that assumed that the past was a slate to be wiped clean, and that society could be rebuilt from the ground up. To make politics work, it was necessary to be attentive to the structures that would allow an ongoing negotiation of different interests.

Some scholars have viewed this as coming from the continuing influence of anti-absolutist thought of the eighteenth century that focused on the importance of intermediary bodies.[44] Others have viewed it as related to a commitment to "moderation."[45] Still others have related it to the influence of Protestant notions of liberal morality.[46] I have argued that it is connected to viewing politics as the arena where incommensurable interests were to be expressed and negotiated.[47] All have emphasized the importance of early liberals responding to the traumas of the French Revolution and the Napoleonic Empire.

Nineteenth-century French liberalism took different forms. Some believed that there was one correct answer to political and social issues, and that reason would ultimately indicate this truth. Guizot and the Doctrinaires were the preeminent exemplars of this view. Others believed that politics was an ongoing process of accommodation and compromise. There always would be conflicting interesting and divergent ideals, and the trick was to determine the correct form of political organization that would allow peaceful political contestation to occur. Benjamin Constant articulated this view.[48]

Both groups wished to protect civil liberties. But neither group wished to restrict liberty to "negative liberty." Rather, liberties were tethered to collectively defined ends; liberals generally recommended "rights" *and* "duties." This was closely associated with criticisms of "individualism." There was a deep respect for individuality—of individual autonomy and self-development—but this was tied to criticism of narrow self-interest. During France's revolutionary era, this was combined with a critique of aristocratic pretentions and "aristocratic racism." In the early nineteenth century, it was associated with the embrace of ideals of social responsibility and closely related to notions of citizenship that implied obligations to the community, and to the belief in the interdependent nature of individuals in society.[49] By the late nineteenth century this could be associated with calls for rehabilitating the family,[50] or with constructing a workable notion of social solidarity,[51] or more generally with addressing socioeconomic inequities. Social reform, by the late nineteenth century, was often viewed as part of liberal democracy, as we have seen with Halévy.

Another important dimension of French liberal thought, and again one that distinguished it from Anglo-American liberalism, was the conviction that the state was essential. While there was a recognition that the state could be intrusive and abusive—memories of overbearing regimes during the Revolution and the First and Second Empires undergirded this—there was a belief that the state was essential to protect the weak from the powerful. It was the state that, during the Old Regime, had protected the middle and lower classes from the power of nobles. It was the state that, during the nineteenth century, could protect the middle and lower classes from the power of financial, economic, and social elites. Rights were considered to exist *through* the state, not against the state. While the state could be oppressive, it was also an emancipatory force. Collective authority required a higher purpose than simply maximizing individual utilities.

French liberalism also tended to be historical rather than theoretical; comparative rather than abstract. Another way to characterize this is to say that it was "pragmatic" in the sense that liberals believed that different situations required different responses. The embrace of an absolute notion of rights was believed to be a formula that could overwhelm the needs of the sovereign people; the embrace of an absolute notion of popular sovereignty could overwhelm the rights of individuals. In short, politics was inherently complex; and complexity required that careful consideration be given to the divergent forces in play.[52]

Finally, it is essential to emphasize the importance for French liberals of the issue of culture. The French Revolution taught liberals that even with the protection of civil liberties and with the embrace of popular sovereignty instantiated in representative institutions, stability would be threatened if furious passions ran wild. Therefore, to combat idealism, fanaticism, and fear, they argued that it was necessary to encourage other sentiments or emotions. It was important to contain the fears that led individuals to retreat from public engagement and, at the other extreme, to contain the impulses for aggressive acts of revenge. Therefore, culture, in the anthropological sense of ways of life involving the complex of values and habits characteristic of different societies, became a focus of attention. This was not entirely new, of course, as Montesquieu, Rousseau, and others had often discussed the importance of the "spirit" of societies and the close correspondence of this spirit with different types of political regimes. Liberals were descendants of these earlier writers. French liberals focused on moeurs, which included religious beliefs, republican "virtue," and the wider patterns of sociability that encouraged these generous sentiments. In short, there is a central moral and psychological dimension to French liberalism. Constitutional arrangements and civil protections were viewed as critically important, but so were social spaces where positive human sentiments could be nurtured to promote the social experience that enhanced communal solidarity. They tended to oppose the power of the Catholic Church in France but were not aggressively anti-clerical, instead insisting on religious toleration.

Élie Halévy shared these concerns. He was, in many respects, a late nineteenth-century representative of this distinctive French liberal tradition. He defended the legitimacy of the state, arguing that it was one of the guardians of individual rights and of the general interest. He insisted on measuring the strong influence of cultural and historical traditions. He worked within the French liberal framework that assumed causative forces would be illuminated by a comparative perspective. What distinguished his liberalism from that of some of his well-known predecessors (of, say, Benjamin Constant and Alexis de Tocqueville) was his sensitivity to the socioeconomic issues thrown up by modern industrialization, and to the attendant sociocultural dilemmas that such modernity inevitably brought. Halévy was convinced of the central importance of modern economic changes but recognized the need to confront the attendant problems with a dialogue that included all participants in this society. He also was attentive to how the quest for empire and the growth of militaries had been transformed by industrialization, and worried about how these were exacerbating the quest for national power and grandeur. While he placed his faith in the progress of rational reflection, he also recognized the importance of sentiment and contingency. He was a cosmopolitan but respectful of national peculiarities and the pull of cultural traditions. It was his sensitivity to these multiple dimensions that distinguished his writings, and it is these same qualities that continue to make them relevant to ongoing debates concerning political and social policy.

One of Halévy's lifelong interests, as we have seen, was the relationship of liberalism and socialism, ideologies that had emerged in the early nineteenth century, and that, each in its own way, confronted the positive and negative consequences of modern individualism. Though legitimately classified as a liberal, Halévy was also very sympathetic to nonauthoritarian versions of socialism, especially before World War I. As he put it to Bouglé in 1913, "Socialism encompasses the secret of the future." But it had internal tensions that led it in contrary directions. Halévy wondered if socialism would lead to "a universalized Swiss republic or to European Caesarism."[53]

As analyzed above, Halévy admired the cooperatist, associationist, and emancipatory dimensions of the European socialist tradition, and he was deeply respectful of the ways that Marx had historicized and modified the theories of the British economists. He was critical, however, of the materialism upon which many socialist doctrines were situated and suspicious of the organizational dimension of some socialist theories and socialist movements (a dimension he traced back to the doctrines of the Saint-Simonians). His complex relationship to socialism is revealed in his published articles before World War I (where he advocated a redistribution of income), in his voluminous correspondence (where he reflected on socialist thinkers and contemporaries), and in the manuscript versions of his early lectures on the history of socialism. He was sensitive to a tension he perceived at the heart of European socialism: the drive for emancipation of those segments of society most affected by the spread of industrialization, on the one hand, and the drive for technocratic and authoritarian organizations to bring about this emancipation, on the other. He celebrated and supported the socialist drive for the emancipatory side of socialism but worried that it was frequently overwhelmed by the authoritarian drive for social organization, a worry that grew after World War I.

These issues were central to how Halévy faced the Third Republic. He was attracted to socialist arguments that economic relations were historically conditioned, to socialist claims that wealth distribution was inequitable, and to socialist critiques that economic organization was unjust. To move ahead, he believed that it would be necessary to avoid extremes. He steered a course between, on the one hand, the revolutionary socialism and syndicalism that animated much of the French Left before World War I and, on the other hand, the conservatism of many French elites. He insisted that modern industrial economies created class divisions that could not be ignored, and that economic and political conflicts could not be overcome with wishful thinking; in short, he argued that class conflict was a natural element of modern economies. It was this recognition of the economic conflict at the heart of industrial societies that led him to reject "solidarism," which he believed posited a naive hope in consensus and social agreement.[54]

This was no ordinary liberalism. It was informed by an engaged reflection on the nature of public institutions; it recommended a careful analysis of how these institutions were related to economic forces. There should be no "sacrifice of individuality to the collectivity," as he put it in a letter to Bouglé in 1895.[55] But there should also be no acceptance of unregulated competition.[56] It was necessary to think of each society, as had the Saint-Simonians, "as an association, not for the abolition of competition but for its organization."[57] But, in Halévy's opinion, this would require, not the ascendancy of a Saint-Simonian technocratic elite, but the participation of workers and working-class groups in the reorganization of economic relations and wealth distribution. It would require continuous negotiation.

Another thing that makes the analyses by Halévy so powerful today is his concern for the fragility of liberal democracy. During World War I, as seen above, he was worried that the war was causing profound deformations. After the war, he was convinced that new tensions between individuals and the state, between reason and enthusiasm, between moderation and radicalism were growing, and, lamentably, that European politics were dangerously tipping in favor of charismatic leaders who, leading powerful states, were stirring up dangerous nationalistic passions. Given events in Europe and the United States today, it is difficult not to see Halévy's sensitivity to the new and potentially destructive forces within modern states as prescient, and to view his calls for calm reason, prudent opposition, and toleration as appealing. In 1929, in his famous lectures at Oxford, he implored the audience to develop a "fanaticism of humanity powerful enough to counter-balance or to absorb our fanaticisms of nationality."[58] In his last address, in 1936, he spoke of the dangers of ideological intolerance and the ease with which the demons of nationalism were stirred up. "When we apply to ourselves the methods of historical research and come to discover the reasons for our convictions, we often realize that they are accidental, that they spring from circumstances beyond our control. And perhaps there is a lesson of tolerance in this. If one has really understood this, one is led to ask if it is worthwhile for us to massacre each other for convictions whose origins are so fragile."[59]

# NOTES

## INTRODUCTION

1. Élie Halévy, *La formation du radicalisme philosophique*, 3 vols. [first published 1901–1904], new edition directed by Monique Canto-Sperber, 3 vols. (Paris: PUF, 1995); *Histoire du peuple Anglais au XIXe siècle*, 6 vols. (Paris: Hachette, 1911–1946). There is an English translation of all of these volumes.

2. A version of these lectures was published posthumously: Élie Halévy, *Histoire du socialisme européen*, preface by Raymond Aron (Paris: Gallimard, 1948). References are to Élie Halévy, *Oeuvres complètes*, vol. 3: *Histoire du socialisme européen*, under the direction of Vincent Duclert and Marie Scot (Paris: Les Belles Lettres, 2016). There is no English translation.

3. Élie Halévy, *L'ère des tyrannies*, preface by Célestin Bouglé (Paris: Gallimard, 1938). References are to Élie Halévy, *Oeuvres complètes*, vol. 2: *L'ère des tyrannies*, under the direction of Vincent Duclert and Marie Scot (Paris: Les Belles Lettres, 2016).

4. Élie Halévy, *La théorie Platonicienne des sciences* (Paris: Alcan, 1896).

5. Françoise Mélonio, *Tocqueville et les Français* (Paris: Aubier, 1993), p. 283.

6. Raymond Aron, "L'itinéraire intellectuel d'Élie Halévy," *Bulletin de la Société français de philosophie*, vol. 64 (1971), reprinted in *L'ère des tyrannies* (Paris: Gallimard, 1990), pp. 271–78.

7. This phrase comes from Halévy's essay "L'ère des tyrannies," *Oeuvres complètes*, vol. 2: *L'ère des tyrannies*, p. 280.

8. In 1936, when Halévy looked back on his political stance before the war, he stated: "I was not a socialist. I was a 'liberal' in the sense that I was anticlerical, democrat, republican; to employ a single word that was heavy with meaning: a 'Dreyfusard.'" "L'ère des tyrannies," *Oeuvres complètes*, vol. 2, p. 283. He also frequently claimed in his correspondence that he was a liberal. See, for example, Élie Halévy, *Correspondance (1891–1937)*, texts collected and presented by Henriette Guy-Loë (Paris: Fallois, 1996), pp. 72, 176, 333, etc.

9. François Furet, "Préface," Élie Halévy, *Correspondance (1891–1937)*, p. 31.

10. The first two volumes of *La formation du radicalisme philosophique* were published in 1901; volume 3 was published in 1904.

11. The first volume, *L'Angleterre en 1815*, was published in 1912; volumes 2 and 3 of *Histoire du peuple anglais au XIX siècle* were published in 1923; the final two volumes, the "epilogue" focusing on the period 1895–1914, were published in 1926 and 1932. All were published by Hachette.

12. Élie Halévy, "La naissance du Méthodisme en Angleterre," *Revue de Paris* (July-August 1905), pp. 519–39, 841–67; *Thomas Hodgskin, précurseur anglais de Marx* (Paris: Sté nouvelle de librairie et d'éditions, 1903); *L'Angleterre et son empire* (Paris: Pages libres, 1905).

13. Historians of Britain invariably speak of Halévy and his scholarship with great respect. J. Bartlet Brebner, for example, wrote: "Halévy's writings are rewarding at several levels because the philosophical severity and subtlety of his mind and methods were accompanied by a singularly lucid, unornamented, and yet evocative prose style. Thus the Penguin editions of his *History*, in tens of thousands of small paper-bound copies, passed from hand to hand in Great Britain to reach a popular audience just before the War of 1939." J. Bartlet Brebner, "Elie Halévy," in *Some Modern Historians of Britain* (New York: Dryden Press, 1951), pp. 235–54, this quote p. 236.

14. Furet, "Préface," p. 34.

15. "Papiers Élie Halévy" and "Fonds Élie Halévy," École normale supérieure (Paris).

16. Michèle Bo Bramsen, *Portrait d'Élie Halévy* (Amsterdam: B. R. Grüner, 1978).

17. Myrna Chase, *Élie Halévy: An Intellectual Biography* (New York: Columbia University Press, 1980).

18. Raymond Aron, "Le socialisme et la guerre," *Revue de métaphysique et de morale*, 46:2 (April 1939), pp. 283–307 (reprinted in *Oeuvres complètes*, vol. 2, pp. 688–707); "L'itinéraire intellectuel d'Élie Halévy" (1970) and a different version of "Le socialisme et la guerre," (1939), both reprinted in *L'ère des tyrannies* (Paris: Gallimard, 1990), pp. 271–84.

19. Charles C. Gillispie, "The Work of Élie Halévy: A Critical Appreciation," *Journal of Modern History*, 22:3 (1950), pp. 232–49.

20. Melvin Richter, "A Bibliography of Signed Works by Élie Halévy," *History and Theory*, 7 (1978), pp. 46–70; "Étude critique: Élie Halévy," *Revue de métaphysique et de morale* (April-June 1997), pp. 271–93; and, "Elie Halévy come storico delle idee, la loro ricezione e le paradossali conseguenaze," in *Elie Halévy e l'era delle tirannie*, edited by Maurizio Griffo and Gaetano Quagliariello (Rome: Rubbettino Soveria Mannelli, 2001), pp. 143–58.

21. François Bédarida, "Élie Halévy et le socialisme anglais," *Revue historique*, 254 (1976), pp. 371–98.

22. Halévy, *La formation du radicalisme philosophique*.

23. Halévy, *Correspondance (1891–1937)*, François Furet, "Préface," pp. 19–54.

24. *Entre le théâtre et l'histoire: La famille Halévy (1760–1960)*, under the direction of Henri Loyrette (Paris: Fayard, 1996).

25. Ludovic Frobert, "Le jeune Halévy et Karl Marx," *Mil neuf cent, Revue d'histoire intellectuelle*, 17 (1999), pp. 45–65; *Élie Halévy: République et économie (1896–1914)* (Lille: Presses universitaires Septentrion, 2003); and "Élie Halévy's First Lectures on the History of European Socialism," *Journal of the History of Ideas*, 68:2 (2007), pp. 329–53.

26. Stéphan Soulié, *Les philosophes en République: L'aventure intellectuelle de la Revue de métaphysique et de morale et de la Société française de philosophie (1891–1944)* (Rennes: Presses universitaires de Rennes, 2009).

27. Vincent Duclert, "Élie et Daniel Halévy dans l'Affaire Dreyfus: Le savant, le poète et le politique," in *Entre le théâtre et l'histoire: La famille Halévy, 1760–1960*, pp. 220–35; "Élie Halévy retrouvé: World War I and the Crisis of Democratic Thought from the Dreyfus Affair to the Age of Tyrannies," *Tocqueville Review/La revue Tocqueville*, 36:1 (2015), pp. 167–84; and the introductions and notes for the *Oeuvres complètes*.

28. Marie Scot (with Françoise Dauphragne), "Les archives d'Élie Halévy: À la redécouverte de l'atelier halévien," *Histoire@Politique: Politique, culture, société*, 19 (2013); and the introductions and notes for the *Oeuvres complètes*.

29. I organized an international conference that met in Durham, North Carolina, on 20 October 2013. Some of the papers were published in *Modern Intellectual History*, 12:1 (2015), pp. 121–18. Vincent Duclert and Marie Scot organized a conference that met in Paris on 27–28 November 2016. Some of the papers are published as *Études: Élie Halévy et L'ère des tyrannies*, V. Duclert and M. Scot, eds. (Paris: Les Belles Lettres, 2019).

30. Élie Halévy, *Oeuvres complètes*, under the direction of Vincent Duclert and Marie Scot (Paris: Les Belles Lettres, 2016–). Three volumes have appeared: vol. 1: *Correspondance et écrits de guerre*, lxxvi + 553 pp.; vol. 2: *L'ère des tyrannies*, 762 pp.; vol. 3: *Histoire du socialisme européen*, xiv + 900 pp. Planned volumes: vol. 4: *Métaphysique et morale*; vol. 5: *Textes de jeunesse*; vol. 6: *Études anglaises*; vol. 7: *L'Europe libérale au XIXe siècle*; vol. 8: *Politique et République*; vol. 9: *Nouvelle correspondance générale*; vol. 10: *Histoire du peuple anglais*; vol. 11: *Radicalisme philosophique*.

31. Ludovic Frobert initiated this chronological approach to Halévy's writings about socialism. See note 25 above. After I had copied by hand many of the early lectures located in the archive, Frobert kindly supplied me with a typed version. We had hoped to publish these in English translation, but were not able to find a publisher.

CHAPTER I

Epigraphs: Alain, *Correspondance avec Élie and Florence Halévy* (Paris: Gallimard, 1958), pp. 21–22, 325.

1. There is an informative book that was associated with the 1996 exhibit: *Entre le théâtre et l'histoire: La famille Halévy, 1760–1960*, under the direction of Henri Loyrette (Paris: Fayard, 1996).

2. For details about the Halévy family, see ibid., especially the chapter by Henriette Guy-Loë, pp. 196–219; François Furet, "Préface," Élie Halévy, *Correspondance (1891–1937)*, texts collected and presented by Henriette Guy-Loë (Paris: Fallois, 1996), pp. 19–54; Michèle Bo Bramsen, *Portrait d'Élie Halévy* (Amsterdam: B. R. Grüner, 1978), pp. 1–23; Myrna Chase, *Élie Halévy: An Intellectual Biography* (New York: Columbia University Press, 1980), pp. 1–17; Diana R. Hallman, *Opera, Liberalism, and Antisemitism in Nineteenth-Century France: The Politics of Halévy's* La Juive (Cambridge: Cambridge University Press, 2002), pp. 73–107; Jean-Claude Yon, "Introduction," Ludovic Halévy, *L'invasion: Souvenirs et récits* (Paris: Mercure de France, 2014), pp. 7–22.

3. Believing that the Empire was liberalizing in 1870 following the appointment of Émile Ollivier, Anatole Prévost-Paradol accepted the post of *minister plénipotentiaire de France* to the United States, receiving much criticism from republican opponents of Napoleon III. He had scarcely arrived in Washington when the Franco-Prussian War broke out; when he received the news, he committed suicide.

4. Marcelin Berthelot wrote many books about chemistry. He was also very active in public and political affairs. He was the head of the Comité scientifique pour la défense de Paris during the Franco-Prussian War (1870–1871), minister of education (1886–1887), and briefly minister of foreign affairs (1895–1896).

5. Ludovic Halévy, *L'invasion: Souvenirs et récits*. Ludovic Halévy's most well-known book was probably *Abbé Constantin*, published in 1882.

6. On Daniel Halévy (1872–1962), see Alain Silvera, *Daniel Halévy and His Times: A Gentleman-Commoner in the Third Republic* (Ithaca: Cornell University Press, 1966); and Sébastien Laurent, *Daniel Halévy: Du libéralisme au traditionalisme* (Paris: Grasset, 2001).

7. Furet, "Préface," Élie Halévy, *Correspondance (1891–1937)*, p. 19.

8. Célestin Bouglé, "Annuaire de l'Association des anciens élèves de l'École normale" (1938), cited by Jeanne Michel-Alexandre, "Introduction," Alain, *Correspondance avec Élie and Florence Halévy*, p. 11.

9. Élie Halévy, "Journal" (18 May 1888); in Alain, *Correspondance avec Élie and Florence Halévy*, pp. 21–22.

10. Ibid., p. 22.

11. "Journal" (1 December 1890), ibid., p. 23.

12. Élie Halévy to Célestin Bouglé (16 November 1897), in Élie Halévy, *Correspondance (1891–1937)*, p. 203.

13. See, for example, Phyllis Stock-Morton, *Moral Education for a Secular Society: The Development of* Morale Laïque *in Nineteenth-Century France* (Albany: State University of New York Press, 1988); Pierre Rosanvallon, *Le sacre du citoyen: Histoire du suffrage universel en France* (Paris: Gallimard, 1992), pp. 341–90; and Philip Nord, *The Republican Moment: Struggles for Democracy in Nineteenth-Century France* (Cambridge, Mass.: Harvard University Press, 1995), pp. 64–114.

14. Halmann, *Opera, Liberalism, and Antisemitism in Nineteenth Century France*, p. 73.

15. This contrasted with the situation in the Germanies during the nineteenth century, where "assimilation" did not often extend to intermarriage. Intermarriage was more common in France. For the German story, see David Sorkin, *The Transformation of German Jewry, 1780–1840* (Oxford: Oxford University Press, 1987).

16. Élie Halévy to Daniel Halévy (16 March 1893), Élie Halévy, *Correspondance (1891–1937)*, p. 133.

17. Élie Halévy to Célestin Bouglé (14 July 1895), ibid., p. 165.

18. Élie Halévy to Célestin Bouglé (4 December 1895), ibid., p. 170.

19. Élie Halévy to Célestin Bouglé (16 July 1900]), ibid., p. 282.

20. Élie Halévy to Xavier Léon (26 March [1898]), ibid., p. 238.

21. Léon Brunschvicg, "Le philosophe," *Élie Halévy, 1870–1937* (Paris: École libre des sciences politiques, [1938]), p. 20.

22. For these years, see Stéphan Soulié, *Les philosophes en République: L'aventure intellectuelle de la* Revue de métaphique et de morale *et de la* Société française de philosophie *(1891–1914)* (Rennes: Presses universitaires de Rennes, 2009), pp. 31–54.

23. See chapter 2.

24. See Henri Bonnet, *Alphonse Darlu, maître de philosophie de Marcel Proust* (Paris: Nizet, 1961).

25. Robert Dreyfus, "L'ami," *Revue de Paris* (1 October 1937), in *Élie Halévy, 1870–1937*, p. 43. See the similar reflection by André Sigfried, who also found Halévy during these years "a little intimidating": "Souvenirs personnels," *Revue d'économie politique* (March-April 1938), in *Élie Halévy, 1870–1937*, p. 15.

26. Julien Benda, "Un grand praticien de l'esprit et du coeur," in *Élie Halévy, 1870–1937*, p. 65.

27. Though not so popular now, Alain was immensely influential for the following generation of French intellectuals. His students included André Maurois, Jean Prévost, Simone Weil, Georges Canguilhem, and Raymond Aron. One indication of his renown is that there are four volumes of Alain's writings (5,800 pages of text) published in the Pléiade series: *Propos I* (Paris: Gallimard/Pléiade, 1956); *Les arts et les dieux* (Paris: Gallimard/Pléiade, 1958); *Les passions et la sagesse* (Paris: Gallimard/Pléiade, 1960); *Propos II* (Paris: Gallimard/Pléiade, 1970). There is

more on Alain in chapters 7 and 8. On the influence of Alain, see Jean-François Sirinelli, *Génération intellectuelle: Khâgneux et normaliens dans l'entre-deux-guerres* (Paris: Fayard, 1988).

28. Sirinelli points out that neo-Kantianism remained dominant at the École normale through the mid-1920s. See *Génération intellectuelle*, pp. 488–89.

29. Émile Boutroux (1845–1921) published an influential book in 1874, *De la contingence des lois de la nature*, that was part of the neo-Kantian wave but in fact differed from Kant on a few critical issues. He did not accept Kant's claim that the phenomenal world could be understood as conforming to the laws of causality; and he argued that time (one of Kant's *a priori* intuitions) existed outside the structures of understanding. The first claim, concerning causality, was at the center of his 1874 book. Boutroux argued that physical determinism was valid only on the macro-physical level, while on the micro-physical level there was no absolute necessity—there was, rather, indeterminacy-contingency. This left a space for free will in the phenomenal world that Kant's philosophy never permitted. And it allowed space for religion, as the teleological end of "perfection" that was the goal of evolution. On Boutroux's philosophy, see Joel Revill, "Émile Boutroux, Redefining Science and Faith in the Third Republic," *Modern Intellectual History*, 6 (2009), pp. 485–512.

Boutroux rejected positivism as it was narrowly construed at the time. So did Halévy, as we see in chapter 2. How they rejected it, however, was quite different. Boutroux pushed back against positivism by advancing his philosophy of contingency. Halévy took a stance against positivism by respecting the transcendental methodology of Kant, by accepting the Kantian dichotomy between the phenomenal and the noumenal, and by insisting on the Kantian dichotomy between "is" and "ought." This did not entail embracing religion. As Brunschvicg and Halévy put it in 1894, the embrace of reason "doesn't allow for luck or miracles." Léon Brunschvicg and Élie Halévy, "L'année philosophique 1893," *Revue de métaphysique et de morale*, 2 (1894), p. 489.

The philosophical differences between Boutroux and Halévy would be joined, during World War I, by opposing stances on the importance and implications of nationalism, as we see in Chapter 7.

CHAPTER 2

Epigraph: Élie Halévy to Xavier Léon (31 August [1891]), *Correspondance Élie Halévy (1891–1937)* (Paris: Fallois, 1996), p. 65.

1. See, for example, Thomas E. Willey, *Back to Kant: The Revival of Kantianism in German Social and Historical Thought* (Detroit: Wayne State University Press, 1978); and Klaus Christian Köhnke, *The Rise of Neo-Kantianism: German Academic Philosophy Between Idealism and Positivism*, trans. R. J. Hollingdale (Cambridge: Cambridge University Press, 1991). Kant's major works had been translated into French by this time. See Jean-Pierre Lefebvre, "L'introduction de la philosophie allemande en France au XIXe siècle: La question des traductions," in *Tranferts les relations interculturelles dans l'espace Franco-Allemand (XVIIIe et XIXe siècles* (Paris: Éditions recherche sur les civilisations, 1988), pp. 464–76, esp. p. 468.

2. Among the works that focus on late nineteenth-century French thought, I've found the following especially helpful for situating Halévy: Dominique Parodi, *La philosophie contemporaine en France: Essai de classification des doctrines* (Paris: Alcan, 1919); William Logue, *From Philosophy to Sociology: The Evolution of French Liberalism, 1870–1914* (Dekalb: Northern Illinois University Press, 1983); Jean-Louis Fabiani, *Les philosophes de la république* (Paris: Editions de

minuit, 1988); Christophe Prochasson, "Philosophe au XXe siècle: Xavier Léon et l'invention du système R2M (1891–1902)," *Revue de métaphysique et de morale* (1993), pp. 109–40; Louis Pinto, "Le détail et la nuance: La sociologie vue par les philosophes dans la *Revue de métaphysique et de morale*, 1893–1899," *Revue de métaphysique et de morale* (1993), pp. 141–74; Christophe Prochasson, *Les intellectuels, le socialisme et la guerre, 1900–1938* (Paris: Seuil, 1993); Gary Gutting, *French Philosophy in the Twentieth Century* (Cambridge: Cambridge University Press, 2001); Jean-Fabien Spitz, *Le moment républicain en France* (Paris: Gallimard, 2005); Joshua M. Humphreys, "Servants of Social Progress: Democracy, Capitalism and Social Reform in France, 1914–1940 " (Ph.D. dissertation, New York University, 2005); Joel Revill, "Taking France to the School of the Sciences: Léon Brunschvicg, Gaston Bachelard, and the French Epistemological Tradition" (Ph.D. dissertation, Duke University, 2006); Stéphan Soulié, *Les philosophes en République: l'aventure intellectuelle de la* Revue de métaphysique et de morale *et de la* Société française de philosophie *(1891–1914)* (Rennes: Presses universitaires de Rennes, 2009); Frédéric Worms, *La philosophie en France au XXe siècle: Moments* (Paris: Gallimard, 2009).

3. Alphonse Darlu (1849–1921) received his agrégé in philosophy in 1871. He became a professor at the Lycée Condorcet in 1885 and *inspecteur général de l'instruction publique* in 1901.

4. The *Revue philosophique* predated the *Revue de métaphysique et de morale* and was, therefore, the chief competitor for the new journal. The *Revue* did well while Ribot was the editor. A new challenge presented itself when Lucien Lévy-Bruhl, a popular and well-connected philosopher-anthropologist, took over the *Revue philosophique* in 1916. For an analysis of the relations between the journals, see the article of Dominique Merllié, "Les rapports entre la *Revue de métaphysique* et la *Revue philosophique*: Xavier Léon, Théodule Ribot, Lucien Lévy-Bruhl," *Revue de métaphysique et de morale* (1993), pp. 59–108.

5. In a letter to Célestin Bouglé in late 1892, Halévy wrote that he defined philosophy as "an effort or a method for describing being in ideas. I say a method because philosophy, no longer taking an ontological point of view, will be purely and simply the general method of thinking, the method that the thinker uses to build a system from nature, or the method that a legislator uses to construct a system of laws." Élie Halévy to Célestin Bouglé [probably September or October 1892], *Correspondance (1891–1937)*, p. 72.

6. Célestin Bouglé, "L'ancien normalien," in *Élie Halévy, 1870–1937* (Paris: École libre des sciences politiques, [1938]), p. 47.

7. Élie Halévy to Xavier Léon (31 August [1891]), *Correspondance (1891–1937)*, p. 65.

8. Léon Bruschvicg, "Élie Halévy (6 septembre 1870–21 août 1937)," *Revue de métaphysique et de morale* (1937), pp. 679–91; reprinted in Élie Halévy, *Oeuvres complètes*, vol. 2: *L'ère des tyrannies* (Paris: Les belles lettres, 2016), pp. 669–79, this quote, p. 670.

9. *Revue de métaphysique et de morale*, 2 (1894), p. 113; cited by Prochasson, "Philosophe au XXe siècle," p. 123. There is no evidence that Léon wrote such a book.

10. Stéphan Soulié, in his recent historical account of the *Revue*, has provided a precise characterization of this aspect of the journal: "The 'moral question,' the problem of the constitution of a secular morality that is not a State morality, and which respects the prerogatives of individual conscience without renouncing the affirmation of the existence of an absolute principle, went to the heart of the preoccupations of the *Revue* and of the *Société française de philosophie.*" Soulié, *Les philosophes en République*, p. 49.

The insistence on the close relationship between philosophy and science also informed the stance the *Revue* took on educational reform.

11. Xavier Léon to Octave Hamelin (4 April 1893); cited ibid., p. 214.

12. "Introduction," *Revue de métaphysique et de morale*, 1 (1893), pp. 1–5; these phrases, p. 4.

13. In addition to the works in note 2 above, see Efraim Podoksik, "Neo-Kantianism and Georg Simmel's Interpretation of Kant," *Modern Intellectual History*, 13:3 (2016), pp. 597–622. Halévy will come to see this Kantian unity as not sufficiently attentive to historical differences and to pragmatic sociopolitical issues. We return to this later.

14. Élie Halévy to Célestin Bouglé (28 April 1903), Fonds Halévy, carton 8.

15. Poincaré defended this position many times. In a late essay, to offer one example, he wrote: "There is not a single law which we can enunciate with the certainty that it has always been true in the past with the same approximation as today; in fact, not even with the certainty that we will never be able to demonstrate that is has been false in the past. And yet, there is nothing in this to prevent the scientist from maintaining his belief in the principle of immutability, since no law will ever be relegated to the rank of being transitory, only to be replaced by another law more general and more comprehensive; since that law will owe its disgrace merely to the advent of this new law so that there will have been no interregnum and the principles will remain intact." Henri Poincaré, "The Evolution of Laws," in *Mathematics and Science: Last Essays*, translated by John W. Bolduc (New York: Dover, 1963), p. 13; originally published as *Dernières pensées* (Paris: Flammarion 1913). On Poincaré's "conventionalism," see Leszek Kolakowski, *The Alienation of Reason: A History of Positivist Thought*, trans. Norbert Guterman (Garden City, NY: Doubleday, 1968), pp. 134–53; and Peter Galison, *Einstein's Clocks, Poincaré's Maps: Empires of Time* (New York: Norton, 2003).

16. Léon Brunschvicg, "L'oeuvre d'Henri Poincaré: Le philosophe," *Revue de métaphysique et de morale*, vol. 21 (1913), pp. 597–98; cited in Soulié, *Les philosophes en République*, p. 227.

17. Élie Halévy to Xavier Léon (31 August [1891]), *Correspondance (1891–1937)*, p. 65.

18. Léon Brunschvicg and Élie Halévy, "La philosophie au Collège de France," *Revue de métaphysique et de morale*, 1 (1893), pp. 369–81.

19. These phrases, ibid., p. 370.

20. Ibid., pp. 373–74.

21. Ibid., p. 375.

22. Ibid., p. 377.

23. Ibid., p. 375.

24. Ibid., p. 374.

25. Ibid., p. 375.

26. The "positivist—metaphysical (Kantian)—spiritualist" triangle is the common manner of characterizing the tendencies within French philosophy during this historical era. Isaac Benrubi, for example, in 1933 divided French philosophy into three schools: empirical and scientific positivism; critical and epistemological idealism; and metaphysical and spiritualist positivism. Isaac Benrubi, *Les sources et les courants de la philosophie contemporaine en France* (Paris: Alcan, 1933), p. 4. In an address to the faculty of Columbia University in April 1938, Célestin Bouglé reasonably claimed that "idealistic rationalism" deriving from Descartes and Kant was dominant in France between 1880 and 1920. It was opposed by the "intuitionism" of Henri Bergson, the "naturalism-biologism" of Alfred Espinas, the Thomism of Catholics, and the materialism of Marxists. See Bouglé, *The French Conception of "Culture Générale" and Its Influences upon Instruction* (New York City: Teachers College, Columbia University, 1938), p. 44. On Fouillée, see Parodi, *Le philosophie contemporaine en France*, pp. 40–48; Logue, *From*

*Philosophy to Sociology*, pp. 129–50; and the recent article by Larry S. McGrath, "Alfred Fouillée Between Science and Spiritualism," *Modern Intellectual History*, 12:2 (2015), pp. 295–323.

27. Léon Brunschvicg and Élie Halévy, "L'année philosophique 1893," *Revue de métaphysique et de morale*, 2 (1894), pp. 473–96, 563–90, this quote p. 483.

28. Ibid., p. 484.

29. "Quelques remarques sur l'irréversibilité des phénomènes psychologiques," *Revue de métaphysique et de morale*, 4 (1896), pp. 756–77.

30. Ibid., pp. 776–77.

31. Brunschvicg reported that as early as 1900 Halévy insisted, in an address to the Congrès international de philosophie, on distinguishing his "associationism" from "the sensualist idea." "The associationist idea" took into account "the intellectual origins of the impressions of pleasure and pain." Léon Bruschvicg, "Élie Halévy: le philosophe," in *Élie Halévy, 1870–1937*, p. 21.

32. Élie Halévy, "L'explication du sentiment," *Revue de métaphysique et de morale*, 5 (1897), pp. 703–24.

33. This phrase, ibid., p. 711.

34. Ibid., p. 718.

35. Ibid., pp. 719–20.

36. For the distinction between "conscience réfléchie" and "conscience immédiate," see ibid., pp. 721–24.

37. Élie Halévy, "Quelques remarques sur la notion d'intensité en psychologie," *Revue de métaphysique et de morale*, 6 (1898), pp. 589–607.

38. Élie Halévy, "De l'association des idées," in *Philosophie générale et métaphysique* (Paris: Armand Colin, 1900), pp. 219–35.

39. Élie Halévy to Célestin Bouglé (14 October 1897), *Correspondance (1891–1937)*, p. 202.

40. Ibid., pp. 223–24, emphasis in original.

41. Ibid., p. 227.

42. Letter of Alain to Élie Halévy (16 September 1898), in Alain, *Correspondance avec Élie et Florence Halévy*, p. 81.

43. Immual Kant, "Transcendental Doctrine of the Elements," part 2, introduction, *The Critique of Pure Reason*, translated by Norman Kemp Smith (New York: St. Martin's Press), pp. 92–99.

44. Léon Brunschvicg and Élie Halévy, "La philosophie au Collège de France," p. 377.

45. Élie Halévy, *La théorie platonicienne des sciences* (Paris: Alcan, 1896).

46. Ibid., p. iv.

47. Ibid., p. iv.

48. Ibid., p. xv.

49. Ibid., p. vii.

50. The dialogic nature of Halévy's stance is suggested in a letter to Bouglé, where Halévy wrote the following: "La totalité . . . ne peut être conçue comme une totalité de vérités abstraites . . . , ni comme une totalité des choses. . . . Elle ne doit pas non plus (semble-t-il) être niée, comme le veut Kant, de telle sorte que, par un postulat pratique, l'unité, l'identité de l'idéal et du réel soit substituée à la réciprocité d'action de ces deux termes, dans l'univers scientifique. La totalité est une réciprocité d'action de deux termes hétéogènes: cela se peut démontrer par un raisonnement métaphysique, ainsi que la multiplicité infinie des formes que revêt cette réciprocité d'action. Par là sont déterminées les lois de notre pensée et de notre

action, nos devoirs théoriques et nos devoirs pratiques." Élie Halévy to Célestin Bouglé ([probably Decemer 1892?]), *Correspondance, (1891–1937)*, pp. 112–13. The dialogic nature of Halévy's rationalism/idealism is argued by Ludovic Frobert, "Élie Halévy and Philosophical Radicalism," *Modern Intellectual History*, 12:1 (2015), pp. 127–50.

There was an interesting exchange concerning the correct interpretation of Plato in the pages of the *Revue* between Halévy and Charles Bénard in 1893. Halévy critically reviewed Bénard's *Platon, sa philosophie, précédé d'un aperçu de sa vie et de ses écrits* (Paris: Alcan, 1892) in *Revue de métaphysique et de morale*, 1:3 (1893), pp. 288–301. Bénard responded: "Pour moi, j'aime mieux ce Platon inconséquent, même un peu christianisé que le Platon sceptique ou demi-sceptique de la nouvelle Académie, ou que le Platon panthéiste, hegelien ou semi-hégélien que l'on propose. En tout cas, je crois avoir suivi la vraie méthode historique." "Supplement," *Revue de métaphysique et de morale*, 1:4 (1893), pp. 3–5.

Others faulted Halévy for ignoring a historical analysis of Plato. Frédéric Rauh, for example, a scholar closely connected with the *Revue*, wrote that Halévy had left "complètement de côté la question de la chronologie et de l'authenticité des dialogues. . . . Il y a là un dédain au moins apparent de la critique philosophique et historique." Letter of 1896, cited by Renzo Ragghianti, *Alain: Apprentissage philosophique et genèse de la Revue de Métaphysique et de Morale* (Paris: Harmattan, 1995), p. 15.

51. Brunschvicg and Halévy, "L'année philosophique 1893," p. 478.

52. Brunschvicg, "Élie Halévy: le philosophe," p. 20.

53. Élie Halévy to Célestin Bouglé (30 March 1900), cited in Alain, *Correspondance avec Élie et Florence Halévy*, p. 406.

54. Élie Halévy to Xavier Léon (20 March [1898]), *Correspondance (1891–1937)*, pp. 237–38.

55. On Bergson's thought, I have found especially useful: Parodi, *La philosophie contemporaine en France*, pp. 251–344; Thomas Hanna, ed., *The Bergsonian Heritage* (New York: Columbia University Press, 1962); Leszek Kolakowski, *Bergson* (Oxford: Oxford University Press, 1985); Worms, *La philosophie en France au XXe siècle*, pp. 31–170.

56. Henri Bergson, *Essai sur les données immédiates de la conscience* (Paris: Alcan, 1889).

57. There is a good analysis of the philosophical differences between Bergson and Brunschvicg in Worms, *La philosophie en France au XXe siècle*, pp. 31–64. For Bergson's relationship with the *Revue*, see also Ragghianti, *Alain: Apprentissage philosophique et genèse de la Revue de Métaphysique et de Morale*, pp. 227–48.

58. The fact that Bergson still maintained that truths could be grasped, albeit by intuition and not by reason, was one of the issues that fundamentally separated him from subsequent philosophers of "existence" who rejected all notions of certitude. On this issue, as Frédéric Worms has argued, Bergson shared with Brunschvicg a belief in the intelligibility of the world and of the ultimate unity of mind. Worms, *La philosophie en France au XXe siècle*, pp. 23–64. That is, the philosophers of pre–World War I France did not make the move, subsequently made by Heidegger, Sartre, and others, that ontology should replace epistemology. These later thinkers would argue that neither Bergsonian intuitionism nor neo-Kantian rationalism correctly took the measure of the *limit* of our understanding of Being and, therefore, of our destiny in the world.

59. Bergson, *Essai sur les données immédiates de la conscience*; cited by Kolakowski, *Bergson*, p. 16.

60. Brunschvicg and Halévy, "L'année philosophique 1893," p. 486.

61. Letter of Louis Couturat to Élie Halévy (26 September 1896); cited by Ragghianti, *Alain: Apprentissage philosophique et genèse de la Revue de Métaphysique et de Morale*, p. 228.

62. Letter of Halévy (22 October 1908); cited by Ragghianti, ibid.

63. Élie Halévy to Célestin Bouglé (22 March [1901]), *Correspondance (1891–1937)*, p. 298.

64. Soulié, *Les philosophes en République*, p. 230.

65. *Revue philosophique* (November 1892); cited by Parodi, *La philosophie contemporaine en France*, p. 94.

66. "Tout est réductible à des explications physico-chimiques." Théodule Ribot, *La psychologie des sentiments* (Paris: Alcan, 1896), p. 5.

67. "Le fond de la vie affective d'est l'appétit ou son contraire, c'est-à-dire des mouvements ou arrêts de mouvements; que dans sa racine, elle est tendance, acte à l'état naissant ou complet, indépendante de l'intelligence." Ibid. p. 429.

Reservations concerning Ribot's psychological theories, similar to Halévy's, were expressed in the pages of *Revue de métaphysique et de morale* by Frédéric Rauh. See Rauh's article "Les diverses formes du caractère d'après M. Ribot," *Revue de métaphysique et de morale*, 1 (1893), pp. 492–506. Rauh was critical of Ribot's theory "pour éliminer l'intelligence comme élément fondamental du caractère" (p. 497).

On Ribot's relationship to positivism, see Vincent Guillin, "Théodule Ribot's Ambiguous Positivism: Philosophical and Epistemological Strategies in the Founding of French Scientific Psychology," *Journal of the History of the Behavioral Sciences*, 40:2 (2004), pp. 165–181. For an account of the early nineteenth-century relationship of French psychology to philosophical arguments concerning materialism and "physiology," see Jan Goldstein, *Console and Classify: The French Psychiatric Profession in the Nineteenth Century* (Cambridge: Cambridge University Press, 1987), pp. 240–75.

68. Brunschvicg and Halévy, "La philosophie au Collège de France," *Revue de métaphysique et de morale*, 1 (1893), pp. 373–74.

69. Élie Halévy to Célestin Bouglé (6 janvier 1897), Fonds Halévy, École normale supérieure (Paris), carton 8.

70. Durkheim saw sociology and "modern education" (versus "classical education") as the best means of protecting the Third Republic and of resolving the crisis opened up in France by the revolutionary tradition. He wrote in *Les règles de la méthode sociologique* (1895), for example: "It is no longer a question of pursuing desperately an objective that retreats as one advances, but of working with steady perseverance to maintain the normal state, of re-establishing it if it is threatened, and of rediscovering its conditions if they have changed. The duty of the statesman is no longer to push society toward an ideal that seems attractive to him, but his role is that of the physician: he prevents the outbreak of illnesses by good hygiene, and he seeks to cure them when they have appeared." Émile Durkheim, *The Rules of Sociological Method*, trans. S. A. Solovay and J. H. Mueller (New York: Free Press, 1964), p. 75. Halévy could only applaud such a stance, as I indicate in chapters 5 and 6.

71. As Jean-Louis Fabiani has put it, "It is the unquestioned acceptance of the belief that intellectual activity (it matters little whether it is the product of an inquiry or of a metaphysical reflection) is capable without mediation, by its own efficacy, of producing in society the effects of a moral reform." Jean-Louis Fabiani, "Métaphysique, morale sociologie: Durkheim et le retour à la philosophie," *Revue de métaphysique et de morale* (1993), pp. 175–191; this quote, p. 180.

72. Durkheim attempted to provide an empirical sociological answer to a philosophical question of epistemology. He argued that collective *répresentations* were the like Kantian "categories," and that they, therefore, provided an empirical answer to Kant's idealism. This, however, was a faulty philosophical move: to mistake a claim about the "content of the mind" for Kant's epistemological claim about the "capacity of the mind."

73. Durkheim famously argued in *Les règles de la méthode sociologique*: "The determining cause of a social fact should be sought among the social facts preceding it and not among the states of the individual consciousness." Durkheim, *The Rules of Sociological Method*, p. 110.

74. Brunschvicg and Halévy, "L'année philosophique 1893," p. 566.

75. This issue would also be the basis of Halévy's criticism of his friend Bouglé's sociology. In a letter in January 1899, he wrote: "Je pense que tu diminues à l'excès l'importance des causes intellectuelles du progrès des sociétés. . . . J'ai été choqué de retrouver chez toi la notion de densité sociologique, déjà trouvée autrefois chez Durkheim." Élie Halévy to Célestin Bouglé (5 January [1899?]), *Correspondance (1891–1937)*, pp. 259.

76. Brunschvicg and Halévy, "L'année philosophique 1893," p. 568.

77. Élie Halévy to Célestin Bouglé (6 February [1906]), *Correspondance (1891–1937)*, p. 374.

78. For the latter point, see Durkheim's review of Labriola's book in *Revue philosophique*, 44 (1897), pp. 645–51. There is a good discussion of Durkheim's methodological and conceptual evolution during the 1890s in Steven Lukes, *Émile Durkheim: His Life and Work* (New York: Harper and Row, 1972), pp. 226–36.

79. In 1902, Halévy wrote to Bouglé about the individual-social nexus: "S'il faut prolonger la discussion sur l'individualisme, je répondrai que les mots en isme portent malheur à ceux qui les imploraient. L'individuel n'étant tel que par son opposition au social, tu pourras toujours m'objecter qu'une explication 'genre Frazer' se réfère à des propriétés de la nature humaine qui n'ont rien de spécialement 'individuel.' Mais elles deviennent 'spécifiquement individuels,' lorsqu'il s'agit d'expliquer par elles un phénomène social, et lorsque, *par suite*, la pensée apparaît, nécessairement comme l'attribut d'un certain nombre d'êtres individuels qui s'arrangent pour vivre ensemble." Élie Halévy to Célestin Bouglé (16 April 1902), Fonds Halévy, carton 8.

The same year (1902), Durkheim wrote to Xavier Léon about a critical review that had appeared in the *Revue*: "What I deplore is precisely that [your review] should have thought it necessary to give a personal character to the criticism of a work that is essentially collective and impersonal and which I try to keep as impersonal as possible." Letter dated 21 September 1902; cited by Lukes, *Émile Durkheim*, p. 293. While Durheim framed his complaint as a discomfort about the personal nature of the criticism, the irritation clearly went deeper, and related to the challenge made to Durkheim's methodology and its philosophical underpinnings. Durkheim in response temporarily refused to allow his inaugural lecture in Paris to be published in the *Revue*.

80. Brunschvicg and Halévy, "L'année philosophique 1893," p. 568.

81. Durkheim wrote in *Division du travail social*: "La conscience est un mauvais juge de ce qui se passe au fond de l'être, parce qu'elle n'y pénètre pas" (Paris: Alcan, 1893), p. 394.

82. Brunschvicg and Halévy, "L'année philosophique 1893," p. 569. A similar critique of Durkheim and "l'école sociologique" was advanced in 1919 by Dominique Parodi (close to the *Revue*) in his *La philosophie contemporaine en France*, pp. 150–60. Parodi argued that this sociological theory amounted to "a sort of idealism . . . a sort of social mysticism. . . . It weakens the confidence that we are able to have in reason" (pp. 151–52).

83. Steven Lukes has a lucid discussion of Durkheim's "sociology of morality." See his *Émile Durkheim*, pp. 410–34.

84. In the 1930s, Brunschvicg is reported to have characterized Durkheim's propensity to view as legitimate any society's collective representations as "society adoring itself." Cited by

Lukes, *Émile Durkheim*, p. 339 note. Lukes writes that Raymond Aron, in a personal communication addressed to him, recalled Brunschvicg telling him (Aron) in the late 1930s that "Nuremberg is religion according to Durkheim, society adoring itself."

85. "Enseignement" (unsigned article), *Revue de métaphysique et de morale*, 3 (1895), p. 233.

86. Ibid. p. 232.

87. This is the conclusion of Jean-Louis Fabiani. Fabiani points out that Durkheim "fait de la philosophie une province de la sociologie." "Métaphysique, morale sociologie: Durkheim et le retour à la philosophie," p. 191. Fabiani makes a similar point in *Les philosophes de la république*, pp. 11–18, 97–101, 154–55. It was more than an academic turf war, however. It involved fundamental differences of approach to issues of individual psychology and of society.

88. Brunschvicg and Halévy, "L'année philosophique 1893," p. 496.

89. Ibid., p. 489.

90. Ibid., p. 491.

91. Ibid., p. 235.

92. Tarde's best-known book is *Les lois de l'imitation: Étude sociologique* (Paris: Alcan, 1890). For a sympathetic analysis of his life and thought, see Jean Milet, *Gabriel Tarde et la philosophie de l'histoire* (Paris: Vrin, 1970).

93. Garbiel Tarde, "La logique sociale des sentiments," *Revue philosophique*, 36 (1893), p. 561.

94. Cited by Steven Lukes, *Émile Durkheim*, p. 307.

95. On the Tarde-Durkheim debate, see Lukes, *Émile Durkheim*, pp. 302–13; and Milet, *Gabriel Tarde et la philosophie de l'histoire*, especially pp. 247–57.

96. See, for example, the critique of Tarde by Bouglé in his book *Idées égalitaires* (Paris: Alcan, 1899), pp. 81–83.

97. Célestin Bouglé, "Un sociologue individualiste: Gabriel Tarde," *Revue de Paris* (15 May 1905), pp. 294–316.

98. Alfred Espinas in *Revue philosophique*, 50 (1900), p. 449, cited by Milet, *Gabriel Tarde et la philosophie de l'histoire*, pp. 43–44.

99. This comparison is noted by Françoise Mélonio, *Tocqueville et les Français* (Paris: Aubier, 1993), esp. pp. 263–69.

100. Halévy's friend Graham Wallace had a similar conception. "The mind of man is like a harp, all of whose strings throb together; so that emotion, impulse, inference, and the special kind of inference called reasoning, are often simultaneous and intermingled aspects of a single mental experience." Wallace, *Human Nature in Politics* [1908], 4th edition (London: Constable, 1948), p. 99.

101. Élie Halévy to Célestin Bouglé ([probably 8 January 1902]), *Correspondance (1891–1937)*, p. 318, emphasis in original.

102. My discussion draws from the analysis by Cheryl Welch of "inquietude" in Tocqueville's thought. See Cheryl Welch, "A New *Democracy in America*," *French Politics, Culture and Society*, 21 (2003), pp. 131–38.

103. See the letter of Élie Halévy to Célestin Bouglé (30 March [1901]), *Correspondance (1891–1937)*, pp. 298–99.

104. For these phrases, see the letters of Élie Halévy to Célestin Bouglé (2 March [1903] and 10 August [1902]), ibid., pp. 332, 324.

105. See the letters of Élie Halévy to Célestin Bouglé (29 October 1901 and 5 January [1902]), ibid., pp. 311, 319. See also *Histoire du peuple anglais au XIXe siècle, épilogue (1895–1914),*

vol. 1: *Les impérialistes au pouvoir (1895–1905)* (Paris: Hachette, 1926), p. 89, where Halévy writes of the "état de frénésie patriotique" in England during the Boer War.

106. Élie Halévy to Célestin Bouglé (29 October 1901), *Correspondance (1891–1937)*, p. 311.

107. See the letter of Élie Halévy to Célestin Bouglé (8 January [1903]), ibid., p. 331.

108. See the letter of Élie Halévy to Célestin Bouglé (19 December [1901]), ibid., p. 318.

109. Élie Halévy to Célestin Bouglé (16 [July 1900]), ibid., p. 282.

110. Papiers Élie Halévy, École normale supérieure (Paris); carton 33, folder 13. This is probably the manuscript that he mentioned in a letter to Bouglé. Élie Halévy to Célestin Bouglé (10 November 1904): "J'ai même écrit quelques pages de l'ouvrage sur les principes de la morale, dont seul tu connais l'existence: mais je sens qu'il me manquera l'impulsion décisif, pour me forcer à écrire cela tout au long, avec une introduction et une conclusion." Fonds Halévy, carton 8.

111. Ibid. Most of the manuscripts are not dated; however, this fragment is dated 21 April 1904.

112. See, for example, Élie Halévy to Célestin Bouglé ([20 February 1895]), *Correspondance (1891–1937)*, p. 145; Élie Halévy to Célestin Bouglé (18 [June 1895]), ibid., p. 159.

113. Papiers Élie Halévy, École normale supérieure (Paris); carton 33, folder 13.

114. Stefan Collini has argued that similar notions were major elements of political and social thought in Victorian England. Stefan Collini, *Public Moralists: Political Thought and Intellectual Life in Britain, 1850–1930* (Oxford: Oxford University Press, 1991).

115. Élie Halévy to Célestin Bouglé (4 May 1897), Fonds Halévy, École normale supérieure (Paris); carton 8.

116. Élie Halévy to Daniel Halvy (17 March 1893), *Correspondance (1891–1937)*, p. 133. A decade later, contemplating how to teach "Christian morals" to the young, Halévy would again recommend the ancients: "J'ai trouvé un procédé à te suggérer: enseigne-la leur chez les moralistes grecs, depuis Socrate jusqu'aux stoïciens. Ils y apprendront qu'il faut s'aimer les uns les autres; ils y apprendront en outre qu'il faut se posséder soi-même." Élie Halévy to Célestin Bouglé (15 March 1903), Alain, *Correspondance avec Élie et Florence Halévy*, p. 329.

117. "Séance Générale: 11ième Congrès de philosophie—Genève," *Revue de métaphysique et de morale*, 12 (1904), pp. 1103–13.

118. Ibid. p. 1108.

119. In a letter to Bouglé in 1905, Halévy mentioned that he had "written a hundred pages . . . on individualism." Élie Halévy to Célestin Bouglé (8 March [1905]), *Correspondance (1891–1937)*, p. 363. Unfortunately, these pages have not been found.

120. "Séance Générale," p. 1113.

121. Élie Halévy, *La formation du radicalisme philosophique*, vol.3: *Le radicalisme philosophique* [1904], new edition directed by Monique Canto-Sperber (Paris: PUF, 1995), p. 243.

122. Papiers Élie Halévy, École normale supérieure (Paris); carton 33, folder 20.

123. Élie Halévy, *Histoire du peuple anglais au XIXe siècle*, vol. 2: *Du lendemain de Waterloo à la veille du Reform Bill (1815–1830)* (Paris, 1923), pp. vi–vii.

124. Ibid. p. vi.

125. Élie Halévy to Célestin Bouglé ([24 November [1901]]), *Correspondance (1891–1937)*, p. 315.

126. Élie Halévy to Ludovic Halévy ([22 July 1903]), ibid., p. 339.

127. The phrase "spontaneous collectivism" is in the first lecture for his class on the history of European socialism. Papiers Élie Halévy, École normale supérieure (Paris). For Halévy's positive assessment of societies where individuals are co-propietors, see "Les principes

de la distribution des richesses," *Revue de métaphysique et de morale*, 14 (1906), pp. 545–95, this phrase, p. 571.

128. These phrases from Élie Halévy to Célestin Bouglé (14 May [1903]), *Correspondance (1891–1937)*, p. 333; and, Élie Halévy to Célestin Bouglé ([2 November 1903]), ibid., p. 347.

129. "Séance Générale, p. 1112.

130. Élie Halévy, *La formation du radicalisme philosophique*, vol. 3: *Le radicalisme philosophique*, pp. 236–37.

131. Élie Halévy to Célestin Bouglé ([7 February 1899]), *Correspondance (1891–1937)*, p. 261.

132. Élie Halévy to Célestin Bouglé (21 September 1904), ibid., p. 356.

133. Élie Halévy to Célestin Bouglé (4 February [1903]), ibid., p. 332.

134. Léon Brunschvicg and Élie Halévy,"L'année philosophique 1893," p. 564.

135. Ibid. p. 571.

136. Ibid.

137. Élie Halévy to Célestin Bouglé (17 December 1905), *Correspondance (1891–1937)*, p. 373.

138. Ibid. p. 574.

139. This is also the position of Paul Lapie, another contributor to the *Revue de métaphysique et de morale*. See his article "L'année sociologique 1894," *Revue de métaphysique et de morale*, 3 (1895), pp. 308–39. See also Louis Pinto, "La sociologie vue par les philosophes dans la *Revue de métaphysique et de morale*, 1893–1899," *Revue de métaphysique et de morale* (1993), pp. 141–74.

140. For this issue, see Halévy's interchange with Georges Sorel in *Bulletin de la société française de philosophie* (meeting of 20 March 1902), pp. 94–122.

141. Élie Halévy to Célestin Bouglé (4 December 1901), *Correspondance (1891–1937)*, p. 316.

142. Élie Halévy to Célestin Bouglé (19 December 1901), ibid., p. 318.

143. Brunschvicg and Halévy, "La philosophie au Collège de France," pp. 376–77. Halévy would give these issues extensive analysis in an article published in 1906: "Les principes de la distribution des richesses," *Revue de métaphysique et de morale*, 14 (1906), pp. 545–95.

144. Brunschvicg and Halévy, "L'année philosophique 1893," p. 579.

145. Ibid., p. 579.

146. Ibid., pp. 588–89.

147. Ibid., pp. 589–90.

148. See Joel Revill, "A Practical Turn: Élie Halévy's Embrace of Politics and History," *Modern Intellectual History*, 12:1 (2015), pp. 151–71.

149. For an overview of this controversy, see Harry Paul, "The Debate over the Bankruptcy of Science in 1895," *French Historical Studies*, 5 (1968), pp. 299–327. For the impact of the controversy on Halévy and the *Revue*, see Revill, "A Practical Turn: Élie Halévy's Embrace of Politics and History," pp. 164–71.

150. Ferdinand Brunetière,"Après une visite au Vatican," *Revue des deux mondes*, CXXVII (January 1895), pp. 97–118.

151. Marcelin Berthelot, "La science et la morale," *Revue de Paris* (1 February 1895), pp. 449–69.

152. Marcelin Berthelot was Halévy's cousin. He was also an avowed Kantian. Therefore, the issue stirred up both personal and ideological issues for Halévy. At first reluctant to commit the *Revue* to anticlericalism, he ultimately saw no choice. "I've been thinking about the

announcement [for the 'Questions pratiques' section]," he wrote to Bouglé, "which serves notice for better or worse that we are devoted to anticlericalism, and that bothers me, because anticlericalism is neither a position nor an opinion. However, it's the fault of the clerical party." Élie Halévy to Célestin Bouglé (30 January 1895), *Correspondance (1891–1937)*, p. 144.

153. Alphonse Darlu, "Science, morale et religion," *Revue de métaphysique et de morale*, 3 (1895), pp. 239–51.

154. Frederic Rauh, "Science, morale et religion," *Revue de métaphysique et de morale*, 3 (1895), pp. 366–74.

155. Ludovic Frobert has emphasized the importance of this. See his *Élie Halévy: République et économie (1896–1914)* (Lille: Presses universitaires Septentrion, 2003).

156. *Revue de métaphysique et de morale*, 9 (1901), supplement, p. 4, emphasis in original. All the *Revue* reviews were anonymous, but it is reasonable to assume that Halévy wrote this one, as he was the resident expert on British political economy.

157. Élie Halévy to Xavier Léon (probably 12 or 19 November 1902), *Correspondance (1891–1937)*, p. 328; Élie Halévy to Xavier Léon (14 January 1905), ibid., p. 360.

158. This phrase from Élie Halévy, *Histoire du peuple anglais au XIXe siècle*, vol. 1: *L'Angleterre en 1815* (Paris: Hachette, 1912), pp. 25, 564.

CHAPTER 3

Epigraphs: Élie Halévy, *La formation du radicalisme philosophique*, 3 vols. [1901–4], new edition directed by Monique Canto-Sperber (Paris: PUF, 1995). There is an English translation: *The Growth of Philosophic Radicalism*, translated by Mary Morris (London: Faber and Faber, 1952). References are to the new French edition, with page references to the English edition in brackets. This quote, *La formation du radicalisme philosophique*, vol. 3: *Le radicalisme philosophique*, pp. 229–30 [497].

Halévy, *La formation du radicalisme philosophique*, vol. 3, p. 232 [499].

1. Ibid.

2. "Il faut . . . observer que la nature humaine est essentiellement instable et variable. Sans même se commettre à cette affirmation, il faut dire que l'homme a une histoire dans la mesure où sa nature est instable et variable. Le problème que l'historien doit résoudre, consiste à savoir pourquoi, parmi ses variations, quelques unes réuississent. Tandis que le plus grand nombre échoue." Papiers Élie Halévy, École normale supérieure (Paris), carton 33, folder 32.

3. See the discussions of this issue by Frances Acomb, *Anglophobia in France 1763–1789: An Essay in the History of Constitutionalism and Nationalism* (Durham: Duke University Press, 1950); and by David A. Bell, *The Cult of the Nation in France: Inventing Nationalism, 1680–1800* (Cambridge, MA: Harvard University Press, 2001), esp. pp. 78–106, 140–68.

4. Voltaire's *Letters Concerning the English Nation* (1733) is probably the most famous of these early reflections about England.

5. There is an extensive literature here. Among others, see: Lucien Jaume, *L'individu effacé: Ou le paradoxe du libéralisme français* (Paris: Fayard, 1997); K. Steven Vincent, *Benjamin Constant and the Birth of French Liberalism* (New York: Palgrave Macmillan, 2011); Aurelian Craiutu, *A Virtue for Courageous Minds: Moderation in French Political Thought, 1748–1830* (Princeton: Princeton University Press, 2012).

6. See, especially, Seymour Drescher, *Tocqueville and England* (Cambridge, MA: Harvard University Press, 1964).

7. For a recent penetrating discussion, see J. A. W. Gunn, *When the French Tried to Be British* (Montreal: McGill-Queen's University Press, 2009).

8. Rousseau was critical of the English and their presumptions of liberty. In *Du Contact Social,* he wrote: "The English people think they are free, they are wrong; they are free only during the election of members of Parliament. As soon as they are elected, there is slavery, there is nothing. In the short moments of their liberty, the use that they make of it merits that they lose it" (book III, chap. XV). In his *Considérations sur la gouvernement de Pologne*, Rousseau wrote: "Representatives are difficult to deceive, but easy to corrupt, and it rarely happens that they are not. We have under our eyes the example of the Parliament of England" (chap. VII). In a letter to M. de Bastide (16 June 1760), he wrote: "When you print *Paix perpétuelle*, please, Sir, do not forget to send me the proofs. . . . There is a note where I say that in twenty years the English will have lost their liberty, I believe that it is necessary to put *the rest of their liberty,* because there are too many fools that believe they still have some."

9. For a recent analysis of the Physiocrats, see Paul Cheney, *Revolutionary Commerce: Globalization and the French Monarchy* (Cambridge, MA: Harvard University Press, 2010).

10. Papiers Élie Halévy, École normale supérieure (Paris).

11. See, especially, Hippolyte Taine, *Notes sur l'Angleterre* (Paris: Hachette, 1874); and Émile Boutmy, *Essai d'une psychologie politique du peuple anglais au XIXe siècle* (Paris: Colin, 1901). Halévy rejected, however, the racialist dimension of Taine and Boutmy's descriptions. In 1892, for example, he wrote to René Berthelot: "Pour l'instant, je me livre, sur le compte des Anglais, à de profondes méditations ethnographiques; et j'en viens à cette conclusion que la race est peu de chose, le milieu, météorologique et sociologique, tout, ou peu s'en faut. Car des deux côtes de la Manche, d'Irlande à Londres d'une part, de Brest à Calais de l'autre, il y a un mélange à peu près identique de sang celtique, germain et scandinave. La différence d'histoire, d'institutions, un bras de mer ont fait la différence de moeurs et de caractère. Les Irlandais et les Écossais sont celtes; et cependant le sang-froid écossais et l'imagination irlandaise sont les deux pôles entre lesquels oscille l'Angleterre." Élie Halévy to René Berthelot (Friday evening [25 November 1892]), *Correspondance (1891–1937)*, p. 101.

12. Ernst Renan, *Qu'est-ce qu'une nation?* (Paris : Calmann Lévy, 1882). For this phrase by Théodule Ribot, see his *La psychologie allemande contemporaine* (Paris: Librairie Germer Baillière, 1879), p. 51.

13. This phrase, Élie Halévy, *Histoire du people Anglais au XIXe siècle, épilogue (1895–1914)*, vol. 2: *Vers la démocratie sociale et vers la guerre (1905–1914)*, pp. 372–73.

14. Élie Halévy to Mme Ludovic Halévy (24 [October 1892]), *Correspondance (1891–1937)*, p. 80.

15. Élie Halévy to his family ([19 November 1892]), *Correspondance (1891–1937)*, p. 94.

16. Élie Halévy to René Berthelot (Friday evening [25 November 1892]), Fond Halévy, École normale supérieure (Paris), carton 11. A portion of this letter is in *Correspondance (1891–1937)*, p. 101.

17. Élie Halévy to Mme Ludovic Halévy (26 November 1892), *Correspondance (1891–1937)*, p. 102.

18. Élie Halévy to Célestin Bouglé (28 April [1898]), ibid., p. 243.

19. Élie Halévy to Daniel Halévy ([probably 16 November 1900]), ibid., p. 284.

20. Élie Halévy to Ludovic Halévy (5 June 1902), ibid., p. 324.

21. Élie Halévy to Célestin Bouglé (19 April 1905), ibid., p. 363.

22. Halévy, *Histoire du peuple anglais au XIXe siècle*, vol. 1: *L'Angleterre en 1815* (Paris: Hachette, 1912), p. 40.

23. Élie Halévy to Bertrand Russell (Friday 18 [September 1903]; and 12 December 1903), *Correspondance (1891–1937)*, pp. 345–46, 348–49. Also, see the discussion in Ludovic Frobert, *Élie Halévy: République et économie (1896–1914)* (Lille: Presses universitaires Septentrion, 2003), pp. 114–18.

24. Élie Halévy, *L'Angleterre et son empire* (Paris: Pages libre, 1905), pp. 121–22.

25. Élie Halévy to Célestin Bouglé (14 September 1905), *Correspondance (1891–1937)*, p. 370.

26. Élie Halévy to Célestin Bouglé ([13 November 1895]), ibid., p. 169.

27. Élie Halévy to Célestin Bouglé (26 June [1896]), ibid., p. 180.

28. Élie Halévy to Célestin Bouglé (22 [July 1896]), ibid., p. 180.

29. Jean-Marcel Jeanneney, "L'historien du socialisme," in *Élie Halévy, 1870–1937* (Paris: École libre des sciences politiques, [1938]), p. 66.

30. Élie Halévy to Ludovic Halévy (15 May 1898), "Document 4: Lettres d'Elie Halévy," in *La formation du radicalisme philosophique*, vol. 3, p. 423.

31. Halévy wrote to Bouglé in December 1900 that he had found "a large number of interesting citations" that allowed him to conclude that "the chronology of the Bentham's works is certainly established." Élie Halévy to Célestin Bouglé (16 [December 1900]), *Correspondance (1891–1937)*, p. 291.

Leslie Stephen published a three-volume study of the Utilitarians just before Halévy's, but he seems to have relied exclusively on published works. Leslie Stephen, *The English Utilitarians*, 3 vols. (London: Duckworth, 1900). Halévy read the volumes when they appeared and judged them "excellent." He also believed, however, that his book, "despite the identity of subjects, does not resemble his, and completes it on many points." Élie Halévy to Ludovic Halévy (18 November 1900), *Correspondance (1891–1937)*, p. 285. Leslie Stephen wrote admiringly of Halévy's books when he read them. Leslie Stephen to Elie Halévy (2 June 1901 and 30 November 1903), "Document 5: Lettres de Leslie Stephen et de Henri Bergson," in *La formation du radicalisme philosophique*, vol. 3, pp. 433–34.

32. Halévy referred to the defense of his thesis in letters to Bouglé. He tells Bouglé that Henri Michel seemed to have no real informed sense of his thesis, beyond vague political opinions. Concerning Charles Seignobos, on the other hand, "he had the sense that [he] genuinely esteemed my volume; and that is what counts." Élie Halévy to Célestin Bouglé (16 March [1901]), *Correspondance (1891–1937)*, p. 296.

33. In 1950, Charles Gillispie claimed that Halévy "accomplished an all too rare feat, and one particularly rare in intellectual history—he has added to historical literature a secondary work so perceptive and so clear that it provides the reader more illumination on its subject than a study of the sources would do." Charles C. Gillispie, "The Work of Elie Halévy: A Critical Appreciation," *Journal of Modern History*, 22 (1950), pp. 232–49; this quote, p. 237.

Scholarly opinion on Bentham and the Utilitarians has been more critical since the mid-twentieth century, with some scholars disputing Halévy's interpretation of Bentham and of Utilitarianism more generally. For a judicious discussion of this new literature, see Melvin Richter, "Etude critique: Elie Halévy," *Revue de métaphysique et du morale* (1997), pp. 271–93. For a judicious critique of the critiques, see Ludovic Frobert, "Elie Halévy and Philosophical Radicalism," *Modern Intellectual History*, 12:1 (2015), pp. 127–50. For more about the scholarly recepion, see my Conclusion.

34. Élie Halévy, *La formation du radicalisme philosophique*, vol. 1: *La jeunesse de Bentham*, p. 12 [3].

35. Ibid., p. 113 [89].

36. Ibid., p. 12 [4].

37. Ibid., pp. 94–95 [74–75].

38. Halévy, *La formation du radicalisme philosophique*, vol. 3: *Le radicalisme philosophique*, p. 80 [375–76].

39. Halévy, *La formation du radicalisme philosophique*, vol. 2: *L'évolution de la doctrine utilitaire de 1789 à 1815*, pp. 144–45 [266–67].

40. Halévy, *La formation du radicalisme philosophique*, vol. 1: *La jeunesse de Bentham*, p. 133 [105].

41. Ibid., p. 117 [92–93].

42. Ibid., p. 120 [95].

43. Ibid., p. 121 [96].

44. All the quotes in this paragraph, ibid., pp. 122–23 [97].

45. Ibid., pp. 124–25 [99], emphasis added.

46. Henri Bergson complimented Halévy especially for seaching and discovering these "latent postulates" in the thought of the thinkers he discussed. Henri Bergson to Halévy (2 January 1904), "Document 5: Lettres de Leslie Stephen et de Henri Bergson," in *La formation du radicalisme philosophique*, vol. 3, p. 435.

47. Halévy, *La formation du radicalisme philosophique*, vol. 1: *La jeunesse de Bentham*, p. 125 [99], emphasis added.

48. Ibid., pp. 128–29 [102].

49. See Chapter 5 for more about Halévy's support of government action and more generally of some varieties of "socialism."

50. Halévy, *La formation du radicalisme philosophique*, vol. 1: *La jeunesse de Bentham*, pp. 148–49 [118–19].

51. Ibid., p. 136 [108].

52. Halévy, *La formation du radicalisme philosophique*, vol. 3: *Le radicalisme philosophique*, p. 16 [324–25].

53. Ibid., p. 17 [326].

54. Ibid.

55. Ibid., p. 201 [474].

56. Ibid.

57. Ibid., p. 206 [478].

58. Ibid., p. 231 [498].

59. Élie Halévy to Célestin Bouglé (15 May [1898]), *Correspondance (1891–1937)*, p. 247.

60. Ibid., pp. 237–38 [503–4].

61. Ibid., p. 231 [499].

62. Ibid., p. 232 [499].

63. Ibid.

64. Élie Halévy to Célestin Bouglé (13 November 1895), *Correspondance (1891–1937)*, p. 169.

65. There is an excellent discussion of this by Melvin Richter, "Elie Halévy come storico delle idee, la loro ricezione e le paradossali conseguenaze," in *Elie Halévy e l'era delle tirannie*, edited by Maurizio Griffo and Gaetano Quagliariello (Rome: Rubbettino Soveria Mannelli, 2001), pp. 143–58.

66. Élie Halévy to Célestin Bouglé (26 June [1896]), *Correspondance (1891–1937)*, p. 180.

67. Halévy noted that there was a focus in French theory on "acquired rights," while British theory tended to focus on "interests." See, for example, *La formation du radicalisme philosophique*, vol. 1: *La jeunesse de Bentham*, p. 159 [127]. For a broader consideration of the

French-British comparative issue, see Greg Conti and Cheryl Welch, "The Reception of Elie Halévy's *La formation du radicalisme philosophique* in England and France," *Modern Intellectual History*, 12:1 (2015), pp. 197–218.

68. Halévy, *La formation du radicalisme philosophique*, vol. 1: *La jeunesse de Bentham*, pp. 47–48 [35–36].

69. Halévy, *La formation du radicalisme philosophique*, vol. 3: *Le radicalisme philosophique*, p. 17 [326].

70. Halévy, *La formation du radicalisme philosophique*, vol. 2: *L'évolution de la doctrine utilitaire de 1789 à 1815*, p. 157 [277] ; and *La formation du radicalisme philosophique*, vol 3: *Le radicalisme philosophique*, pp. 32–39 [337–42].

71. Halévy, *La formation du radicalisme philosophique*, vol. 3: *Le radicalisme philosophique*, p. 244 [509].

72. Léon Brunschvicg made this point in his posthumous hommage to Halévy. "Le philosophe pose le problème. A un historien seul il appartiendra de la résoudre. Elie Halévy sera cet historien." Léon Brunschvicg, "Le philosophe," in *Élie* Halévy, 1870–1937, p. 24.

73. See Élie Halévy to Célestin Bouglé (22 March [1901]), *Correspondance (1891–1937)*, pp. 297–98.

CHAPTER 4

Epigraphs: Élie Halévy, "L'ère des tyrannies," meeting of la Société française de philosophie (28 November 1936), in *Oeuvres complètes*, vol. 2: *L'ère des tyrannies: Études sur le socialisme et la guerre* (Paris: Les belles lettres, 2016), p. 283.

1. The front page of *La libre parole* for November 10, 1894, is reprinted in Michael Burns, *France and the Dreyfus Affair: A Documentary History* (Boston: Bedford/St. Martins, 1999), p. 35.

2. Daniel Halévy, *Regards sur l'affaire Dreyfus,* textes réunis et présentés par Jean-Pierre Halévy (Paris: Fallois, 1994), p. 35; quoted by Vincent Duclert, "Élie et Daniel Halévy dans l'affaire Dreyfus: Le savant, le poète et le politique," *Entre le théâtre et l'histoire: La famille Halévy (1760–1960)* (Paris: Fayard, 1996), pp. 220–35, this quote p. 221.

3. Bernard Lazare, *Une erreur judiciare: L'affaire Dreyfus* (Paris: Stock, 1897).

4. Élie Halévy, *La théorie platonicienne des sciences* (Paris: Alcan, 1896).

5. Much of the following is drawn from Vincent Duclert, "Élie et Daniel Halévy dans l'affaire Dreyfus: Le savant, le poète et le politique," pp. 220–35.

6. Halévy wrote to Célestin Bouglé on 16 November 1897: "Je te demande un avis sur une question grave, la question Dreyfus. Je me suis refusé à croire, *jusqu'à dimanche*, à la possibilité de son innocence. . . . Je suis presque certain que Dreyfus, même si coupable (tu m'entends) a été victime d'une machination effroyable, que la raison d'État et des intérêts électoraux commandent de dissimuler." Élie Halévy to Célestin Bouglé (16 November 1897), in Élie Halévy, *Correspondance, 1891–1937* (Paris: Fallois, 1996), p. 203.

7. Years later, Élie recounted the central role played by Lucien Herr in the mobilization of Dreyfusards. See the bulletin *Union pour la vérité* (17 December 1932).

8. The petitions appeared in *L'Aurore* et *Le Siècle* on 14 and 15 January 1898. Halévy's correspondence from mid-November 1897 to September 1899 (when Dreyfus accepted the presidential pardon) is filled with discussion of the affair. See Halévy, *Correspondance, 1891–1937*, pp. 203–68.

9. See the correspondence and the subsequent analyses of the affair in *Savoir et engagement: Écrits normaliens sur l'affaire Dreyfus*, under the direction of Vincent Duclert (Paris: Éditions rue d'Ulm, 2006). Many of the letters in this collection were sent to Élie Halévy by his colleagues from the ENS.

10. Joel Revill, "Taking France to the School of the Sciences: Léon Brunschvicg, Gaston Bachelard, and the French Epistemological Tradition" (Ph.D. dissertation, Duke University, 2006); see pp. 65–90 for a discussion of the editors of the *Revue* facing the Dreyfus Affair.

11. Élie Halévy to Célestin Bouglé (4 December 1897), *Correspondance, 1891–1937*, p. 214.

12. Élie Halévy to Célestin Bouglé (31 March 1898), ibid., pp. 239–40. There is another reference to "anti-Semites of the Right and the Left" in Élie Halévy to Célestin Bouglé (8 December 1898), ibid., p. 256.

13. Élie Halévy used this phrase in a letter to Léon Brunschvicg (9 October 1898), ibid., p. 255.

14. Élie Halévy to Célestin Bouglé (22 [February or March? 1899, probably]), ibid., pp. 263–65.

15. See the letter of Élie Halévy to Célestin Bouglé (15 and 18 August 1899), ibid., pp. 265–66.

16. See the letter of Élie Halévy to Daniel Halévy ([13 February? 1898]), ibid., p. 225.

17. Alain, *Mars ou la guerre jugée*, in the Pléiade edition: *Les passions et la sagesse* (Paris: Gallimard, 1960). See especially pp. 589, 622.

18. Vincent Duclert, "Élie et Daniel Halévy dans l'affaire Dreyfus: Le savant, le poète et le politique," pp. 222–24.

19. See Sébastien Laurent, *Daniel Halévy du libéralisme au traditionalisme* (Paris: Grasset, 2001), pp. 95–187.

20. See Jean-François Sirinelli and Pascal Ory, *Les intellectuels en France, de l'affaire Dreyfus à nos jours* (Paris: Colin, 1986); Jean-François Sirinelli, *Intellectuels et passions françaises: Manifestes et pétitions au XXe siècle* (Paris: Fayard, 1990); and Venita Datta, *Birth of a National Icon: The Literary Avant-Garde and the Origins of the Intellectual in France* (Albany: SUNY Press, 1999).

21. Vincent Duclert emphasizes this point. See his "Élie et Daniel Halévy dans l'affaire Dreyfus: Le savant, le poète et le politique," pp. 232–35; and his "Introduction: Un événement historique, politique, philosophique," in *Savoir et engagement: Écrits normaliens sur l'affaire Dreyfus*, pp. 13–23.

22. Élie Halévy, *Histoire du peuple anglais au XIXe siècle: Épilogue (1895–1914)*, vol. 1: *Les impérialistes au pouvoir (1895–1905)* (Paris: Hachette, 1926), p. iv.

23. E. I. Watkin to Élie Halévy, *Correspondance, 1891–1937*, p. 686, note 2.

24. Élie Halévy to E. I. Watkin (1 November 1927), ibid., p. 685.

25. Ibid., p. 687.

26. See the discussion by Christophe Prochasson, "Philosopher au XXe siècle: Xavier Léon et l'invention du 'système R2M' (1891–1902)," *Revue de métaphysique et de morale* (1993), pp. 126–27.

27. Vincent Duclert, "Élie et Daniel Halévy dans l'affaire Dreyfus: Le savant, le poète et le politique," p. 233.

28. Élie Halévy, "L'ère des tyrannies," p. 283.

29. Élie had written to his friend Bouglé, "If the woman whom the Gods have made for me finds herself one day on my path, and opens her arms for me, would I be able to resist the

order of the Gods? But I will not search for her in any path." Cited in *Correspondance, 1891–1937*, p. 304.

30. Élie Halévy to Célestin Bouglé (22 March [1901]), ibid., p. 298.

31. Both are statements of Henriette Guy-Loë, the niece of Florence: the first in "Élie Halévy, une biographie," *Entre le théâtre et l'histoire: La famille Halévy (1760–1960)*, p. 205; the second in a book about her parents, *André Noufflard, Berthe Noufflard, leur vie et leur peinture* (Paris: Imprimerie de la vallé d'Eure, 1982), p. 45, cited by Claude Nabokov-Joxe, "Les dames Halévy," *Entre le théâtre et l'histoire: La famille Halévy (1760–1960)*, p. 339.

32. Élie Halévy to Mme Ludovic Halévy (20 October 1901), *Correspondance, 1891–1937*, p. 310.

33. Élie Halévy to Célestin Bouglé (29 October 1901), ibid., p. 311.

34. Élie's father Ludovic died in 1908, and his mother continued to reside in the Haute-Maison in Sucy-en-Brie during most of the year. The Maison Blanche was built by Georges Vaudoyer, a brother of Daniel Halévy's wife, in the park surrounding the Haute-Maison. The Maison Blanche is now the property of the village of Sucy-en-Brie.

35. See Steven C. Hause with Anne R. Kenney, *Women's Suffrage and Social Politics in the French Third Republic* (Princeton: Princeton University Press, 1984), p. 268. Cécile Brunsch-wing, the wife of Élie's friend and colleague Léon Brunschvicg, was more active in these circles. She became leader of the Union française pour le suffrage des femmes (UFSF) before World War I.

36. Both Florence Halévy and Henriette [Noufflard] Guy-Loë were instrumental in preserving, organizing, editing, and publishing Halévy's articles, papers, and correspondence. Florence assisted with the initial publication of *L'ère des tyrannies*, preface by Célestin Bouglé (Paris: Gallimard, 1938), and *Histoire du socialisme européen*, preface by Raymond Aron (Paris: Gallimard, 1948). Henriette was instrumental in the publication of Halévy's *Correspondance (1891–1937)*, text compiled and presented by Henriette Guy-Loë (Paris: Fallois, 1996). Henriette serially, over the years, also arranged for boxes of papers to be brought to the École normale supérieure, to be archived. See the account by Marie Scot (with Françoise Dauphragne), "Les archives d'Élie Halévy: A la redécouverte de l'atelier halévien," *Histoire@Politique: Politique, culture, société*, 19 (2013).

CHAPTER 5

Epigraphs: Élie Halévy, "Journal" (18 May 1888). In Alain, *Correspondance avec Élie et Florence Halévy* (Paris: Gallimard, 1958), p. 22.

Élie Halévy to Célestin Bouglé (1 October 1913), in *Correspondance (1891–1937)*, texts collected and presented by Henriette Guy-Loë (Paris: Éditions de Fallois, 1996), p. 442.

Élie Halévy, *Histoire du socialisme européen*, originally published with a preface by Raymond Aron (Paris: Gallimard, 1948). References are to *Oeuvres complètes*, vol. 3: *Histoire du socialisme européen*, under the direction of Vincent Duclert and Marie Scot (Paris: Les belles lettres, 2016), this quote, p. 49.

1. Halévy, *Histoire du socialisme européen*, 49.

2. Alain, *Correspondance avec Florence et Élie Halévy*; Élie Halévy, *Correspondance (1891–1937)*; Élie Halévy, *Correspondance et écrits de guerre 1914–1918*, under the direction of Vincent Duclert and Marie Scot (Paris: Colin, 2014). Additional correspondence is located in the archives at the École normale supérieure (Paris) and the London School of Economics.

3. Papiers Élie Halévy, École normale supérieure de la rue d'Ulm (ENS). These early notes have now been published as "Les conférences rédigés dans les années 1900," in *Oeuvres complètes*, vol. 3: *Histoire du socialisme européen*, pp. 367–459.

4. Ludovic Frobert, *Élie Halévy: Republique et économie, 1896–1914* (Lille: Presses du Septentrion, 2003); and Ludovic Frobert, "Elie Halévy's First Lectures on the History of European Socialism," *Journal of the History of Ideas*, vol. 68 (2007), pp. 329–53. Also important are the introduction and notes of Vincent Duclert and Marie Scot in *Oeuvres complètes*, vol. 3: *Histoire du socialisme européen*.

5. For example: Judith Stone, *The Search for Social Peace: Reform Legislation in France, 1890–1914* (Albany: SUNY Press, 1985); Douglas E. Ashford, *The Emergence of the Welfare States* (Oxford: Basil Blackwell, 1986); K. Steven Vincent, *Between Marxism and Anarchism: Benoît Malon and French Reformist Socialism* (Berkeley: University of California Press, 1992); H. S. Jones, *The French State in Question: Public Law and Political Argument in the Third Republic* (Cambridge: Cambridge University Press, 1993); Christian Topalov, ed., *Laboratoires du nouveau siècle: La nébuleuse réformatrice et ses réseaux en France, 1880–1914* (Paris: EHESS, 1999); Janet Horne, *A Social Laboratory for Modern France: The Musée Social and the Rise of the Welfare State* (Durham: Duke University Press, 2002); the issue of *Mil neuf cent: Revue d'histoire intellectuelle*, 30 (2012), entitled "Le réformisme radical: Socialistes réformistes en Europe (1880–1930)"; Emmanuel Jousse, *Hommes révoltés: Les origines intellectuelles du réformisme en France* (Paris: Fayard, 2017); Julian Wright, *Socialism and the Experience of Time: Idealism and the Present in Modern France* (Oxford: Oxford University Press, 2017).

6. Élie Halévy, "Les principes de la distribution des richesses," *Revue de métaphysique et de morale*, vol. 14 (1906), pp. 545–95; this quote, p. 594.

7. Élie Halévy to Célestin Bouglé (1 October 1913), *Correspondance (1891–1937)*, p. 442.

8. See, especially, "Les principes de la distribution des richesses."

9. In a letter to Bouglé, Halévy stated, "The logic of socialism is profoundly anarchic and individualist, and assigns as the goal of society, as the reality of society, the satisfaction of all individual interests, and the economic, intellectual, and moral emancipation of all individuals." But he also recognized that some socialists were only what he termed "alleged individualists" who called for the "sacrifice of individuality to the collectivity" and discounted the importance of liberty to "defend the abstract ideas of the nation, the family, and others." Élie Halévy to Célestin Bouglé (7 May 1895), *Correspondance (1891–1937)*, p. 156.

10. Élie Halévy, "L'ère des tyrannies," in *Oeuvres complètes*, vol. 3: *L'ère des tyrannies: Études sur le socialisme et la guerre*, under the direction of Vincent Duclert and Marie Scot (Paris: Les belles lettres, 2016), p. 279.

11. Alain, *Corresponance avec Élie et Florence Halévy*, p. 22.

12. Élie Halévy to Célestin Bouglé (following a letter of 5 November 1894), *Correspondance (1891–1937)*, p. 143.

13. Élie Halévy to Daniel Halévy (21 April 1895), ibid., p. 153.

14. Élie Halévy to Daniel Halévy (7 May 1895), ibid., p. 155.

15. Élie Halévy to Célestin Bouglé (5 January [1902]), ibid., pp. 318–19. Constantin Pecqueur (1801–1888) was an important socialist thinker of the 1840s, gaining his highest visibility when he worked closely on the Luxembourg Commission with Louis Blanc and François Vidal. Though recognized earlier by Benoît Malon, *Constantin Pecqueur, doyen du collectivisme français* (Paris: Bibliothèque de la Revue socialiste, 1886), he is only now receiving serious scholarly attention. See: *De la République de Constantin Pecqueur (1801–1888)*, under the direction of Clément Coste, Ludovic Frobert, and Marie Lauricella (Besançon: Presses universitaires de

Franche-Comté, 2017); and Ludovic Frobert, "What Is a Just Society? The Answer According to the Socialistes Fraternitaires Louis Blanc, Constantin Pecqueur, and François Vidal," *History of Political Economy*, 46:2 (2014), pp. 281–306.

16. Élie Halévy to Célestin Bouglé (2 November 1903), *Correspondance (1891–1937)*, p. 347.

17. Élie Halévy, review of Gaston Isambert's *Les idées socialistes en France de 1815 à 1848* (1905), in *Annales de sciences politiques*, 21 (1906), pp. 407–9; this quote p. 408.

18. "Séance du 20 février 1912," *Bulletin de la Société française de philosophie* (Paris: Armand Colin, 1912), pp. 173–97. Halévy argued that Proudhon was an economic and juridical individualist. "More republican than democratic, and in preparing the doctrine, for the anarchists owe him so much, he opposed to the theory of the social contract [of Rousseau] the theory of the economic contract, of the contract of exchange, and wants a society constituted through a fidelity to individual contracts, freely concluded and always freely revocable" (p. 174).

19. Halévy suggested that there were passages where Proudhon recognized a "metaphysique of the group," and he argued that this indicated an internal contradiction in Proudhon's thought. To bring these two divergent views together, Halévy suggested, Proudhon introduced the hypothesis of progress, "the idea which has been the dogma of European philosophy of the nineteenth century" (ibid., p. 176). Bouglé argued that this did not sufficiently take into account the "sociology" of Proudhon. Halévy responded that Proudhon was "an eccentric, a loner," and was first and foremost an "individualist" (ibid., pp. 177–93, these phrases pp. 189 and 191). Though not critical for the argument here, I think Bouglé, who published several studies of Proudhon, had a better understanding of Proudhon's thought than did Halévy.

20. Élie Halévy to Célestin Bouglé (24 November [1905]), *Correspondance (1891–1937)*, p. 371.

21. "Séance du 20 février 1912," *Bulletin de la Société française de philosophie*, p. 193.

22. Élie Halévy to Dominique Parodi (8 February 1901), *Correspondance (1891–1937)*, p. 295.

23. Élie Halévy to Dominique Parodi (22 January 1904), ibid., p. 350.

24. Élie Halévy to Célestin Bouglé (24 November [1901]), ibid., p. 315.

25. Halévy, "Les principes de la distribution des richesses," this phrase, p. 571.

26. The phrase "spontaneous collectivism" is in the first lecture for Halévy's class on the history of European socialism, discussed later. For the comment to Bouglé, see Élie Halévy to Célestin Bouglé (19 December 1901), *Correspondance (1891–1937)*, p. 318.

27. Halévy, "Les principes de la distribution des richesses," this phrase, p. 566.

28. Élie Halévy to Célestin Bouglé (10 March 1907), Fond Halévy, École normale supérieure (Paris). On the issue of the debate concerning the organization of public employees, see Jones, *The French State in Question*.

29. Élie Halévy to Célestin Bouglé (22 October 1910), *Correspondance (1891–1937)*, p. 408.

30. Élie Halévy, *Histoire du peuple anglais au XIXe siècle*, vol. 1, *L'Angleterre en 1815* (Paris: Hachette, 1912), p. 554. Similarly, in 1893, Halévy wrote: "The economist did not ask himself if this state was realizable: he supposed this realized state, because it was the condition of the possibility of his science; he did not pose the critical problem of knowing if the abstractions of political economy were legitimate in the same way as those of physics, astronomy, and geometry." Halévy, "La philosophie au Collège de France," *Revue de métaphysique et de morale*, 1 (1893), pp. 376–77.

31. Papiers Élie Halévy, École normale supérieure (Paris), now published as "Les conférences rédigés dans les années 1900," *Oeuvres complètes*, vol. 3: *Histoire du socialisme européen*, pp. 367–459.

32. J.-M. Jeanneney, "L'historien du socialisme," in *Élie Halévy, 1870–1937* (Paris: École libre des sciences politiques, [1938]), pp. 66–69. Jeanneney recalled that the specific focus of Halévy's lectures on socialism shifted. Sometimes Halévy focused on Marx, sometimes on French socialism, sometimes (after the war) on the Russian Revolution or other contemporary topics.

33. Daniel Guérin to Célestin Bouglé (19 December [1937]); cited by François Bédarida, "Elie Halévy et le socialisme anglais," *Revue Historique*, 254:2 (1975), pp. 371–98; this quote, p. 372.

34. Halévy, "Les conférences rédigés dans les années 1900," p. 373.

35. The quotations in the next few paragraphs come from ibid., pp. 373–80.

36. "It is not a question here of wondering if Marxism truly is an original doctrine, if it is not made of parts borrowed a little from all sides, if its philosophy of history does not often speak the language of the Hegelian dialectic, its theory of value the language of the political economy of Ricardo, if it has not borrowed from Sismondi his theory of overproduction and crisis, from Pecqueur his theory of the industrial concentration. . . . All this proves the truly synthetic character of the doctrine. In it are absorbed, fused together, systematized, all the discernable elements in the fermentation of anterior ideas." Ibid. p. 377.

37. This lesson corresponds to the text in "Annexe I" of *Histoire du socialisme européen*, pp. 317–31. References are to this source.

38. Ibid., p. 324.

39. Ibid., p. 328.

40. This lesson corresponds to the text in "Annexe II" of *Histoire du socialisme européen*, pp. 333–45. References are to this source.

41. Élie Halévy to Célestin Bouglé (1st November 1908), *Correspondance (1891–1937)*, p. 398.

42. Except for a few introductory comments, this lesson corresponds to the text in part II, chapter 3, of *Histoire du socialisme européen*, pp. 125–38. References are to this source.

43. Élie Halévy to Célestin Bouglé (9 November 1901), *Correspondance (1891–1937)*, p. 313.

44. Élie Halévy to Célestin Bouglé (22 November 1901), ibid., p. 314.

45. Élie Halévy to Xavier Léon (14 September 1913), ibid., p. 441.

46. "Je lis Pecqueur. As-tu lu Pecqueur? Tout ce que Marx a écrit sur la concentration capitaliste est copié chez Pecqueur. Le succès est un mystère. Car pourquoi le mérite de la théorie revient-il et reviendra-t-il toujours à Karl Marx?" Élie Halévy to Célestin Bouglé (5 January [1902]), ibid., pp. 318–19.

47. Élie Halévy to Célestin Bouglé ([23 May 1902]), ibid., pp. 321–22. Halévy would go on to claim that Hodgskin was "inventeur de la théorie marxiste de la plus-value." Élie Halévy to Célestin Bouglé (6 [November 1902]), ibid., p. 327.]

48. Élie Halévy, *Thomas Hodgskin (1787–1869)* (Paris: Sté nouvelle de librairie et d'éditions, 1903). Halévy signals Bouglé in November 1902 that his volume on Hodgskin is finished. Élie Halévy to Célestin Bouglé (24 [November 1902]), *Correspondance (1891–1937)*, p. 329. A few months later, he suggested to Bouglé that his book on Hodgskin would be "intéressant pour les spécialistes du Marxisme, un peu intéressant pour le reste des mortels." Élie Halévy to Célestin Bouglé (15 mars 1903), Fond Halévy, carton 8.

49. Halévy, *Histoire du socialisme européen*, p. 67.

50. Halévy, *Thomas Hodgskin*, pp. 196 and 191.

51. This quote from Marx and Engels, *The Communist Manifesto*. This translation, *Karl Marx, Selected Writings*, ed. David McLellan (Oxford: Oxford University Press, 1997), p. 238.

52. Halévy noted the similarities and differences between Hodgskin and Marx in the conclusion to *Thomas Hodgskin*, pp. 191–209.

53. Halévy, *Histoire du socialisme européen*, p. 118.

54. Élie Halévy to Célestin Bouglé (24 November 1902), *Correspondance (1891–1937)*, p. 329. Halévy was just as emphatic in his third volume of the history of English Radicalism. "It should not be said that men were born free and founded the State to increase their security at the expense of their liberty. It should be said that men wanted to be free, and that, in so far as they wanted to be free, they constituted the State to increase simultaneously their security and their liberty." *La formation du radicalisme philosophique*, vol. 3: *Le radicalisme philosophique* [1904], new edition directed by Monique Canto-Sperber (Paris: PUF, 1995), p. 243.

55. Halévy, "Les principes de la distribution des richesses," passim.

56. Halévy to Célestin Bouglé (14 September 1905), *Correspondance (1891–1937)*, p. 370.

57. Halévy, "Les principes de la distribution des richesses," p. 580.

58. Ibid., p. 592.

59. Ibid., p. 567.

60. Ibid., p. 566.

61. Ibid., pp. 566–67.

62. Ibid., p. 567.

63. Ibid., pp. 570–71.

64. Ibid., p. 590.

65. Ibid., p. 594.

66. Similarly, in a 1904 summary of a session of the second Congress of Philosophy, devoted to Pareto and his conception of the individual and the social, Halévy distanced himself from a "liberalism" that wished radically to restrict the intervention of the state. "Séance générale du congrès de philosophie—Genève," *Revue de métaphysique et de morale*, 12 (1904), pp. 1103–13.

67. Ibid., p. 595.

68. Ibid., p. 591.

69. Ibid.

70. Èlie Halévy to Célestin Bouglé (14 May [1903]), *Correspondance (1891–1937)*, p. 333.

71. Èlie Halévy to Célestin Bouglé (2 November 1903), ibid., p. 347.

72. The article, "La doctrine économique Saint-Simonienne," was published in *Revue du Mois* (10 December 1907), pp. 641–76, and (10 July 1908), pp. 39–75. Though it was published in 1907–8, Halévy informed Bouglé in November 1908 that he had written the two -part article two years earlier. Èlie Halévy to Célestin Bouglé (1 November 1908), *Correspondance (1891–1937)*, p. 397. Both articles were reproduced in *L'ère des tyrannies*, pp. 83–149 [21–104]. References are to this source.

73. See, for example, Élie Halévy to Célestin Bouglé (17 [December 1905]), *Correspondance (1891–1937)*, p. 373.

74. Élie Halévy, "La doctrine économique Saint-Simonienne," p. 84 [21].

75. Ibid., p. 85 [21].

76. Whether Saint-Simon or Auguste Comte was responsible for the doctrinal transitions during these years is still disputed by scholars. See, especially, Sébastien Charléty, *Histoire de Saint-Simonisme, 1825–1864* (Paris: Hachette, 1896); and Mary Pickering, *Auguste Comte: An Intellectual Biography*, vol. 1 (Cambridge: Cambridge University Press, 1993), esp. pp. 60–139.

77. This is Halévy quoting Saint-Simon's *Système industriel*. "La doctrine économique Saint-Simonienne," p. 113 [58].

78. Ibid., pp. 128–31 [78–82].

79. Ibid., pp. 112–13 [58–59].

80. Ibid., p. 109 [54].

81. Ibid., p. 144 [97].

82. Ibid., pp. 111–12 [56–57].

83. Ibid., p. 145 [99].

84. And toward the goal of "exploitation of the inhabited globe. That is the true purpose of political economy." Ibid. p. 122 [70]. Halévy seems to have shared this view of the purpose of economic activity.

85. Ibid., p. 127 [76].

86. Ibid., p. 123 [72].

87. See the discussion in Chapter 2 above.

88. I also discuss this in "Élie Halévy on England and the English," *Modern Intellectual History*, 12:1 (2015), pp. 173–96, and in Chapter 6 here.

89. "La politique de paix sociale en Angleterre" [1919]; "Le problème du contrôle ouvrier" [1921]; "État présent de la question sociale en Angleterre" [1922]. All three are reprinted in *L'ère des tyrannies*. See the discussion in my Chapter 8.

90. Élie Halévy to Célestin Bouglé (10 March 1913), in Alain, *Correspondance avec Élie et Florence Halévy*, p. 336.

91. In 1906, Halévy referred to the English Labour Party as "a party of mutualists." Élie Halévy to Célestin Bouglé (10 May [1906]), *Correspondance (1891–1937)*, p. 377.

92. Élie Halévy, "Les principes de la distribution des richesses," p. 591.

93. This phrase is in a letter of Élie Halévy to Florence Halévy (28 December 1906), *Correspondance (1891–1937)*, p. 382. See also "La naissance du Méthodisme en Angleterre," *Revue de Paris*, vol. 14 (July-August 1906), pp. 38–40.

94. Élie Halévy to Célestin Bouglé (26 September 1912), *Correspondance (1891–1937)*, p. 428.

95. Élie Halévy to Célestin Bouglé (following a letter of 5 November 1894), ibid., p. 143.

96. Élie Halévy to Ludovic Halévy (19 [February] 1898), ibid., p. 229. Henri Rocheford (1831–1913) was a Communard, who then turned to the radical Right: a Boulangist, anti-Semitic, anti-Dreyfusard.

97. Élie Halévy to Célestin Bouglé (14 September [1905]), ibid., p. 370. Gustave Hervé (1871–1944) was a violent socialist opponent of the military before World War I, who circa 1912 turned to militant ultranationalism.

98. Élie Halévy to Célestin Bouglé (25 December 1905), ibid., p. 373.

99. Élie Halévy to Célestin Bouglé (10 May [1906]), ibid., p. 377.

100. Élie Halévy to Florence Halévy (28 December 1906), ibid., p. 382.

101. Élie Halévy to Célestin Bouglé (19 October 1908), Fonds Halévy, carton 8.

102. Élie Halévy to Célestin Bouglé (18 January 1904), Fonds Halévy, carton 8.

103. Élie Halévy to Célestin Bouglé (15 June 1913), *Correspondance (1891–1937)*, p. 438.

104. Élie Halévy to Célestin Bouglé (1 October 1913), ibid., p. 442.

105. These phrases: *Histoire du peuple anglais au XIXe siècle*, vol. 1: *L'Angleterre en 1815*, pp. 559, 564.

106. Halévy, "La naissance du Méthodisme en Angleterre," *Revue de Paris* (July-August 1906), p. 38.

107. Élie Halévy to Célestin Bouglé (20 May 1905), Fonds Halévy, carton 8.

108. Halévy, "La naissance du Méthodisme en Angleterre," p. 40.

109. Élie Halévy to Mme Ludovic Halévy (24 [October 1892]), *Correspondance (1891–1937)*, p. 80.

110. Élie Halévy to Célestin Bouglé (29 May 1906), Fonds Halévy, carton 8, emphasis in original.

111. In October 1898, Halévy referred to the "une bande de cabotins hurleurs" who led the crowds during the affair. See Élie Halévy to Léon Brunschvicg (9 [October 1898]), *Correspondance (1891–1937)*, p. 255.

112. Élie Halévy to Xavier Léon (9 [February 1898]), ibid., p. 223.

113. Élie Halévy to Daniel Halévy ([probably 13 May 1898]), ibid., p. 246.

114. Élie Halévy to Célestin Bouglé (15 [June 1894]), ibid., p. 143.

115. Élie Halévy to Célestin Bouglé (27 Februarry [1904]), ibid., p. 352. See also Élie Halévy to Célestin Bouglé (29 [April 1906]), ibid., p. 375, where Halévy laments how "the French esprit changes daily."

116. See, for example, Élie Halévy to Célestin Bouglé (16 November 1897), ibid., p. 203.

117. Élie Halévy to Célestin Bouglé (10 May [1906]), ibid., p. 377.

118. See Halévy's comments from Séance de la Société française de philosophie (28 November 1936), "L'ère des tyrannies," in *L'ère des tyrannies*, pp. 283–84 [269–71].

## CHAPTER 6

Epigraphs: Élie Halévy to Florence Halévy [2 July 1903], Élie Halévy, *Correspondance (1891–1937)*, texts collected and presented by Henriette Guy-Loë (Paris: Fallois, 1996), p. 336.
Élie Halévy, *Histoire du peuple anglais au XIXe siècle*, vol. 1: *L'Angleterre en 1815* (Paris: Hachette, 1912), p. 559 [587]. There is an English translation: *A History of the English People in the Nineteenth Century*, vol. 1: *England in 1815*, second revised edition, translated by E. I. Watkin and D. A. Barker (London: Benn, 1949), but many passages are not as precise as the originals. References, therefore, are to the original French edition, with page references to the English edition in brackets. All translations are my own.

1. Élie Halévy, *La formation du radicalisme philosophique*, 3 vols. [published 1901–4], new edition directed by Monique Canto-Sperber, 3 vols. (Paris: PUF, 1995).

2. Élie Halévy, *L'Angleterre et son empire* (Paris: Pages libres, 1905).

3. Élie Halévy, "La naissance de Méthodisme en Angleterre," *Revue de Paris* (1 and 15 August 1906), pp. 519–39, 841–67. References are to the translation by Bernard Semmel, *The Birth of Methodism in England* (Chicago: University of Chicago Press, 1971).

4. Elie Halévy, *Histoire du peuple anglais au XIXe siècle*, vol. 1: *L'Angleterre en 1815*. Strangely enough, Halévy had his manuscript rejected by Colin, and he briefly agonized about getting it published. See his letters to Lucien Herr (26 December 1910, 30 December 1910, 8 January 1911, 12 January 1911), *Correspondance (1891–1937)*, pp. 412–19.

5. For a clear statement of this thesis, see *Correspondance (1891–1937)*, p. 364. In a letter to Lucien Herr (30 December 1910), Halévy summarized the thesis of *L'Angleterre en 1815*: "C'est le 'réveil évangélique' du XVIIIe siècle qui explique le caractère tempéré du 'libéralisme' et de l''individualisme' anglais au XIXe siècle, qui a peu à peu rendu impossible en Angleterre la formation de partis réactionnaires et révolutionnaires à la manière continentale." Ibid., p. 413.

6. This phrase comes from a subsequent volume of Halévy's history of England: *Histoire du peuple anglais au XIXe siècle*, vol. 2: *Du lendemain de Waterloo à la veille du Reform Bill (1815–1830)* (Paris: Hachette, 1923), vi.

7. See, for example, Élie Halévy to Ludovic Halévy ([25 October 1899]), *Correspondance (1891–1937)*, pp. 270–71.

8. Halévy, *L'Angleterre et son empire.*

9. Ibid., p. 48, for the comment that Disraeli "invented imperialism"; p. 64 for the definition of "Asiatic imperialism."

10. Ibid., p. 121.

11. Ibid., pp. 121–22.

12. Ibid., p. 123.

13. Élie Halévy to Ludovic Halévy [26 April 1897], *Correspondance (1891–1937)*, p. 192.

14. Élie Halévy to Ludovic Halévy (24 April 1897), ibid., p. 191.

15. Élie Halévy to Ludovic Halévy [26 April 1897], ibid., p. 192.

16. Élie Halévy to Ludovic Halévy [5 May 1897], ibid., p. 196.

17. Halévy, "La naissance du Méthodisme en Angleterre."

18. *The Birth of Methodism in England*, p. 56.

19. Ibid., p. 62.

20. Ibid., p. 49.

21. These phrases, ibid., pp. 38–39.

22. Ibid., p. 49.

23. Ibid., p. 70.

24. Ibid., p. 76.

25. Ibid., p. 77.

26. Ibid., p. 51.

27. Especially important here are E. P. Thompson, *The Making of the English Working Class* (New York: Pantheon, 1964), and E. J. Hobsbawm, *Primitive Rebels* (New York: W. W. Norton, 1965), esp. pp. 128–32. Bernard Semmel provides an overview of this historiography: "Introduction: Elie Halévy, Methodism, and Revolution," *The Birth of Methodism in England*, pp. 1–29.

28. See, for example, the book by Brent Sirota, *The Christian Monitors: The Church of England and the Age of Benevolence, 1680–1730* (New Haven: Yale University Press, 2014).

29. Halévy, *The Birth of Methodism in England*, p. 76.

30. Halévy, *Histoire du peuple anglais au XIXe siècle*, vol. 1, *L'Angleterre en 1815.*

31. Élie Halévy to Lucien Herr (30 December 1910), *Correspondance (1891–1937)*, p. 413; emphasis in original.

32. Halévy, *Histoire du peuple anglais au XIXe siècle*, vol. 1, *L'Angleterre en 1815*, p. v [xi].

33. Ibid., pp. 31–32 [35].

34. Ibid., p. 38 [41].

35. Ibid., p. 113 [119].

36. J. Bartlet Brebner, "Elie Halévy," in *Some Modern Historians of Britain: Essays in Honor of R. L. Schuyler*, ed. H. Ausubel, J. B. Brebner, and E. M. Hunt (New York: Dryden Press, 1951), pp. 235–54; this phrase, p. 242.

37. Halévy, *Histoire du peuple anglais au XIXe siècle*, vol. 1, *L'Angleterre en 1815*, p. 144 [152]. Halévy made similar statements about the meager importance of constitutional issues in England in his correspondence. See, for example, Élie Halévy to Célestin Bouglé (15 May [1898]), *Correspondance (1891–1937)*, 247, where he stated that he was "assez sceptique sur la profondeur et l'importance des questions constitutionnelles."

38. These phrases, Halévy, *Histoire du peuple anglais au XIXe siècle*, vol. 1, *L'Angleterre en 1815*, pp. 307 [325], 338 [357].

39. Ibid., p. 364 [383].

40. Ibid., p. 366 [387].

41. As we have seen, Halévy's had discussed these dimensions of English Methodism in "La naissance du Méthodisme en Angleterre," esp. pp. 536–39.

42. These phrases, ibid., pp. 525–26.

43. Ibid., p. 528.

44. Ibid., p. 526.

45. Halévy, *Histoire du peuple anglais au XIXe siècle*, vol. 1, *L'Angleterre en 1815*, p. 564 [590–91].

46. Ibid., p. 427 [451].

47. This phrase, ibid., p. 550 [578].

48. See Chapter 3 above.

49. Halévy, *La formation du radicalisme philosophique*, vol. 2: *L'évolution de la doctrine utilitaire de 1789 à 1815*, pp. 192–93.

50. Halévy, *La formation du radicalisme philosophique*, vol. 1: *La jeunesse de Bentham, 1776–1789*, pp. 23–24.

51. Ibid., pp. 24–25.

52. Ibid., p. 38.

53. Ibid., pp. 94. As Halévy pointed out, Bentham's model prison, the "panopticon," was a radical extension of this belief in imposed order and reform (ibid., pp. 104–6).

54. See chapter 2 above.

55. Halévy, *La formation du radicalisme philosophique*, vol. 1: *La jeunesse de Bentham, 1776–1789*, p. 125.

56. Halévy, *Histoire du peuple anglais au XIXe siècle*, vol. 1 : *L'Angleterre en 1815*, p. 553 [581]

57. For example, when discussing the economic theories of Smith, Paine, and Godwin, Halévy emphasized the divergent conclusions reached by these thinkers, all of whom started with similar utilitarian assumptions. "C'est ici le lieu de marquer le caractère paradoxal que présente le marche des idées dans l'histoire." *La formation du radicalisme philosophique*, vol. 2 : *L'évolution de la doctrine utilitaire de 1789 à 1815*, p. 90.

58. Ibid.

59. Halévy, *La formation du radicalisme philosophique*, vol. 3: *Le radicalisme philosophique*, pp. 205–6.

60. Ibid., pp. 223–24.

61. Halévy, *Histoire du peuple anglais au XIXe siècle*, t. 1: *L'Angleterre en 1815*, p. 401 [424–25].

62. Ibid., p. 401 [425].

63. Ibid., p. 404 [427–29].

64. Ibid., p. 427 [451–52].

65. Ibid., p. 558 [586].

66. Ibid., p. 559 [587].

67. During the late 1920s and early 1930s, Halévy returned to his history of the English people, but rather than pick up his chronological analysis by focusing on Victorian England (he had completed only the volumes up to 1841), he decided to focus on the decades before World War I—a period that he judged to be the "epilogue" of the nineteenth century. See *Histoire du peuple anglais au XIXe siècle, épilogue (1895–1914)*, 2 vols. (Paris: Hachette, 1926 and 1932). For analysis of these volumes, see my Chapter 9.

68. Referring to the changes in England in the first decade of the twentieth century, Halévy wrote: "De grandes vagues venues des pays chauds, juives, catholiques, mais surtout païennes, venaient battre, effriter la vieille falaise protestante et nordique." *Histoire du peuple anglais au XIXe siècle, épilogue (1895–1914)*, vol. 2: *Vers la démocratie sociale et vers la guerre (1905–1914)*, p. 76.

69. See the analysis in my Chapters 8 and 9.

70. "Avant-propos," *Histoire du peuple Anglais au XIXe siècle, épilogue (1895–1914)*, vol. 1: *Les impérialistes au pouvoir (1895–1905)*, pp. i–vi, this quote p. vi.

71. See the discussion in Chapter 3 above.

72. This phrase, Halévy, *Histoire du people Anglais au XIXe siècle, épilogue (1895–1914)*, vol. 2: *Vers la démocratie sociale et vers la guerre (1905–1914)*, pp. 372–73.

73. Mention of Sidney and Beatrice Webb in Halévy's correspondence begins in 1900 and extends into the early 1930s. See Halévy, *Correspondance (1891–1937)*, pp. 290, 322, 336, 377, 378, 414, 416, 615, 648–49, 667, 682, 718, and 719. In June 1921, for example, Halévy reported to his mother that he and Florence had spent three days at Dumford House with the Webbs, "who treat us as old friends." Élie Halévy to Mme. Ludovic Halévy (6 June 1921), ibid., pp. 648–49.

74. Halévy, "L'ère des tyrannies," pp. 283–84 [270–71].

75. On Graham Wallas, see Martin J. Weiner, *Between Two Worlds: The Political Thought of Graham Wallas* (Oxford: Clarendon Press, 1971); and Peter Clarke, *Liberals and Social Democrats* (Cambridge: Cambridge University Press, 1978).

76. Graham Wallas was also an active teacher. In 1890, he became a university extension lecturer and frequently organized conferences at the London School of Economics. From 1914, he occupied the chair of political science at the LSE.

77. The first letter from Halévy to Wallas that I am aware of is dated 3 December 1908, but it seems clear that they had come to know each other before this. Élie Halévy to Graham Wallas (3 December 1908), *Correspondance (1891–1937)*, p. 399. There are letters from Wallas to Halévy from March 1908 to August 1929 in the Wallace Papers [1/91] at the London School of Economics.

78. For my understanding of the New Liberals, I am much indebted to Peter Clarke, *Liberals and Social Democrats*; Stefan Collini, *Liberalism and Sociology: L. T. Hobhouse and Political Argument in England, 1880–1914* (Cambridge: Cambridge University Press, 1979); and P.F. Clarke's introduction to J. A. Hobson, *The Crisis of Liberalism: New Issues of Democracy* [originally published 1909] (New York: Harper and Row, 1974). Though Wallas and the New Liberals shared a good deal, Collini situates Wallas on the margins of the New Liberals. Wallas, he writes, "could never have been easily classed as a New Liberal." Collini, *Liberalism and Sociology*, p. 76.

79. The first mention of a dinner is in a letter of Halévy to his wife, Florence (5 January [1911]), *Correspondance (1891–1937)*, p. 417. For mention of other meetings and exchanges, see ibid., pp. 433, 443, 515, 568, 623, 648, 649, 651, 708, and 711.

80. "We must always remember that the problems which Socialism attempts to solve, deal with conditions which themselves are constantly changing." Graham Wallas, "Property Under Socialism," *Fabian Essays* (London: Allen and Unwin, 1889), pp. 123–39, these quotes pp. 123 and 138.

81. Ibid., p. 125.

82. As Wallas put it in *The Great Society*, "We must submit to the Division of Labour; and the Division of Labour will involve, if it is to be effective, a certain degree of compulsion." Graham Wallas, *The Great Society: A Psychological Analysis* (London: Macmillan, 1914), p. 367.

83. Wallas, "Property Under Socialism," p. 138.

84. Graham Wallas, *Human Nature in Politics* (London: Constable, 1908); and Wallas, *The Great Society*. Wallas had already published *The Life of Francis Place, 1771–1854* (London: Longmans, 1898).

85. A. L. Rowse calls Wallas "a pioneer in the application of psychology to political thinking." "Foreword," *Human Nature in Politics*, 1948 edition (London: Constable, 1948), p. xv. Weiner argues that the psychological and moral dimensions of Wallas's orientation were residues of Wallas's evangelical background. Stefan Collini demurs. See Collini's review of Weiner's *Between Two Worlds* in the *Historical Journal*, 15:4 (1972), pp. 827–30.

86. Wallas, *Human Nature in Politics*, p. 103.

87. Ibid., pp. 90–91, 105.

88. Wallas, *The Great Society*, cited by Jose Harris, "Epilogue: French Revolution to *fin de siècle*: Political thought in retrospect and prospect, 1800–1914," in *The Cambridge History of Nineteenth-Century Political Thought*, ed. G. S. Jones and G. Claeys (Cambridge: Cambridge University Press, 2011), pp. 893–933; these phrases of Wallas cited on p. 923.

89. In a letter to Wallas in 1918, Halévy mentioned both *Human Nature in Politics* and *The Great Society*, Élie Halévy to Graham Wallas (12 May 1918), *Correspondance (1891–1937)*, p. 569.

90. See my Chapter 8.

91. See Melvin Richter, *The Politics of Conscience: T. H. Green and His Age* (Cambridge, MA: Harvard University Press, 1964).

CHAPTER 7

Epigraphs. Élie Halévy to Xavier Léon (24 March 1916), Élie Halévy, *Oeuvres complètes*, vol. 1: *Correspondance et écrits de guerre*, edited by Vincent Duclert and Marie Scot (Paris: Les belles lettres, 2016), p. 139.

Élie Halévy to Xavier Léon (25 February 1917), ibid. p. 224.

1. Élie Halévy to Xavier Léon (26 November 1914), ibid., p. 44. Sciences Po had eight hundred enrolled students in 1914, while at the beginning of 1915 there were only seventy-two. This figure from Pascal Ory and Jean-François Sirinelli, *Les intellectuels en France de l'affaire Dreyfus à nos jours* (Paris: Colin, 1992), p. 62.

2. Élie Halévy to Xavier Léon (28 July 1915), *Correspondance et écrits de guerre*, p. 91. Halévy referred to a politician like Paul Painlevé as "un insect, d'une espèce bourdonnante." Élie Halévy to Xavier Léon (14 October 1915), ibid., p. 110.

3. Élie Halévy to Xavier Léon (11 October 1915), ibid., p. 108.

4. Élie Halévy to Xavier Léon (28 July 1915), ibid., pp. 91–92.

5. Vincent Duclert, "Élie Halévy et la guerre," in ibid., pp. xxxi–lii; this quote, p. xxxvi.

6. Élie Halévy to Xavier Léon (23 September 1914), ibid., p. 19.

7. Élie Halévy to Xavier Léon (25 May 1915), ibid., p. 77.

8. Élie Halévy to Louise Halévy (24 September 1917), Archives Henriette Guy-Loë, Fonds Halévy; cited by Marie Scot, "Écrire en guerre, écrits de guerre," in ibid., pp. liii–lxxvi, this quote, p. lviii.

9. Élie Halévy to Louise Halévy (12 December 1916), *Correspondance et écrits de guerre*, p. 200.

10. Marie Scot, "Écrire en guerre, écrits de guerre," p. lx.

11. Élie Halévy to Xavier Léon (15 May 1916), *Correspondance et écrits de guerre*, p. 147.

12. See, for example, Élie Halévy to Mrs. Russell (28 August 1916); and Élie Halévy to Graham Wallace (29 August 1916), ibid., pp. 173–76.

13. Élie Halévy to Xavier Léon (27 July 1916), ibid., p. 165.

14. Élie Halévy to Xavier Léon (22 January 1916), ibid., p. 125.

15. Élie Halévy to Xavier Léon (31 August 1915), ibid., p. 103; see also Élie Halévy to Xavier Léon (3 February 1916), ibid., p. 128.

16. See Élie Halévy to Louise Halévy (19 November 1914), ibid., p. 42; Élie Halévy to Xavier Léon (27 January 1915), ibid., p. 58.

17. Élie Halévy to Xavier Léon (10 July 1915), ibid., p. 88.

18. Élie Halévy to Daniel Halévy (15 September 1915), ibid., pp. 105–06.

19. Élie Halévy to Xavier Léon (26 November 1914), ibid., p. 43.

20. For example, Élie Halévy to Xavier Léon (6 December 1916), ibid., pp. 196–97.

21. Élie Halévy to Daniel Halévy (13 July 1915), ibid., p. 89.

22. Élie Halévy to Xavier Léon (5 June 1915), ibid., p. 80.

23. Élie Halévy to Xavier Léon (19 October 1915), ibid., p. 112.

24. Élie Halévy to Xavier Léon (28 July 1915), ibid., pp. 91–92.

25. Élie Halévy to Xavier Léon (13 December 1916), ibid., p. 201.

26. Élie Halévy to Xavier Léon (23 July 1917), ibid., p. 262.

27. Élie Halévy to Xavier Léon (4 November 1915), ibid., pp. 114–15.

28. Élie Halévy to Xavier Léon (24 March 1916), ibid., pp. 137–39.

29. Élie Halévy to Xavier Léon (20 August 1916), ibid., pp. 170–73; this phrase, p. 171.

30. Élie Halévy to Xavier Léon (16 December 1916), ibid., p. 202.

31. See the letters of Élie Halévy to Xavier Léon (12 March, 17 March, 28 March 1917), ibid., pp. 230–40.

32. Élie Halévy to Xavier Léon (24 April 1917), ibid., p. 245.

33. Élie Halévy to Xavier Léon (12 May 1917), ibid., p. 249.

34. Élie Halévy to Xavier Léon (28 March 1917), ibid., pp. 239.

35. Élie Halévy to Xavier Léon (31 October 1917), ibid., p. 298.

36. Élie Halévy to Xavier Léon (22 November 1917), ibid., p. 300.

37. Élie Halévy to Xavier Léon (19 October 1915), ibid., p. 112.

38. Halévy would also oppose French annexationist demands during the postwar peace negotiations. See Élie Halévy to Xavier Léon (30 December 1918) and Élie Halévy to Paul Mantoux (8 January 1919), *Élie Halévy Correspondance (1891–1937)*, texts collected and presented by Henriette Guy-Loë (Paris: Fallois, 1996), pp. 595 and 598.

39. Élie Halévy to Célestin Bouglé (29 October 1901), ibid., p. 311.

40. Élie Halévy to Célestin Bouglé (5 February [1904]), ibid., p. 350.

41. In 1902, Halévy wrote to Bouglé that "the human species tends toward peace and unity." Élie Halévy to Célestin Bouglé (3 October 1902), ibid., p. 327. In 1904, again to Bouglé, he wrote: "It is necessary to consider humanity disposed of an almost inexhaustible fund of enthusiasm; and that reflection, if it understands the true limits of its power, will accomplish the modest and useful task of ruling and controlling enthusiasm." Élie Halévy to Célestin Bouglé (21 September 1904), ibid., p. 356.

42. Élie Halévy to Mme Ludovic Halévy (18 December 1910), ibid., p. 410.

43. Élie Halévy to Célestin Bouglé (18 July 1912), ibid., p. 425.

44. Élie Halévy to Célestin Bouglé (18 February 1904), ibid., p. 351.

45. Élie Halévy to Célestin Bouglé (20 [June 1905]), ibid., p. 366.

46. Élie Halévy to Célestin Bouglé (18 July 1912), ibid., p. 425.

47. Originally appearing in the *Berliner Tageblatt* on 4 October 1914, it was published in Paris in *Le Temps* on 13 October 1914. The "Manifesto" was signed by distinguished scholars and writers, including Ernst Haeckel, Gerhart Hauptmann, Engelbert Humperdinck, Karl Lamprecht, Friedrich Naumann, Max Planck, and Wilhem Wundt.

48. See the discussion by Martha Hanna, *The Mobilization of Intellect: French Scholars and Writers During the Great War* (Cambridge, MA: Harvard University Press, 1996), pp. 78–105.

49. In addition to the book by Martha Hanna, see Christophe Prochasson and Anne Rasmussen, *Au nom de la patrie: Les intellectuels et la première guerre mondiale (1910–1919)* (Paris: Découverte, 1996); and Ory and Sirinelli, *Les intellectuels en France de l'affaire Dreyfus à nos jours*, pp. 61–75.

50. Debate over Kant's ethics and Kant's relationship to nationalism and cosmopolitanism were important elements in the intellectual controversy in France during the war. See, especially, Hanna, *The Mobilization of Intellect*, pp. 106–41.

51. Élie Halévy to Xavier Léon (16 September 1914), *Correspondance et écrits de guerre*, p. 16.

52. Élie Halévy to Xavier Léon (21 October 1914), ibid., p. 31.

53. Ibid., pp. 31–32.

54. Émile Boutroux (1845–1921) was a philosopher of science who is best known for his *De la contingence des lois de la nature* (1874). He began teaching at the École normale in 1877. His neo-Kantianism, but not his spiritualism, influenced Halévy and others of his circle, especially Brunschvicg. See Joel Revill, "Émile Boutroux, Redefining Science and Faith in the Third Republic," *Modern Intellectual History*, 6:3 (2009), pp. 485–512. The defense of French "classicism" against narrow Prussian/German "nationalism" became a common theme among French intellectuals during the war. See the discussion by Hanna in *The Mobilization of Intellect*, pp. 142–76. Halévy wished to defend Kant, and even proposed the publication of a translation of Kant's "Project for Perpetual Peace" in the *Revue*. See Élie Halévy to Xavier Léon (4 April 1915), *Correspondance et écrits de guerre*, pp. 66–68.

55. Émile Boutroux, "Allemande et la guerre," *Revue des deux mondes*, 23 (1914), pp. 385–401.

56. Henri Bergson (1859–1941) had published in the *Revue* before the war, and he was, arguably, the most famous intellectual in France at the time.

57. Bergson was strident in his attacks of Germany and German culture. He opened the 8 August 1914 session of the Académie des sciences morales et politiques with the following statement: "[Notre académie] accomplit un simple devoir scientifique en signalant dans la brutalité et le cynisme de l'Allemagne, dans son mépris de toute justice et de toute vérité, une régression à l'état sauvage." Cited by Jean-François Sirinelli, *Intellectuale et passions françaises* (Paris: Fayard, 1990), p. 36. See also the discussion in Hanna, *The Mobilization of Intellect*, pp. 85–97. Bergson would assume a conciliatory attitude toward Germany after the war, taking positions with the League of Nations and the International Committee for Intellectual Cooperation.

58. Élie Halévy to Xavier Léon (21 October 1914), *Correspondance et écrits de guerre*, pp. 30–32 ; this phrase, p. 32.

59. Élie Halévy to Xavier Léon (15 December 1914), ibid., p. 50.

60. Two numbers of the journal carried 1914 dates (September and November 1914), but they did not in fact appear until July and November 1915. The journal began regular publication in 1916; only the year 1915 is absent from the collected numbers of the *Revue*. On the *Revue* during the war, see the discussion in Marie Scot, "Écrire en guerre, écrits de guerre,"

pp. lx–lxviii; and Yaël Dagan, "'Justifier philosophiquement notre cause': *La revue de métaphysique et de morale, 1914–1918,*" *Mil neuf cent,* 23 (2005), pp. 49–74.

61. Élie Halévy to Xavier Léon (23 September 1914), *Correspondance et écrits de guerre,* p. 20. It was a constant refrain. See, for example, Élie Halévy to Xavier Léon (4 February 1915), ibid., p. 59.

62. Élie Halévy to Xavier Léon (8 December 1914), ibid., pp. 46–47.

63. Élie Halévy to Xavier Léon (12 September 1915), ibid., pp. 104–5; this phrase, p. 105.

64. Élie Halévy to Xavier Léon (8 September 1916), ibid., p. 176.

65. Élie Halévy to Xavier Léon (21 September 1916), ibid., p. 180.

66. Élie Halévy to Xavier Léon (23 December 1914), ibid., p. 55.

67. Élie Halévy to Xavier Léon (9 October 1916), ibid., p. 184.

68. See Élie Halévy to Xavier Léon (10 June 1917), ibid., p. 253–55; and Élie Halévy to Xavier Léon (18 September 1917), ibid., pp. 283–85.

69. Élie Halévy to Xavier Léon (26 November 1914), ibid., p. 45.

70. Élie Halévy to Xavier Léon (4 April 1915), ibid., p. 67.

71. Élie Halévy to Xavier Léon (16 November 1915), ibid., p. 117.

72. See the discussion by Yaël Dagan, "'Justifier philosophiquement notre cause,'" pp. 60–70.

73. Dominique Parodi, "La force du Droit, à propos de l'étude de Th. Ruyssen," *Revue de métaphysique et de morale,* vol. 23 (1916), pp. 277–93.

74. Charles Andler, "Les origins philosophiques du pangermanisme," *Revue de métaphysique et de morale* (1916), pp. 659–95. Xavier Léon continued to maintain, contrary to Andler, that Fichte was a Jacobin, not a chauvinistic nationalist.

75. *Revue de métaphysique et de morale,* vol. 25 (1918).

76. Élie Halévy to Xavier Léon (17 July 1917), *Correspondance et écrits de guerre,* p. 260.

77. Élie Halévy to Xavier Léon (19 September 1918), ibid., p. 393. Alphonse Darlu, learning of the project to devote a number of the *Revue* to Protestantism, warned that it was "dangereux à un double point de vue: le protestantisme est né sur la terre allemande; le protestantisme c'est pour le catholique, donc le Français, en majeure partie de l'hérésie. N'est-ce pas en ce moment compromettre la *Revue* à un double titre?" Alphonse Darlu to Xavier Léon (3 June 1917), cited in *Correspondance (1891–1937),* p. 546 note.

78. Élie Halévy to Xavier Léon (25 September 1918), *Correspondance et écrits de guerre,* p. 294.

79. *Revue de métaphysique et de morale,* vol. 25 (1918), pp. 529–31.

80. The first mention by Halévy of this translation is in a letter to Xavier Léon dated 16 February 1917. Élie Halévy to Xavier Léon (16 February 1917), *Correspondance et écrits de guerre,* p. 218. Halévy announces the completion of the translation on 1 August 1917. Élie Halévy to Xavier Léon (1 August 1917), ibid., p. 265. Halévy mentions that he wishes to check his translation against the French translation of Sorbière (1649) and against an unspecified English-language translation in a letter in August 1918. Élie Halévy to Xavier Léon (16 August 1918), ibid., p. 386.

81. Thomas Hobbes, *On the Citizen,* ed. and trans. by Richard Tuck and Michael Silverthorne (Cambridge: Cambridge University Press, 1997); this quote in "Preface to the Reader," p. 12.

82. Ibid., chap. 1, sec. 13, p. 30.

83. Ibid., chap. 2, sec. 1, pp. 32–34.

84. Ibid., chap. 5, sec. 7, p. 72.

85. Richard Tuck, "Introduction," in ibid., pp. xxxi–xxxiii. As Tuck points out, Hobbes argues in chapter 10 that monarchy is preferred over aristocracy or democracy, but he "is usually careful to allow that sovereignty may be vested in a group of men as well as in one man" (p. xliii).

86. Hobbes makes the abolition of sovereignty extremely difficult—unanimous agreement of *all* citizens *and* the sovereign. See ibid., chap. 6, sec. 20, pp. 89–90.

87. Élie Halévy to Bertrand Russell (15 April 1919), *Correspondance (1891–1937)*, p. 618. Original text in English.

88. Hobbes discusses in chapter 12 of *De Cive* the critical difference between "a people," on the one hand, and "a crowd," on the other. *On the Citizen*, pp. 131–41.

89. There is an excellent overview in Dagan, " 'Justifier philosophiquement notre cause.' "

90. On Bouglé during the war, see Joshua M. Humphreys, "Servants of Social Progress: Democracy, Capitalism and Social Reform in France, 1914–1940" (Ph.D. dissertation, New York University, 2005), pp. 83ff.

91. On Brunschvicg during the war, see Joel Revill, "Taking France to the School of the Sciences: Léon Brunschvicg, Gaston Bachelard, and the French Epistemological Tradition" (Ph.D. dissertation, Duke University, 2006), chap. 4. Halévy, in a letter to Léon, expressed moderate disapproval of Brunschvicg's position during the crisis leading up to the war. "Don't persecute the unfortunate Brunschvicg. The best tactic toward him is to avoid all species of political subjects. His situation is not easy. Here he is living side-by-side . . . with Boutroux, Delbos, Darlu [all, at this time, fervent nationalists]." Élie Halévy to Xavier Léon (27 July 1914), *Correspondance et écrits de guerre*, p. 8.

92. Before the war, Parodi published *Traditionalisme et démocratie* (Paris: Alcan, 1909) and *Le problème moral et la pensée contemporaine* (Paris: Alcan, 1910). He also participated in the discussion on the "crisis of liberalism" in the *Revue* (1902–1903), and organized debates at the Société française de philosophie on questions of morals and education. Following the deaths of Léon in 1935 and of Halévy in 1937, Parodi took over running the *Revue*. On the "crisis of liberalism" debate and Parodi's position in this debate, see Eric Brandom, "Liberalism and Rationalism at the *Revue de Métaphysique et de Morale*, 1902–1903," *French Historical Studies*, 39:4 (2016), pp. 749–80.

93. For the details of Dominique Parodi's wartime activities and writings, I have drawn from the articles by Stéphan Soulié, "Philosophie en République et expérience de la Grande Guerre: Le cas Dominique Parodi," *Histoire@Politique*, 25 (2015), pp. 159–75; and "Dominique Parodi: Un philosophe au service de la diplomatie française pendant la Première Guerre mondiale," *Sezione: Dossier: Le relazioni culturali e intellettuali tra Italia e Francia dalla Grande Guerra al Fascismo*, 14 (2018), pp. 1–29.

94. The theory of the "two Germanies"—good versus bad, Protestant versus Catholic, progressive versus retrograde, south versus north—emerged in France in 1870. See Claude Digeon, *La crise allemande de la pensée française, 1870–1914* (Paris: PUF, 1959). It became a common trope during World War I. See Hanna, *The Mobilization of Intellect*, pp. 106–41.

95. "Pragmatism," for Parodi, referred to the lamentable tendency, especially prevalent in wartime, to valorize the mysticism of action over thought and reason. It should not be confused with the "pragmatism" of, say, William James.

96. Parodi, "La force du Droit, à propos de l'étude de Th. Ruyssen," pp. 281 and 291.

97. "Warrior enthusiasm" is Halévy's phrase. See Élie Halévy to Daniel Halévy (15 September 1915), *Correspondance et écrits de guerre*, pp. 105–6.

98. See chapter 2.

99. Élie Halévy to Xavier Léon (28 July 1915), *Correspondance et écrits de guerre*, p. 91.

100. See the letter of Élie Halévy to Xavier Léon (12 December 1918), ibid., p. 402, discussed in my chapter 8.

101. Élie Halévy to Xavier Léon (3 August 1916), ibid., p. 168.

102. Soulié, "Dominique Parodi," p. 24.

103. Vincent Duclert, "Élie Halévy et la guerre," p. 19.

104. Most of the letters from Halévy, unfortunately, were destroyed in a fire during the occupation of France during World War II. For what we have, see Alain, *Correspondance avec Élie et Florence Halévy* (Paris: Gallimard, 1958).

105. Among Alain's students were André Maurois, Jean Prévost, Simone Weil, Georges Canguilhem, and Raymond Aron.

106. See, for example, the four volumes of Alain's writings (5,800 pages of text) published in the Pléiade series (Paris: Gallimard/Pléiade, 1956–1970). Among the books about Alain, see André Maurois, *Alain* (Paris: Gallimard, 1950); Georges Pascal, *L'idée de philosophie chez Alain* (Paris: Bordas, 1970); Renzo Ragghianti, *Alain: Apprentissage philosophique et genèse de la* Revue de Métaphysique et de morale (Paris: Harmattan, 1995); *Alain, littérature et philosophie mêlée*, under the direction of Michel Murat et Frédéric Worms (Paris: Éditions rue d'Ulm, 2012); and Jérôme Perrier, *Alain ou la démocratie de l'individu* (Paris: Les belles lettres, 2016).

107. Élie Halévy to Xavier Léon (4 April 1915), *Correspondance et écrits de guerre*, p. 66.

108. Most of *Mars ou la guerre jugée* was written between 14 January and 17 April 1916, just before Alain was injured. References are to the version in the Pléiade edition. Alain, *Les passions et la sagesse*, (Paris: Gallimard/Pléiade, 1960), pp. xxx–xxxiii and 547–705.

109. References to Alain's *Souvenirs de guerre* are to Alain, *Les passions et la sagesse* pp. xxv–xxx and 429–545.

110. Alain to Florence Halévy (10 March 1916), *Correspondance avec Élie et Florence Halévy*, p. 225.

111. Alain to Élie Halévy (4 April 1916), ibid., p. 227.

112. François Furet, "Preface," *Correspondance (1891–1937)*, p. 43.

113. Alain to Élie Halévy (25 March 1915), *Correspondance avec Élie et Florence Halévy*, p. 193.

114. Alain (August 1914), cited by Raymond Aron in his 1970 article "Le socialisme et la guerre," reprinted in the edition of Halévy's *L'ère des tyrannies* (Paris: Gallimard, 1990), this quote, p. 279.

115. For this phrase, Élie Halévy to Xavier Léon (2 April 1916), *Correspondance et écrits de guerre*, p. 140.

116. Alain, *Souvenirs de guerre*, p. 475.

117. Ibid., pp. 541–42.

118. Ibid., p. 446.

119. Ibid., p. 440. In *Mars ou la guerre jugée*, there is a similar statement about soldiers: "The marks of terror or of despair, always and without exception visible in the corners of their eyes and on their temples," p. 636.

120. Alain, *Mars ou la guerre jugée*, p. 95; see also Alain to Florence Halévy (4 April 1916), *Correspondance avec Élie et Florence Halévy*, p. 228.

121. Alain, *Mars ou la guerre jugée*, p. 569.

122. Ibid. pp. 578–79 and 608–09.

123. Alain, *Souvenirs de guerre*, p. 457.

124. Alain, *Mars ou la guerre jugée*, p. 655.

125. Alain to Élie Halévy (4 August 1934), *Correspondance avec Élie et Florence Halévy*, p. 301.

126. Alain, *Mars ou la guerre jugée*, p. 690.

127. Alain to Florence Halévy (10 March 1916), *Correspondance avec Élie et Florence Halévy*, p. 225.

128. Alain to Florence Halévy (29 February 1916), ibid., p. 226.

129. Élie Halévy to Xavier Léon (8 September 1916), *Correspondance et écrits de guerre*, p. 176.

130. Élie Halévy to Xavier Léon (11 February 1915), ibid., p. 60.

131. Alain to Florence Halévy (13 June 1915), *Correspondance avec Élie et Florence Halévy*, pp. 205–6. Alain said the same thing in *Mars ou la guerre jugée*, pp. 676–78 and 702–05.

132. Alain to Élie Halévy (12 January 1915), *Correspondance avec Élie et Florence Halévy*, p. 172.

133. Alain to Florence Halévy (22 February 1916), ibid., p. 224.

134. Alain to Élie Halévy (25 March 1919), ibid., p. 260.

135. Alain to Xavier Léon (28 November 1894), ibid., p. 392).

136. Emmanuel Blondel suggests that this moral focus emerged more clearly in Alain's writings during the war. See his "Écrire pour la paix," in *Alain, littérature et philosophie mêlée*, ed. Murat and Worms, pp. 203–16.

137. Alain to Élie Halévy (Sunday [March or April 1894]), *Correspondance avec Élie et Florence Halévy*, p. 57.

138. Alain to Élie Halévy (16 November 1894), ibid., p. 260.

139. Alain to Élie Halévy (4 February 1916), ibid., p. 222.

140. Alain to Florence Halévy (18 January 1917), ibid., p. 250.

141. Élie Halévy to Louise Halévy (13 November 1914), *Correspondance et écrits de guerre*, pp. 38–39.

142. Élie Halévy to Xavier Léon (12 September 1915), ibid., p. 104.

143. Élie Halévy to Xavier Léon (22 November 1917), ibid., p. 300.

144. Élie Halévy to Xavier Léon (20 November 1916), ibid., p. 194.

145. Alain to Marie-Monique Morre-Lambelin (18 July 1915), *Alain: Lettres au deux amies*, texts assembled and prefaces by Emmanuel Blondel (Paris: Les belles lettres, 2014), p. 307.

146. Alain to Marie-Monique Morre-Lambelin (30 July 1915), ibid., p. 316.

147. Alain to Marie-Monique Morre-Lambelin (26 December 1916), ibid., p. 620.

148. Alain to Marie-Monique Morre-Lambelin (29 December 1916), ibid., p. 623.

149. Élie Halévy to Xavier Léon (17 April 1917), *Correspondance et écrits de guerre*, p. 242.

150. Élie Halévy to Célestin Bouglé (10 April 1915), ibid., p. 69.

## CHAPTER 8

Epigraph: Élie Halévy to Bertrand Russell (15 April 1919), *Correspondance (1891–1937)*, texts collected and presented by Henriette Guy-Loë (Paris: Éditions de Fallois, 1996), p. 618. Original text in English.

1. Élie Halévy to Xavier Léon (28 May 1925), ibid., p. 675.

2. See Élie Halévy to Xavier Léon (19 October 1915), ibid., p. 500, where he states that France is "the greatest among the powers of the second class."

3. Robert Wohl, *The Generation of 1914* (Cambridge, MA: Harvard University Press, 1979), esp. pp. 5–41.

4. Maurice Barrès, *Un homme libre*, cited by Wohl, *The Generation of 1914*, p. 37.

5. For a recent analysis of this side of French intellectual life, see Frederick Brown, *The Embrace of Unreason: France, 1914–1940* (New York: Knopf, 2014).

6. Élie Halévy to Louise Halévy (18 August 1917), in *Oeuvres complètes*, vol. 1: *Correspondance et écrits de guerre*, under the direction of Vincent Duclert and Marie Scot (Paris: Les belles lettres, 2016), pp. 276–77.

7. Paul Mantoux to Élie Halévy (July 1918), cited in *Correspondance (1891–1937)*, p. 587.

8. Ibid.

9. Élie Halévy, "Le problème des élections anglaises," *Revue politique et parlementaire*, 98 (January-March 1919), pp. 227–46; "Après les élections anglaises," *Revue de Paris* (March-April 1919), pp. 207–24; "La nouvelle loi scolaire anglaise," *Revue de Paris*, 26 (September-October 1919), pp. 596–621; "Du peuple anglais et de M. Lloyd George," *Revue hebdomadaire*, 29 (4 December 1920), pp. 119–21. The first and fourth are reproduced in *Oeuvres complètes*, vol. 2: *L'ère des tyrannies* (Paris: Les belles lettres, 2016), pp. 344–66.

10. The French version of this lecture was published under an English title, "The Problem of Nationality," in *Proceedings of the Aristotelian Society*, new series, 20 (1919–1920), pp. 237–42. It was published in French, after Halévy's death, as "Le problème des nationalités," in the *Revue de métaphysique et de morale*, 46 (1939), pp. 147–51, and in *Commentaire*, 57 (1992), pp. 125–27. It is reproduced in *Oeuvres complètes*, vol. 2: *L'ère des tyrannies*, pp. 367–72. References are to this edition.

11. See the letters of Élie Halévy to Louise Halévy (6 April and 9 April 1919) and Élie Halévy to Xavier Léon (12 April 1919), in *Oeuvres complètes*, vol. 2: *L'ère des tyrannies*, pp. 411–14. Halévy's interview notes have been published in *Oeuves complètes*, vol. 3: *Histoire du socialisme européen* (Paris: Les belles lettres, 2016), pp. 765–804.

12. Élie Halévy, "La politique de paix sociale en Angleterre: Les 'Whitley Councils'" (originally published in the *Revue d'économie* politique, [4 June] 1919); "Le problème du contrôle ouvrier" (originally given at the conference of the Comité national d'études politiques et sociales, 7 March 1921); "État présent de la question sociale en Angleterre" (originally published in the *Revue politique et parlementaire*, [July] 1922). All three were reprinted in *L'ère des tyrannies* (Paris: Gallimard, 1938). References, however, are to the new *Oeuves complètes*, vol. 2: *L'ère des tyrannies*. These articles are discussed in detail later in this chapter.

13. During this first postwar visit, they remained in England for more than six months, from 28 November 1918 to mid-June 1919.

14. H. A. L. Fisher wrote that he had "never known anyone from France who knew better how to handle our language in conversation." Halévy, he noted, often presented at conferences without notes. He "had the art of speaking in English as in French with a rare and delicious perfection." H. A. L. Fisher, "L'historien de l'Angleterre moderne," in *Elie Halévy, 1870–1937* (Paris: École libre des sciences politiques, [1938]), p. 88.

15. This is a point made by several historians. See Christophe Prochasson and Anne Rasmussen, *Au nom de la patrie: Les intelletuels et la première guerre mondiale (1910–1919)* (Paris: Découverte, 1996), p. 8; and Pascal Ory and Jean-François Sirinelli, *Les intellectuels en France de l'affaire Dreyfus à nos jours* (Paris: Colin, 1986), p. 62.

16. "Les 'souvenirs' de Lord Morley," *Review de métaphysique et de morale*, 25 (1918), pp. 83–97.

17. Alain shared this concern. He also claimed that the war, unfortunately, had increased the "strong socialist organization, so effective in France and in Germany for realizing a better distribution of products." Alain, *Mars ou la guerre jugée*, in Alain, *Les passions et la sagesse* (Paris: Gallimard/Pléiade, 1960), this quote p. 655.

18. Élie Halévy to Xavier Léon (3 July 1915), *Correspondance et écrits de guerre*, p. 99.

19. Élie Halévy to Graham Wallas (12 May 1918), ibid., p. 261, original in English.

20. Élie Halévy to Xavier Léon (14 January 1918), *Correspondance (1891–1937)*, p. 600. A week earlier, Halévy had written to Léon that nationalism "is a thing as frightening as victory." Élie Halévy to Xavier Léon (7 January 1918), ibid., p. 597.

21. Élie Halévy to Alfred Zimmern (19 August 1919), ibid., p. 624.

22. Élie Halévy to Xavier Léon (30 December 1918), ibid., p. 595.

23. Élie Halévy to Xavier Léon (12 December 1918), ibid., p. 593.

24. Élie Halévy to Xavier Léon (5 December 1918), ibid., p. 591.

25. Élie Halévy to Xavier Léon (12 December 1918), ibid., p. 593.

26. For the criticism of Wilson's support of the Monroe Doctrine, see Élie Halévy to Xavier Léon (26 April 1919), ibid., p. 619.

27. Élie Halévy to Xavier Léon (14 January 1919), ibid., p. 600.

28. In a letter to his brother in May 1919, Halévy suggested that the Russian Revolution was not as bloody as some were recounting and, further, that French cries of atrocities, given France's own history, "cela m'impatiente." Élie Halévy to Daniel Halévy (9 May 1919), ibid., p. 622.

29. Élie Halévy to Xavier Léon (25 January 1919), ibid., p. 604.

30. Élie Halévy to Mme Ludovic Halévy (27 January 1919), ibid., p. 605.

31. Élie Halévy to Mme Ludovic Halévy (12 February 1919), ibid., p. 607.

32. Élie Halévy to Xavier Léon (13 February 1919), ibid., p. 608.

33. Élie Halévy to Xavier Léon (9 February 1919), ibid., p. 606.

34. Élie Halévy to Xavier Léon (26 May 1920), ibid., p. 633.

35. Élie Halévy to Xavier Léon (11 May 1922), ibid., p. 656.

36. Élie Halévy to Xavier Léon (10 May 1921), ibid., p. 644.

37. Élie Halévy to Xavier Léon (8 April 1921), ibid., p. 641.

38. Élie Halévy to Xavier Léon (7 January 1919), ibid., p. 596.

39. This paragraph draws from "Le problème des élections anglaises" (references to this article are to *Oeuvres complètes*, vol. 2: *L'ère des tyrannies*, pp. 344–63); "Après les élections anglaises," *Revue de Paris* (March-April (1919), pp. 207–24; and "Du Peuple anglais et de M. Lloyd George," *Revue hebdomadaire*, 29 (4 December 1920), pp. 119–21 (references to this article are to *Oeuvres complètes*, vol. 2: *L'ère des tyrannies*, pp. 363–66).

40. Halévy, "Le problème des élections anglaises," this quote p. 354.

41. Ibid., p. 361.

42. Halévy, "Du peuple anglais et de M. Lloyd George." Halévy made the same point in an article published in 1923: "L'opinion anglaise et la France," *Revue politique et parlementaire*, 117 (1923), pp. 354–71. References to this article are to *Oeuvres complètes*, vol. 2: *L'ère des tyrannies*, pp. 394–409.

43. Élie Halévy, "Les origines de la discorde Anglo-Allemande," *Revue de Paris*, 28 (1921), pp. 563–83.

44. Halévy, "L'opinion anglaise et la France."

45. "N'oublions pas cependant quelle est la nature vraie de ce public. Une foule qui manque d'état major dirigeant, qui sent vivement mais pense peu, qui montre moins de goût,

dans son journal préféré, pour les nouvelles politiques ou diplomatiques qu'elle n'en montre pour la chronique judiciaire ou la chronique des sports." Ibid., p. 398.

46. "Franco-German Relations Since 1870" (lecture delivered 29 October 1923), *History*, 9 (1924), pp. 18–29.

47. Ibid. p. 19.

48. Halévy, "Les origines de la discorde Anglo-Allemande," pp. 563–83; "Les origines de l'Entente," *Revue de Paris*, 31 (1924), pp. 293–318.

49. Ibid. See also Élie Halévy to Xavier Léon (14 January 1919), *Correspondance (1891–1937)*, p. 600, where he writes: "It seems, again, that in all these matters, President Wilson is a good guide."

50. Élie Halévy to Xavier Léon (19 March 1919), ibid., p. 614.

51. "Le problème des nationalités."

52. Ibid. p. 372.

53. "Trois fragments sur les perspectives de paix après guerre," in *Oeuvres complètes*, vol. 2: *L'ère des tyrannies*, pp. 372–90.

54. Premier fragment: "Note pour l'établissement d'une paix durable en Europe occidentale," *Oeuvre complètes*, vol. 2: *L'ère des tyrannies*, pp. 373–76; this quote, p. 375.

55. Troisième fragment: "Fédération internationale," *Oeuvres complètes*, vol. 2: *L'ère des tyrannies*, pp. 383–90; these phrases, pp. 387.

56. Ibid., pp. 386–87.

57. .Ibid., pp. 387–90.

58. See, on this issue, Peter Galison, *Einstein's Clocks, Poincaré's Maps: Empires of Time* (New York: Norton, 2003). Galison argues that Einstein and Poincaré largely talked past each other.

59. Émile Meyerson (1859–1933) was a Polish-born French epistemologist, chemist, and philosopher of science.

60. Brunschvicg defended Kant's "Copernican revolution" but failed to address the truly devastating implication of Einstein's new theory—how fundamentally it undermined Kant's claim that we have a priori intuitions of space and time. He, in essence, gave a "conventionalist" defense of Kantianism. Einstein responded that "every philosopher has his own Kant." Bergson's argument fell back on his notion of "intuition," claiming that there was no conflict between "relativistic simultaneity" and "intuitive simultaneity," and that there was an intuited universal time. Bergson, in essence, reintroduced a traditional concept of time through the back door. Einstein responded that there was no difference between physical time and philosophical time. Meyerson stressed the continuity between classical mechanics and Einstein's theory of relativity. He, in essence, did not wish to register the frontal attack on conventional theories of time and mechanics that relativity theory represented.

Thanks to Joel Revill for helping me understand the debates at the 1922 meeting. Revill has argued that at this meeting the French philosophers presented their understanding of relativity "within the confines of their own projects," but that it nonetheless was an important moment in "the reconceptualization of philosophy that took place in the interwar years." It was a moment where philosophical differences were clearly exposed—the separation between, on the one hand, the intuitionism of Bergson that pointed toward phenomenology and existentialism, and therefore toward those who, following Husserl and Heidegger, insisted on the primacy of ontology (Levinas, Sartre, and Merleau-Ponty), and, on the other hand, the rationalism of Brunschvicg that pointed toward those who insisted on the centrality of epistemology

(Bachelard, Canguilem, and Cavaillès). Joel Revill, "Taking France to the School of the Sciences: Léon Brunschvicg, Gaston Bachelard, and the French Epistemological Tradition" (Ph.D. dissertation, Duke University, 2006), esp. chap. 4.

61. Before the visit, Einstein wrote to Langevin (who had sent Einstein the invitation), "You know that I am, without reserve, animated by internationalist sentiments, and that the fact that I am installed in the Prussian Academy of Science has no impact on my beliefs." In a letter to Einstein after the visit, Langevin indicated how happy he was to have "worked with you to repair, insofar as we could, the immense harm caused by the war." Luce Langevin, "Paul Langevin et Albert Einstein d'après une correspondance et des documents inédits," *La pensée*, 161 (1972), pp. 11–16.

62. Jean-Fabien Spitz, *Le moment républicain en France* (Paris: Gallimard, 2005); Spitz, "The 'Illiberalism' of French Liberalism: The Individual and the State in the Thought of Blanc, Dupont-White and Durkheim," in *French Liberalism from Montesquieu to the Present Day*, ed. R. Geenens and H. Rosenblatt (Cambridge: Cambridge University Press, 2012), pp. 252–68.

63. Élie Halévy to Célestin Bouglé (24 November 1902), *Correspondance (1891–1937)*, p. 329.

64. See, especially, Élie Halévy, "Les principes de la distribution des richesses," *Revue de métaphysique et de morale* 14 (1906), pp. 545–95.

65. See, for example, Élie Halévy to Célestin Bouglé (16 November 1897 and 24 November 1905), *Correspondance (1891–1937)*, pp. 203 and 372.

66. Élie Halévy to Célestin Bouglé (1 October 1913), ibid., p. 442.

67. See chapter 5 above and my article "Élie Halévy and French Socialist Liberalism," *History of European Ideas*, 44:1 (2018), pp. 75–97.

68. In a letter to Bouglé, Halévy stated that "the logic of socialism is profoundly anarchic and individualist, and assigns as the goal of society, as the reality of society, the satisfaction of all individual interests, and the economic, intellectual, and moral emancipation of all individuals." But he also recognized that some socialists were only what he termed "alleged individualists" who called for the "sacrifice of individuality to the collectivity" and discounted the importance of liberty to "defend the abstract ideas of the nation, the family, and others." Élie Halévy to Célestin Bouglé (7 May 1895), *Correspondance (1891–1937)*, p. 156.

69. "Socialism, since its birth in the early years of the nineteenth century, has suffered from an internal contradiction. On the one hand, it is often presented by its partisans as the outcome and fulfillment of the Revolution of 1789, which was a revolution of liberty, as a liberation from the last remaining subjection after all the others have been destroyed: the subjection of labor by capital. But, it is also, on the other hand, a reaction against individualism and liberalism; it proposes a new compulsory organization in place of the outworn institutions that the Revolution had destroyed." "L'ère des tyrannies." References are to the new *Oeuvres complètes*, vol. 2: *L'ère des tyrannies* (Paris: Les belles lettres, 2016), this quote p. 279. References in brackets are to the page numbers of the English translation (though sometimes altered) by R. K. Webb (New York: Anchor, 1965), this quote [265].

70. When the Halévy returned to England in November 1918, he interviewed workers and labor leaders. Much of this information was incorporated into the articles and the address discussed below. Halévy's interview notes have been published in *Oeuvres complètes*, vol. 3: *Histoire du socialisme européen* (Paris: Les belles lettres, 2016), pp. 765–804.

71. "[The war is] probably unfavorable to the progress of the liberal forms of socialism (syndicalism, etc.), on the other hand it reinforces, significantly, state socialism. I see things in

this manner, but others may see it differently, and the subject merits reflection." Élie Halévy to Xavier Léon (3 July 1915), *Correspondance et écrits de guerre*, p. 99.

72. Halévy, "La politique de paix sociale en Angleterre: Les 'Whitley Councils'"; "Le problème du contrôle ouvrier"; "État présent de la question sociale en Angleterre."

73. Halévy, "La politique de paix sociale en Angleterre," p. 152 [105].

74. Ibid. p. 155 [110].

75. Ibid. pp. 157–58 [112–13].

76. Ibid. p. 159 [115].

77. Ibid. p. 172 [132].

78. Élie Halévy to Daniel Halévy (12 March 1919), *Correspondance (1891–1937)*, p. 612. Similarly, in his 1919 article on the British elections, Halévy noted the influence of the "revolutionary instincts" of the workers. Halévy, "Le problème des élections anglaises," p. 362. As we shall see, Halévy soon changed his view of the desires and power of the British working class.

79. Halévy, "La politique de paix sociale en Angleterre," p. 176 [137], emphasis in original.

80. Ibid. p. 177 [137–38], emphasis in original.

81. Ibid. p. 178 [139], emphasis in original.

82. Ibid. pp. 180–82 [143–45], emphasis in original.

83. Élie Halévy to Xavier Léon (12 April 1919), *Correspondance (1891–1937)*, p. 618.

84. Halévy, "La politique de paix sociale en Angleterre," pp. 190–91 [157].

85. Halévy, "Le problème du contrôle ouvrier," pp. 193–94 [160].

86. Ibid., p. 201 [169]. As he put it in a letter to Bouglé: "In so far as the Whitley Councils are concerned, not only are they aborting, as I had predicted, but the National Conference, on which I had attempted to place some hope, seems to have silently expired." Élie Halévy to Bouglé (28 April 1920); cited by Michèle Bo Bramsen, *Portrait d'Élie Halévy* (Amsterdam: Grüner, 1978), p. 267.

87. Halévy, "Le problème du contrôle ouvrier," p. 209 [179–80].

88. Ibid. p. 201 [169].

89. Élie Halévy to Xavier Léon (8 April 1921), *Correspondance (1891–1937)*, p. 641.

90. Halévy, "État présent de la question sociale en Angleterre," p. 213 [183–84].

91. Ibid. p. 218 [191].

92. Ibid. p. 221 [195].

93. Ibid. p. 226 [202].

94. Halévy, "Les principes de la distribution des richesses," pp. 545–95.

95. Halevy suggested in 1936, in the "The Era of Tyrannies," that a "reconciliation between socialism and liberalism" had appeared possible before World War I. But he concluded that this possibility had ended with the outbreak of the war. *L'ère des tyrannies*, p. 284 [271]. Bouglé wrote in his preface to the original edition of the *L'ère des tyrannies*, "The catastrophe of 1914 did more for socialism than the spread of the Marxist system," p. 62 [xxiii]. What he should have said, in my opinion, is that the war did more for *organizational* socialism than the doctrines of Marx. He also stated, more accurately, that Halévy believed that what remained of syndicalism was "a syndicalism reduced to its barest elements, forcibly sobered and, one might say, domesticated by étatism," p. 64 [xxv].

96. In a letter to Michel Alexandre in 1930, Halévy discussed the possible republication of his 1906 article "Les principes de la distribution des richesses." He was obviously honored but not sure he agreed entirely with the position he had taken. "Before authorizing the reproduction, I would be obliged to reread it. Rereading, I would wish to totally rewrite it. And, I

would not have the time to rewrite it. *Commit piracy against me.* So much the worse for you if an excessive admiration for this old article leads you astray." Élie Halévy to Michel Alexandre (20 October 1930), *Correspondance (1891–1937)*, p. 704.

97. Halévy, "Sismondi: Critique de l'optimisme industrialiste," in *L'ère des tyrannies*, pp. 66–82.

98. Halévy, "Socialisme et le problème de parlementarisme démocratique," originally presented at Chatham House (24 April 1934) and published in *International Affairs* (1934); reprinted in *L'ère des tyrannies*, pp. 263–76 [249–64]; this quote p. 266 [251]. I was made aware of this quote by Joel Revill, "The Bitterness of Disappointed Expectations: Elie Halévy and European Socialism," *Proceedings of the Western Society for French History*, 35 (2007).

99. Halévy, "Socialisme et le problème de parlementarisme démocratique," this quote p. 270 [257]. The average workman, Halévy writes (pp. 269–70 [256–57]), "wants higher wages, shorter hours and better conditions of work. When the socialist party explains to him abstractly, in terms almost unintelligible to him, that he is not able to obtain all of that except by the nationalization of the means of production, distribution and exchange, he does not take the trouble to understand these difficult ideas. He is content to obtain a portion of what he desires thanks to a first form of socialism that I will call not socialism but fiscalism. . . . [It] leaves in tact the system which has profit as its foundation. . . . Fiscalism does what it can to make the capitalist's life difficult, but it does nothing to change the system which rests on making a profit."

100. Halévy, *The Era of Tyrannies* (New York: Anchor, 1965), p. xiv.

101. *Revue des sciences politiques*, 46 (1923), pp. 624–25; reprinted in *Oeuvres complètes*, vol. 3: *Histoire du socialisme européen*, pp. 857–58.

102. *Revue des sciences politiques*, 49 (1926), pp. 140–41; reprinted in *Oeuvres complètes*, vol. 3: *Histoire du socialisme européen*, pp. 864–65.

103. Halévy, *Histoire du peuple anglais au XIXe siècle, épilogue (1895–1914)*, vol. 1: *Les impérialistes au pouvoir (1895–1905)* (Paris: Hachette, 1926), pp. 204–8.

104. Halévy, *Histoire du peuple anglais au XIXe siècle, épilogue (1895–1914)*, vol. 2: *Vers la démocratie sociale et vers la guerre (1905–1914)* (Paris: Hachette, 1932), pp. 425–71, this quote p. 463.

105. Alain's enthusiastic reading of this article is mentioned in a letter to Halévy ([July or August 1906]), *Correspondance avec Élie et Florence Halévy* (Paris: Gallimard, 1958), p. 103.

106. Ludovic Frobert makes this point, in "Éthique et économie après 1918" (unpublished typescript).

107. Alain, *Propos* (Paris: Gallimard/Pléiade, 1970), vol. 2, pp. 98–99.

108. Halévy, *Histoire du peuple anglais au XIXe siècle*, vol. 2: *Du lendemain de Waterloo à la veille du Reform Bill (1815–1830)* (Paris: Hachette, 1923); and *Histoire du peuple anglais au XIXe siècle*, vol. 3: *De la crise du Reform Bill à l'avènement de Sir Robert Peel (1830–1841)* (Paris: Hachette, 1923). There are English translations: *A History of the English People in the Nineteenth Century*, vol. 2: *The English Awakening 1815–1830*, second revised edition, translated by E. I. Watkin and D. A. Barker (London: Benn, 1949); and *A History of the English People in the Nineteenth Century*, vol. 3: *The Triumph of Reform, 1830–1841*, second revised edition, translated by E. I. Watkin and D. A. Barker (London: Benn, 1950). Many of the passages in the translation are not as precise as the originals. References, therefore, are to the original French editions, with page references to the English editions in brackets. All translations are my own.

109. I think it is going too far to suggest, as does Stefan Collini, that for Halévy "it would not be altogether unfair to say that history was political science pursued by other means." See

Collini, "Idealizing England, Élie Halévy and Lewis Namier," in *English Pasts: Essays in History and Culture* (Oxford: Oxford University Press, 1999), pp. 67–84, this quote p. 68.

110. Halévy, *Histoire du peuple anglais au XIXe siècle*, vol. 2: *Du lendemain de Waterloo à la veille du Reform Bill (1815–1830)*, pp. xi–xii [x].

111. Ibid., p. xi [x].

112. Ibid. p. 26 [29].

113. Halévy, *Histoire du peuple anglais au XIXe siècle*, vol. 3: *De la crise du Reform Bill à l'avènement de Sir Robert Peel (1830–1841)*, p. 93 [100].

114. Ibid., p. 316 [332].

CHAPTER 9

Epigraph: Élie Halévy, "The World Crisis (1914–1918): An Interpretation," Rhodes Memorial Lectures, Oxford University, 1929. These lectures were published in 1930 by the Clarendon Press. They appeared in French in *L'ère des tyrannies*, published in 1938 by Gallimard. Because they were originally in English, references are to the English edition of *The Era of Tyrannies*, translated by R. K. Webb (New York: Doubleday, 1965), pp. 209–47, with page references to the new French edition, *L'ère des tyrannies, Oeuvres complètes*, vol. 2 (Paris: Les belles lettres, 2016), pp. 232–62, in brackets. This quote, p. 247 [262].

1. Halévy, *Histoire du peuple anglais au XIXe siècle: Épilogue (1895–1914)* vol. 1: *Les impérialistes au pouvoir (1895–1905)* (Paris: Hachette, 1926). The English translation changed the title of this volume to *Imperialism and the Rise of Labour* (London: Ernest Benn, 1929). Halévy, *Histoire du peuple anglais au XIXe siècle: Épilogue (1895–1914)* vol. 2: *Vers la démocratie sociale et vers la guerre (1905–1914)* (Paris: Hachette, 1932). The English translation changed the title of this volume to *The Rule of Democracy (1905–1915)* (London: Ernest Benn, 1934). Many of the passages in the translation are not as precise as the originals. References, therefore, are to the original French edition, with page references to the English 2nd revised edition, translated by E. I. Watkin (London: Ernest Benn, 1951–1952), in brackets. All translations are my own.

2. "The World Crisis (1914–1918): An Interpretation."

3. The subheading is a direct translation of the original title, *Histoire du peuple anglais au XIXe siècle: Épilogue (1895–1914)*, vol. 1: *Les impérialistes au pouvoir (1895–1905)* (Paris: Hachette, 1926).

4. See Chapter 6.

5. Halévy, *L'Angleterre et son empire* (Paris: Pages libres, 1905), p. 121.

6. See, for example, the letter of to Célestin Bouglé (20 August 1903), *Correspondance (1891–1937)*, pp. 344–45.

7. Halévy, "Les souvenirs de Lord Morley," *Revue de métaphysique et de morale*, vol. 25 (1918), pp. 83–97.

8. Élie Halévy to Ludovic Halévy (24 April 1897), *Correspondance (1891–1937)*, p. 191.

9. Élie Halévy to Ludovic Halévy [26 April 1897], ibid., p. 192.

10. Élie Halévy to Ludovic Halévy (5 May 1897), ibid., p. 196.

11. Élie Halévy to Célestin Bouglé (23 January 1913), ibid., p. 434: "I return to my old idea: what can the Ligue des Droits de l'Homme do for the cause of the *indigénes algérien*? That is a question of general humanity and of justice, not a question of party, about which it is visibly impossible to excite this old, perhaps moribund body."

12. Halévy, *Histoire du peuple anglais au XIXe siècle: Épilogue (1895–1914)*, vol. 1 : *Les impérialistes au pouvoir (1895–1905)*; see pp. 3, 13–15, 278–83 [5, 15–16, 293–99].

13. Subsequent scholars have given the volume high praise. For example, J. Bartlet Brebner writes: "No one has given us an equally good account of that time. When the volumes appeared in 1926 and 1932, they were greeted by French and British historians in terms of perfection. . . . Since its publication, many students have looted Halévy's history of the years 1895–1918 for its information and ideas. They have not greatly altered its underlying pattern of interpretation except perhaps insofar as they have accepted the impact of outright democracy in terms of a more continuous tradition than he. Even so, it is doubtful whether the student of today could find any better single guide than Halévy through those twenty-three years." J. Bartlet Brebner, "Elie Halévy," in *Some Modern Historians of Britain: Essays in Honor of R. L. Schuyler*, ed. H. Ausubel, J. B. Brebner, and E. M. Hunt (New York: Dryden Press, 1951), pp. 235–54; this passage, p. 250.]

14. Halevy is unusually blunt in his assessment of Joseph Chamberlain, whom he refers to as "this terrible fellow [*ce diable d'homme*]," *Histoire du peuple anglais au XIXe siècle: Épilogue (1895–1914)*, vol. 1 : *Les impérialistes au pouvoir (1895–1905)*, p. 225 [236].

15. Ibid., p. 345 [362]. There are similar comments about the moderation of the English On p. 87 [92] ibid., for example, Halévy writes that the English are "a race in which the moral temperament is neither excitable nor cruel, a race that remains, even in violence, pacific and calculating."

16. Ibid. p. 345 [362].

17. Ibid. pp. v–vi [viii–ix].

18. Ibid. p. 16 [18].

19. This phrase, ibid., p. 89 [94].

20. This phrase, ibid., p. 100 [105].

21. Ibid., p. 247 [258].

22. Ibid., p. 90 [95].

23. Sebastien Charléty mentioned this assignment in "L'hommage de l'École," in *Élie Halévy, 1870–1937* (Paris: École libre des sciences politiques, [1938]), p. 5.

24. Élie Halévy, "Documents diplomatiques français," *Revue de Paris*, 36 (1929), pp. 45–63.

25. Halévy commented about the difficulty he had going from London to Oxford to receive an honorary doctorate. See Élie Halévy to Mme Ludovic Halévy (14 May 1926), *Correspondance (1891–1937)*, pp. 680–81.

26. "The World Crisis of 1914–1918: An Interpretation," p. 210 [235].

27. Ibid., p. 228 [248].

28. Ibid., pp. 233–34 [252].

29. Ibid., p. 214 [237].

30. Ibid., p. 215 [238].

31. Ibid., p. 222 [243].

32. Ibid., p. 245 [260–61].

33. Ibid., p. 239 [256].

34. Ibid., pp. 246–47 [262].

35. Ibid., p. 247 [262].

36. The subheading is a direct translation of the original title, *Histoire du peuple anglais au XIXe siècle: Épilogue (1895–1914)*, vol. 2: *Vers la démocratie sociale et vers la guerre (1905–1914)*.

37. On the "feminist revolt," see ibid., pp. 471– 512 [486–527]. On the Irish question, see esp. pp. 512–49 [527–66].

38. Ibid. p. 238 [246–47].

39. Ibid. p. 238 [247].

40. These phrases, ibid. p. 266 [275].

41. Halévy, "Les principes de la distribution des richesses," *Revue de métaphysique et de morale*, 14 (1906), pp. 545–95, discussed in chapter 5 above.

42. Halévy, *Histoire du peuple anglais au XIXe siècle: Épilogue (1895–1914)*, vol. 2: *Vers la démocratie sociale et vers la guerre (1905–1914)*, this phrase, p. v [v].

43. Ibid., p. 452 [467].

44. Ibid., p. 452 [468].

45. Ibid., pp. 266–93 [275–304].

46. Ibid., p. 267 [276].

47. Ibid., p. 464 [479].

48. Ibid., p. 320 [331].

49. Ibid., p. 348 [361].

50. Ibid., pp. 50, 359–61 [52, 371–74].

51. See esp. ibid., pp. 603–32 [621–50].

52. Ibid., p. 565 [582].

53. Ibid., pp. 373–76 [386–89].

54. Ibid., pp. 391–93 [404–7].

55. Ibid., p. 467 [482].


CHAPTER 10

Epigraphs: Élie Halévy to Xavier Léon (4 June 1934), *Correspondance (1891–1937)*, p. 726. Élie Halévy to René Berthelot (8 August 1935), ibid., p. 730.

1. See Julian Jackson, *The Politics of Depression in France, 1932–1936* (Cambridge: Cambridge University Press, 1985).

2. Julian Jackson, *France: The Dark Years, 1940–1944* (Oxford: Oxford University Press, 2001), this quote p. 65.

3. Robert Paxton, "When France Went Dreadfully Wrong," review of Frederick Brown, *The Embrace of Unreason: France, 1914–1940*, *New York Review of Books* (14 August 2014). More generally, for these years, see Julian Jackson, "1940 and the Crisis of Interwar Democracy," in Martin S. Alexander, ed., *French History Since Napoleon* (London: Arnold, 1999), pp. 222–43; and Jackson, *France: The Dark Years*, pp. 43–111.

4. In June 1936, Colonel de La Rocque transformed the Croix de feu into an authoritarian-populist political party (some have argued that it was fascist), Parti social français. The same month, Jacques Doriot formed the Parti populaire français, a party that in 1937 adopted the fascist salute and favored an entente with Nazi Germany.

5. The most popular vehicles for radical right-wing attacks on the Republic in the late 1930s were the journal *Je suis partout* (edited by Pierre Gaxotte, Robert Brasillach, and Lucien Rebatet) and the mass-circulation papers *Gringoire* and *Candide*.

6. François Goguel, *La politique des partis sous la IIIe République*, 3rd ed. (Paris: Seuil, 1958), pp. 318–19.

7. Jackson, *France: The Dark Years*, pp. 93 and 101.

8. David L. Schalk, *The Spectrum of Political Engagement: Mounier, Benda, Nizan, Brasillach, Sartre* (Princeton: Princeton University Press, 1979), these phrases, p. 15.

9. See the books by Samuel Moyn, *Origins of the Other: Emmanuel Levinas Between Revelation and Ethics* (Ithaca: Cornell University Press, 2005), and Stefanos Geroulanos, *An Atheism That Is Not Humanist Emerges in French Thought* (Stanford: Stanford University Press, 2010).

10. Élie Halévy to Gabrielle Léon (15 June 1937), *Correspondance (1891–1937)*, pp. 746–47.

11. Élie Halévy to Jacques Émile Blanche (10 July [1931]), ibid., pp. 706–7.

12. Halévy, "L'équilibre anglais et l'Europe," in *Oeuvres complètes*, vol. 2: *L'ère de tyrannies*, pp. 589–606.

13. Ibid., p. 597.

14. This phrase, ibid., p. 602.

15. Ibid., p. 602.

16. Ibid., p. 603.

17. Ibid.

18. Ibid., p. 604.

19. Ibid., p. 605. In a 1931 letter to his niece, Halévy addressed the issue of the power of individuals to affect larger events. "The question that Tolstoy posed is that of the influence of individuals on history; he concludes, and I am inclined to agree with him, that individuals have very little influence, and that general events have general causes." Élie Halévy to Henriette Noufflard (13 April 1931), *Correspondance (1891–1937)*, p. 705.

20. Théodore Ruyssen (1868–1967) entered the École normale supérieure the same years as Halévy (1889). Subsequently, they passed the agrégation in the same year (1892)—Alain was first, Halévy second, Ruyssen third. Ruyssen's speciality was the history of philosophy and international law. Before World War I, he published books on Kant and Schopenhauer, among others. After the war, he became an active supporter of the League of Nations. He was president of l'Association de la paix par le droit from 1896 to 1948.

21. Halévy, "Le nationalisme absolutiste a été la cause profonde de la guerre européenne," in *Oeuvres complètes*, vol. 2: *L'ère de tyrannies*, pp. 606–12.

22. Ibid., p. 607.

23. Dominique Parodi (1870–1959) was a friend of Halévy's, and a frequent contributor to the *Revue*. Parodi had been, like Halévy, a student of Darlu at the Lycée Condorcet and had entered the École normale supérieure the year after Halévy. He shared the neo-Kantian orientation of the founders of the *Revue* and published books on philosophical and political subjects, as well as many articles in the *Revue*. In 1935, after the death of Xavier Léon, he became the *secrétaire de rédaction* of the *Revue*.

24. Halévy, "Le nationalisme absolutiste a été la cause profonde de la guerre européenne," p. 612.

25. Élie Halévy to Baron de Meyendorff (3 April 1937), *Correspondance (1891–1937)*, p. 743.

26. Ibid.

27. Sébastien Laurent, *Daniel Halévy: Du libéralisme au traditionalisme* (Paris: Grasset, 2001), pp. 287–432.

28. Élie Halévy to Daniel Halévy (3 July 1931), *Correspondance (1891–1937)*, p. 705.

29. These notes are in various cartons of the Papiers Halévy, École normale supérieure (Paris). See cartons VI-1 and IX-1 for outlines and notes about the Russian Revolution and the Soviet Union. See carton IX-4 for outlines and notes about Italian Fascism. Some versions

found their way into Halévy's lectures on the history of European socialism. See *Oeuvres complètes*, vol. 3: *Histoire du socialisme européen*, pp. 269–314.

30. There are outlines for lectures on "la révolution bolchevik" from different years (1922, 1924, 1926, 1930, 1934). There are differences, especially in those that were written after the end of the New Economic Policy. The summary provided here gives priority to the outline dated 27 February 1934, but there is a great deal of continuity. These are located in carton VI-1 of the Papiers Halévy, ENS (Paris). The notes from students, published as a chapter in *Histoire du socialisme européen*—entitled "l'expérience socialiste en Russie Soviétique"—covers similar ground but extended to 1936, when the notes were taken.

31. "The Russians are dreadful and sublime people. One is able, therefore, to feel sentiments of distaste and sentiments of admiration, or mixed sentiments of distaste and admiration. But the Russian people are not what is important. What is important is the Marxist doctrine [of the leaders]." Élie Halévy to Jacques Émile Blanche (10 July [1931]), *Correspondance (1891–1937)*, p. 706.

32. Halévy, *Histoire du socialisme européen*, p. 280.

33. Ibid., p. 283.

34. Ibid., p. 286.

35. Carton IX-1, Papiers Halévy, ENS (Paris).

36. Lydia Bach, *Moscou: Ville rouge* (Paris: Librairie Valois, 1929), William Henry Chamberlin, *The Russian Revolution* (London: 1935), and Alexander Meyendorff, *The Background of the Russian Revolution* (New York: Henry Holt, 1929).

37. See *Florence et Élie Halévy: Six jours en URSS (septembre 1932): Récit de voyage inédit*, presented by Sophie Coeuré (Paris: Presses de l'École normale supérieure, 1998).

38. Élie Halévy to Étienne Mantoux (20 September 1934), *Correspondance (1891–1937)*, p. 727.

39. The most accessible account is in *Histoire du socialisme européen*, pp. 287–92.

40. See "Une interprétation de la crise mondiale de 1914–1918," p. 241. As Halévy recounted to his mother, "Most of the listeners in Oxford knew nothing of it [Mussolini's revolutionary role]; and appeared surprised as much as diverted when they saw, under my direction, the Italian devil jump out of his box." Élie Halévy to Mme Ludovic Halévy (28 July 1929), *Correspondance (1891–1937)*, p. 696.

41. Halévy, *Histoire du socialisme européen*, p. 290.

42. This phrase, ibid., p. 292.

43. See the letter of Élie Halévy to Gabrielle Léon (15 June 1937), *Correspondance (1891–1937)*, pp. 747. See also Serge Audier, "Le 'socialisme libéral' de Carlo Rosselli et le réformisme," *Mil neuf cent: Revue d'histoire intellectuelle*, 30 (2012), pp. 115–32.

44. This description, Halévy, *Histoire du socialisme européen*, p. 296.

45. Élie Halévy to Xavier Léon (3 May 1933), *Correspondance (1891–1937)*, pp. 713–14. More generally, see the chapter in *Histoire du socialisme européen*, pp. 293–99.

46. Élie Halévy to Xavier Léon (18 May 1933), *Correspondance (1891–1937)*, p. 715.

47. Élie Halévy to Xavier Léon (27 May 1933), ibid., p. 716.

48. Sismondi, *Nouveaux principes d'économie politique, ou de la richesse dans ses rapports avec la population* (1819), cited by Halévy, "Introduction" to *Sismondi* (Paris: Alcan, 1933). This introduction is reproduced in *L'ère de tyrannies*, pp. 66–82 [1–20]; this quote pp. 72–73 [7].

49. Halévy, "Introdution" to *Sismondi*, p. 74 [9].

50. Ibid., p. 79 [15].

51. This point about Sismondi's stance was made by Halévy in his earlier writings about Saint-Simon and the Saint-Simonians. "La doctrine économique saint-simonienne," originally in *Revue du Mois* (1908); reprinted in *L'ère de tyrannies*, pp. 83–149 [21–104]. Halévy discussed Sismondi on pp. 115–18 [61–65].

52. Halévy, "Introduction" to *Sismondi*, p. 74 [9–10].

53. Halévy, "Socialism and the Problem of Democratic Parliamentarianism," originally an address given at Chatham House, London, 24 April 1934, reprinted in *L'ère de tyrannies*, pp. 263–76 [249–64].

54. Ibid., p. 270 [256].

55. Ibid., p. 270 [257].

56. Ibid., p. 273 [260].

57. Ibid.

58. Ibid., p. 280 [266].

59. Ibid., p. 289 [277].

60. Ibid., p. 293 [282].

61. Ibid., pp. 279–80, note 2 [266–67].

62. Ibid., pp. 280–81 [267].

63. Ibid., p. 294 [283].

64. Ibid., p. 289 [278].

65. Ibid., p. 290 [279].

66. Originally published in *La crise sociale et les idéologies nationales* (Paris: Alcan, 1936), it is reprinted in *Oeuvres complètes*, vol. 2: *L'ère des tyrannies*, pp. 513–23.

67. On the first page of "The Era of Tyrannies" Halévy stated: "In its original form, socialism was neither liberal nor democratic, but organizational and hierarchical." *L'ère des tyrannies*, p. 279 [265].)

68. Ibid., pp. 287–88 [275].

69. Ibid., p. 288 [276].

70. Ibid.

71. Ibid.

72. Ibid., pp. 290–91 [279].

73. Élie Halévy to Baron de Meyendorff (7 August 1936), *Correspondance (1891–1937)*, p. 732.

74. "L'ère des tyrannies: Appendice II: Suite de la discussion," *L'ère des tyrannies*, p. 318 [311–12].

75. Ibid., p. 295 [285].

76. Ibid., p. 293 [282].

77. Ibid., p. 291 [280].

78. Halévy, *Histoire du peuple anglais au XIXe siècle, épilogue*, vol. 2, pp. 373–76.

79. A central theme of Halévy's 1929 lecture "Une interprétation de la crise mondiale de 1914–1918," in *L'ère des tyrannies*, pp. 232–62.

80. In a letter to Meyendorff in April 1937, he wrote: "More unquieting [than the political situation in France] is the financial situation. Even in this century of fools, I do not see how one is able to dispense eighty billion with a quarter of receipts; how, in any event, one is able to do it without a directed and firm economic system." Halévy to Baron de Meyendorff (3 April 1937), *Correspondance (1891–1937)*, p. 743.

81. Myrna Chase has argued that Halévy believed that "the intellectual origins of communism and fascism were rooted in 'socialism.'" Myrna Chase, *Élie Halévy: An Intellectual Biography* (New York: Columbia University Press, 1980), p. 203. I believe that Halévy considered the

"intellectual origins" of these regimes as more complex, having to do with complicated cultural traditions and the differing historical forces at work.

82. Élie Halévy to Célestin Bouglé (20 April 1934), *Correspondance (1891–1937)*, p. 725. Michelle Bo Bramsen has argued that Halévy was not so pessimistic. Michèle Bo Bramsen, *Portrait d'Élie Halévy* (Amsterdam: B. R. Grüner, 1978).

83. Élie Halévy to Xavier Léon (4 June 1934), *Correspondance (1891–1937)*, p. 726.

84. Élie Halévy to Célestin Bouglé (20 August 1934), ibid., p. 726. Halévy did not complete the volumes on the Victorian era before his death in 1937. His notes were worked up, however, by Paul Vacher into a volume of Halévy's *Histoire du peuple anglais au XIXe siècle: Le milieu du siècle (1841–1852)* (Paris: Hachette, 1946). The English translation, *Victorian Years 1841–1895*, incorporated an additional section by R. B. McCallum that covered 1852 to 1895.

Paul Vacher (1887–1966) was educated at the Sorbonne and the École libre des sciences politiques. In 1922, in part because of support from Halévy, he was appointed to the chair of French history and institutions at the University of London; in 1945, he assumed the chair in eighteenth-century history at the Sorbonne. See John C. Rule, "Paul Vacher: Historian," *French Historical Studies*, 5:1 (1967), pp. 98–105.

85. Alain to Florence Halévy (Sunday at the end of September 1936). Alain, *Correspondance avec Élie et Florence Halévy* (Paris: Gallimard, 1958), p. 314.

86. Élie Halévy to René Berthelot (30 June 1937), *Correspondance (1891–1937)*, p. 748.

87. Élie Halévy to Raymond Aron (2 August 1937), in *L'ère des tyrannies*, p. 663.

88. Halévy, "Une interprétation de la crise mondiale de 1914–1918," p. 261.

89. Henriette Guy-Loë, in *Correspondance (1891–1937)*, p. 724.

90. Alain, for example, wrote to Florence: "In the future one will judge him [Élie] as one ought to; one will appreciate the incredible grandeur which I have known so well, and a level of judgment without rival. Take this discourse as a witness of my profound friendship, which will last as long as I do. Heavens! We are not immortal! Therefore something ends. Everything ends and everything will end." Alain to Florence Halévy (31 August 1937), *Correspondance avec Élie et Florence Halévy*, p. 316.

91. Many of these were brought together in a publication by Sciences Po entitled *Élie Halévy, 1870–1937* (Paris: École libre des sciences politiques, [1938]). It includes pieces by Sébastien Charléty (originally in *Sciences politiques*), André Siegfried (originally in *Revue d'économie politique*), Léon Brunschvicg (originally in *Revue de métaphysique et de morale*), Robert Dreyfus (originally in *La revue de Paris*), Célestin Bouglé (originally read at the ENS), Paul Vaucher (originally in *Revue historique*), Julien Benda (originally in *La nouvelle revue françise*), Jean-Marcel Jeanneney, Ernest Barker (originally in *English Historical Review*), Basil Williams, and H. A. L. Fisher.

CONCLUSION

Epigraphs: Élie Halévy, "L'ère des tyrannies" [1936], in *Oeuvres complètes*, vol. 2: *L'ère des tyrannies*, under the direction of Vincent Duclert and Marie Scot (Paris: Les belles lettres, 2016), p. 286 [274].

Raymond Aron, "L'itinéraire intellectuel d'Élie Halévy," *Bulletin de la société française de philosophie* [1971], reprinted in *L'ère des tyrannies* (Paris: Gallimard, 1990), pp. 271–84; this quote, p. 277.

Charles C. Gillispie, "The Work of Élie Halévy: A Critical Appreciation," *Journal of Modern History*, 22:3 (1950), pp. 232–49; this quote, p. 233.

1. Élie Halévy, *La théorie platonicienne des sciences* (Paris: Alcan, 1896).

2. Élie Halévy, *La formation du radicalisme philosophique*, 3 vols. [1901–1904], new edition directed by Monique Canto-Sperber, 3 vols. (Paris: PUF, 1995).

3. Élie Halévy, *Histoire du socialisme européen* [1948], in *Oeuvres complètes*, vol. 3: *Histoire du socialisme européen* [1948], under the direction of Vincent Duclert and Marie Scot (Paris: Les belles Llettres, 2016), pp. 457–58; "L'ère des tyrannies," pp. 275–95.

4. Melvin Richter has pointed this out. See his "Elie Halévy come storico delle idee, la loro ricezione e le paradossali conseguenaze," in *Elie Halévy e l'era delle tirannie*, edited by Maurizio Griffo and Gaetano Quagliariello (Rome: Rubbettino Soveria Mannelli, 2001), pp. 143–58.

5. Élie Halévy, *La formation du radicalisme philosophique*, vol. 1: *La jeunesse de Bentham*, pp. 21–22, cited by Richter, "Elie Halévy come storico delle idee, la loro ricezione e le paradossali conseguenaze," p. 145.

6. For a judicious exploration of the tensions at the heart of Halévy's analysis of Utilitarianism and of the ways he saw these developing in nineteenth-century English thought, see Ludovic Frobert, "Élie Halévy and Philosophical Radicalism," *Modern Intellectual History*, 12:1 (2015), pp. 127–50.

7. In *L'Angleterre en 1815*, Halévy wrote: "It is therefore necessary, in the search for causes, to make a new step forward, to analyze a final order of social phenomena: beliefs, emotions, and opinions, as well as the institutions and the groups where these beliefs, these emotions, and these opinions take on a reality that directly strikes scientific observation." Élie Halévy, *Histoire du peuple anglais au XIXe siècle*, vol. 1: *L'Angleterre en 1815* (Paris: Hachette, 1912), p. 364.

8. This phrase, Halévy, *La formation du radicalisme philosophique*, vol. 3: *Le radicalisme philosophique*, pp. 205–6.

9. Max Weber, *The Protestant Ethic and the Spirit of Capitalism*, original German edition 1904–1905.

10. The phrase "disastrous eloquence" is from a letter of Élie Halévy to Florence Halévy (28 December 1906), *Correspondance (1891–1937)*, texts collected and presented by Henriette Guy-Loë (Paris: Fallois, 1996), p. 382. The phrase "parliamentary paralysis" is from a letter of Élie Halévy to Xavier Léon (28 May 1925), ibid., p. 675.

11. Élie Halévy, "La doctrine économique de Saint-Simonienne" [1908], in *Oeuvres complètes*, vol. 2: *L'ère des tyrannies*, pp. 83–149; and "L'ère des tyrannies" [1936], pp. 285–86.

12. Raymond Aron, "L'itinéraire intellectuel d'Élie Halévy," pp. 271–74.

13. In a letter to Bouglé in 1901, Halévy wrote: "Sociology ought to be accompanied by a study of the reciprocal relations of beliefs (philosophical, religious, scientific, moral) and of social forms." Élie Halévy to Célestin Bouglé (19 December 1901), in Alain, *Correspondance avec Élie et Florence Halévy* (Paris: Gallimard, 1958), p. 327.

14. For an excellent analysis of the favorable reception of Halévy's three volumes in England and the very different reception in France, see Greg Conti and Cheryl Welch, "The Receptions of Élie Halévy's *La formation du radicalisme philosophique* in England and France," *Modern Intellectual History*, 12:1 (2015), pp. 197–218.

15. Charles C. Gillispie, "The Work of Élie Halévy: A Critical Appreciation," *Journal of Modern History*, 22:3 (1950), pp. 232–49, this quote p. 237.

16. Talcott Parsons, "Utilitarianism: Sociological Thought," *The International Encyclopedia of the Social Sciences*, 16 (1968), pp. 229–36, this quote p. 230.

17. *The Collected Works of Jeremy Bentham* is the new authoritative edition being prepared by the Bentham Project, in the Faculty of Laws, University College London. Originally published by the Athlone Press (1968–1981), it was taken over in 1983 by Oxford University Press. To date, thirty-three of the projected seventy volumes have been published. As Melvin Richter pointed out, more than five hundred papers on Bentham alone appeared between 1950 and 1997. Melvin Richter, "Étude critique: Élie Halévy," *Revue de métaphysique et de morale*, April–June 1997), pp. 271–93, this quote p. 282.

18. See, for example, David Weinstein, *Utilitarianism and the New Liberalism* (Cambridge: Cambridge University Press, 2007).

19. William Thomas, *The Philosophic Radicals: Nine Studies in Theory and Practice, 1817–1841* (Oxford: Oxford University Press, 1979), esp. pp. 7–10.

20. William Thomas, "Recollections of A. J. P. Taylor," *Contemporary European History*, 3 (1994), p. 66; cited by Conti and Welch, "The Receptions of Élie Halévy's *La formation du radicalisme philosophique*," p. 197 note.

21. Frederick Rosen, *Jeremy Bentham and Representative Democracy: A Study of the Constitutional Code* (Oxford: Oxford University Press, 1983); Rosen, "Elie Halévy and Bentham's Authoritarian Liberalism," *Enlightenment and Dissent*, 6 (1987), pp. 59–76; Rosen, *Bentham, Byron, and Greece: Constitutionalism, Nationalism, and Early Liberal Political Thought* (Oxford: Oxford University Press, 1992), pp. 3–7.

22. For example, Jean-Pierre Dupuy's "postface" to the first volume of the new edition of *La formation du radicalisme philosophique*, pp. 329–59. Ludovic Frobert has argued that Dupuy's criticism "reveals a startling anachronism." Frobert, "Élie Halévy and Philosophical Radicalism," this quote p. 127.

23. H. S. Jones, *Victorian Political Thought* (London: Macmillan, 2000), p. 5.

24. Stefan Collini, "Idealizing England: Élie Halévy and Lewis Namier," in *English Pasts: Essays in History and Culture* (Oxford: Oxford University Press, 1999), pp. 67–84, this quote p. 73. William Thomas has referred to the doctrine of the Philosophic Radicals as "perplexed and contradictory." Thomas, *The Philosophic Radicals*, p. 4.

25. Melvin Richter prudently concludes that "the new knowledge of Bentham derived from the first reliable complete edition of his works has not produced unanimity among English-speaking authorities about the present day status of *La formation du radicalisme philosophique*." "Étude critique: Élie Halévy," p. 286. Emmanuelle de Champs has argued that the thesis of *La formation du radicalisme philosophique* should be connected to Halévy's wider intellectual agenda. "Elie Halévy: Bentham et l'Angleterre," in *Bentham et la France: Fortune et infortunes de l'utilitarisme* (Oxford: Voltaire Foundation, 2009), pp. 227–42.

26. J. D. Walsh, "Elie Halévy and the Birth of Methodism," *Transactions of the Royal Historical Society*, 25 (1975), pp. 1–20, this quote p. 1. See also the discussion by Bernard Semmel, "Introduction: Elie Halévy, Methodism, and Revolution," in his translation of Halévy's *Birth of Methodism* (Chicago: University of Chicago Press, 1971).

27. This quote, Walsh, "Elie Halévy and the Birth of Methodism," p. 6.

28. Ibid., p. 9.

29. Christopher Hill, *Society and Puritanism in Pre-Revolutionary England* (London: Secker and Warburg, 1964).

30. Michael Walzer, *The Revolution of the Saints: A Study in the Origins of Radical Politics* (Cambridge, MA: Harvard University Press, 1965).

31. E. P. Thompson, *The Making of the English Working Class* (New York: Vintage, 1963), esp. pp. 26–54, 350–400.

32. E. J. Hobsbawm, "Methodism and the Threat of Revolution in Britain," in *Labouring Men: Studies in the History of Labour* (New York: Basic Books, 1964), pp. 23–33; and *Primitive Rebels* (New York: Norton, 1965).

33. I'd like to thank my colleagues Brent Sirota and Chad Ludington for their guidance concerning recent scholarship.

34. Raymond Aron, "Le socialisme et la guerre" (1939), in *Oeuvres complètes*, vol. 2: *L'ère des tyrannies*, pp. 688–707.

35. Of the recent studies, see especially Robert Paxton, *The Anatomy of Fascism* (New York: Knopf, 2004).

36. See also H. S. Jones, "The Era of Tyrannies: Élie Halévy and Friedrich Hayek on Socialism," *European Journal of Political Theory*, 1 (2002), pp. 53–69.

37. See, most recently, Emmanuel Jousse, *Hommes révoltés: Les origines intellectuelles du réformisme en France* (Paris: Fayard, 2017); Julian Wright, *Socialism and the Experience of Time: Idealism and the Present in Modern France* (Oxford: Oxford University Press, 2017); and, volume 30 (2012) of *Mil neuf cent: Revue d'histoire intellectuelle*, devoted to "socialistes réformistes en Europe (1880–1930)." More than twenty-five years ago, I made a contribution: *Between Marxism and Anarchism: Benoît Malon and French Reformist Socialism* (Berkeley: University of California Press, 1992).

38. See Joshua M. Humphreys, "Servants of Social Progress: Democracy, Capitalism and Social Reform in France, 1914–1940" (Ph.D. dissertation, New York University, 2005).

39. On this longer tradition, there are good recent works. See, for example: Ludovic Frobert, "What is a Just Society? The Answer According to the Socialistes Fraternitaires Louis Blanc, Constantin Pecqueur, and François Vidal," *History of Political Economy*, 46:2 (2014), pp. 281–306; Ludovic Frobert and George Sheridan, *Le Solitaire du ravin: Pierre Charnier (1795–1857) canut lyonnais et prud'homme tisseur* (Lyon: ENS éditions, 2014); *De la République de Constantin Pecqueur (1801–1888)*, under the direction of Clément Coste, Ludovic Frobert, and Marie Lauricella (Besançon: Presses universitaires de Franche-Comté, 2017); and, *Une imagination républicaine: François-Vincent Raspail (1794–1878)*, under the direction of Jonathan Barbier and Ludovic Frobert (Besançon: Presses universitaires de Franche-Comté, 2017).

40. See the discussion above in Chapter 6.

41. I draw here from Stefan Collini's analysis of Hobhouse in *Liberalism and Sociology: L. T. Hobhouse and Political Argument in England, 1880–1914* (Cambridge: Cambridge University Press, 1979).

42. See, especially, Graham Wallas, *Human Nature in Politics* (London: Constable, 1908); and Wallas, *The Great Society: A Psychological Analysis* (New York: Macmillan, 1914).

43. There is a vast literature on earlier French liberalism. See, among others: Pierre Rosanvallon, *Le moment Guizot* (Paris: Gallimard, 1985); André Jardin, *Histoire du libéralisme politique de la crise de l'absolutisme à la constitution de 1875* (Paris: Hachette, 1985); George Armstrong Kelly, *The Humane Comedy: Constant, Tocqueville, and French Liberalism* (Cambridge: Cambridge University Press, 1992); Lucien Jaume, *L'individu effacé: Ou le paradoxe du libéralisme français* (Paris: Fayard, 1998); Aurelian Craiutu, *Liberalism Under Siege: The Political Thought of the French Doctrinaires* (Lanham, MD: Lexington Books, 2003); Helena Rosenblatt, *Liberal Values: Benjamin Constant and the Politics of Religion* (Cambridge: Cambridge University Press, 2008); Annelien de Dijn, *French Political Thought from Montesquieu to Tocqueville: Liberty in a Levelled Society* (Cambridge: Cambridge University Press, 2008); Andrew Jainchill, *Reimagining*

*Politics After the Terror: The Republican Origins of French Liberalism* (Ithaca: Cornell University Press, 2008); K. Steven Vincent, *Benjamin Constant and the Birth of French Liberalism* (New York: Palgrave Macmillan, 2011); Aurelian Craiutu, *A Virtue for Courageous Minds: Moderation in French Liberal Thought* (Princeton: Princeton University Press, 2012); Raf Geenens and Helena Rosenblatt, eds., *French Liberalism from Montesquieu to the Present Day* (Cambridge: Cambridge University Press, 2012).

44. De Dijn, *French Political Thought from Montesquieu to Tocqueville*.

45. Craiutu, *A Virtue for Courageous Minds*.

46. Rosenblatt, *Liberal Values*.

47. Vincent, *Benjamin Constant and the Birth of French Liberalism*.

48. Lucien Jaume is a good guide on the diverging strains of French liberalism. See his *L'individu effacé: Ou le paradoxe du libéralisme français* and his "The Unity, Diversity and Paradoxes of French Liberalism," in *French Liberalism from Montesquieu to the Present Day*, pp. 36–54.

49. On this issue, see Pierre Rosanvallon, *The Demands of Liberty: Civil Society in France Since the Revolution*, trans. A. Goldhammer (Cambridge, MA: Harvard University Press, 2007); and Rosanvallon, *The Society of Equals*, trans. A. Goldhammer (Cambridge, MA: Harvard University Press, 2013).

50. In the thought, for example, of M. F. Le Play, *La réforme sociale en France*, 3 vols. (Paris: Dentu, 1872).

51. For example, with Léon Bourgeois's "solidarism." On solidarism see Léon Bourgeois and Alfred Croiset, *Essai d'une philosophie de la solidarité* (Paris: Alcan, 1907); J. E. S. Hayward, "Solidarity: The Social History of an Idea in Nineteenth-Century France," *International Review of Social History*, 4 (1959), pp. 261–84; J. E. S. Hayward, "The Official Social Philosophy of the French Third Republic: Léon Bourgeois and Solidarism," *International Review of Social History*, 6 (1961), pp. 19–48; and William Logue, *From Philosophy to Sociology: The Evolution of French Liberalism, 1870–1914* (Dekalb: Northern Illinois University Press, 1983), esp. pp. 185–204. Halévy, as mentioned below, rejected solidarism as naively wishing away class divisions.

52. Andrew Jainchill has argued that "liberal republicans," seeing this complexity, have believed that political institutions should be rooted in social forces. See Jainchill, *Reimagining Politics After the Terror*. I have argued that it led to prudence and judgment rather than commitment to a strict political program. See my *Benjamin Constant and the Birth of French Liberalism*.

53. Élie Halévy to Célestin Bouglé (1 October 1913), *Correspondance (1891–1937)*, p. 442.

54. Halévy wrote that "doctinally solidarism does not exist." See Halévy's review of Bouglé's *Le solidarisme* (Paris: Giard, 1907) in *Revue de métaphysique et de morale*, 15 (1907), supplément. 5. On solidarism, see note 51 above.

55. Élie Halévy to Célestin Bouglé (7 May 1895), *Correspondance (1891–1937)*, p. 156.

56. Halévy argued that the market is "a political institution . . . it is necessary that there are rules, a police, in brief an intervention of the state." "Les principes de la distribution des richesses," 567.

57. Halévy, "La doctrine économique Saint-Simonienne," p. 145.

58. Halévy, "The World Crisis (1914–1918): An Interpretation." These were the Rhodes Memorial Lectures given in English at Oxford University in 1929. Reference, therefore, is to the English edition of *The Era of Tyrannies*, trans. R. K. Webb (New York: Doubleday, 1965), pp. 209–47, this quote p. 247. In the new French edition, *Oeuvres complètes*, vol. 2: *L'ère des tyrannies* (Paris: Les belles lettres, 2016), pp. 232–62, this quote, p. 262.

59. Halévy, "L'ère des tyrannies," p. 283 [270].

ACKNOWLEDGMENTS

I have been very fortunate to have received advice and assistance from many individuals and organizations. I first encountered Élie Halévy when, decades ago, I informed my graduate mentor, Martin Malia, that I had decided to narrow my thesis from "The Quest for Community in the Thought of Lamennais, Tocqueville, and Proudhon" to a thesis on Proudhon and early French socialism. He insisted that I read Halévy's *Histoire du socialisme européen*, the series of lectures and notes posthumously pulled together by Halévy's widow and friends and published in 1948. I did so but honestly was not impressed. I put the book aside, driven by interests and perspectives that had more to do, I suspect, with the era of the late 1960s and 1970s in Berkeley than anything else. While working on the dissertation, I was more drawn to the works of Halévy's close friend Célestin Bouglé, to the books of Maxime Leroy and Armand Cuvillier, and to the more recent works of Maurice Agulhon and Jacques Julliard, to name a few.

I was reintroduced to Halévy when I was asked in 1996 by Malachi Hacohen to co-teach a graduate class at Duke University on French liberalism. One of the readings for the class was Halévy's 1929 essay "The World Crisis of 1914–1918: An Interpretation." I was deeply impressed and made a mental note to look at more of his work, though at the time I was contemplating a book that focused on the thought of Germaine de Staël and Benjamin Constant. When I finished that project, I turned back to Halévy, read more of his essays and books, and was struck by their brilliance. His 1907 extended analysis of Saint-Simonian economic doctrine, to mention one example, remains, in my opinion, one of the best essays in intellectual history ever written. I was hooked, and surprised to discover that there was no recent comprehensive study of this preeminent intellectual of the French Third Republic. I had found a new project.

At a very early stage, I contacted people who had worked on Halévy. Melvin Richter kindly sent me copies of the dictionary entries and journal articles written by Halévy that he had collected over the years. In 2012, when I presented one of my first papers on Halévy, I shared a panel with Ludovic Frobert, a deeply knowledgeable scholar of social and economic thought who had already published articles and a book devoted to Halévy's economic views. I also contacted Joel Revill, whose Ph.D. dissertation had chapters devoted to the *Revue de métaphysique et de moral*. Mel, Ludo, and Joel have remained conscientious interlocutors since our first discussions about Halévy, and all three agreed to come to a conference devoted to Halévy that I organized in October 2013, held on the campus of Duke University. Joining us were other scholars who shared our interest, including Michael Behrent, Vincent Duclert, Malachi Hacohen, Cheryl Welch, and Julian Wright. The conference, supported by the Triangle Intellectual History Seminar, the Duke Center for European Studies, and the History Department of North Carolina State University, helped expand my view of the worlds in which Halévy moved.

In May 2011, I made my first foray into the Halévy archive at the École normale supérieure, where ninety-five cartons of his notes, papers, and correspondence are located. On this visit, I had the extreme good luck to meet Françoise Dauphragne, herself deeply immersed in Halévy's writings, and responsible for the Halévy archive. She directed me to the manuscripts of his early lectures on socialism and to other boxes of Halévy's papers, some organized, many not. I have returned to the archive at the École normale many times and have benefited from the assistance of Françoise Dauphragne, Estelle Boeuf-Belilita, Sandrine Iraci, and others on the ENS staff. The expenses for my third visit in May 2013 were in part covered by a research award from North Carolina State University, for which I am very grateful. That same year, I also consulted Halévy's correspondence with English intellectuals at the London School of Economics. Again, my thanks to the LSE archivists, especially Catherine McIntyre, for making this a productive visit.

In the fall of 2014, I spent a wonderful four months at the Institute for Advanced Study in Princeton. There, I benefited from the extraordinary scholarly community of the IAS and drafted much of the section on Halévy's early socialism. It is a pleasure to be able to thank the superb staff of the IAS, Michael van Walt van Praag for welcoming me into his International Relations and International Law seminar, Jonathan Israel for allowing me to join his early modern seminar, Joan Wallach Scott and Michael Walzer for engaged discussions, and fellow residents who made it such a wonderful experience: Marco Barducci, Gurminder Bhambra, Suzannah Clark, John Holmwood, Nannerl Keohane, Maurizio Meloni, Olindo De Napoli, Nader Sohrabi, Owen Stanwood, and especially Nicole Reinhardt. While there, I also had the pleasure of a meeting with Fritz Stern, another Halévy enthusiast.

In the spring of 2015, I was a resident (thanks, I am sure, to Ludovic Frobert) at the Institute d'étude avancée, Collegium de Lyon. Ludovic and I had planned to devote time to the translation of Halévy's early lectures on socialism (unpublished at the time, never published in English, now published in volume 3 of the new *Oeuvres complètes*), but we failed to find a publisher, so the project was abandoned. Frustrated on that front, I was able, while at the collegium, to write most of the section of this book on World War I and the immediate postwar period. The collegium in the spring of 2015 was in the process of settling into new offices at l'Université Lyon II (it has since moved again), but in spite of the disorganization this created, it was a wonderful experience communing with the other scholars in residence, especially with Michael Sonenscher and Jean-Marie Hombert.

Vincent Duclert met with me that spring during one of my visits to the archive in Paris, and he invited me to a conference that he and Marie Scot were organizing for the eightieth anniversary (to the day!) of the presentation of Halévy's essay on the era of tyrannies. This magnificent conference, held in November 2016 at Halévy's residence in Sucy-en-Brie and at Sciences Po in Paris, provided the opportunity to meet members of Halévy's family as well as other scholars, including Michele Bo Bramsen, Michele Battini, Marco Bresciani, Sophie Coeuré, Venita Datta, Duncan Kelly, Steve Sawyer, Stéphan Soulié, and Frédéric Worms.

On my numerous trips to Paris, Tomek Ulatowski has greeted me with generous accommodation, with engaged conversation about the state of Europe and the world, with exhausting matches of tennis, and, above all, with his good will. I am lucky to have such a long-standing friend, one who has also patiently and sympathetically supported me through the stumbles of my personal life.

I wish, in addition, to express my enduring gratitude to the Triangle Intellectual History Seminar, which has been my intellectual home since its creation in the spring of 1995. The monthly sessions during the academic year, held at the National Humanities Center, have provided an exceptionally congenial, but also rigorous, scholarly forum for the discussion of intellectual and cultural history. I wish to extend my special thanks to the other coordinators: James Chappel, Malachi Hacohen, Lloyd Kramer, Anthony LaVopa, Emily Levine, Martin Miller, Noah Strote, and David Weinstein.

I have presented papers related to Halévy at various conferences: the Social Science History Association (2012); Western Society for French History (2012, 2013); Triangle Intellectual History Seminar (2013, 2015); Institute for Advanced Study (2014); CUNY Intellectual History Seminar (2014); Collegium de Lyon (2015); British Society for the Study of French History (2015); Paris Colloque "Élie Halévy et l'ère de tyrannies" (2016); and the Society for French Historical Studies (2017). I wish to thank all of those who made comments and/or joined the discussions. In addition to those mentioned above, these include Susan Ashley, Jonathan Beecher, Aurelian Criautu, Sandria Freitag, David Gilmartin, Doris Goldstein, Paul Hanson, Chad Ludington, Larry McGrath, Julie Mell, John Merriman, Thomas Ort, Donald Reid, Nicholas Robins, Helena Rosenblatt, Sophia Rosenfeld, Julia Rudolph, David Schalk, Jerrold Seigel, George Sheridan, Brent Sirota, Jay Smith, and Ken Vickery. I undoubtedly have forgotten some who have offered advice and assistance. Please accept my apology for my poor memory; it does not diminish my gratitude.

The librarians at North Carolina State University have been helpful, courteous, and efficient locating material not found in one of the libraries of the North Carolina Triangle. Again, I am most grateful.

James Banker and Richard Sonn read chapters in the final stage of writing and offered helpful and supportive feedback. Helena Rosenblatt and Aurelian Craiutu read a near-final version of the entire manuscript. I am especially indebted to them for their valuable comments about organization, emphasis, and lacunae. I also found extremely useful the suggestions for revision provided by the anonymous readers for the University of Pennsylvania Press. Damon Linker and Noreen O'Connor-Abel have been ideal editors: engaged, supportive, responsive, efficient.

Chapter 5 is derived in part from an article published in *History of European Ideas*, 44:1 (2018), copyright Taylor & Francis. Chapter 6 is derived in part from an article published in *Modern Intellectual History*, 12:1 (2015), copyright Cambridge University Press. Chapter 8 is derived in part from a chapter published in *Élie Halévy Études* I: *Élie Halévy et l'Ère des tyrannies: Histoire, philosophie et politique au XXe siècle* (Paris: Les Belles Lettres, 2019). I thank these publications for permission to incorporate portions of this material here.

Figures 2–5 are printed with the permission of the Société historique et archéologique de Sucy-en-Brie, and of the chairman of this society, Michel Balard. Figures 6–7 and the cover image are printed with the permission of the Association des amis d'Élie et Florence Halévy, and of the president of this association, Vincent Duclert. Technical assistance was provided by Zack Dean of North Carolina State University CHASS IT. My brother, Peter Vincent, graciously stepped in at the last minute to enhance the quality of some of the photographic images. I am very grateful to all.

After I began this project, I had the good fortune to meet a wonderful woman, Ana Edelmira Gray, who is now my companion and wife. She has brought me more joy and contentment, and greater understanding of the world beyond Europe and North America, than I ever thought possible. It is with great pleasure that I dedicate this book to her.